SCIENCE AND CULTURE SERIES

JOSEPH HUSSLEIN, S.J., Ph.D., GENERAL EDITOR

EXPERIMENTAL PSYCHOLOGY

Experimental Psychology

By

HUBERT GRUENDER, S.J., PH. D.

Professor of Psychology
Saint Louis University

THE BRUCE PUBLISHING CO.

New York   MILWAUKEE   *Chicago*

Imprimi potest:

S. H. HORINE, S.J.,
Praepositus Provincialis Provinciae Missourianae

Nihil obstat:

H. B. RIES,
Censor librorum

Imprimatur:

✠ SAMUEL A. STRITCH,
Archiepiscopus Milwaukiensis

Die 29 Martii, 1932

(Second Printing — 1935)

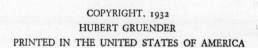

PREFACE BY THE GENERAL EDITOR

The question which men are asking themselves at the present time in regard to the comparatively new science of experimental psychology can be briefly summed up in the words: "What has it accomplished?"

The extravagant hopes entertained by some are contrasted by the no less extreme misgivings in the minds of others. To all such questionings the author has sought to give an authentic answer, stripped of all bias. That answer, certainly, should be of interest alike to the general reader, to the specialist in the field, and to the students in our numerous colleges and universities. For the latter, the present work may serve as a text or a reference book in advanced courses of psychology.

Supreme insistence has been placed throughout the volume on the central fact that experimental psychology is strictly a natural science, and as such must be subject to strictly scientific methods. Rightly, therefore, we may deprecate the attitude of those who would intrude here with unwarranted metaphysical assumptions, which of necessity will react to the detriment of the science and rob its presentation of that deep human interest inherent in the subject.

How true this is may be illustrated by a circular issued at the first publication of the *Foundations of Experimental Psychology.* Twice in his own memory, the writer of the document states, has a class of senior students, in one of our largest universities, voted psychology to be "the emptiest, most useless, and most uninteresting of all subjects studied during the previous four years." Similar experiences are referred to as not uncommon elsewhere. Let those responsible forego their metaphysical bias, adhere to strictly scientific methods, and psychology will be the most interesting of sciences.

A leading characteristic of the present volume is its close ad-

herence to the methods of a refined common sense, equally de-
manded in all the natural sciences. Violations of these methods
by psychological experts has not seldom tended to bring their
science itself into disrepute. In all his own conclusions the author never loses grip of what we may fitly call a saving sanity
of judgment.

As an outstanding feature of his book may be mentioned in
particular his treatment of thought processes and the will, contained in the last four chapters. This will prove a welcome contribution to American psychological literature. Reference should
especially be made here to his presentation, on its experimental
side, of the distinction between the higher and lower processes,
as well as to his lucid exposition of the experimental evidence
regarding the nature and properties of the will act.

One of the typically modern subjects brought up for minute
investigation, under the heading of "Instinct," is Koehler's experimentation with apes. The specific example chosen is that of an
ape fitting together two short sticks to make a longer one, in
order to reach the object he desired. The factual testimony in the
case is open to challenge, but the author freely waives this point,
satisfactorily explains the nature of the act, and gives its correct
interpretation.

But the phases of experimental psychology which have perhaps
most intimately engrossed the author's attention for many years
are those concerned with color sensations and tone sensations.
The method used by him in investigating the phenomena of
simultaneous contrast will be of interest not only to the casual
reader, but in a more particular way to the technical psychologist.
Special attention should here be called to his musical nomogram.

It is ordinarily believed that a thorough discussion of tone sensations is intelligible to musicians only. This, the author holds,
is not the case, and he confidently trusts that the lay reader will
find no difficulty in following his musical illustrations. A more
complete development of this subject, however, is reserved by
him for a future volume on *Appreciation of Music,* to appear
in this Series.

The present book, in fine, restricts itself to the normal working of the human mind. This aspect, obviously, must be basic in the study of experimental psychology. The general reader, the students in our colleges and universities, and all others interested in this subject will find here an accurate exposition and evaluation of the data ascertained by strictly scientific methods, in the province of normal psychology.

JOSEPH HUSSLEIN, S.J., PH.D.,
General Editor, Science and Culture Series
St. Louis University,
January 4, 1932.

FOREWORD

This book is the outgrowth of a series of lectures given to graduate students at the St. Louis University. The lectures have been so recast that they can be read with profit by the general reader, or may serve the needs of students in more advanced courses in experimental psychology.

It has been my aim to develop the critical attitude of the student: to insist that he take nothing for granted, and that he make no assumptions of any kind, except those that are at the basis of all science.

In the preparation of this volume I have gleaned from many sources. Sometimes I have made explicit reference to them in the text, but it was impossible to do so consistently. It may suffice to state here once and for all that I have used not only original sources, but also the leading textbooks and laboratory manuals available in English and in German, and in some way or other I am indebted to them all. It should be added, however, that an explicit reference to a definite author does not imply in consequence that the viewpoint or theoretic interpretation of that author is accepted by the present writer.

Perhaps a word is needed to explain why I have given such prominence to German psychological literature, particularly in the chapters on Thought. I was first introduced to the subject of experimental psychology by the Rev. Joseph Froebes, S.J., professor of psychology in Valkenburg, Limburg, Holland, and in 1912 pursued my studies under the leaders of the Würzburg school, the late Professor Kuelpe and Dr. Buehler, both of whom at that time taught in the University of Bonn, Germany. I thus became acquainted with their experimental investigations of the thought processes and took an active part in one of these investigations. Hence it is that I refer frequently to the work of this school.

Another and even more weighty reason is that their remarkable investigations of the thought processes have not received in this country the degree of attention which they deserve. We have indeed a critical account of the Würzburg researches from the pen of Titchener, but his treatment is decidedly biased, written from the standpoint of a sensationalist. *Audiatur et altera pars* would seem to be a sufficient justification for the prominence given to the German literature on this subject.

In accordance with the aim of the book the usual references to psychological literature at the end of each chapter are reduced to the absolute minimum They are meant in literal strictness for *further* reading and not for parallel reading. Among the books generally mentioned is the *Lehrbuch der Experimentellen Psychologie* of Fr. Froebes, S.J. It is a complete survey of the whole field and contains an exhaustive list of the psychological literature.

Unless otherwise stated, the illustrations are made from original drawings.

THE AUTHOR.

CONTENTS

xiii

Chapter I

THE SCOPE OF PSYCHOLOGY

1. The word "psychology" is derived from two Greek words, *psyche* (soul) and *logos* (science), and means the science of the soul. It is a curious fact that this word is of rather recent origin. The first traces of it are found in the writings of Melanchthon (d. 1560). As a title of a book it was used first by Goclenius (1590) and at about the same time by Casmann, who wrote an *Anthropological Psychology* (1594). The word came into general use only after Wolf, whose *Empirical Psychology* appeared in 1738.

Aristotle wrote several treatises which we now call psychological; namely, "On the Soul," "On Sensation and the Sensible," "On Memory and Reminiscence," "On Sleeping and Waking," "On Dreams." They were used by the old schoolmen as texts and were explained in numerous commentaries. The most noteworthy of the latter are the treatises of St. Thomas and Suarez "On the Soul."

2. **Definition of Psychology.** Psychology may be defined as *the science of our conscious life.*

It is a *science,* that is, an exact and systematic body of knowledge concerning the subject which it undertakes to investigate. This involves three things; namely: (1) An exact knowledge of the facts with which psychology deals. Such knowledge is gained by accurate observation, particularly observation under controlled conditions, that is, by experiment. (2) An exact knowledge of the laws which govern these facts. This is obtained by a systematic correlation of the facts observed. (3) An exact knowledge of the causes of the facts and the laws which govern them. By "cause" we understand anything and everything that makes the why and wherefore of the facts and laws intelligible to us.

The subject matter of psychology or the object with which it is directly concerned, is *"our conscious life,"* that is, a definite group of vital processes distinguished from all others by *two characteristics indicated by the two accepted meanings of the term "consciousness,"* as will be explained presently. Such are the thoughts, feelings, moods, perceptions, fancies, memories, aspirations, resolves, regrets, fears, likes and dislikes, in short, the whole drama enacted within the sanctum of each one's private Self.

All these vital processes are called "conscious," in the first place, *because of the manner in which we get first-hand information concerning them,* namely, by "consciousness," that is, the explicit turning of the attention of the thinking subject on its own acts: this is the first meaning of the term "consciousness." Introspection and internal experience are but other names for this turning of my attention on my own acts. Accordingly, we can also say that psychology is directly concerned with the facts of internal experience, while the physical sciences deal with the facts of external experience. When we are working in physics or chemistry, our attention is turned outward; it is in the world outside of myself that I find the objects that directly interest me. In psychology our attention is turned inward; it is within myself that I find the objects which I study for their own sake. Expressing the same idea in yet another way, we can say that the objects of the physical sciences can be seen, heard, felt, in short, observed directly by everyone by means of his senses, while the objects of psychology cannot be seen, heard, or felt by anyone, not even by the use of his own senses. I can look into a mirror and see my own eyes, but I cannot see my own seeing. The only way in which I can get first-hand information concerning this and all other acts in the foregoing provisional list (thoughts, feelings, moods, etc.) is by turning my attention on these facts of the inner world.

There is, however, another reason why all the vital processes mentioned are called "conscious," namely *because all of them involve essentially an "awareness of an object,"* this awareness of the object (external or internal) being the second meaning which common usage attaches to the term "consciousness." Accordingly, the objects with which psychology is directly concerned are characterized not only by their privacy (indicated by the first meaning of the term "consciousness") but also by their unique double aspect: their *subjective-objective* character. They are *subjective* facts, because they are essentially modifications of the thinking subject or Ego. They are *objective,* because they have just as essentially a reference to an object (external or internal). Thus, when I think, I think of something; when I see, I see something; when I hate, I hate something; when I resolve, I resolve to do something.

From this unique double aspect of the facts of "our conscious life" it is clear that *we cannot even describe them as mere phenomenal facts except with this double reference to the experiencing Ego and to the object of which I become aware.* Thus, the fact that I perceive a tree belongs undoubtedly to the direct object of psychology. So does the fact that I am thinking of that peculiar object which has worried boys and girls ever since the time of Pythagoras, namely, the relation between the hypotenuse and the other two sides of a right-angled triangle. But I cannot possibly describe these phenomenal facts and discriminate them from other facts of internal and external experience without expressing both the "I" and the "object" of these conscious acts. If I eliminate either the one or the other in the description of these facts, I no longer express the facts with which psychology is directly concerned. Indeed, I do worse than that: I do violence to these facts: I deprive them of two essential features without which they never occur in my experience.

What has been said concerning the phenomenal description of "our conscious life" does not mean that we are expected to express a theory concerning the constitution of the "Ego" or the nature of the "object" of our conscious acts. Nor are we supposed to express an opinion concerning the nature of the very acts of perception and thought or any other conscious process which we specify and discriminate from one another by indicating their respective objects. All such theories and opinions do not belong to the phenomenal description of facts. If we include such the-

ories in our description of facts — as has been done, and it makes
no difference under what pretext this is done — we are inventing
and not describing; we are positively hampering the science of
psychology by our metaphysical prepossessions.

3. The Indirect Object of Psychology. Psychology, like
every other science, has also an indirect object, and this comprises
anything and everything that is capable of throwing light on the
main business in hand, but only inasmuch as it is capable of doing so. In this sense it is perfectly correct to state, as has been
said, that the whole world of our external experience, the entire
furniture of earth and the choir of heavenly bodies, in short,
everything that is contained within the domain proper to every
other science, belongs to the object of psychology, that is, to its
indirect object. This does not mean that the boundary lines between the various sciences and in particular between psychology
and the various physical sciences are ill defined. It only means
that all sciences are interconnected and what is the direct object
of one science belongs to the indirect object of another science,
provided that, and insofar as, it throws light on the main business
in hand.

Accordingly in the study of our conscious life an occasional
sally into the domains proper to other sciences is unavoidable.
Thus, for instance, in psychology we are not directly concerned
with the properties of light: this belongs to the domain of physical optics. We are, however, interested in color sensations aroused
by light and it is impossible to understand color sensations without correlating them with the physical properties of light. Hence
we shall do so and we shall find to our surprise that this correlation is something of a tangle. This tangle must be unraveled if
we are to describe and explain color sensations. Hence our ex-
cursion into physical optics may turn out to be a rather extended
trip in this foreign domain. We shall not quarrel about the word
by which we designate our stay in the domain of physical optics,
but stay we must until we have unraveled the tangle.

Prominent among the things that can throw light on our subject matter proper are the bodily conditions under which our conscious life actually occurs. That there is some connection be-tween our conscious life and the physiological processes going on in our body, particularly the nervous system, has been recognized from time immemorial. The nature of this connection has been stated differently by different schools of psychology, each one pro-pounding its own theory. We cannot possibly judge about the value of any particular theory in the very beginning of psychol-ogy. We shall let facts guide us in the discussion of these theories. Hence when referring from the very start to "the bodily condi-tions of our conscious life," we take the word *condition* not in the technical sense of scholastic philosophy as opposed to *cause,* but in a much wider sense including both *conditions* and *causes,* in the technical sense. In short, we leave the finer terminology to be determined by the accurate study of the facts both of "our conscious life" and of physiology. Such a study of the facts, how-ever, is impossible without a sally into the domain of physiology and particularly the physiology of the nervous system. And sally forth we shall, without any scruples as to obliterating the bound-ary lines between psychology and physiology. Aristotle and the great schoolmen had no such scruples in discussing our conscious life. Our mode of procedure, then, is in principle the same as that of Aristotle. But modern advances in physiology have made it possible to apply this principle more consistently and in greater detail than was possible when the science of physiology was still in its infancy.

This would seem to be the proper place for discussing the ques-tion whether *subconscious processes* come within the scope of experimental psychology. Some authors ascribe a rather impor-tant rôle to these processes, particularly in the explanation of cer-tain pathological conditions. We shall have occasion to point out that subconscious processes occur, but we know of them only by inference. Persons who are said to be guided by them can give us no introspective report concerning them. This means that sub-conscious processes are not "conscious" in the first sense of the word: they are not revealed by introspection. They are, however, "conscious" in the second sense, that is, *they involve a dim awareness of some object of suppressed hope, desire, fear,* and the like. The investigators try to find out by indirect methods what the objects of such "bottled-up ideas" are. And this brings us to the answer to the foregoing question. Subconscious processes undoubtedly come within the scope of experimental psychology. It is largely a matter of terminology whether we shall say that subconscious processes belong to the indirect object of psychology, or that they belong to the direct object but must be investigated by indirect methods. We shall deal with them in the chapter on Attention.

4. Human and Animal Psychology. The term "our" by which we qualify "conscious life" in the definition of psychology, needs a few words of comment. By this qualification we mean two things. The first is that the conscious life of animals is not included in the object with which psychology is directly concerned. We have indeed sufficient evidence that animals have at least some of the acts which we call "conscious" in the second sense of the word, that is, animals also become "aware of objects" outside of them. But in no case have we any first-hand information or immediate knowledge of these acts: we know of their existence only by inference from the outward manifestations of these inner acts. In the interpretation of these outward signs the analogy between animal behavior and that of man looms large. Of "consciousness" in the first and original sense of the word, that is, the capacity of the thinking Ego to turn his attention explicitly on his own acts, we have no evidence whatever in the case of animals. In a word, *we can know of the "conscious" life of animals only by constructing it after the analogy of man,* and here we must beware of the danger of "humanizing brutes." Of course, the "conscious life" of animals can be made the subject of a special science known as "animal psychology." It is practically a systematic study of animal behavior and an interpretation of this behavior in the light of what we know of human behavior. In a general treatise of psychology, however, the "conscious life" of animals belongs to its indirect object. We shall deal with it in the two chapters on Instinct.

It is true that in literal strictness I have no immediate knowledge of the conscious life of any man outside myself. But not only is the analogy between my behavior and that of another man more thoroughgoing than that between human and animal behavior; there is another difference of even greater importance. *Other men can give me an introspective report* of what they experience immediately, and insofar the information which I have concerning the conscious life of other men is not a matter of construction but one based upon immediate knowledge. From this it will be seen that *the "privacy" of our conscious life must not be exaggerated,* a point to which we shall return when discussing behaviorism. It has been said that the data of all other sciences are common property, whereas those of psychology, as defined in the foregoing, are not. This is false. *Once I give an introspective report of the thoughts, sensations, memories, etc., which I have observed under definite conditions, these conscious processes of mine thereby become common property;* and the same is true of the conscious processes of any other man. The only proviso is that all introspective reports should be made in purely empirical terms and not be vitiated by any theoretic bias. But theoretic bias must be guarded against also in gathering reliable data of any other science. We mean to emphasize, then, that the direct object of psychology is not "my" conscious life but the conscious life of every human individual. This is the second thing which is meant by the term "our" in the definition of psychology.

5. The Sources of Psychology. From what has been said it is clear that the primary source of psychology is *self-observation,* particularly self-observation under controlled conditions, that is, *psychological experiment.* The introspective reports of others, provided their accuracy be insured, are no distinct source of psychology but are part of what is meant by "self-observation."

Another source of information is the *observation of others,* and this is sometimes referred to as an *"objective source"* of psychology in opposition to "self-observation" which is called a "subjective source." We shall not quarrel about these words, provided they are not meant to convey a slur on the value of the "subjective source." It has been recognized from the time of Aristotle that the observation of the outward behavior of others is a valuable supplement to self-observation, just as it is a mere truism to say that accurate self-observation is sometimes difficult and liable to error. But all experimental work, whether in the physical, chemical, or psychological laboratory, has its difficulties. In the study of each particular problem a method must be devised to overcome the specific difficulties of that problem. This can be done and has been done successfully in the psychological laboratory to meet the difficulties of self-observation just as it has been done in the physical or physiological laboratory to secure the accuracy of external observation. One of the various means of securing the accuracy of self-observation is the "objective" study of the outward behavior of the observer who reports a definite internal experience of his. All this is nothing new in psychological literature. The important thing to recognize is that *the study of the outward behavior is of its very nature secondary in importance, depending essentially for its interpretation on the data of "self-observation."*

The sources of information concerning the indirect object of psychology are the same as those of the other sciences from which we borrow our information. And if we cannot borrow the information which is expected to throw light on our subject proper, or if a refinement in the methods of other sciences is required for our purposes, we shall scruple very little about using the methods and sources of other sciences in order to secure the information needed in the discussion of our subject proper.

In practical terms this means that in the psychological laboratory we use instruments just like those used in the physical and physiological laboratories. In fact, most of our instruments are found also in the catalogs of physical and physiological instruments. Only very few instruments are specially devised for the psychological laboratory. But the purpose which guides us in the use of physical instruments is radically different from that which guides the physicist in his laboratory work. We want to throw light on the facts of the inner world while the physicist aims at throwing light on the facts of the outer world.

6. Observation and Experiment. We stressed self-observation under controlled conditions, that is, psychological experiment, as a source of psychology. The obvious reason for this is that anyone is thus enabled to create identically the same conditions and to verify for himself the accuracy of the introspective reports of the observers. *This stressing of psychological experiment, however, must not be interpreted to mean that self-observation outside the psychological laboratory is valueless.* It may be so in particular cases but it is not essentially so. Laboratory procedures are devised only to secure accuracy of observation. There are a number of facts of internal experience which require no laboratory arrangements for their exact observation. Thus, for instance, we need not go into the psychological laboratory in order to learn that we use words not merely to beat the air but in order to communicate our ideas to others. Similarly, everyone knows independently of, and prior to, any laboratory findings that he not only hears the words spoken by someone else but at least at times becomes aware also of the objects of which the words are the conventional signs. It is riding a hobbyhorse to death to insist that these facts should be ascertained in the psychological laboratory. And to reject these facts because they are ascertained outside the psychological laboratory, is suicidal. For no laboratory work in psychology is possible without the use of language: the experimenter gives instructions to the observer and he supposes that they are understood or he is at pains to find out whether they are understood; the observer must give an introspective report and it is valueless unless it is understood by the experimenter. Hence, the above two facts of everyday experience are, and must be, supposed before we can make any laboratory experiments. To cast even a doubt on these facts renders all psychological experiment — in fact, all experiment of any kind — impossible. Now these plain facts are the starting point of some plain inferences concerning the nature of our conscious life. We shall not detail these plain inferences here. What we insist on here is only this: If such plain inferences are rejected because they are based on facts ascertained outside the laboratory, we are dealing with a case of bias.

It will not do to justify this bias by insisting that experiment is an essential feature of scientific work. This contention is plainly false. *There are some sciences whose subject matter cannot be investigated by means of experiment.* Such are, for instance, geology and astronomy. *Nor can every problem of even an experimental science be approached from the side of experiment.* In such a case, we welcome any information concerning our problem, no matter how we get it. All we insist on is that the information be accurate. That this is possible even without the use of any instrument whatever is plain from the fact that many mere chance observations have done much for the advancement of various experimental sciences. This is too well known to need further comment. Hence, even if the observation outside the laboratory be of the "chance" or "random" kind, it is not essentially valueless, though it may be so in particular cases.

This leads us to a more fundamental consideration. Experiment is defined as "controlled observation" and the "controlling" of observation is understood to mean that we arbitrarily create and change the condition under which a definite phenomenon is known or suspected to occur. *All observation which is done without this control of the said conditions is sometimes called indiscriminately "chance" or "random" observation. This is very wrong.* When the astronomer observes an eclipse of the sun, he does not create the conditions under which the eclipse occurs: he is not experimenting but only observing. But it is far from correct to say that his observations are of the "chance" or "random" kind. He is prepared for the accurate observation of the eclipse and this excludes all that is meant by the terms "chance" and "random." In psychology we can be likewise prepared for the accurate observation of a number of facts whose conditions are realized in an ideal manner outside the laboratory, at any rate much better than they could be created in the laboratory. In such a case we simply do what the astronomer does: we observe, and see to it that we observe accurately. The accuracy of our observation is not necessarily improved upon because we sit in front of a brass instrument, and the time of our observation is measured by a huge stop watch, known as a chronoscope. And the observation can be repeated very frequently and by many different observers, as the ideal conditions of the fact to be observed occur so frequently. All that is needed is that the observers know the conditions under which a definite fact, say free choice, is supposed to occur. Some people are bad observers inside the laboratory as well as outside the laboratory. But a trained observer is just as good in the performance of his task outside the laboratory as inside. And metaphysical prepossessions do just as much harm inside the laboratory as outside. The point is to get rid of these metaphysical prepossessions.

In one word, we value psychological experiment, but we insist that a hobbyhorse must not be ridden to death and that bias, parading on this hobbyhorse, is a bad guide in the scientific investigation of our conscious life. Much of what is said by modern writers against the "old-fashioned psychology" of Aristotle and the great schoolmen, is bias parading on a hobbyhorse.

7. Psychology and Philosophy. No science can be satisfied with a mere description of facts; it must inquire into their causes. If in the inquisition of causes we proceed as far as legitimate inference from the facts and laws will carry us, we are said to investigate the *ultimate causes* of them and our inquiry is an integral part of philosophy. If, however, we are satisfied with ascertaining the *proximate causes* of our conscious life, psychology is an empirical science. Most modern writers profess to treat psychology as an empirical science, and such is also our intention.

It should be added, however, that it is very difficult to abstain altogether from an inquisition into the ultimate causes of our conscious life, nor has this ever been done consistently. A great many modern writers, while professing to abstain from the discussion of philosophical questions, *settle them dogmatically from the beginning by making unwarranted assumptions.* As a result, many modern books on psychology are a peculiar mixture of real

science and crude metaphysical speculation. What James said of
the psychology of his day is true today. We quote:

"When, then, we talk of 'psychology as a natural science,' we
must not assume that that means a sort of psychology that
stands at last on solid ground. It means just the reverse; it means
a psychology particularly fragile, and into which the waters of
metaphysical criticism leak at every joint, a psychology all of
whose elementary assumptions and data must be reconsidered in
wider connections and translated into other terms."[1]

*In the present book, then, we shall stress the empirical aspect
of our conscious life,* but we shall not attempt the impossible. We
must refer at times to the metaphysical assumptions that have
been made by those who claim to be empirical psychologists.
When we do so, our discussion will be so far philosophical.

References for Further Reading

J. Froebes, S.J., *Lehrbuch der Experimentellen Psychologie*, Vol. I (1923), pp.
1-20.

H. Gruender, S.J., *Introductory Course in Experimental Psychology*, pp. 7-15.

C. S. Myers, *Text-Book of Experimental Psychology*, Chap. I, pp. 1-9.

---

[1] *Psychology*, p. 467 sq.

Chapter II

SENSATIONS

1. The Nature of Sensations and Their Traditional Classification. Our conscious life begins with sensations so that "if a man has no sensation, he cannot learn or understand anything," as Aristotle correctly remarks.[1] Hence, the scientific investigation of our conscious life begins naturally with an account of our sensations. *By "sensations" we mean those conscious processes which are the immediate results of objects affecting our sense-organs and by which we become aware of the sensible qualities of these very objects.*

In our adult life we have rarely, if ever, sensations pure and simple as here defined. Of course, sensible objects affect our sense-organs, namely, the organs of sight, hearing, smell, taste, and touch. But the conscious processes thus aroused are *promptly supplemented and interwoven with memories, associations, and intellectual interpretations of all kinds.* The sum total of these conscious processes, as we get them in our adult life, are known in modern terminology as *sense-perceptions.* For the present we are not concerned with sense-perceptions but with sensations. To get at them, we must artificially separate the memories, associations, and intellectual interpretations from the nucleus around which they cluster. And this nucleus, thus stripped of all accretions, is a simple awareness of the color of an object or of its sound, smell, or flavor, according as the object affects the organ of sight, hearing, smell, or taste.

The traditional fifth sense-organ, that of *touch,* is really a collective name for various sense-organs distributed over our whole skin and its underlying tissues. It is only under artificial conditions that these different organs can be stimulated separately.

---

[1] *De Anima,* III, 8.

Normally, several or all of these organs are acted upon when a body comes in contact with our skin. Hence, it is very natural that all these different organs should be known collectively as the "sense of touch." It is thus that by the traditional fifth sense we become aware of several sensible qualities of bodies. According to the physical condition of the body which comes in contact with our skin, that body "feels" warm or cold, hard or soft, light or heavy, wet or dry, smooth or rough, yielding or resisting, blunt or sharp, in motion or at rest; and sometimes it causes pain. In other words, the traditional sense of "touch" differs from the other senses in this, that it yields several specifically different sensations, as was already recognized by Aristotle[2] and St. Thomas.[3] Under the conditions of everyday life these sensations come to us usually in the form of *"touch blends,"* that is, combinations of several sensations of "touch." It would seem that all such "touch blends" are resolvable into four fundamental sensations; namely, the sensation of *pressure* or touch proper, and the sensations of *heat, cold,* and *pain.*

It should be noted, however, that Aristotle, in classifying sensations according to the traditional five sense-organs, took into consideration only *external sensations,* that is, those sensations which give us first-hand information concerning the sensible qualities of the external world. The Aristotelian classification of these sensations is as satisfactory today as it was at the time of Aristotle, provided we understand it with the qualification made by him. To this day external sensations are known as *sensations of the special senses,* and the special senses meant are the traditional five sense-organs. Details concerning the different sense-organs which mediate the various sensations of "touch" are very little understood even today.

2. Organic Sensations. What really complicates the classification of sensations is the fact that besides external sensations there is another group known as "organic sensations." For our

---

[2]*De Anima,* II, 7. Cf. Hicks, p. 77.
[3]St. Thomas, 9. 78, a. 3, ad 3.

own body, too, is sensible, not only to the sense of sight and touch, but also in other ways, namely, *through changes which occur within our organism*. Although many of these changes are purely physiological transactions, at least as long as we are in good health, some of them normally affect certain sense-organs and as a result we become aware of the condition of our own body.

A good many of these organic sensations are of little psychological interest and are better left to the physiologists for a more detailed discussion. Such are the sensations of hunger, thirst, nausea, dizziness, "pins and needles," itching, tingling, and others of a rather obscure nature.

The sensation of pain, usually enumerated among the sensations of "touch," is really an organic sensation. For it is not the sensible quality of an external object but a condition of our own body, of which we become aware when we feel pain. From this it will be seen that even today the distinction between external and organic sensations is far from clearly drawn.

The most important group of organic sensations is that known collectively under the name of *kinesthetic sensations,* which is but a Greek substitute for the term "sensations of movement." They are mediated by sense-organs situated in the very muscles that contract, in their tendons, and in the joints of the limbs that are moved. When we grasp an object, push or pull it, when we walk or take setting-up exercises, when we play a musical instrument or typewrite a manuscript, not only the organs situated in the skin, but also those in the muscles, tendons, and joints are stimulated, and thus it is that the sensations of movement occur intimately connected with the sensations of "touch." In other words, sensations of movement are normally constitutive elements of the "touch blends" previously referred to. Hence, it is that many psychologists discuss the sensations of movement in connection with the fifth traditional sense-organ. This seems justified because the sensations arising from the muscles, tendons, and joints have some reference to the sense of touch and may be appropriately called sensations of "internal touch"; for they are really due to the contact and pressure of one portion of the body upon another.

We have called kinesthetic sensations a group of sensations. For even after their artificial separation from cutaneous sensations they are a tangle which may be further resolved into three different sensations, namely, those of *muscular ache, tendinous strain,* and *articular friction.* It is particularly the sensations of articular friction, supplemented by visual sensations or images of the limb moved, which figure largely in the perceptions of movement as we get them in everyday life. Intimately connected with kinesthetic sensations are those arising from bodily positions and known as *static sensations.*

From all we have said so far it is clear that in our present state of knowledge it is impossible to make an accurate classification of all our sensations. The following list is an attempt in this direction or, rather, a summary of what we have said on this topic.

	Tentative List of Sensations	*Sensible Qualities*
EXTERNAL SENSATIONS	Visual	colors
	Auditory	sounds
	Olfactory	odors
	Gustatory	flavors
	"Touch"	pressure, weight / heat / cold
ORGANIC SENSATIONS	Cutaneous	pain
	Kinesthetic	muscular ache / tendinous strain / articular friction
	Static	bodily position, dizziness
	Alimentary	hunger, thirst, nausea
	Circulatory	itching, "pins and needles," tingling

TABLE I

3. The Importance of Kinesthetic Sensations. Kinesthetic sensations together with the "touch blends" of which they are a part, are important for three reasons. The first is, because these sensations are *the starting point in the acquisition of skilled movements* of all kinds and particularly in the acquisition of the most complex of all skilled movements, namely, those of articulate speech. This will be explained more fully in a subsequent chapter. When the baby goes through all sorts of random movements, he gets his first lesson in the control of his own body, and when he babbles with delight, he gets his first lesson in his mother tongue.

The second reason is, because kinesthetic sensations together with the "touch blends" give us *first-hand information concerning our own body* and lead us to distinguish it from bodies that are not "mine."

The third reason is, because kinesthetic sensations and the "touch blends" help us considerably in *the building up of our perception of space.* So important are they that even persons born blind can acquire a very accurate perception of space: they build up an exclusively tactual perception of space. We shall deal with this more fully in subsequent chapters.

What we said concerning sensations in general, holds also of kinesthetic sensations in particular, namely, that we must separate them from all associations and intellectual interpretations which in our adult life cluster around them. It is not a matter of mere repetition that we emphasize this. We do so lest we get mixed up with some metaphysical speculations which have been current in modern psychology in this connection.

We said that by organic sensations we become aware of our own body. But no matter how many of these organic sensations are combined or fused, *they must not be construed to be the perception of the Ego as we get it by introspection.* By organic sensations we become aware of our own body *only insofar as it is sensible,* just as by external sensations we become aware of external bodies only insofar as they are sensible. Sensations of articular friction, "touch blends" and any other blends of sensations are one thing, and the intellectual perception of the Ego as we get it by introspection is another. *Hence, when attempts*

*are made to resolve the intellectual perception of the Ego into
its component sensations, we are dealing with a metaphysical pre-
possession.* It is such a metaphysical speculation when James says
"the 'Self of selves, when carefully examined, is found to consist mainly of the collection of these peculiar motions in the head
or between the head and throat."[4]

Animals also undoubtedly have organic sensations, sensations
of articular friction, "touch blends" and other blends of sensations. But it is an unwarranted use of the argument from analogy
when we ascribe to them the awareness of the Ego as we get it
by introspection. On the basis of experience we have defined introspection as the explicit turning back of the attention of the
thinking subject on its own acts. Sensations of articular friction
do not imply such an explicit turning back of the thinking subject on its own acts. Whether articular sensations may be supplemented by such an act of introspection in the case of animals,
will depend, of course, on the question whether animals are
"thinking subjects" at all. If there are arguments which prove
that animals lack intelligence, then these very arguments justify
us in saying that animals lack also such an act of introspection.
All talk, therefore, about a rudimentary sort of introspection and
a rudimentary perception of the Ego in the case of animals, is
based on a confusion of ideas, if it is not worse than that, namely,
a matter of monistic bias.

In ascribing, then, to animals organic sensations such as we
experience, we must strip these sensations from all associations
and intellectual interpretations which in our adult life cluster
around them. How much of this cluster can be said to supplement the nucleus of sensations in the case of animals, is a matter
of construction which will engage our attention in a future
chapter.

**4. Unwarranted Assumptions Concerning the Nature of
Sensations.** Sensations are the starting point of our whole conscious life. This fact has led to an assumption concerning the na-

---

[4]*Principles of Psychology,* I, p. 301.

ture of sensations and the part they play in our conscious life, which has had the profoundest influence on modern psychology. We mean the hypothesis known by the name of *sensationalism*. It holds that *sensations are the structural units of our whole conscious life, even of the most abstract thought.* Hence, sensationalism is intimately connected with *structuralism*, that is, the attempt to trace the pattern or mode of connection imposed upon the elements of our conscious life and thus to account for the origin of all higher conscious processes in terms of their supposed structure. As "structure" is the nearest English equivalent of what some German psychologists call *Gestalt*, it will be seen that sensationalism as actually taught today, is really one of the many varieties of the *theory of Gestalt*, namely, that variety which admits no units of structure except sensations.

We shall deal with sensationalism at great length in the chapters on Thought. For the present it must suffice to say that this hypothesis is far from self-evident and that we cannot accept it unchallenged. Neither can we allow that this assumption be made "provisionally" as a starting point. For, as James has said of this and other assumptions of modern psychology, "when these assumptions have once established themselves (as they have a way of doing in our very descriptions of the phenomenal facts) it is almost impossible to get rid of them afterwards or to make anyone see that they are no essential feature of the subject. . . . One of the obscurest of the assumptions of which I speak is the assumption that *our mental states are composite in structure,* made up of smaller states conjoint. This hypothesis has outward advantages which make it almost irresistibly attractive to the intellect, and yet *it is inwardly quite unintelligible. Of its unintelligibility, however, half the writers on psychology seem unaware.*"[5]

Intimately connected with the hypothesis of sensationalism or structuralism is another assumption concerning the nature of sensations which must be briefly mentioned here. *It has been said that a sensation has no object,* while a perception has, and that

---

[5]*Principles of Psychology,* I, p. 145.

this is the real difference between sensation and perception. There is absolutely no foundation for such an assertion in our experience: it is a metaphysical speculation which may fit well into the scheme of sensationalism and structuralism, but it does not fit the facts.

Whatever else a sensation may be, it is a conscious process and, as we have explained in Chapter I (p. 3), every conscious process involves essentially an awareness of an object. Even sensationalists cannot possibly describe a particular sensation and discriminate it from other sensations except by indicating its characteristic "quality." But the quality of a sensation has an essential reference to the sensible quality of the body which normally arouses the sensation. In fact, the quality of a sensation is nothing else than the sensible quality of a body, not indeed the quality as it is in itself, but as it appears to the senses. Every attempt to explain the "quality" of a sensation differently is tantamount to the metaphysical speculation known in philosophy as idealism.

There is, however, a grain of truth in the metaphysical speculation which we here reject: it is the very distinction which we made just now between *the sensible quality* of a body *as it is in itself*, and *as it appears to the senses*. In other words, though a sensation involves essentially an awareness of the sensible quality of a body, this awareness does not amount to a knowledge concerning the intimate nature of this sensible quality. This was stated with all the emphasis desirable by St. Thomas, when he said that a knowledge concerning the intimate nature of the sensible qualities of bodies is not a matter of sensation but of intellectual interpretation.[6] Aristotle says in substance the same.[7]

Still another assumption has been current in modern psychological literature. It is known by the name of *interpretationism* or as the *theory of eccentric projection*. The hypothesis put forward is that all our sensations appear to us at first as purely subjective phenomena and are afterwards and by a process of interpretation or further elaboration "extradited" or "projected" into the outer

---

[6] Cf. St. Thomas, I, q. 78, a. 3, in c.
[7] Cf. *De Anima*, II, 6; Tr. by Hicks, p. 77.

world as properties of bodies. There is nothing in our adult experience to warrant such an hypothesis. When in an unsophisticated, healthy mood we watch a baseball game, we know nothing of such an elaboration, interpretation, eccentric projection, or extradition of our sensations. Nor does our distinction between the *sensible quality* of a body *as it is in itself* and *as it appears to our senses,* imply an eccentric projection such as is postulated in the theory referred to. We see the baseball, that is, we experience the ball *as it affects our organ of sight:* this, and no more and no less. What the experience of a newborn babe may be when his sense-organs are bombarded for the first time, we can know only by inference. James has probably described this experience correctly when he calls it a big, blooming, buzzing confusion, but this big, blooming, buzzing confusion is the physical universe *as it appears* to the philosopher-to-be. He will have to swallow a good deal of unwholesome idealistic literature before he comes to think of "projecting" or "extraditing" his sensations.

The last assumption concerning the nature of sensations which must be briefly mentioned here is known as the *local-sign theory.* It will come up for a detailed discussion in later chapters. Here it may suffice to say that the hypothesis voiced is that all our sensations, including those of sight and touch, are *originally devoid of all spatial content.* But visual sensations, it is stated, always occur in connection with eye movements and the kinesthetic sensations arising from them. These kinesthetic sensations gradually become "signs" for us by which we are guided in the spatial "projection" of visual sensations, pretty much as a librarian is guided by the labels on the backs of books in placing each book on the proper shelf. In short, the local-sign theory is a scheme of building up our visual perception of space with nothing to start with, or a trick of arriving at a big capital by adding zeros to zeros. The result of adding zeros to zeros is, of course, zero. We must, and do, start with a capital, however small it may be. In other words, it is not true that all our sensations are originally devoid of all spatial content. At least this is not true of visual sensations. Whatever else the original content of a visual sensation may be, it surely includes the awareness of the color of a body. A "colored mathematical point" does not occur in the world in which we live or in our visual experience of this world: it belongs to the realm of chimeras where circles are square. Hence, some spatial content is included in every color sensation.

There is, however, a grain of truth in the local-sign theory and it is this: in the elaboration of the original spatial content of visual sensations we need "signs" or "criteria." In fact, the remarkable perfection of our visual perception of space is entirely due to the use of these criteria. It must be emphasized, however, that the "criteria" of the local-sign theory have practically nothing to do with our visual space perception. All details concerning the original data of our visual experience, and the manner of their elaboration, will be dealt with in Chapters VI, VII, and VIII. It is because of the great complexity of our visual space perception that we eliminate this topic entirely from the chapters dealing with visual sensations. The latter will be discussed under the heading of "color sensations."

5. The Nervous System of Man. We must now consider the bodily structures which make sensations possible — namely, the sense-organs. They are really parts of the nervous system and can be understood only in this connection. A rough illustration, which must not be pressed beyond a mere analogy, will assist the student in understanding the general arrangement of the nervous system of man. It may be compared to the *telephone system* which brings the remotest parts of a city into ready communication.

The central station is really a complicated system of switchboards and represents *the central nervous system* — that is, the spinal cord and the brain. Here certain connections of vital importance are ready-made and correspond to the telephone connections necessary to give the fire alarm or to call for police protection; other connections can be established as occasion requires.

The telephone wires together with their terminal attachments, the transmitter and the receiver, correspond to *the peripheral nervous system*. The eye, ear, nose, mouth, and skin are the transmitters into which the external world speaks; the terminal organs which mediate organic sensations are the transmitters into which our own body speaks. The peripheral nerves correspond to the telephone wires, but here our analogy is less perfect. One and the same telephone wire may carry a message in both directions, toward, or away, from the central station. This is not true of the peripheral nerves. The latter are really of two kinds, known respectively as *afferent* and *efferent nerves*. The former carry a message from the eye, ear, skin, etc., to the central nervous system; the latter are paths conducting impulses from the central nervous system to the muscles and the glands. It would be more accurate to compare the peripheral nerves to cables, for they consist of a great many insulated fibers, usually of both the afferent and the efferent type. Accordingly, these insulated nerve-fibers really correspond to the telephone wires except that, unlike the latter, they carry a message only in one direction, either toward, or away from, the central station.

As all organs of the body, so also the nervous system consists of cells. The most important of these are called *ganglion cells* or *neurons* (Fig. 1). They differ in shape and are accordingly designated multipolar, bipolar, or unipolar. *Multipolar neurons* (Figs. 1 and 2) consist of a cell body with numerous protoplasmic processes, called *dendrites,* and another process, usually of greater length and known as the *axis cylinder, axon,* or also *nerve-fiber.* It is the function of the dendrites to "pick up" a message or neural current, and that of the axon or nerve-fiber to "conduct" the message further. Before reaching its destination the axon (or nerve-fiber), as a rule, gives off one or more collateral branches, called *collaterals,* and at last terminates in a very fine end brush, known as *telodendrion* (see Figs. 1 and 4). It is by means of these end brushes and the dendrites and the collaterals mentioned that the different neurons are physiologically connected with one another and joined so as to form the nervous system. There are also spherical and spindle-shaped ganglion cells with only two processes, one of which acts like a dendrite, the other as an axis cylinder. These *bipolar cells* are found chiefly in (the gray matter of) the brain. *Unipolar* neurons have only one prolongation which divides into an axis cylinder and a dendrite so that, functionally, a unipolar neuron is bipolar.

The connection between neuron and neuron is called a *synapse,* whose function has been likened to that of a spark gap or also to

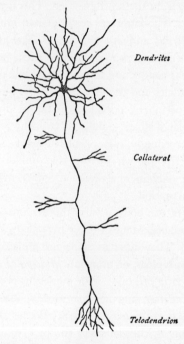

Dendrites

Collateral

Telodendrion

FIG. 1. Schematic Representation of a Neuron (from *Villiger*).

that of a resistance box. Following out the latter comparison we may say that a *synapse offers resistance to the passage of a nervous impulse from one neuron to another.* Congenitally this resistance is lesser in one direction than in another. Wherever this occurs, we speak of *congenital ruts or grooves* in the nervous system such as are used in physiological reflexes and to a great extent in instinctive actions. This will be explained more fully later. The resistance which a synapse offers may also be gradually reduced by the frequent repetition of actions which are at first difficult. Whenever this occurs, we speak of *acquired ruts or grooves* in the nervous system. This will be explained at great length when we deal with the formation of habits and the man-

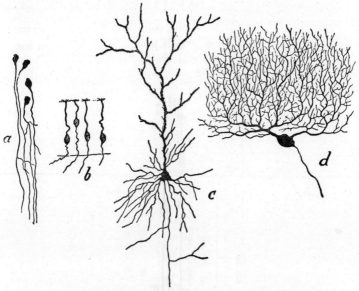

FIG. 2. Nerve cells of different types: *a*, unipolar cells; *b*, bipolar cells; *c* and *d*, multipolar cells; *c*, pyramidal cell (from *Villiger*).

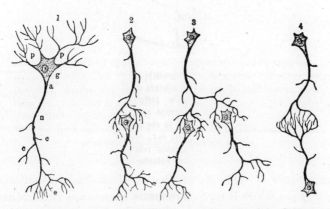

FIG. 3. Schematic representation of synaptic connections between neurons (after C. von Langer and Toldt, from *Ranke*).

ner in which we acquire voluntary control over our body. Here it suffices to state that the kinesthetic sensations arising from congenitally determined movements are the starting point for the

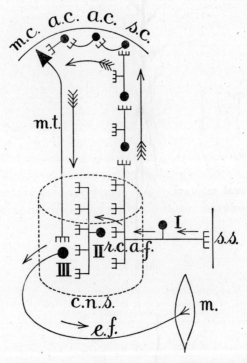

Fig. 4. Neural Connections (schematic); *s.s.* I, II, III, *m*, the reflex arc; *s.s.* sensory surface (receptor); I, afferent neuron; II, correlation neuron; III, efferent neuron; *m*, muscle (effector); *r.c.*, reflex collateral; *c.n.s.*, some level of central nervous system; *a.f.*, afferent fiber; *e.f.*, efferent fiber; *s.c.*, sensory center in the cortex of the brain; *a.c.*, association center; *m.c.*, motor center; *m.t.*, motor tract (pyramidal tract); *small arrows* indicate the congenital reflex path, *the long feathered arrows* the path of voluntary movements.

performance of voluntary movements of all kinds. The neural mechanism which is used in voluntary movements is schematically indicated in Figure 4 and will be explained more fully in later chapters.

6. The Sense-Organs. This premised, we are ready to define a sense-organ. By this term we mean *not only the terminal attachments of the nervous system* which are situated at the surface of our body and on which sensible bodies (our own body included) act, *but also the nervous paths which connect these structures with the brain and the very portions of the brain thus connected.* For unless the impulse set up in the peripheral structure be propagated to its appropriate central station in the cortex (or outer layer) of the brain, the conscious process known as a sensation will not be aroused.

As a matter of fact, the impulse set up in the sensory surface (s.s. in Fig 4) say of the skin, may be "short-circuited" by means of "reflex collaterals" (r.c.) along the path indicated by the short arrows, and then the result of the activity of sensible objects on the peripheral sense-organ is a purely physiological transaction known as a *physiological reflex.* This will be explained more fully in Chapter XII. Not only do reflexes occur, but some of them are necessary for the normal functioning of our sense-organs: they consist in adjustments of these organs to their respective stimuli. An instance in point is the appropriate contraction of the pupil of the eye necessary for distinct vision. From this it will be seen that physiological reflexes are a normal adjunct of sensations. For the radical behaviorist such purely physiological transactions are the "units of behavior," as will be explained more fully in a later chapter.

Before a sensation can arise, the nervous impulse must travel upward along the path indicated by the feathered arrow until it reaches the corresponding sensory center (s.c.) in the cortex of the brain. Introspectively we are not aware of the fact that we have in our brain centers of vision, hearing, etc. All we know from unsophisticated experience is that we see, hear, etc. *We localize, indeed, the object seen, but we do not localize the act of vision.* The localization of sensations in the brain is an inference based, at least in part, upon the findings of the anatomist in the dissecting room. There the path that leads, for instance, from the eye to the cortex of the occipital lobe is traced. From these *ana-*

tomical findings to the statement that visual sensations are localized in the occipital lobe, is a good distance which must be bridged over by experimental findings of different kinds. They are furnished by *physiologists* and *pathologists* but are too complex to be explained here.

7. **The physiological conditions of the sensory associations which supplement our actual sensations** are diagrammatically indicated in Figure 4. The excitement set up in a sensory center of the brain (s.c.) is propagated to other centers known as association centers (a.c.). It is thus that the various sensory associations arise which usually supplement our actual sensations. This will be dealt with more fully in later chapters.

According to sensationalists, even our intellectual interpretations of the sensible object present are reduced to such sensory associations. In fact, all thinking is assumed to be thus fully accounted for. *This supposed,* the further explanation of thought is physiological and takes one of two forms, known respectively as *materialism* and *psychophysical parallelism*. Materialism identifies thought with nerve processes; psychophysical parallelism maintains that thought runs parallel to nerve processes in such a way that *definite thoughts are the invariable concomitants of definite neural processes*. The latter hypothesis is the more prevalent today. *Neither hypothesis fits into the psychology of Aristotle.*

As experimentalists we have nothing to do with such metaphysical speculations and leave their discussion to philosophy. The reader who is interested in these philosophical discussions is referred to a book published by the present writer under the title *Psychology Without a Soul.*

Here it may suffice to state that both *materialism and psychophysical parallelism suppose sensationalism. We can test the latter hypothesis very readily by the facts of our experience* and we shall do so in the chapters on Thought. *Thus we shall be able to deal effectively with materialism and psychophysical parallelism without getting involved in any metaphysical speculation.*

8. **The True Nervous End-Organs of External Sensa-**

tions and Their Accessory Structures. Only comparatively small portions of eye, ear, nose, mouth, and skin constitute *the true nervous end-organs of external sensations.* By the latter term we mean *those peripheral attachments of the sensory nerves which are specially adapted to respond each to a definite stimulus known as its "adequate" stimulus.* Stimulus denotes any action proceeding from sensible objects about us. The term "adequate" is applied to that stimulus for which each nervous end-organ is specially adapted or to which it is specially "attuned."

The adequate stimuli for the five traditional sense-organs are: light waves for the organ of sight; sound waves for the organ of hearing; the chemical action of volatile emanations coming in contact with the interior of the nostrils for the organ of smell; the chemical action of soluble substances put into the mouth for the organ of taste; and mechanical pressure, heat, and cold, for the organs of touch. To other than their adequate stimuli the various sensory end-organs do not respond at all or only in an abnormal manner, and hence such stimuli are known as "inadequate" stimuli. *Each sensory end-organ, then, owing to its special adaptation for its own adequate stimulus, selectively singles out this stimulus from the many which are continually acting upon us,* and thus becomes a source of specific information concerning the world about us.

The true nervous end-organ of vision is the thin layer of rods and cones in the retina of the eye. Each rod and each cone is attached in a somewhat complicated manner to a corresponding fiber of the optic tract pretty much as a telephone transmitter is attached to its conducting wire. It will not do to talk directly into a telephone wire: we must speak into the transmitter. Just so the fibers of the optic tract will not respond to the action of light, if it falls on them directly. The only portion of our retina which is altogether blind is that where the bundle of optic fibers passes out of the eyeball on its path to the brain. In this "blind spot" there are no rods and no cones so that light hits the optic fibers directly. If a normal visual sensation is to be aroused, light must fall on the terminal attachments of the optic fibers. It is the rods and cones which are sensitive to light and which set up an impulse in the optic fibers connected each with corresponding rods and cones.

The true nervous end-organs of the ear, nose, and mouth respectively are the organ of Corti in the inner ear, too complex to be described here in detail, the olfactory epithelium, and the taste buds on the back of the tongue. It is these structures attached to the fibers of the auditory, olfactory, and gustatory nerves respectively, which act like telephone transmitters.

The true nervous end-organs of "touch" are a great variety of structures found in our skin and connected each with an afferent fiber. But we know very little in detail concerning their function. In some cases the free endings of afferent fibers seem to serve as telephone transmitters.

By far the greater portions of what are popularly known as "sense-organs," consist of contrivances designed to modify their respective adequate stimuli and to bring them to bear on the true nervous end-organs in such a way as is required for normal sensations. These contrivances are known as *accessory structures.* Thus, for instance, the greater portion of the eye consists of contrivances designed to refract the rays of light reflected or emitted by the objects about us, and to focus these rays on those cones which must be acted upon, if we are to have a normal vision, say, of a rose and its surrounding green leaves.

The upper portion of Figure 5 illustrates what would happen if the refracting media of the eye were absent. Let R represent a definite point on a rose, and G a definite point on the green leaf which is near the rose. Sunlight reflected from R is diffused in all directions, and if a retina is in the path of this diffused light, every rod and cone will be affected by it indiscriminately. The same is true of light reflected from G. In other words, in the absence of the refracting media of the eye all objects about us would affect indiscriminately all the rods and cones of the eye. There would indeed be a confused visual sensation but we could not discriminate between the rose and the green leaf: all visual discrimination of objects would be impossible.

The lower portion of Figure 5 illustrates what actually takes place, because of the refracting media with which the eye is supplied. Identically the same light as it is reflected from point R in its passage through the refracting media of the eye comes to a point again on the retina (R') and thus only a definite cone is

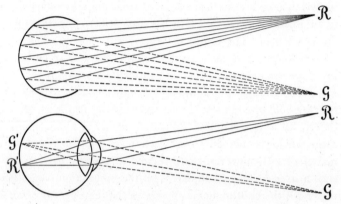

FIG. 5. Diagram to illustrate the function of the accessory structures of the eye.

stimulated by this light. Something similar is true of the light reflected from point G. In a word, our eye is constructed after the manner of a photographic camera. The result of this is that the rose affects only definite cones and the green leaf affects other definite cones. The stimulation of the cones thus corresponds to the spatial distribution of the objects seen and each cone is affected by identically the same kind of light as it proceeds from the corresponding part of the object seen.

The accessory structures of the ear are rather complicated and are as yet not fully understood. It is a matter of theory how sound waves really come to stimulate the organ of Corti. We shall deal with this difficult subject when discussing auditory sensations (see Fig. 17). Still less is known concerning the accessory structures of the other sense-organs. As many of the sensations mediated by these organs are of little psychological interest, we had better leave the detailed discussion of these end-organs and their accessory structures to physiologists. *It is all these doubtful matters which are referred to in the "theories" of this or that sensation.*

9. The Limits of Sensation. Weber's Law.

The discussion of the end-organs of sensation and of the adequate stimuli by which they are normally aroused to action lead us naturally to an aspect of sensation which has been widely discussed under the heading of "The Limits of Sensation." There are lights too weak to arouse a visual sensation; sounds too faint to be heard; pressures too light to be felt, and so forth. *A stimulus which is just strong enough to produce a conscious sensation is known as the threshold of sensation.* If man were but a machine, we should expect that a fixed minimal amount of energy in some particular form would be needed to set each sense-organ agoing. As a matter of fact, however, the threshold of sensation is far from such a fixed quantity. It differs with the multifarious conditions under which the stimulus is applied to the sense-organs of man. In the case of visual stimuli, in particular, the threshold varies considerably with the conditions which we shall discuss under the heading of The Phenomena of Simultaneous Contrast (p. 66). And in the case of all stimuli the direction of our voluntary or involuntary attention has a great deal to do with the threshold of sensation.

There is also a threshold in making an addition of one stimulus to another. This is known as *the differential threshold*. Here again we are not dealing with a fixed quantity of light, heat, etc., but this quantity differs with the concrete conditions under which the addition is made. Supposing, however, that all other factors of a visual sensation, for instance, are kept constant, it has been found that the amount of light reflected from a body must be increased in *a definite ratio*, if that body is to appear *noticeably brighter* In other words, no matter what the amount of light is by which a body is illuminated, we must add to that amount (say L) a definite fraction of that amount (a definite fraction of L). if the body is to appear noticeably brighter. It is stated that this fraction of L is 1/100, and *it is this fraction which is known as the differential threshold of a visual sensation.* A similar condition prevails in the case of other sensations but the fraction which constitutes the differential threshold of these sensations, differs with each sensation.

There is also an *acme of sensation.* That is to say, there is a maximal amount of light, heat, pressure, and so forth, beyond which we cannot go without causing pain and eventually injuring the sense-organ. This acme, in turn, is not a fixed quantity of light, heat, etc., but it differs with the conditions under which the stimulus is applied to the sense-organ. Thus, for instance, immediately upon awaking at midnight, the light of a match may be blinding and above the acme of a visual sensation. Soon after, however, we can stand a good deal more light, and at noontime the light of a match is considerably below the differential threshold: it adds nothing to the brightness of objects seen.

Between the threshold and the acme of a visual sensation, then, we can arrange a series of lights, L1, L2, L3, L4, etc., in such a way that each L differs from the just preceding L by a definite fraction (1/100) of that preceding L. This done, we can correlate this series of lights with a corresponding series of visual sensations, S1, S2, S3, S4, etc., in such a way that each S differs from the S just preceding by a noticeable increase in brightness. *This correlation between the two series, understood in the sense of a rough empirical formula, is known as Weber's law.* The following table is a schematic representation of this law as it applies to visual sensations.

Series of Sensations Described	Series of Lights Described
S1	L1
S2	$L2 = L1\ (1 + 1/100)$
S3	$L3 = L2\ (1 + 1/100)$
S4	$L4 = L3\ (1 + 1/100)$

TABLE II

The intensity of other sensations (except perhaps those of taste and smell) can be similarly correlated with a series of corresponding stimuli.

It should be emphasized, however, that the exact fraction by which the stimulus must be increased, is not particularly exact, even if all other factors of the sensation investigated are kept constant. In other words, Weber's law is a mere approximation and far from the precision which characterizes the laws of physics and chemistry.

Weber's law, moreover, can be easily misconstrued in other ways. Suppose, for instance, that A, B, and C denote three different amounts of light. I observe and compare two physically equal surfaces illuminated respectively by A and B, and I notice no difference in the brightness of the two surfaces. Then I compare the same two surfaces illuminated respectively by B and C, and again I notice no difference in their brightness. Lastly, I compare the same two surfaces illuminated respectively by A and C, and I notice a difference in their brightness. From this it has been concluded that two quantities (A and C) may be equal to the same third quantity (B) and still not be equal among themselves.

If we misconstrue the meaning of Weber's law, this paradox follows. But if we realize what the law really says, no such absurdity can be deduced from it. Weber's law really deals only with the *noticeability* of a difference between two sensations. In other words, it states the conditions under which (all other things being equal) the difference in the intensity of a sensation becomes noticeable. These conditions were not fulfilled when I compared A with B, or C with B, but they were fulfilled when I compared A with C.

10. Fechner's "Law" and Titchener's "Quantitative Analysis" in Psychology. Fechner, treating the fraction of the stimulus which constitutes the differential threshold as if it were mathematically exact, and assuming that each noticeable increase in the intensity of a sensation is a "unit" of that sensation, and assuming a number of other things which he had no right to assume, has extended the rough empirical formula of Weber into a metaphysical speculation which, by way of courtesy, is sometimes referred to as Fechner's "law." It states that the intensity of a sensation increases as the logarithm of the stimulus and this (according to Fechner) means that a sensation increases in arithmetic proportions when its stimulus increases in geometric proportions. If all this is granted, it follows that sensations can be measured in units and are susceptible of mathematical treatment. These speculations are the basis for the statement that psychology is really a part of physics and may be appropriately called *"psychophysics."*

Titchener has tried to put Fechner's mathematical formula on an experimental basis, which is, to say the very least rather doubtful. Discussions of this kind constitute a great part of what Titchener calls *"quantitative analysis"* in psychology. *We are not particularly interested in these discussions.*

References for Further Reading

J. Froebes, S.J., *Lehrbuch der Experimentellen Psychologie.* Vol. I (1923), pp. 21–40; 445–484.

J. Lindworsky, S.J., *Experimentelle Psychologie* (1921), pp. 16–20.

H. Gruender, S.J., *Introductory Course in Experimental Psychology,* Chap. XIV.

H. v. Helmholtz, *Handbuch der Physiologischen Optik* (ed. 2, 1896), pp. 384–394.

H. v. Helmholtz, *English Translation* of 3d German edition, edited by J. P. C. Southall, Vol. II, pp. 172–204.

Chapter III

COLOR SENSATIONS

1. Color in the Physical Sense. The reader who has carefully followed our discussion of sensations in general will understand why Aristotle insists that "in considering each separate sensation we must first treat of the sensible objects."[1] In treating, then, of visual sensations, we must begin with their objects — visible bodies. As Aristotle correctly remarks, a body is "visible because it contains within itself the cause of visibility, namely, color. Hence, color is universally capable of exciting change in the actually transparent, that is, light; this being, in fact, the true nature of color. Hence, color is not visible without light, but the color of each object is always seen in light."[2] If we substitute "ether" for "the actually transparent," this Aristotelian account of color states with absolute precision what modern science means by the color of a body.

When we speak of color in the physical sense, we mean the color of a body: we mean that peculiarity of the object which renders it capable of being seen. Before explaining in detail what this peculiarity is, we wish to call attention to an improper use of the term "physical color." This term is sometimes applied to light and then we speak of "colored light." Such a use of the term is inappropriate for the simple reason that we never see light but we see bodies in light. When a beam of direct sunlight enters through an opening in the shade of a window, we really see the dust particles in the air which scatter the light, or we see a portion of the wall of the room thus directly illuminated by light. In the absence of all dust particles in the air and of all

[1]*De Anima*, II, 6.
[2]*Op. cit.*, II, 7.

36

bodies scattering the light, we should never become aware of this light, unless we look directly at the sun, and then we see the sun. Hence, visual sensations are really not "sensations of light," but sensations by which we become aware of the color of bodies. When, therefore, we inquire into the nature of "color in the physical sense," we inquire into the nature of a physical property of bodies. The notable fact, however, is that the term "physical color" is sometimes applied by physicists to light.

As applied to light, "physical color" is synonymous with wave length within the limits of the visible spectrum (which is only a comparatively small portion of solar radiant energy). Thus, "yellow" light for the physicist means radiant energy of a wave length of 567.1 Angströms (an Angström being the ten-millionth part of a millimeter); "white" light is synonymous with unfiltered sunlight. *A good deal of confusion in the discussion of color phenomena would be avoided if the physicist always substituted for such terms as "white," "yellow," or any other "colored" light just what he means, namely, unfiltered sunlight and radiant energy of this or that wave length.*

The color of a body in the physical sense may be defined as *the specific property which that body has in virtue of its molecular and atomic constitution to emit, transmit, absorb, or reflect certain portions of radiant energy and thus to determine the kind and amount of light that impinges upon the organ of sight, and causes a definite color sensation.* In particular, a "physically white" body is one that absorbs none of the light that falls upon it but diffusely reflects (or scatters in all directions) all of this light. Newly fallen snow is a fairly ideal example of this physical condition; a piece of mat typewriting paper approaches it. A "physically black" body is one that absorbs all incident light and reflects none; a piece of black velvet approaches this physical condition. A "physically gray" body is one that absorbs a portion of the incident light, but *not selectively,* and diffusely reflects all the rest. Hering's series of gray papers represent different degrees of this physical condition. The leaf of a tree is "physically green" in the sense that the chlorophyll particles within the cells of the leaf absorb *selectively* those portions of solar radiant energy which supply the energy for the vital processes of the tree, and diffusely reflect the rest, namely, a mixture of many different wave lengths, in which, however, the middle portion of the visible spectrum (the "green" light of the physicist) preponderates, and this mixture, as a matter of fact, causes the sensations of "leaf green."

From this it will be seen that *color in the physical sense is a property of bodies as truly objective and independent of any sensation as is the physical and chemical constitution of bodies.* In fact, the physical color of a body is a necessary resultant of its physical and chemical constitution and hence a specific property of that body. As most bodies are opaque at least to the radiations of the visible spectrum, the selective absorption and reflection (which constitutes their color) takes place at their surfaces or more correctly, in the outermost molecular layers of that body. Hence, it can also be said that *the physical color of an opaque body depends upon the molecular constitution and the structure of its surface.*

2. Color in the psychological sense is the *physical color of a body as it appears* in a visual sensation aroused by that body. In other words, it is that *characteristic appearance* which a body has when light modified by the reflecting surfaces of that body actually stimulates the organ of sight, and which is readily distinguished from the seen spatial attributes of that body and cannot be described in any other way than by saying: That body *looks red, looks pale green,* etc.

The characteristic appearance which different colored bodies in nature have, presents an immense variety. It has been estimated by Sir Frederick W. Herschel that the mosaic workers in Rome have distinguished in the neighborhood of 30,000 colored stones by their characteristic appearance. Psychologists add at least several thousands to this number when they figure out the sum total of colors which can be discriminated under laboratory conditions. Our vocabulary simply gives out when we try to designate by specific names all those we distinguish. Dealers in colored silk resort to special trade names such as "ashes of roses," "pearl gray," "royal purple," "quaker drab," etc., or sell their colored wares simply by number. All such trade names and numbers are of no psychological interest but are necessary for commercial purposes. Simply saying that "red" silk is wanted, will not do; for *there are thousands of reds;* the customer must pick out from a specimen card the precise red he or she wants and then order it by trade name or number.

Evidently there is need of some classification of the vast number of distinguishable colors. And to this problem we must turn our attention. Behaviorists have poked fun at the vast number of colors that psychologists distinguish under laboratory conditions, and they reject the problems arising from these distinctions as questions that have no human interest. To which the answer is that *not only introspectionists but men and women in the ordinary walks of life are intensely interested in color discriminations.* The very devices used by tradesmen in selling their colored wares show how fine this discrimination is. So long as artistic pursuits appeal to men, so long are color discriminations and the problems arising from them of human interest. Leonardo da Vinci can surely not be accused of dealing with questions of lunar politics, but he was intensely interested in color discriminations and the problem of the classification of colors. What is of such intense human interest, is worth discussing from a scientific standpoint. Evidently a scientist cannot be satisfied with trade names and catalog numbers of tradesmen; such devices are for the psychologist of as little value in an orderly arrangement of colors as accession numbers of books or their bindings are for the librarian in an orderly arrangement of books.

3. **The Stimulus-Response Method of Behaviorists and the Problem of Color Classification.** The first thing to be noted in answer to the question before us is that the stimulus-response method of behaviorists is an utter failure in dealing with

a problem of such intense human interest as color discrimination and classification. The stimulus-response method consists in this: knowing the stimulus, we can predict the response, and knowing the response we can tell the nature of the stimulus which evoked the response. Wherever else this method may be applied successfully, it surely cannot be applied in the case of color sensations. In other words, *the specific character of a color sensation cannot be defined by the nature of the light which normally arouses it and no satisfactory classification of colors can be accomplished on the basis of the physical properties of light: wave length, amplitude, and form of the light wave.* In proof of these statements it will suffice to point out *three salient facts of physiological optics.*

The first fact is that identically the same color sensation can be aroused by many physically different kinds of light. Every "color equation" is an experimental demonstration of this fact. $W = 567.1 + 464.5$ is a typical example of a color equation, made by Helmholtz. The symbol on the left side of the equation (W) stands for a definite amount of unfiltered sunlight, that is, the physical mixture of all the wave lengths of the visible spectrum. The numbers on the right side of the equation indicate the wave lengths (in Angströms) of two different kinds of light; the longer wave being one of the various "yellow" lights of the physicist, the shorter one, one of his various "indigo-blue" lights. The sign of addition denotes the physical mixture of these two kinds of monochromatic light. The sign of equation ($=$) does not mean what it means in a mathematical or physical formula. For then our color equation would be just as absurd as the statement that $365 = 7 + 2$. The real meaning of this symbol as understood in a "color equation" is *the physiological equivalence of two physically different kinds of light* indicated on the left and on the right side of the equation respectively. Both kinds of light reflected from identically the same surface (say, a piece of physically white paper) arouse identically the same sensation, namely, that of a definite white. What holds of the color equation mentioned in the foregoing, holds of every other color equation, and we make them by the thousands in the psychological laboratory.[3]

From this it will be seen that *the correlation of color sensations with their physical stimuli is something of a tangle which can be unraveled only under laboratory conditions.* And it deserves emphasis that this correlation is a tangle, even if all other conditions of color sensations be kept uniform. We shall try to bring some order into this tangle when discussing in a later paragraph the laws of color mixture. It is not difficult to establish these laws as simple empirical rules, but it is very difficult to explain them. The very laws of color mixture introduce us to the most central problem of color sensations, and it is this: *Why is it that there are so many physically different kinds of light which are physiologically equivalent in arousing one and the same color sensation?* Whosoever ignores this aspect of color equations ignores the most unique feature of color sensations, that feature by which visual sensations are so radically distinguished from auditory sensations. We have as yet no theory of color vision which makes the tangled correlation of color sensations with their physical stimuli intelligible to us. But one thing is sufficiently clear, namely, that *the stimulus-response method of behaviorists ignores the central problem of color sensations.* And for those who are not behavioristically inclined the most important conclusion from the above data is this: *Any theory of color vision which attempts to define or classify color sensations by simply correlating them with the physical properties of light, is wide of the mark.*

---

[3]The simplest way of making a "color equation" is by means of the color wheel or the so-called "color mixer." Thus, for instance, we may mount on one color wheel a compound disk consisting of two sectors, one yellow, the other indigo blue. On another color wheel we mount a compound disk consisting of a white and a black sector. If the two sectors of each compound disk are appropriately adjusted, and both compound disks are rotated with sufficient speed, the two disks *look exactly alike:* it is impossible to tell the one from the other. We state this fact in the form of a "color equation" such as *170° Yellow + 190° Indigo Blue = 60° White + 300° Black. What really happens when we use the color wheel* is fully explained in the first chapter of the writer's *Introductory Course in Experimental Psychology,* pp. 16–25. From the explanations there given, the reader will also see why we call the color wheel a "so-called color mixer."

The second fact of physiological optics which leads to identically the same conclusion is this: *Unfiltered sunlight as reflected from a physically white piece of paper does not always produce the sensation of white.* Conditions can be readily created in the psychological laboratory under which *identically the same amount of unfiltered sunlight, reflected from identically the same physically white piece of paper, arouses the sensation of yellow or blue or green, in fact, any color under the sun.* The conditions here referred to are known by the name of *simultaneous contrast.* The phenomena of simultaneous contrast have sometimes been referred to as "abnormal," and there is a grain of truth in this statement, as we shall point out in the paragraph dealing with these phenomena. But this grain of truth must not be exaggerated to mean that the phenomena of simultaneous contrast are mere oddities which can be safely ignored in discussing normal color vision. Such a statement is far from correct. When carefully examined, these phenomena show that the very contrary is the truth: *Our normal vision would not be what it is if it were not for the facts of simultaneous contrast.* For the purposes of the present discussion the important point to note is this: *The characteristic appearance of a colored body depends not only on the kind and amount of light which that body reflects into our eye and which affects definite rods and cones, but also on the kinds and amounts of light which are reflected by surrounding bodies and reach another set of rods and cones.* The plain inference is: We cannot define the characteristic appearance of a colored body by the properties of light which that body sends into the eye.

The third fact of physiological optics which tells the same story is one which is *just as unique as it is familiar to us: the sensation of black.* If the characteristic appearance of a colored body is to be defined by the physical properties of the light which that body reflects into the eye, then the sensation of black is, to put it mildly, a stumblingblock. For there is no "physically black light." A physically black body is one that absorbs all incident light and reflects none.

There are two ways of avoiding this difficulty. The first is to say — and it has been said — that *the sensation of black is really no visual sensation at all.* It will be hard for the reader to make up his mind that in reading this page he has no visual sensations of the black letters at all. From the back of my head I have no visual sensation, but it cannot be said that from the back of my head I have the sensation of black. Having no visual sensation at all is one thing, and having the sensation of black is quite another. *So far as our internal experience is concerned, the sensation of black is exactly on a par with any other color sensation, say that of green: both have a positive content character and we distinguish them from each other precisely by their positive content character.*

Granting, then, the positive character of the sensation of black, the other alternative is, that *this positive sensation has no physical cause at all.* This would mean that the sensation of black is really an abnormal phenomenon, that is, a plain illusion. It is, to say the very least, rather incongruous to classify our ability to read the black letters of this page among the illusions. Nor is it true that the sensation of black arises in the absence of all light. Laboratory findings show that the sensation of black never arises except under the conditions of simultaneous (or successive) contrast: it is in every instance *an indirect effect of light.* In a word, *the sensation of black, though the most familiar of our color sensations, is the most unique of all the phenomena of simultaneous contrast.*

From all this it follows that the assumption of the foregoing two alternatives is wrong. That is to say, *it is wrong to maintain that the characteristic appearance of a colored body can be defined by the physical properties of the light which that body reflects into the organ of sight.*

4. The Purely Psychological Classification of Colors and the Six Colors Which Serve as Fixed Points of Comparison. Accordingly, *the more thoroughly we forget all we know about the physical properties of light, the more satisfactory will be our classification of colors.* Our classification of colors must be *purely psychological.* And this means: *We must be*

*guided exclusively by the similarities and differences which we
ascertain by introspection* when comparing the characteristic appearance of differently colored bodies. To proceed scientifically in
this process of comparison, we must have definite standards of
comparison. *It was Leonardo da Vinci who first pointed out the
fact that there are six colors which serve as such standards of
comparison.* They are: white, black, red, yellow, green, and blue.

*The six colors mentioned might be appropriately called "the
six psychological primaries."* The only objection to this terminology is that the term "primary colors" is so hackneyed and has
passed through so many meanings. In popular literature the all-
important "primaries" signify no one knows exactly what. Print-
ers have a set of primaries; those interested in color photography
have another set of primaries. Both of these primaries are of *industrial value;* this and no more. Young had his primaries; Helmholtz and Hering had each his own primaries. Their significance
is *hypothetical,* that is, they have exactly the same value as the
theories of color vision proposed by these men, and this value, as
we shall see, is not particularly great. When, therefore, the above
six colors of Leonardo da Vinci are called "psychological primaries," it should be clearly understood that no theoretic, physical,
or industrial consideration enters into the meaning of this term.
What is meant is *the plain fact that in classifying colors the six
colors mentioned serve as definite points of comparison.* They
are for the psychologist what the meter stick and the gram are
for the physicist. These units of measurement are standards of
comparison without which the length and weight of physical
bodies could not be indicated with accuracy. Just so the six colors
of Leonardo da Vinci are fixed points of comparison without
which it would be impossible to classify colors. The only difference is *that the meter stick and the gram are more or less arbitrary standards, whereas there is nothing arbitrary about the six
standards of comparison in classifying colors.*

5. Neutral and Chromatic Colors. Using, then, the *six
colors of Leonardo da Vinci* as definite points of comparison, we

find that the 30,000 (or more) distinguishable colors fall readily into two groups, namely, neutral and chromatic colors. *Those of the first group have a similarity to both white and black and to none of the four other colors.* As these four other colors (red, yellow, green, blue) are designated as four *tones* of colors, all colors of the first group are called *tone-free* or *neutral.* Koenig calculated that there are about 660 tone-free colors which according to their increasing similarity with white and black respectively can be arranged *along a straight line* (Fig. 6). At one end of this line we place the most brilliant white and at the other the darkest black. The intermediate positions are occupied by the different shades of neutral gray. In popular parlance not only the fixed end points of this straight line but also those intermediates which approach closely these end points are called white or black. Hence, in popular parlance there are many different whites and blacks.

| Black | Dark Gray | Medium Gray | Light Gray | White |

Fig. 6. The Classification of Neutral Colors.

Every chromatic color has three attributes; namely, a *definite tone,* a *definite degree of saturation,* and a *definite brightness.* Only when *the purely psychological meaning* of these three attributes is understood, can we undertake to classify chromatic colors and correlate them with those of the neutral series.

6. The Three Attributes (or Determinants) of Each Chromatic Color: Tone, Saturation, and Brightness. The first and most fundamental attribute of each chromatic color is known as its tone. The term "tone" is a figure of speech by which we designate *that attribute of a color by which it is distinguished from every neutral color and which we express by such terms as* "red," "bluish red," "yellowish green," etc. Under suitable laboratory conditions Koenig has discriminated in the visible spectrum alone as many as 165 tones, and there are many more tones than those exhibited in the visible spectrum. Nor is there any reason why all tones should be found in the spectrum, unless we attempt to define tone in terms of wave length; and this brings confusion into our whole color scheme.

Saturation is a figure of speech by which we designate the second attribute of every chromatic color. Defined in purely introspective terms, saturation means *the relative clearness of tone*. Thus the purplish-red tone of a cardinal's robe is *very clear* so that its color cannot possibly be mistaken for a neutral color. This is what we mean when we call it *saturated*. The color of news print is often slightly yellowish, but its yellow tone is *not very clear* so that the color of a newspaper can be easily mistaken for a neutral whitish gray. We call, therefore, the yellow color of a newspaper an *unsaturated* one. The important thing to note is that *the terms "saturated" and "unsaturated" must not be interpreted to contain a reference to the physical nature of the stimulus by which the color sensation is aroused*. Such a literal interpretation of these figures of speech would again bring confusion into our color scheme.

The third attribute of every chromatic color sensation is one which it has in common with neutral colors, namely, *brightness*. No chromatic color is as brilliant or visibly luminous as the white of newly fallen snow nor is it as dark as black velvet. *So far as visible luminosity is concerned, every chromatic color lies somewhere between white and black,* just as all the neutral grays do. Hence, *each chromatic color has a similarity both to white and black, and insofar, can be matched with a definite neutral gray: both are equidistant from both white and black.* The direct matching of a chromatic color with a definite gray is very difficult, as we must abstract from the tone of the chromatic color. Hence, various indirect methods have been devised. This being understood, we define the brightness of a chromatic color in introspective terms as its *relative similarity to both white and black.*

7. **The Color Square.** The *most saturated* colors can be arranged along the sides of what is known as the *color square.* At each of the four corners of this square we place one of the four tones of Leonardo da Vinci which serve as fixed points of

comparison in classifying all the other tones, namely, a pure red, a pure yellow, a pure green, and a pure blue, and in the order here indicated. The "purity" of these tones is again a figure of speech and *we must beware of giving this term a physical meaning* such as it has in physics or chemistry. In other words, no reference to the physical properties of light is meant by "purity," *nor is anything physiological or theoretic even hinted at.* By a *"pure" red* we mean a red that is *neither yellowish nor bluish;* by a *"pure" yellow,* one that is *neither greenish nor reddish;* by a *"pure" green,* one that is *neither bluish nor yellowish;* by a

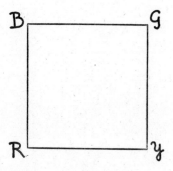

FIG. 7. The Color Square.

"pure" blue, one that is *neither reddish nor greenish.* In the accompanying diagram (Fig. 7) these pure tones of Leonardo da Vinci are indicated respectively by the letters R, Y, G, B.

Between R and Y we arrange all their *intermediates,* that is, *all those tones which have a similarity to both R and Y,* and they follow one another in the order of their relative similarity in both directions. Thus, to mention only those tones for which we have specific names, *we pass from red over scarlet, vermillion, orange, gold, to pure yellow.* In a like manner, we arrange the intermediates between Y and G, G and B, and B and R. Thus, for instance, *we pass from a pure blue over indigo, violet, bluish purple, reddish purple, carmine, magenta, crimson, to a pure red.* Accordingly, indigo and reddish purple, for instance, are intermediate tones, but *they should not be called "mixed colors."* The physical properties of the light by which these color sensations can be aroused have nothing whatever to do with our classification of them, lest we bring confusion into our color scheme.

8. The Color Octahedron. Through the center of our color square (Gr. in Figure 8) we erect a vertical line and place the most brilliant white (W) at its upper end, and the darkest black (Bl) at its lower end and arrange along this line all the neutral

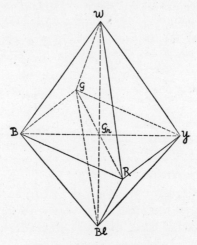

FIG. 8. The Color Octahedron.

grays, as we have explained before, a medium gray (Gr) thus occupying the very center of the square.

Each color tone is next connected by a straight line with W and by another with Bl and along these lines we place all those chromatic colors which are *intermediate between the points connected.* Thus along the line R W we place all the tints of a pure red in the order of their increasing similarity to white and decreasing similarity to pure red. *This straight line, then, represents a series of colors whose saturation is continually decreasing and whose brightness is continually increasing.* The same is true of the straight lines connecting Y and W, G and W, B and W. *All the intermediate tones should be likewise connected each with W* and every one of these lines (not indicated in the diagram) represents *a series of colors whose saturation is decreasing and whose brightness is increasing the more we approach W*.

The line R Bl represents the shades of pure red, that is, a series of chromatic colors *whose saturation is decreasing and whose brightness is likewise decreasing*. The same is true of the lines connecting Y, G, B, each with Bl.

We next fill the whole inside of the color octahedron, and here, as a matter of fact, we place the bulk of colors as they are found in the works of nature and art. The method of procedure in filling the inside of the octahedron is to arrange the colors in a number of series, each series being represented by a straight line. Thus, for instance, along the line Y Gr we arrange all the intermediates between a pure saturated yellow and that neutral gray which is equally bright. Thus we get *a series of colors whose brightness remains identically the same but whose saturation decreases in proportion as we approach Gr*. In a similar manner, all the other tones should be connected each with that neutral gray which is equally bright, and thus we get in every instance a series of colors whose brightness is identically the same but whose saturation decreases continually. Our diagrammatic representation of this method of filling the inside of the octahedron *needs a qualification,* as we shall point out in the next section.

We have thus arranged the sum total of all distinguishable colors in *a tridimensional diagram*. From the position each particular color occupies on the inside or outside of the octahedron its three attributes can be ascertained.

9. The Specific Brightness of the Most Saturated Colors. There is only one thing which we have failed thus far to represent diagrammatically, and this is what is known as *the specific brightness of the most saturated colors*. We have represented the four tones of Leonardo da Vinci and all their intermediate tones as connected with *identically the same Gr,* that is, as *equally bright*. Now this is not correct. Thus, for instance, the most saturated pure yellow is plainly brighter than the most saturated blue.

Attempts have been made to remedy this defect in our diagram by tilting the color square, thus bringing Y nearer to W, and B nearer to Bl. But *this tilting of the square really brings confusion into our whole color scheme.* Thus the line YGr no longer represents what it is meant to represent, namely, *a series of colors whose brightness is identically the same and whose saturation decreases continually.* And the *intermediates* between the corners of the color square are *poorly taken care of.* Thus, for instance, the most saturated greenish blue is decidedly brighter than is indicated by tilting the color square.

The real remedy would be, to connect each corner of the square with a different neutral gray, and each intermediate tone likewise with that neutral gray which is equally bright. *But then the color square is gone.* The plain fact is that the specific brightness of the most saturated colors *cannot be represented* in our tridimensional scheme. Nor is there any incongruity in this, unless we assume that all knowledge we have of colors can be diagramed. At any rate, warping and distorting the color square will not remedy matters; nor have any laboratory determinations been made that would enable us to find the correct shade of neutral gray with which each tone ought to be connected. Hence, we had better leave the color octahedron as it is.

It has also been suggested that all the corners of the octahedron should be rounded off. Whatever benefit may be derived from this, *it obscures the fundamental principle of our psychological classification, namely, the fixed points of comparison.*

Recently it has also been suggested that *we really use seven points of comparison in classifying colors, the seventh point being gray.* The answer is that the only *unsatisfactory* point in our diagram is the *gray* which is placed at the center of the square. There is no such fixed point of comparison and *we can do nothing with a variable point* any more than the physicist can do anything with a variable unit of measurement. Moreover, even if gray were a fixed point, *it would have to be defined in terms of white and black.* Hence, it is not true that we really use seven points of comparison. The color octahedron as diagramed has never been improved upon. It cannot be changed except by ignor-

ing the fundamental principle of a purely psychological classification of colors (the fixed points of comparison) or by intermin-
gling physical considerations with purely introspective data.

10. Normal and Abnormal Color Vision. There is *another
qualification* which must be added when accepting the color
octahedron as representing the classification of colors. We must
add *"as they appear to persons of normal vision."* But there is
such a thing as color-blindness, and the variety of *colors as they
appear to color-blind persons can also be classified.* Before we attempt the classification of the latter, we must settle a question of
even greater importance, namely, the question as to *what we
really mean by normal and abnormal color vision.* Unless this
question can be answered satisfactorily, it would seem that our
purely psychological classification of colors really deals with useless oddities of introspection which we cannot share with anybody else. Thus Watson's objection against introspection would
be justified at least in the case of color vision.

The answer is that *normality and abnormality of color vision
can be determined with scientific precision by means of introspective data.* Of course, I cannot compare directly the color of a
definite body as it appears to me with the color of the same body
as it appears to another man. But *indirectly* we can, namely, *by
means of color equations.* In fact, this is the only way in which
the normality of color vision can be ascertained. As the validity
of color equations depends essentially on the data of introspection, it follows that behaviorists simply cannot deal with such an
eminently practical problem as normality and abnormality of
color vision. *The simple verbal report "I see red" gives no information as to either normality or abnormality.*

*Color equations can be made roughly and with scientific ac-
curacy.* In the first case, we get *rough* information concerning
normality and abnormality; in the latter, we define these two conditions *with scientific accuracy.* The scientific mode of procedure
is as follows: Suppose a great number of students (say, a hundred) make color equations in the laboratory such as are used for
ascertaining the laws of color mixture. Then we find that *all*

*students (100 per cent) agree within very narrow limits in mak-
ing certain equations.* These equations give us no information as
to normality or abnormality.

There are, however, about *5 per cent of men* (and a *very* small
fraction of 1 per cent of women) *who make equations which
will not be acknowledged by the remaining 95 per cent.* Moreover, the said 5 per cent of men disagree not only from the 95
per cent, but they disagree also among themselves. *The 95 per
cent of men we call normal, and the remaining 5 per cent we
call abnormal.* Thus, for instance, some of the 5 per cent of men
will equate *a very unsaturated orange* with a *pure saturated
green;* a definite *bluish green* with a definite *neutral gray;* a
definite *purple* with a very *dark neutral gray;* some other *purples*
with *blue;* again other *purples* with a *dark yellow;* a *pure red*
with a very *dark olive green,* etc.

*Once the normality of color vision is thus ascertained, every
one of the 95 per cent of men can say with perfect assurance that
within very narrow limits his experience is identically the same
as that of every other man among the 95 per cent.* It is indeed
true that the use of color names, such as "red," is very ambiguous,
as there are thousands of reds. But the term is no longer ambiguous when the normality of two persons has been ascertained
and both observe the same colored object under the same conditions. *When one of these two observers then calls the color of
the object "red," both know that the color thus designated occupies for both observers approximately the same place in the
color octahedron.* Thus they understand each other perfectly, and
the difficulty of the behaviorists vanishes.

But what about the remaining 5 per cent of men who disagree
among themselves? To begin with, they know for certain that
their color vision is not like that of the 95 per cent. But what is
the experience of color-blind persons? It has been said that it is
impossible to find this out. The answer is that it is *difficult but
not impossible.* The difficulty in dealing with this problem has
been *increased enormously by mixing up the investigation of
color-blindness with the theories of color vision.* As we have no

satisfactory theory of color vision, the investigation of color-blindness is *the more accurate in proportion as it is divorced from all theoretical considerations*. Let it suffice here to say that, when a sufficient number of color-blind persons is tested by means of accurate color equations — and this is not done in the popular tests for color-blindness — then it is found that color-blind persons fall readily into three groups, *each group being defined by its peculiar color equations*. These three groups have been called by names which imply a definite theory of color vision and are consequently of little or no value.

Discarding all theories, we may say that there are three forms of color-blindness, namely, (1) a rare form, (2) a very rare form, and (3) a common form, and this common form occurs in two sharply divided types. As to the details of these three forms of color-blindness and the two types of common color-blindness the reader is referred to the next chapter and to Chapter VI of the writer's *Introductory Course in Experimental Psychology*.

11. Color-Weakness. The investigation of color-blindness is complicated considerably by another anomaly known as color-weakness. This condition, like that of color-blindness, is known *by its characteristic color equations*. We said above that normal persons agree "within very narrow limits" in making all their color equations, that is, they differ but slightly in the amounts of the different kinds of light they need in making a definite color equation. Lord Rayleigh first called attention to the fact that some persons in combining red and green so as to equate a definite yellow, need considerably more red than normal persons; others need considerably more green than normal persons. Those who need an excessive amount of red, are evidently less sensitive to red than normal persons and are called "red-weak"; those who need an excessive amount of green are called "green-weak."

It should be noted, however, that neither the "red-weak" nor the "green-weak" are color-blind for the simple reason that they do not acknowledge the typical equations of the color-blind, provided these equations are made with accuracy. In fact, all the equations made by color-weak persons are really normal except that unusual amounts are required as components of their mixtures. From all these data we infer that color-weak persons experience red and green just as normal persons do, *provided the stimulus is strong enough.* When, however, the stimulus is weak, an object which appears distinctly reddish to a normal person, appears differently to a color-weak person; the same is true of green objects. Hence, color-weak persons have been appropriately called "abnormal normals" and *they constitute the crux of those who make practical tests for color-blindness.* Unless these tests are made by means of accurate color equations, it is impossible to tell the color-weak from the color-blind. It should be added that *for practical purposes* color-weak persons, though in literal strictness not color-blind, *must be treated as color-blind as they can never be trusted to distinguish weak green signals from red ones.*

We may express the condition of color-weak persons also by saying that their "color threshold," particularly for red and green, differs considerably from that of normal persons. We shall explain this more fully in the next chapter when dealing with the "color threshold."

References for Further Reading

J. Froebes, S.J., *Lehrbuch der Experimentellen Psychologie,* Vol. I (1923), pp. 40–52.

J. Lindworsky, S.J., *Experimentelle Psychologie* (1921), pp. 20–25.

H. Gruender, S.J., *Introductory Course in Experimental Psychology,* Chaps. II and VI.

H. Gruender, S.J., *De Qualitatibus Sensibilibus.*

Chapter IV

COLOR SENSATIONS
(Concluded)

1. The Classification of Colors as They Appear to Color-Blind Persons. Persons who belong in the *rare form* of color-blindness *equate every color with a definite neutral gray*. They are known as *totally color-blind*. About 50 such cases have been examined. A simple straight line with white at one end and black at the other, suffices for the classification of all colors as seen by them.

The *common form* of color-blindness is that of the famous chemist Dalton, who described his own case in 1794. Relying on purely introspective data, Dalton stated that besides *white, black,* and the *intermediate grays,* he saw only two tones, namely, *yellow* and *blue,* but these two tones *in every degree of saturation* (*or relative clearness*). Other color-blind persons have come to the same conclusion on the basis of introspective data. These results agree with the introspective data of a person (described by A. v. Hippel in *Graefe's Archiv*[1]) who was color-blind in one eye, the other being normal.

The correctness of all these introspective reports can also be tested experimentally in every case of ordinary color-blindness. When such persons are asked to classify a set of colored papers (say, those of the Bradley series) by means of the color square or the color octahedron, they are entirely lost. If, however, they are given a diagram which corresponds to Dalton's introspective report (see Figs. 9 and 10), the present writer finds that they have no difficulty in assigning a definite place for each of the Bradley papers on this diagram. The only proviso is that such persons be warned that *they must not be guided by color names* but ex-

---

[1] Vol. 26, pp. 176 sqq. and Vol. 27, pp. 47 sqq.

clusively by the *similarities and differences* they ascertain between any given Bradley color and the *four fixed points of comparison* at the corners of "the color rectangle," *White, Black, Yellow,* and *Blue.* From this it will be seen that two points of comparison drop out; namely, a pure red and a pure green *It is because of*

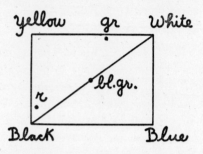

Fɪɢ. 9. The Color Rectangle, representing the classification of colors as they appear to *red-green blind* persons of the *first type.* A paper which appears "pure red" (*r*) to a normal person will be placed somewhere on or near the Yellow-Black line; a "pure green" (*gr.*) will be placed somewhere on or near the Yellow-White line; a definite bluish green of maximal saturation (*bl. gr.*) will be placed on the White-Black line, that is, it appears neutral gray. All colors of the Bradley series will find a place somewhere inside the rectangle or on one of its lines.

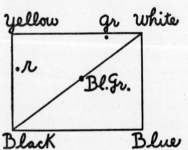

Fɪɢ. 10. The Color Rectangle representing the classification of colors as they appear to *red-green blind* persons of the *second type.* Note that identically the same "pure red" (*r*) is placed by the second type nearer the Yellow than by the first type. *Bl. Gr.* denotes a green which is *more bluish* than the *bl. gr.* of Figure 9. This means that identically the same bluish green appears neutral gray to one type, but colored (that is, either *slightly* yellowish or bluish) to the other type.

this plain fact of experience that color-blind persons of the common form may be correctly called *"red-green blind."* This term,
then, has *no reference to any theory whatever,* and in particular
it has no reference whatever to Hering's theory of color vision.
The pure red and the pure green are classified in terms of yellow;
all the other tones which for normal persons have a similarity to
either red or green, are classified either in terms of yellow or blue
or in terms of neutral gray. The two types of the common form
of color-blindness differ in their classification, but get along perfectly with identically the same diagram. For a more accurate
distinction between the two types the reader is referred to the
writer's *Introductory Course in Experimental Psychology,* Chapter VI.

There is a very rare form of color-blindness which, for theoretical considerations, has been called "yellow-blue blindness." We
know too little about this form to warrant any generalizations.
From the descriptions given it would seem that yellow and blue
drop out as points of comparison in the classification of colors
as seen by such persons. If this is correct, then a "color rectangle"
might be constructed for them like that in Figure 11, with this
difference, that the corners are occupied by red, white, green,
black.

2. The Laws of Color Mixture and Their Significance.
By color mixture we understand the bringing together of rays of
different wave length upon the same point of the retina. The
most accurate way of doing this is by the physical mixture of
different waves before they reach the eye. But there are other
methods. For details of the different methods the reader is referred to the author's monograph *A New Color Mixer.*[2] It is to
be noted that when we use any of these methods of "mixing
colors," there occurs no "fusion" or "blending" of different color
sensations. Thus when we mix the "yellow" light of the physicist
with his "indigo-blue" light, we have not first two color sensations, namely, that of yellow and indigo blue, which then "fuse"

---

[2] Bulletin of Saint Louis University for May, 1922.

or "blend" into the sensation of "white." Introspectively we know nothing of such a fusion and it is a bit of crude metaphysics to suppose that such a fusion occurs. What happens is just what we said in the definition of "color mixture": we bring these two different waves together on the same point of the retina. In other words, we bombard the same retinal elements simultaneously with two kinds of light. Then we observe the result of such a simultaneous bombardment.

It has been said that the laws of color mixture are of no interest to the psychologist just because there occurs no "fusion" of color sensations when we mix colors. True, there occurs no such fusion, and we have insisted on it. But fusions of sensations are not the only thing that interest us in psychology. We are surely interested in the characteristics of color sensations and we should like to get at a satisfactory theory of color vision. One of the principal characteristics of color sensations is the fact that there are so many physically different stimuli which arouse one and the same color sensation. *The laws of color mixture give us more detailed information concerning this unique characteristic of color sensations* and thus present some specific problems to be solved by a satisfactory theory of color vision. Hence, no psychological account of color sensations is complete without a treatment of the laws of color mixture.

3. The first law of color mixture is known as that of so-called "complementary colors." It may be stated in two parts. The first is: *For every long wave of the visible spectrum* (that is, for every wave not shorter than 563.6 Angströms) *a definite short wave can be found so that when the two waves are mixed in appropriate proportions, each component of the mixture will neutralize the chromatic effect of the other and the sensation of neutral white will arise* (see Tables III to V). The second part of the law is this: *If the relative strength of the two components is not appropriately adjusted, the neutralization of one component is incomplete and the result of such a mixture is the sensation of an unsaturated color whose tone is determined by that of the stronger component.*

A glance at the accompanying tables shows that the results of the five experimentalists mentioned do not tally perfectly. The discrepancies are not great and are, no doubt, due in part to experimental error, which is not surprising in experimental work of so delicate a nature as this. They are, however, sufficiently great to indicate a fact which it is important to realize and which

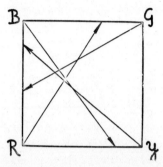

Fig. 11. Some of the so-called "*complementary colors.*" The square R, Y G, B, represents the purely psychological classification of the most saturated colors. Each arrow within the square connects one of *the four tones of Leonardo da Vinci* with its "*complementary.*" There is nothing in these arrows to suggest even faintly any "complementariness," nor is there *any regularity* in the direction in which these arrows point. Note that these "complementary" colors *do not coincide* with the pairs of *Hering's theoretic primaries,* namely, red-green and yellow-blue.

is liable to puzzle a beginner in experimental psychology. *The notable fact is: There are differences in the color-sensitivity of different individuals.* We meet the same fact frequently, when we compare the data of different observers, even if the experimental arrangement is not peculiarly elaborate, as, for instance, in experiments with the color wheel. Where one observer reports "neutral gray," another reports a slight tinge of some color tone. It is only when such individual differences exceed a certain limit, that we speak of "subnormal" color-sensitivity or "color-weakness." The color-sensitivity of the five experimentalists, represented in Tables III, IV, and V, must, in spite of their individual differences, be classed as "normal."

The color which is aroused separately by each of a pair of waves described in the first law, is, strangely enough, said to be "complementary" to the color aroused by the other. This is a figure of speech suggested by the fact that for every angle there is a complementary angle. It should be carefully noted, however, that this figure of speech must not be given any literal

COLOR	WAVE LENGTH	COMPLEMEN- TARY COLOR	WAVE LENGTH	RATIO OF WAVE LENGTHS
RED	656.2	GR. BLUE	492.1	1.334
ORANGE	607.7	BLUE	489.7	1.240
GOLD	585.3	BLUE	485.4	1.206
GOLD	573.9	BLUE	482.1	1.190
YELLOW	567.1	INDIGO BLUE	464.5	1.221
YELLOW	564.4	INDIGO BLUE	461.8	1.222
GR. YELLOW	563.6	VIOLET	433	1.301
				AND DOWNWARDS

TABLE III

Complementary colors as determined by Helmholtz.

meaning whatever either in a physical sense or in a psychological sense. *Not in the physical sense;* for a glance at the table of Helmholtz shows that the ratio between two such waves is not constant as is the ratio between two complementary angles, nor is there anything whatever in the nature of the two waves to suggest even remotely any "complementariness." *Not in the psychological sense;* for, as stated, there occurs *no fusion* or blending of two sensations. Nor is there anything in the psychological nature of two complementary colors, such as *red* and *bluish green, yellow* and *indigo blue,* etc., even to suggest from afar off anything like "complementariness." We simply know, as a matter of empirical rule, that the pairs of colors connected by straight lines in Figure 11, satisfy the conditions of the first law of color mixture. Hence, it would be more accurate if the first law were simply called *the law of neutralization.*

The important information we gather from this law is that there are no specific stimuli for the sensations of white and gray,

TABLE IV

LONG WAVES	COMPLEMENTARY SHORT WAVES ACC. TO				
	v HELMHOLTZ	v KRIES	v FREY	KÖNIG	DIETERICI
675				496.5	
670					494.3
663				495.7	
660					494
656.2	492.1	492.4	485.2		
650				496.7	494.3
638				495.9	
635					494
626		492.2	484.6		493.1
615.3				496	
612.3		489.6	483.6		
610					492.2
607.7	489.7				
599.5		487.8	481.8		
588					485.9
587.6		484.7	478.9		
586.7			478.7		
585.7					485.7
585.3	485.4				
582.6				483.6	
579.7		478.7			
578				476.6	476.6
577.7			473.9		
577		473.9			

TABLE V

LONG WAVES	COMPLEMENTARY SHORT WAVES ACC. TO				
	v HELMHOLTZ	v KRIES	v FREY	KÖNIG	DIETERICI
576				467	
575.6					470
575.5		469.3			
574.5				455	
573.9	482.1				
573				450	
572.9		464.8			
572.8			469.3		
571.5					455
571.4					442
571.3					448
571.1		460.4			
571		452.1			
570.7			464.8		
570.4		440.4			
570.1		429.5			
569			460.4		
568.1			452.1		
567.1	464.5				
566.4			429.5		
566.3			440.4		
564.4	461.8				
563.6	433				
		AND DOWNWARDS			

Complementary colors, as determined by von Kries, von Frey, A. König, and C. Dieterici. The data of Helmholtz are repeated for comparison (see Helmholtz, *Phys. Opt.*, pp. 318 sqq.).

but these sensations arise in every instance by the neutralization of chromatic stimuli. This occurs also in the case of unfiltered sunlight, the only difference being that here a great many (or rather all) pairs of long and short waves that satisfy the first law, work conjointly on the same retinal elements.

There is, no doubt, some regularity back of this phenomenon of neutralization, but it cannot be expressed in either physical or psychological terms. *It is for a theory of color vision to tell us what this regularity is.*

4. The second law of color mixture may be called the law of intermediate colors. It is this: *When two waves are combined which separately arouse color sensations whose tones are not complementary to each other, the result of such a mixture is the sensation of an intermediate color.* By an intermediate color we mean´ here any one of those colors which on the color square lie along the shorter path connecting two noncomplementary colors; and that path is the shorter between noncomplementaries which does not pass over the complementary of either of these two colors (see Fig. 11). Thus red and green are noncomplementary colors. On the color square there are two paths which lead from red to green, namely, *via* blue and *via* yellow. The former path passes over the complementary of both green and red, namely, purplish red and bluish green; the latter avoids these complementaries and is the shorter path connecting red and green. All the colors which lie along this shorter path between red and green (as for instance, orange, yellow, and yellowish green) are intermediate between red and green, as this term is understood in the second law of color mixture, and can be produced by an appropriate mixture of red and green. Which one of the intermediate color sensations will be aroused, simply depends on the relative strength of the two components of the mixture. In other words, the result of such a mixture may be compared to the weighting of a lever at both ends and finding the center of gravity.

From the wording of the second law it will be seen that only the *tone* of the resulting color sensation is specified. The other two attributes of the resulting color, namely, its saturation and brightness, differ from one mixture to another and no universally valid formula is at hand to express the facts observed.

The second law of color mixture presents to us a very hard problem that must be dealt with in a satisfactory theory of color vision. How knotty this problem is, may be brought home to the reader by an illustration. Suppose that the string corresponding to a definite piano key, say the middle c, be broken, and suppose that the second law of color mixture held also for tone sensations. The unique situation before us then would be this: In spite of the broken c string we can still produce the tone c, namely, by striking the key below c and the key above it. And if the strings corresponding to these two keys be also broken, we find a great many other pairs of keys, one below c, the other above it, which can be used as substitutes for the broken c string. A satisfactory theory of color vision will have to tell us why such a condition prevails in the case of color sensations.

5. The third law of color mixture may be called the law of substitution. It may be formulated thus: *If a definite mixture of lights (say r + g) "looks" like a definite other light (say y), then this mixture (r + g) can be substituted for the other light (y), whenever this other light (y) is needed as a component of another mixture.* To illustrate: Suppose we have found that $r + g = y$; we have found further, that $y + i = W$. Then we may also say that $(r + g) + i = W$.

This law has many eminently practical applications. In practical terms it means that, when a definite color, say bluish green, is needed for a definite mixture, *we need not be concerned about the physical constitution of the light* which causes this sensation, but only about the "looks" of the color which is needed. Hence, *in the experimental demonstration of the first and second law of color mixture, it is not necessary to use monochromatic lights —* they are extremely difficult to handle — but we can use sources of colored light which are easily obtained, such as colored papers. Thus, instead of making the difficult equation $567.1 + 464.5 = W$, we can simply use yellow paper which "looks" like 567.1 and an indigo-blue paper which "looks" like 464.5. *The result of the two modes of procedure is exactly the same* And if we should not find in our collection of papers the exact indigo blue needed, but have some red and some blue paper on hand, then we combine these two until the exact shade of indigo blue is found. *And all this is true, even though no colored paper reflects monochromatic light.* In fact, no colored object in nature does, as can be found out experimentally by means of the (direct vision) spectroscope such as is used in any physical or chemical laboratory.

All the comparatively easy methods generally employed in the psychological laboratory for the demonstration of the first two laws of color mixture, are based on the validity of the third law. The reader who desires a more detailed account of such comparatively easy methods of laboratory procedure, is referred to the writer's *Introductory Course in Experimental Psychology.*

Another application of the third law of color mixture is that *color equations can be joined, not only by addition and subtraction, but also by multiplication and division,* as is done in the case of mathematical equations. But the reader should remain aware that in the case of color equations we deal merely with the *physiological equivalence* of the two sides of the equation. Hence, when *multiplication or division* is resorted to, the validity of this mode of procedure must be qualified by another law which we shall discuss under the heading of *the limits of color sensation.*

6. The So-Called Three Primary Colors. One of the various corollaries of the three laws of color mixture which is frequently overemphasized, must be briefly mentioned here. It is the famous law of the so-called three primary colors. This law can also be ascertained independently of such deductions in the form of a simple empirical rule. Thus stated, the law is: *There are a great many trios of light which, on combination in various proportions, will cause the sensation of any color tone as well as the sensations of neutral white and gray.* If colors are desired whose saturation is relatively great, *the most satisfactory trio is that of red, green, and blue-violet lights.* Hence, these three colors have come to be known by the name of "the three primary colors," which seem to be the all-important thing in popular accounts of color sensations. *The grain of truth* contained in these popular accounts is that these three colored lights have undoubtedly *industrial* value. *For the psychologist the empirical rule stated is*

*only one of the numerous facts which must be explained by a
satisfactory theory of color vision.*

7. The Limits of Color Sensation. When dealing with
Weber's law we stated that there is a threshold and an acme of
a visual sensation and we discussed the noticeable variations in
the brightness of a visual sensation which occur within these two
limits. Here we must add that there is also a threshold and an
acme of a color sensation. A definite spectral light, for instance,
may indeed be above the threshold of vision and still remain
below the threshold of color vision. That is to say: monochromatic light of a definite wave length may arouse the sensation of
a neutral gray. *A light just strong enough to cause a sensation
that is noticeably chromatic, is known as the threshold of color
vision.* Similarly, a certain intensity of a spectral light is required
to produce a color sensation whose *tone* is of *maximal saturation*
and of a brightness which is *specific for that tone.* This intensity
of light is known as *the acme of color vision.* If we increase the
intensity of light beyond this point, every spectral light causes a
color sensation which approaches that of *neutral white* until the
acme of vision is reached where *every light produces the sensation of neutral white.*

From this it will be seen that by merely changing the intensity
of a spectral light under conditions which are otherwise uniform,
we change not only the brightness of the visual sensation but we
change also the visual sensation from a neutral to a chromatic
one and vice versa, and we change the degree of saturation of the
color seen. In fact, even the tone of a chromatic sensation may
thus be changed. Thus, for instance, Helmholtz states that "blue"
spectral light below a certain intensity causes the sensation of indigo, "violet" light that of a rose color. It is well known, too, that
beyond the acme of color vision many of the long waves of the
spectrum (the red and orange lights, for instance) cause the sensation of yellow, and many of the short waves (greenish-blue
light, for instance), the sensation of blue. *It is impossible to state
in a universally valid formula the various changes in a color sensation which can be effected by varying the intensity of mono-*

chromatic light, as these changes differ from one wave length to another. The important thing to note is that in effecting all these changes of a color sensation, all its other conditions – and in particular those of contrast – are supposed to be kept constant, so that all these changes are due exclusively to changes in the intensity of one and the same wave length.

It should be added that similar changes in a color sensation occur when we vary the intensity of any mixed light as, for instance, sunlight filtered by some colored screen (colored glasses or celluloid films). *A satisfactory theory of color vision will have to tell us why we can bring about all such changes in a color sensation by merely changing the intensity of identically the same light.*

8. The Phenomena of Simultaneous Contrast. The characteristic appearance of a colored body, as we stated before, depends not only on the kind and amount of light reflected by that body and reaching definite rods and cones, but also on the kinds and amounts of light reflected by surrounding bodies and reaching another set of rods and cones. As the different rods and cones of the retina are really not independent organs of vision but parts of a strictly unitary organ of vision, it is natural to expect that *the physiological disturbance produced in one set of rods and cones should have a modifying effect on the physiological disturbance set up in another set of rods and cones.* And such is, as a matter of fact, the case. It is, however, only under laboratory conditions, *when we regulate with precision the amounts and kinds of light* which affect the different portions of the retina, that we realize how *profound* the *mutual* influence is which two adjacent portions of the retina exert upon each other, and how remarkable are the changes in the appearance of a colored body which are due to these conditions.

The modifying influence of two adjacent portions of the retina upon each other is sometimes designated by the name of *mutual induction,* because of the analogy which these phenomena bear to the phenomena of mutual induction in electricity. Of course, this analogy should not be pressed beyond the point of comparison. Hering's theory of color vision tries to give a more detailed meaning to this mutual induction.

9. **The study of the phenomena of simultaneous contrast is perhaps best approached by considering them as a special case of the general fact of physiological inhibition.** That the physiological effect of light impinging upon a definite portion of the retina can be inhibited either completely or partially by the physiological disturbance set up in the rest of the retina, is a plain fact of experience which can be ascertained very readily without any laboratory arrangements. Thus the stars radiate as much light during the day as during the night; and if we look at the unclouded sky during the day, these stars form a retinal image just as they do at night. But during the day the immense flood of light coming from the rest of the sky and reaching the adjacent portions of the retina, *completely inhibits* the effect of the light of the star we look at: we do not see it. At twilight *this inhibiting effect is not complete* and, as a result, certain stars become visible, but they do not appear as bright as they do at night. *All* the details of the empirical rules concerning the phenomena of simultaneous contrast (and those of successive contrast as well) *can be satisfactorily accounted for as phenomena of partial or complete inhibition.*

Comparatively simple methods for ascertaining the empirical rules concerning simultaneous contrast are described in Chapter V of the writer's *Introductory Course in Experimental Psychology,* to which the reader is referred. Though some of these methods show the various forms of contrast excellently, they are somewhat unsatisfactory, because no accurate measurements can be made of the amounts of light by which the two contrasting surfaces are illuminated. Figure 12 is a diagram of an instrument constructed by the present writer which makes such measurements possible. By means of this instrument *the physical conditions of simultaneous contrast can be expressed in numerical values with a fair degree of accuracy.*

10. **The Contrast Box.** The instrument is a (double) box

(*a, b, c, d*) painted dull white inside. The observer looks through a tube (painted dull black inside) at a piece of dull white paper (*o*) and through a small opening in the latter at another piece of white paper (*i*). *Each of these papers is illuminated independ-*

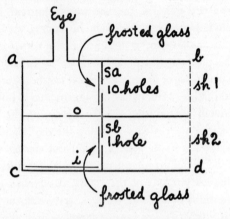

FIG. 12. Contrast Box. This instrument makes it possible to illuminate the infield and the outfield independently. Its construction was suggested to the present writer by Hering's *Doppelschirmanordnung* briefly described in Froebes' *Lehrbuch der Experimentellen Psychologie*, vol. I, p. 67.

ently and the illumination can be varied independently, so that both the amount and the kind of light by which each paper is illuminated can be indicated with precision. When the shutters (*sh 1* and *sh 2*) at the rear of the box are opened, diffused sunlight enters through *one hole* in the screen *sb*, and through *ten*

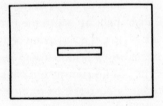

FIG. 13. Field of vision in experiments with the contrast box: a small infield surrounded by a large outfield.

holes in the screen *sa*. In passing through each hole light is further diffused by a piece of frosted glass. As a result, both papers (*o* and *i*) are illuminated very evenly, the illumination being indirect, namely, by diffused reflection from the dull white walls of the box. If, then, both shutters are equally opened, the amount of light by which *o* is illuminated is *ten times as great* as that by

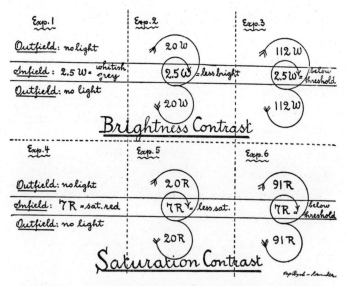

TABLE VI. Experimental data on brightness contrast and saturation contrast. The change in the appearance of the infield is an *indirect* effect of the light illuminating the outfield. The theoretic interpretation of this effect as a *phenomenon of physiological inhibition* is diagrammatically indicated by the arrows.

which *i* is illuminated and *each amount can be determined directly by a scale attached to each shutter.* Thus we can say, for instance, that *o* (the outfield) is illuminated by 85 units of light, while *i* (the infield) is illuminated by 5 units of light. *The kind of light* is regulated by inserting a color filter (colored celluloid or gelatin) in a special groove near the shutter (*sh 1* or *sh 2*).

The field of vision for the observer is as diagrammed in Figure 13. The lower paper (*i*) appears as *a small infield* and the upper

paper (*o*) as *a large outfield*. This is the most favorable condition
for observing the phenomena of contrast. In literal strictness the
"inducing" or "inhibiting" effect of two contrasting surfaces is
mutual, but it is proportional to the size of each contrasting surface. Hence, by choosing a very small infield and a comparatively
large outfield, we reduce the inhibiting effect of the infield on

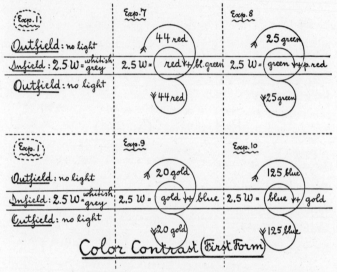

TABLE VII. Experimental data on the first form of color contrast
and their theoretic interpretation as phenomena of physiological inhibition. The facts here stated are the reversal of the facts expressed
by *the first law of color mixture:* one of the components required
for neutralization is rendered ineffective by inhibition.

the outfield to a minimum and we can practically consider the
outfield as the inhibiting surface and the infield as the inhibited
surface.

11. The various forms of simultaneous contrast and the
physical conditions under which they occur are indicated in the
accompanying tables (VI, VII, and VIII). When we illuminate
the infield by 2.5 units of unfiltered sunlight (2.5 W), while the
outfield is not illuminated at all, the infield appears whitish gray
(Exp 1). If we now illuminate the outfield by 20 W, the infield

looks less bright (Exp. 2); and when the outfield is illuminated by 112 W, the 2.5 units of unfiltered sunlight in the infield are below the threshold of vision, and the infield looks black by contrast (Exp. 3). These phenomena are known as *brightness contrast*.

What occurs, then, is *that the illumination of the outfield has a depressing influence on the physiological value of the infield.* The greater the illumination of the outfield, the greater is its inhibiting effect on the physiological value of the infield. The latter is the greatest possible when the outfield is not illuminated at all (Exp. 1).

When the infield is illuminated by 7 units of red light, while the outfield is not illuminated at all, the infield looks red. Under

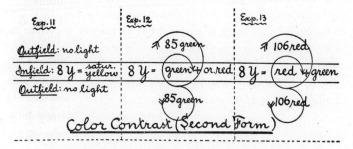

TABLE VIII. Experimental data on the second form of color contrast and their theoretic interpretation as phenomena of physiological inhibition. The facts here stated are the reversal of the facts expressed by *the second law of color mixture:* one of the components of a mixture is rendered ineffective by inhibition.

these conditions the red light of the infield is, as far as its physiological value is concerned, at its best. As soon as the outfield is also illuminated by red light (say, by 20 R), the infield looks darker and less saturated red. When the outfield is illuminated by 91 units of red light, the 7 units of red light in the infield are depressed below the threshold of vision. That is to say, it makes no difference whether we illuminate the infield by 7 units of red light or exclude all illumination, in both cases the infield looks alike, namely, black by contrast. Here again *the stronger light in the outfield has an inhibiting effect on the physiological effect of the infield.* As long as this inhibition is *partial,* the phenomena observed are known as *saturation contrast* (Exp. 4 and 5).

When we illuminate the infield by 2.5 units of unfiltered sunlight (2.5 W), while the outfield is not illuminated at all, the infield appears whitish gray, as we have already stated. If we now illuminate the outfield by some filtered (or "colored") light, *remarkable changes occur in the appearance of the infield.* We shall describe them by stating the actual results of a series of experiments.

When the outfield is illuminated by 44 units of red light, the 2.5 units of unfiltered sunlight in the infield cause the sensation of *a saturated bluish green.* The same 2.5 W in the infield cause the sensation of *a saturated purplish red,* when the outfield is illuminated by 25 units of green light. Identically the same infield will appear *saturated blue,* when the outfield is illuminated by 20 units of golden light, and the infield will appear *saturated gold,* when the outfield is illuminated by 125 units of blue light. In all these cases *there occurs evidently a depressing effect of the outfield on the physiological value of the infield.* Not only is the brightness of the infield decreased, but *the infield assumes the tone complementary to that of the outfield.* This is the *first form of color contrast,* namely, *the change of a neutral color into a chromatic one.*

In further explanation of these remarkable phenomena we can say that, according to the first law of color mixture (p. 59) we can substitute $r + bl. gr.$ for 2.5 W. We cannot indicate the numerical values of the two components of this mixture, but we know that the amounts of both are rather small. When the outfield is illuminated by 44 R, *this strong red light completely inhibits the physiological effect of the small amount of the same red light contained in the illumination of the infield.* The result is that the bluish-green component of the infield illumination is alone effective and, as a further result, the infield looks saturated bluish green. The change of the infield from neutral white to purplish red, blue, and golden yellow, respectively, can be accounted for in a similar manner (without recourse to Hering's theory), namely, as phenomena of *partial inhibition*. The details of this explanation may be gathered from Table VII.

On comparing the experimental data so far described, the reader will note that *the physiological factor which is responsible for the brightness contrast of experiments 2 and 3, and the saturation contrast of experiments 5 and 6 is also responsible for the first form of color contrast in experiments 7 to 10.* In all these cases identically the same light is contained in the illumination of both infield and outfield, and *the stronger light of the outfield inhibits totally or partially the physiological effect of the weaker light of the infield.*

When we illuminate the infield by 8 units of yellow light, while the outfield is not illuminated at all, the infield looks *saturated yellow*. If we now illuminate the outfield by filtered light which is *not* complementary to that of the infield, there occur *changes in the tone of the infield*. These changes of tone are *the second form of color contrast*. Thus, when the outfield is illuminated by 85 units of green light, *the 8 units of yellow light cause the sensation of a saturated orange-red:* and when we illuminate the outfield by 106 units of red light, *the 8 units of yellow light in the infield cause the sensation of a saturated green*. This, again, is an effect of *partial* inhibition.

In further explanation of this second form of color contrast, we may say in experiment 12 that $y = gr. + o.r.$, and in experiment 13, that $y = r + gr$. We do not know the numerical values of the different components of yellow, but both equations are in accord with *the second law of color mixture* (p. 62), When the outfield is illuminated by 85 units of green light, *they completely inhibit the physiological effect of the small amount of green light contained in the illumination of the infield* (see Table VIII). As a result, only the orange-red component of this illumination is effective and the infield appears orange-red. The explanation is similar when the 8 units of yellow light cause the sensation of green. The reader should note that *identically the same physiological factor which is responsible for brightness contrast, saturation con-*

*trast, and the first form of color contrast, is also responsible for
the second form of color contrast.* No matter what form of contrast we ascertain, in all cases *identically the same light is contained in the illumination of both infield and outfield, and the
stronger light of the outfield inhibits totally or partially the physiological effect of the weaker light of the infield.*

**12. It is frequently stated that complementary colors en-
hance each other by simultaneous contrast.** This sweeping
generalization cannot be verified when the amounts and kinds of
light reflected by the infield and outfield are controlled with precision. Thus, for instance, the present writer finds that when the
infield is illuminated by 4 units of bluish-green light, while the
outfield is not illuminated at all, the infield looks noticeably
bluish green. If now the outfield is illuminated by some red light,
the infield becomes darker and less saturated. When the outfield
is illuminated by 100 units of red light, the infield (illuminated
as before by 4 blue-green) is almost below the color threshold,
that is, it looks slightly greenish *black,* while the outfield appears
red, and this red is of a high degree of saturation.

The above generalization is not proved experimentally by plac-
ing a strip of bluish-green paper on a red background and noting
that the tone of the strip is enhanced. For in such an experimental arrangement we cannot control the amounts of light coming
from the infield and from the outfield. It would be easy to diagram hypothetic conditions of this phenomenon which would
allow us to explain it as an effect of partial inhibition. It
must be borne in mind, moreover, that the light reflected from
the bluish-green strip is undoubtedly *at its best* when the outfield is not illuminated at all. Hence, the color of a bluish-green
strip of paper is also enhanced when we place it on black velvet.
In short, *the statement that complementary colors enhance each
other, needs a qualification and it is not easy to find a suitable
qualification.* The same is true of some other statements concerning simultaneous contrast.

It should be noted carefully that all the effects of contrast
mentioned above occur only when the numerical values of the

illumination of the outfield and infield are those indicated in Tables VI, VII, and VIII, and provided the same color screens are used for filtering sunlight as were used in the actual experiments recorded. Every change in these physical conditions brings about a change in the contrast effect. From this it will be seen that all the phenomena of simultaneous contrast that have been accurately ascertained, can be expressed satisfactorily as phenomena of physiological inhibition. We wish to emphasize that we have stated all the conditions under which the various phenomena arise *in purely physical terms and without any recourse to Hering's theory of color vision.* This is of importance, as the phenomena observed are, as a matter of fact, *different* from those that Hering's theory would lead us to expect. It is worthy of note, too, that the *two forms of color contrast,* considered as phenomena of partial inhibition, can be *correlated with the laws of color mixture,* as will be seen from Tables VII and VIII.

13. **The phenomena of successive contrast** are similar to those of simultaneous contrast. Thus, if we look steadily for about 20 seconds at a small red square and then turn our eyes to a neutral gray surface and fixate this again steadily, a portion of the gray surface corresponding in size to the red square, looks bluish green. This is known as a "negative after-sensation." The reader who desires further details concerning these phenomena, is referred to the writer's *Introductory Course in Experimental Psychology.*

Under the conditions of everyday life we hardly ever notice the phenomena of successive contrast for the simple reason that *normally our eyes are in continual motion.* Thus we are normally protected against the disturbing influence of negative after-sensations. Hence, the phenomena of successive contrast are of comparatively little importance in the discussion of normal color vision; they are rather oddities of color vision which we can readily avoid.

The matter is very different in the case of the phenomena of simultaneous contrast. We simply can never avoid them. The best we can do in the laboratory is to control the conditions of

simultaneous contrast. Hence, we should expect that simultaneous contrast is of rather great importance for normal vision. And
so it is.

**14. The importance of the phenomena of simultaneous
contrast for normal vision** can be readily gathered from two
facts. *The first is that the refracting media of our eye are rather
imperfect, very much inferior to a lens in a photographic camera.*
In other words, the retinal images of the objects are normally
rather blurred. In spite of this fact, *our acuity of vision is remarkably good.* As Hering points out, it is due to the rivalry of adjacent retinal areas (i.e., to simultaneous contrast) that the out-
lines of objects do not appear blurred but sharply defined.

The second fact is that daylight illumination varies enormously
in the course of a day and from one month to another, as every
photographer knows. Thus the "black" letters on this page reflect about three times as much light at noon as a corresponding
portion of the white paper does in the early morning. Similar
variations occur in the amount of light reflected by colored objects in nature, as for instance, by a rose. If the sensation aroused
by an object in nature depended exclusively on the actual amount
of light it reflects, both the black letter and the red rose should look
white at noon, for they reflect at noon about fifty times as much
light as they do in the early morning, and about three times as
much as the white paper does in the early morning. But as the
amount of light reflected by the rose increases, the amount reflected by its surrounding green leaves likewise increases, and the
latter exerts an indirect and inhibitory effect on the retinal area
stimulated by the rose. *It is owing to this inhibitory effect or to
the fact of simultaneous contrast that the color of a rose as it
appears to us remains about "constant" despite the enormous
changes in the amounts of light reflected by it.* In the early morning the actual amount of red light (say *r*) reflected by the rose,
is antagonized by the actual amount of green light (say *g*) reflected by the green leaves, and at noon 50 *r* are antagonized by
50 *g,* so that the *actual stimulating value of 50 r at noon is about
the same as the actual stimulating value of r is in the early morn-*

ing. It is thus due principally to simultaneous contrast that the appearance of colored objects does not change from hour to hour and from day to day. *Without simultaneous contrast we should not be able to recognize bodies by their sensible qualities.* From this it will be seen that the phenomena of simultaneous contrast are far from being mere oddities which can be safely ignored in the discussion of normal color vision. On the contrary, they are of fundamental importance. Hence it is that we have treated these phenomena at some length and independently of all theories of color vision.

15. The Young-Helmholtz Theory of Color Vision. We have as yet no satisfactory theory of color vision, that is, a theory which would make *all* the facts of color vision intelligible to us. A notable attempt in this direction is the theory of Thomas Young as modified by Helmholtz. It starts out from *one* of the empirical rules of color mixture, namely, that the sensations of white and gray and those of any distinguishable tone as well, can be produced by the combination in different proportions of three colored lights. The most satisfactory trio of colored lights are red, green, and blue-violet, respectively. Accordingly, Helmholtz supposes that there are in the organ of vision three photochemical substances which, when stimulated separately, would give us the sensations of red, green, and blue-violet, respectively. Light of different wave lengths stimulates these three substances in different proportions and it is thus that the immense variety of color sensations arise. The relative amounts of the physiological processes in these three substances which are assumed to be responsible for any particular color sensation are determined by the relative amounts of red, green, and blue-violet lights which are experimentally ascertained in establishing the above empirical rule of color mixture.

In this theory, as will be seen, Helmholtz makes *no provision for the sensation of black*. This is the first and a very serious difficulty against the theory.

A second difficulty is that *Helmholtz does not explain why so many different kinds of light arouse one and the same sensation of white*. It is true that one way of arousing this sensation is by the mixture in equal proportions of red, green, and blue-violet lights. But the theory of Helmholtz contains nothing which would make the why and wherefore of this empirical rule intelligible to us. If the three substances, stimulated separately, give us the sensations of red, green, and blue-violet, respectively, *we see no intelligible reason why their simultaneous excitation in equal proportions should produce a sensation which has no similarity with either red or green or blue-violet* but is of a quality totally different from these three colors, namely, neutral white. *Helmholtz, then, merely restates in physiological terms one of the numerous facts which need explanation. Similarly, the origin of the sensation of yellow is not accounted for.* Why should the simultaneous excitation in equal proportions of the "red" and the "green" substances give us a sensation which is neither reddish nor greenish but of a totally different quality, namely, yellow? *Here again, Helmholtz merely restates in physiological terms the very fact that needs explanation.*

A third difficulty is that *Helmholtz makes no provision for the phenomena of simultaneous contrast;* hence, he declares them to be illusions and errors of judgment. Laboratory findings do not admit of this interpretation. Since, moreover, the phenomena of simultaneous contrast are of fundamental importance for normal vision, it cannot be said that Helmholtz explains normal color vision.

A fourth difficulty is that *Helmholtz cannot account for the known facts of color-blindness.* He explains color-blindness by the absence of one of the three photochemical substances in the organ of vision, and hence he distinguishes three forms of color-blindness: "red" blindness, "green" blindness, and "blue-violet" blindness. *This division does not agree with the known facts of color-blindness.* Thus, for instance, all "red" blind persons are also "green" blind. Moreover, we have definite information that persons afflicted with the common form of color-blindness experience the sensation of white just as normal persons do. Now according to Helmholtz the coöperation of all three substances is required for this sensation. How, then, do persons who lack one of the three substances, get the sensation of white? *These are some of the principal difficulties which make the theory of Helmholtz unacceptable.*

16. Hering's Theory of Color Vision. Another attempt to explain the facts of color vision is the theory of Hering. He assumes likewise three photochemical substances in the organ of vision, but differs from Helmholtz by correlating the two antagonistic part-processes of dissimilation (breaking down) and assimilation (building up) in these three substances with one of the six color sensations which enable us to classify all color sensations. Thus the process of dissimilation in the "white-black" substance, caused in different degrees by light of every wave length, is *of itself* associated with the sensation of white. As the sensation of black is an indirect effect of light, or a phenomenon of contrast, the sensation of black is associated with the process of assimilation which arises *automatically* in the white-black substance by a process of self-regulation. Dissimilation in the "yellow-blue" substance, caused by the long waves, is *of itself* associated with the sensation of yellow; assimilation in this substance arises not only by a process of self-regulation, but also by the action of the short waves of the spectrum. In a similar manner dissimilation in the "red-green" substance is correlated with the sensation of red, and assimilation with the sensation of green. It is by the combination in various proportions of the two antagonistic part-processes in these three substances that the immense variety of chromatic color sensations arises. The sensations of neutral white and gray never occur except when the two part-processes in the red-green and yellow-blue substances are in equilibrium. For equilibrium in these two substances is correlated with no sensation. There remains, then, only the process of dissimilation in the white-black substance, and this is in every instance responsible for the sensation of white and that of every shade of neutral gray. Thus, all the phenomena of normal color vision would seem to be explained without incurring the difficulties urged against the theory of Helmholtz. Color-blindness is explained by the absence of one or two of the three substances. Hence Hering distinguishes three forms of color-blindness: red-green blindness, yellow-blue blindness, and total color-blindness. In the last case only the white-black substance is supposed to be present.

There is, however, at least one serious flaw in this otherwise ingenious hypothesis. Hering supposes that the colors at opposite corners of the color square are complementary to each other. Now this is not true. No matter what experimental arrangement we devise in mixing colors, we always find that the complementary of a (psychologically) pure red is a green which is rather strongly bluish; the complementary of a pure green is a purple which lies about midway between a pure red and a pure blue; the complementary of a pure yellow is a somewhat reddish blue, namely, indigo; and the complementary of a pure blue is a yellow which is slightly reddish, namely, gold. Similarly, in experiments on simultaneous contrast, and in those of successive contrast as well, we never get the sensation which, according to Hering, ought to arise. Thus, by contrast with a pure red we never get the sensation of a pure green, etc. *Hering's explanations of these plain discrepancies between facts and theory are rather unsatisfactory.*

Something similar is true of Hering's account of color-blindness. From the assumptions of his theory we should expect that the portion of the spectrum which appears to us *pure green,* should appear *neutral gray* to red-green blind persons. As a matter of fact, however, the neutral band for red-green blind persons lies in the *bluish green.* Moreover, red-green blindness occurs in two sharply divided types, *the neutral band lying nearer the violet end for one type than for the other.* The few facts we really know about what Hering calls yellow-blue blindness hardly agree with Hering's assumptions. In short, *Hering's theory needs a decided modification before it can be accepted as a working hypothesis.*

The most notable modification of Hering's theory is that proposed by Müller. Not only is this theory very complicated but the principal objection against Hering's theory holds also against that of Müller: the colors at opposite corners of the color square are assumed to be complementary to each other.

References for Further Reading

J. Froebes, S.J., *Lehrbuch der Experimentellen Psychologie* (1923), Vol. I, pp. 53–94.

J. Lindworsky, S.J., *Experimentelle Psychologie* (1921), pp. 20–37.

H. Gruender, S.J., *Introductory Course in Experimental Psychology*, Chaps. III–VII.

C. S. Myers, *Text-Book of Experimental Psychology*, Chaps. VI and VII.

H. v. Helmholtz, *Handbuch der Physiologischen Optik* (ed. 2, 1896), pp. 275-384; Engl. Transl. edited by J. P. C. Southall, Vol. II, pp. 61-172.

F. Richardson-Robinson, "A Case of Color-Blindness to Yellow and to Blue," *Am. J. of Psychology*, vol. 34 (1923), pp. 157 sqq.

Chapter V

AUDITORY SENSATIONS

1. Nature and Importance of Auditory Sensations. Auditory sensations are *those conscious processes which result immediately from the action of vibrating bodies upon the ear and by which we become aware of the sounds produced by these bodies.*

The important rôle which these sensations play in our lives may be readily gathered if we consider the privations which are imposed upon the congenitally deaf. The whole realm of music with the exquisite artistic enjoyment it affords, is cut off from them. Nor is this all. The congenitally deaf are likewise deprived of the most ready means of communicating their thoughts with their fellow men — spoken language. Thus a source of keen intellectual enjoyment is denied them. Hence, the study of auditory sensations is of intense human interest. *In treating of auditory sensations we shall put emphasis upon those aspects of sounds which make them available for musical art.*

2. Sound in the Physical Sense. Following the advice of Aristotle we shall begin the study of auditory sensations by describing their objects. Sound, considered as a sensible quality of bodies, may be defined as *that form of energy which bodies have in virtue of their vibratory movement and which renders these bodies capable of affecting the sense of hearing and causing definite auditory sensations.* This description of the physical nature of sound differs only by its modern terminology from that given by Aristotle.

The physicist is not concerned with the auditory sensations aroused by vibrating bodies except insofar as these sensations are the most ready and convenient means of observing the more rapid vibrations which, as a matter of fact, cause auditory sensations. The physicist is directly concerned with the vibrations of bodies and the laws which govern these vibrations and their propagation through elastic media whether solid, liquid, or gaseous. These laws are the same whether the vibrations are slow or rapid, whether they affect the ear or not. Hence it is that the physicist uses the term "sound" in a sense which must appear strange to the psychologist and the philosopher. To the physicist a "sounding" body is a "vibrating" body, and "sound" is synonymous with the very vibrations of a body, whether slow or rapid. Consequently, he distinguishes between audible and *inaudible* sounds. By "audible sounds" he means those vibrations which are within the limits of audio-frequency, that is, those limits of frequency to which the human ear is attuned. "Inaudible sounds" are vibrations which are either too slow or too rapid to affect the human ear.

The limits of audio-frequency are variously indicated by different observers. It may suffice here to state that in orchestral music the slowest vibration employed is that of the lowest note of the double bass violin which has 41 complete vibrations per second, and the most rapid vibration employed is that of the highest tone of the piccolo which has 3,720 complete vibrations per second. It should be added that this highest note is rarely used, at least by the masters. All vibrations of audio-frequency which are below or above these orchestral limits belong to the realm of "noises" and not to that of musically available "tones," a distinction to which we shall return presently.

The vibrations of a sounding body, say a tuning fork, are normally propagated to the outer ear by means of alternate condensations and rarefactions passing through the atmosphere. *It is these air waves which are most commonly meant when the physicist speaks of "sound."* He specifies them by indicating their three properties: *wave length* (or frequency), *amplitude* and *form,* all of which may be varied independently. He investigates the phenomena and the laws of the propagation, reflection, refraction and diffraction of these waves just as he does in the case of light waves. Once the viewpoint of the physicist in dealing with "sound" is understood, there is no reason why the psychologist should quarrel with him about the terminology used. In this chapter we suppose that the student has at least an elementary knowledge of the physics of "sound."

3. Sound as a Stimulus of the Ear. The air waves, upon reaching the eardrum of the outer ear, are converted by the mechanism of the middle ear into similar *vibrations of the liquid* contained within the inner ear. Details concerning the working of the middle-ear mechanism are as yet little understood. Hence, we pass the matter over in silence. A mere description of anatomical details would not serve our purposes. For the same reason we dispense also with a detailed description of the inner ear. Its working is still less understood than that of the middle ear. That is to say, it is a matter of theory how the vibrations of the liquid in the inner ear really stimulate the true end-organs of hearing, the hair cells of the organ of Corti. We are satisfied here with stating that the organ of Corti rests on a delicate membrane, known as the basilar membrane, and that this membrane is in direct contact with the said liquid (see Fig. 17, p. 108). At the end of this chapter we shall consider the theoretic attempts which have been made to explain how the physical stimulus is really applied to the true end-organs of hearing.

The vibrations of a sounding body may, however, also be propagated to the end-organs of hearing by *bone-conduction,* as may be readily ascertained by holding, for instance, a vibrating tuning fork against the teeth. Nor is this mode of stimulating the ear a mere oddity which can be safely ignored in discussing the phenomena of normal hearing. Thus, for instance, the sounds of the human voice reach the ears of *the speaker himself* largely by bone-conduction. Some of the phenomena of auditory sensations cannot be fully understood unless we take the bone-conduction of sound into consideration as an additional factor.

The excitation set up in each hair cell of the organ of Corti is conveyed separately by a corresponding fiber of the auditory tract first to a relay station in the lower part of the brain and then to a cortical center in the temporal lobe. When this takes place, we have a sensation of hearing. We have explained the anatomical and physiological conditions of auditory sensations sufficiently in the chapter on sensations in general. Further details may be gathered from any textbook of human physiology, but are not required for the purposes of the present chapter.

4. Tones and Noises. Their Three Characteristics (Pitch, Loudness, Timbre) Introspectively Considered. It is hard, if not impossible, to discriminate between tones and noises on the basis of the physical nature of the stimuli which are responsible for these two great classes of sensations of sound. Thus, for instance, it has been said that tones are sound sensations which are caused by periodic vibrations while noises are auditory sensations aroused by vibrations that are not periodic. *These definitions are inaccurate for many reasons.* The purest violin tone never occurs without the scratch of the bow and this means that the periodic air vibrations produced by the vibrating string are intermingled with a confused medley of vibrations which are aperiodic. It cannot be said that the scratch is something merely accidental which should be left out of consideration when defining a violin tone. This is not true. Take the scratch away and you no longer have that tone with which the musician deals. Sounds may be produced whose vibration frequencies are above or below the orchestral limits previously mentioned. *Such vibrations are just as periodic as those within the orchestral limits.* But all sounds above these limits lose more and more their tonal character and are best described as hissing sounds, approaching the noise quality of the consonant *s*. When we go below the orchestral limits, a similar loss of tone quality is observed, such sounds being rather rumbling noises, shading off at last into simple puffs. Incongruities like these could be multiplied and we find them no matter what definition of tone or noise we try in purely objective terms. All such attempts end in the statement that the dividing line between tones and noises is not clearly marked.

In order to arrive at a satisfactory discrimination between tones and noises, we must begin with the fact that *every sensation of sound, introspectively considered, has three properties: pitch, loudness, and timbre.* Of these characteristics, pitch is the most fundamental.

It may suffice here to say that *by pitch, introspectively considered, we mean that peculiarity of a sound which is popularly described by saying that the sound is high or low.* This description makes use of a metaphor suggesting a spatial character of sounds. We need not concern ourselves with the origin of this metaphor, which nobody takes in the literal sense. When we say that one sound is "higher" or "lower" than another, everybody understands the characteristic of the sound meant, and this characteristic is known as pitch. Once this characteristic of sound is understood, it is easy to see how a sound of one and the same pitch may vary in intensity or loudness and also in timbre, as will be explained presently.

From these general considerations it will be seen that *we define a definite sound with accuracy in proportion as we are able to indicate its three determinants or properties: pitch, loudness, and timbre.* If, however, in ascertaining and describing a definite sound, we must be satisfied with a vague determination and description of its most fundamental property, pitch, our experience and the definition of this experience will be vague. And this brings us to the only satisfactory distinction that can be made between tone and noise. This distinction is based exclusively on data introspectively ascertained.

We define, then, a tone as a sensation of sound whose pitch can be ascertained and described with accuracy. In ascertaining the pitch of a tone the musician relies exclusively on his ear, that is, on introspective data These data enable him to describe that pitch with an accuracy which leaves nothing to be desired. This description is not couched in terms of wave frequencies — he may be totally ignorant of what the physicist means by frequency, amplitude, or form of wave — it is expressed by *written musical symbols which enable every other musician to reproduce the tone of that pitch with accuracy,* whether he knows anything concerning the correlation of that pitch with the properties of air waves or not. *The written musical symbols may, in fact, be said to be the most pithy and unmistakable introspective report that a musician can give concerning the properties of the sounds which constitute the units of a musical composition.* We shall make use of these introspective reports of a musician in defining the three properties of a tone.

Accordingly, in *defining the pitch* of a tone, we need not be satisfied with the rather vague terms "high" and "low." We define it as *that characteristic of a tone which the musician designates by the position of a tone on, above, below, cr between the lines of the musical staff, the meaning of this position being modified by the other means of musical signature (clef, sharps, flats, etc.).* Translated into spoken language the musical symbol for a tone of a definite pitch denotes, for instance, a sound of the quality "a flat" in the once-accented octave.

A noise, on the other hand, is defined as *a sound whose pitch can be ascertained and described only vaguely by such terms as high, very high, rather low, etc.* Thus, a shriek is plainly higher than a growl. In fact, all the properties of noises are described only in vague terms. In most languages words are used which are imitative of that noise and thus suggest not only its pitch but also its degree of loudness and its timbre. We describe noises as rattling, buzzing, humming, roaring, thundering, rippling sounds, etc., or we speak of thuds, clicks, hisses, murmurs, etc.

It should be noted that *noises are not necessarily unpleasant.* The pleasant or unpleasant character of a sound does not enter into the definition of a noise. The rippling of a brook is decidedly not unpleasant. Hence, too, the fact that noises are not necessarily excluded from music. In fact, the musician deliberately makes use of certain noises, but he does so with discretion. As stated already, the scratch of a violin tone is an essential feature of that tone. But it must not be such that it interferes with the definiteness of the pitch of a violin tone.

From this it will also be seen that *a tone should not be defined as a musical sound* and a noise as an unmusical one. It is true that tones constitute the principal portion of the musician's realm, but it includes also all those noises which are pleasant, at least under the conditions specified by the musical composer. In short, *nothing enters into the definitions of tone and noise but definiteness and indefiniteness of pitch.*

By the *loudness* of a tone we mean *that characteristic which the musician designates by his dynamic symbols, such as pp, f, ff, crescendo, decrescendo,* etc. True, these dynamic symbols are far from being as definite as those designating pitch. But they suffice for the purposes of musical art. They are, moreover, much clearer than any physical determination of the amplitude of the wave or its exact pressure on the eardrum or the "exact" fraction of Fechner's logarythmic formula would be, particularly as this "exact" fraction in the case of tone sensations is notably inexact.

By the *timbre* of a tone we mean *that characteristic of a tone which the musician designates in an orchestral score by prescribing that a definite tone must be played by the clarinet, and not by the cello, by the oboe, and not by the flute.* For a tone of identically the same pitch and loudness sounds very different when played by this instrument or that. Hence an orchestral musician is particularly careful to assign each note to that instrument which will assure the timbre desired. In this regard, again, the musician's language is most accurate, but only when writing orchestral scores. In other compositions he uses vaguer terminology, such as *sfz, dolce,* etc. In ordinary parlance we designate the timbre of a tone by saying that it is *rich, mellow, voluminous, thin, hollow, nasal, metallic, piercing,* etc.

5. The Pitch of a Tone and the Frequency of a Sound Wave. Delicacy of Pitch Discrimination. The Leeway of "Tempered Intonation." The Facts of Tonal Fusion. The psychological meaning of the three properties of a tone being understood, we must now correlate them with the three physical properties of sound waves: frequency, amplitude, and form.

In general it can be said that *the pitch of a tone depends on the frequency of the sound wave:* the greater the frequency of the wave, the higher the tone. *This statement, however, needs several qualifications* which should be clearly noted. In the light of these qualifications the student will understand why we did not allow this physical correlation to enter into the definition of pitch.

The first qualification is this: *Not every change in the frequency of a wave causes a noticeable change of pitch in the psychological sense.* This brings us to the subject of pitch discrimination. Before going into details, it may be well to state that the delicacy of pitch discrimination, like that of color discrimination in persons of normal vision, is not so much a matter of native ability as one of attention and practice. These conditions are verified in the case of a musician. Within the middle region of tones employed by the musician (that is, within the octave c'–c'' and c''–c''') the delicacy of his pitch discrimination is rather remarkable under laboratory conditions. Thus within the doubly accented octave (c''–c''') a practiced musician can distinguish *without fail* a difference of pitch arising from *half a vibration per second.* This means that within the octave mentioned the number of distinguishable tones is about 1,000. If we go above this middle region, the pitch discrimination of a musician is less delicate. It has been estimated that the sum total of tones that can be distinguished by a musician *without fail* is about 4,200.[1] Some investigators state that this total is about 11,000. It should be noted, however, that these investigators, in making their cal-

C' Major Scale Just Intonation of the Violin Tempered Intonation of Piano	c'	d'	e'	f'	g'	a'	b'	c''
Just Intonation of the Violin	264	297	330	352	396	440	495	528
Tempered Intonation of Piano	261.2	293.5	328	348.5	391.5	440	493	522

TABLE IX

culations, do not restrict themselves to discriminations that can be made *without fail.* Hence, 4,200 seems to be the preferable figure. When we go above the orchestral limits, enormous changes in vibration frequency may occur without causing a noticeable

---

[1] See Helmholtz-Ellis, p. 147.

change of pitch even for the best musician. It is with this fact in view that the orchestral limits have been fixed.

It should be added that when the musician is not under laboratory conditions, supposed in the foregoing account, there is a certain leeway even in the middle region of the orchestral range. This is true at least in the sense that the ears of a musician, say a violinist, are not offended if the violinist right next to him produces a tone whose frequency differs from his own by half a vibration or even by two or three vibrations per second. He must be in a rather scientific mood, not particularly desirable during an orchestra performance, if he notices such a thing and declares himself offended. A violinist may be perfectly delighted with the piano accompaniment of his solo. A glance at Table IX will show what actually happens. The piano has "tempered" intonation, that is, it is *scientifically out of tune when properly tuned*. The violinist, however, is rather inclined to give all his tones what is known as "just" intonation. We shall explain these matters more fully when speaking on "tempered" intonation. Simply read the numbers of Table IX, and you know *the leeway in the frequency of a wave which is allowable without offense to the ear*. If it were not for the fact that this leeway exists, the "tempering" of intervals in tuning a piano or organ would be an outrage.

The most important feature, however, of this leeway is that without it modern music with its bold modulations and surprising combinations would be impossible. Modern music depends essentially on the said leeway. It enables the orchestrator to "mistake" one note for another even in its harmonic relations to other tones. Thus, for instance, *c sharp* and *d flat,* when "justly" intoned, differ from each other both physically and psychologically, that is, in wave frequency and noticeable pitch. But all these differences are within the limits of the said leeway. *The modern composer takes advantage of this fact.* He at times deliberately "mistakes" *c sharp* for *d flat,* no matter whether its actual intonation is "just" or "tempered," and is thus enabled to "mistake" the harmonic relations which *c sharp* has to other tones for those which *d flat* has, and these harmonic relations differ considerably from each other. In the musician's language this is expressed by say-ing that *the composer makes use of "enharmonic exchanges."* It is precisely these "enharmonic exchanges" which make it possible for the modern composer to do some surprising things in han-dling his tone material. In a word, *the said leeway in pitch dis-crimination is not only responsible for the compromise in tuning a piano or organ, but it is also one of the foundation stones of modern music.* Without it there would be no modern music. From all this it will be seen that the statement that pitch depends on wave frequency, is a trifle too simple.

The second qualification is this: When we say that the pitch of a definite tone, say that of the open "a" string of the violin is due to 440 vibrations per second, the meaning of this assertion is not that the tone of this pitch is really caused by a *single* wave whose frequency is 440 per second. Far from it. Every tone pro-duced by any musical instrument whatever, consists of a great multiplicity of waves, each of which has a different frequency.

To be concrete, the open "a" string of the violin vibrates in its entirety and its vibration frequency is 440 per second. As a result of the elasticity of the string, each half of it vibrates sepa-rately and its vibration frequency stands to 440 in the ratio of 1:2. Also, every third part of the string has its own vibration whose frequency stands to 440 in the ratio of 1:3. In fact, *every aliquot part of the string tends* to vibrate separately. Hence, the violin tone whose pitch is correlated by the physicist with the vibration frequency of 440 per second, is really due to a great number of vibrations whose frequencies are in serial order 440, 880, 1320, 1760, 2200, 2640, etc. The sum total of these vibrations are known as *harmonics* which bear to one another the ratios 1:2:3:4:5:6, etc. The slowest of these vibrations is spoken of either as the *"first harmonic"* or as the *"fundamental."* The other har-monics are indicated either by their *serial number* or are referred to as *"overtones."* How many of the vibrations corresponding to the overtones actually occur depends on the elasticity, form, ten-sion, rigidity, etc., of the string and to some extent also on the manner in which it is set in motion. So much for the physical facts. The internal experience which is correlated with these facts introduces us to a most remarkable problem. *Why is it that we do not hear a multiplicity of tones?* As far as the internal experience even of a musician is concerned, there is no multiplicity of tones but *a unitary experience,* namely, that of one tone of a definite pitch, and that pitch — so the physicist says — is determined by the vibration frequency of the "first harmonic" or "fundamental." This unitary experience is all the more surprising as the ear — in sharp contrast to the eye — is an analyzing organ answering each vibration separately with a sensation of sound.

We might be inclined to think that the unitary character of our internal experience is sufficiently accounted for by the physical nature of the harmonic vibrations, namely, their relative intensity. The explanation then would be as follows: The vibration of the whole string, being much the stronger, causes a tone sensation of a definite pitch. The vibrations of the several aliquot parts of the string, being much weaker, are below the threshold and thus get no chance to arouse their corresponding tone sensations.

Undoubtedly the relative intensity of the "fundamental" tone as compared with that of the "overtones" has something to do with the unitary character of our experience. But it is not all. Substantially the same phenomenon occurs also when several "harmonic vibrations" of the physicist are combined whose intensity is equal so that every one of them is decidedly above the threshold of sensation. Suppose that three violins produce vibrations whose fundamentals bear to one another the ratio of 4:5:6 In musical terminology this is expressed by saying that these three violins produce a pleasing combination of tones known as a "major chord." *To the vast majority of persons in the audience of an orchestra performance this chord comes as a "unit" with no distinguishable parts in it.* There is a very simple method of settling the accuracy of this assertion experimentally. Suppose a male quartet is singing without accompaniment. *Could you follow the second tenor throughout the composition without fail* so that you could write out its part as young Mozart did when he desired a score of a vocal composition which was otherwise not obtainable? If you cannot, or in proportion as you fail to do so, the four notes which the male quartet sings at any given time come to you as a "unit."

Accordingly, several tones of different pitch may be so intimately combined in our internal experience that they come to us as a "unit." You may call it *Gestalt,* if you like. The usual terminology employed to designate such an intimate combination of tones of different pitch is *tonal fusion.* The essential feature of this *Gestalt* or "tonal fusion" is that — at least here and now — *we fail to analyze our auditory experience into its component parts.* But tones thus "fused" *can* be analyzed, as the experience of Mozart and of musicians in general proves. The only proviso is that musicians should have the same attitude of attention as Mozart had when analyzing a choral composition whose written score was unavailable. He explicitly directed his attention to the component parts, and under these conditions the "unit" or *Gestalt* broke up into its component parts.

Essentially the same thing happens when we hear what we call a "single" tone of a definite pitch, say a′. Here again we deal with a case of *tonal fusion.* The only difference between a "single" tone and a musical "chord" is this: *It is decidedly harder to analyze a "single" tone than a "chord."* But everyone can analyze a "single" tone into its "harmonic" constituents. It is not so much a matter of musical ability as one of attention. If the reader desires to perform this task, he will find the mode of procedure described in the chapter on Attention (p. 122).

The important point to be noted for the purposes of our present discussion is that *tonal fusion has degrees* and these degrees depend on the relative ease of analysis by attention. Hence a "single" tone is known as a case of *perfect fusion;* a "chord" is one of *imperfect fusion.* This consideration is of the utmost importance when we come to the real significance of the bothersome subject of "consonance" and "dissonance." These musical concepts remain puzzles if we try to define them in terms of their physical stimuli. The difficulty vanishes if we define them in the light of the internal experience of a musician and then our account of these phenomena deals really with facts as they occur. The same remark applies to the discussion of musical intervals, scales, and other musical matters. Purely physical considerations do not suffice to make them intelligible to us. *We must in every instance begin with the internal experience of a musician.* This ascertained, we may and must correlate it with the nature of the physical stimulus.

There is really a *third qualification* which should be made when correlating the pitch of a tone with the frequency of the sound wave. We shall discuss it in a later paragraph when explaining the important distinction between *tone* and *musical tone*. These two terms are not synonymous.

6. The Loudness of a Tone and the Amplitude of the Sound Wave. It is frequently stated that the loudness of a tone depends on the *amplitude* of the sound wave. This formula, however, is too simple to cover all cases.

When two waves have the same frequency, the energy of the vibration increases as the square of the amplitude. When, however, two waves differ not only in amplitude but also in frequency, this frequency is an additional factor in determining the energy of the vibration. The pressure of the sound wave on our eardrum increases with this energy. Hence the aforementioned formula has been amended by saying that the loudness of a tone, whether of the same or of a different pitch, depends on *the pressure of the wave on our eardrum*. It is a matter of physics to determine this pressure from both the amplitude and the frequency of the vibration. But here *another qualification is necessary which applies to both formulas.*

Not every change in the energy of a sound wave is correlated with a *noticeable* increase in the loudness of a tone. This is clear from what we said in the chapter on sensations in general under the heading of *Weber's law*. We must increase the energy by a *definite fraction* of the just preceding amount, as we have explained before. What needs emphasis here is, that the exact fraction which constitutes the differential threshold, is particularly inexact in the case of tone sensations. From all this it will be

seen that the correlation of the loudness of a tone with its physical stimulus is *much more complex* than the formula with which
we started out would lead us to suspect. From the standpoint of
a musician such exact correlations are of no interest. For him it
is more important to know that the notes of a piccolo or of a
soprano soloist may dominate the whole orchestra and that the
addition of ten or even fifty voices to a large chorus makes little
difference in the loudness of that chorus. It is only by the artistic
sense of the leader that a proper balancing of all the tones of an
orchestral or choral ensemble can be determined.

7. **The Timbre of a Tone and the Form of the Wave.** We
said before that the tone of a musical instrument can be analyzed
by anyone, whether he is a musician or not, into its harmonic
constituents. This analysis is accomplished by *attention* and is,
of course, restricted to those components which under the actual
conditions of the analysis rise above the threshold of sensation.
The same analysis can also be accomplished by *purely physical
means.* That is to say, it is possible to ascertain the physical components of the sound wave caused by a definite musical instrument, say a violin. Various scientific instruments have been devised for this purpose. The most noteworthy of these is known
by the name of *phonodeik.* It was devised by D. C. Miller and is
described by him in his *Science of Musical Sounds.*[2] It must suffice
here to say that the phonodeik makes a *photographic record of a
sound wave.* By means of suitable attachments this record may
be projected on a screen for public demonstration. Thus it is
possible to see a sound wave and measure its physical components
with remarkable precision.

When explaining the psychological meaning of timbre, we said
that two instruments, say an oboe and a clarinet, may produce
a tone of identically the same pitch and of approximately the
same loudness and still the two tones differ from each other. The
characteristic by which they differ is known as timbre. The phonodeik makes it possible to ascertain in what the physical sound

[2]Pages 78 sqq.

waves differ which cause tones of different timbre. We quote: "The average of several analyses . . . shows that the oboe tone has twelve or more partials, the fourth and fifth predominating, with 30 and 36 per cent respectively of the total loudness. The clarinet tone may have twenty or more partials; the average of several analyses shows twelve of importance, with the seventh, eighth, ninth, and tenth predominating; the seventh partial contains 8 per cent of the total loudness, while the eighth, ninth, and tenth contain 18, 15, and 18 per cent respectively."[3]

As the partial vibrations of a sounding body appear as ripples on the main or fundamental wave, we may express the results of such tone analysis in the following general formula: *The timbre of a tone depends on the form of the wave,* that is, the ripples on the fundamental wave. More precisely expressed, the general formula may be worded thus: The timbre of a tone depends at least principally on *the relative number and intensity of the overtones of a musical tone.* The relative number and intensity of the overtones in turn depend on *the construction of the musical instrument,* the material used, etc., and to some extent on the manner in which the vibrations are produced. Hence the fact that musical composers are at times particularly at pains to indicate how a definite sound of an orchestra score is to be produced. In the case of Wagnerian scores, such directions sometimes include elaborate stage devices.

We have already stated that certain noises are inseparable from the tones of certain instruments. But the physical analysis of such noises is much more difficult, particularly as they are relatively weak. They, too, contribute to the timbre of a tone. Their consideration does not change our general formula. Physically they will appear as irregular ripples on the main wave: they contribute in determining the form of the wave on which timbre depends.

All the facts mentioned lead us to the consideration of a most peculiar aspect of tonal fusion. *Why is it that "overtones" not ex-*

---

[3] Miller, *op. cit.,* p. 201, quoted by permission of the Macmillan Co., publishers.

plicitly attended to should alter the character of the fundamental so as to give it its peculiar "color" or "timbre"? We have no explanation for this effect of fusion. We must be satisfied with stating the fact. There are, however, two things which should be noted in connection with this effect of tonal fusion.

The first is that several tone sensations thus fused *can* be analyzed by attention. In proportion as we succeed in this psychological analysis, *the effect of tonal fusion disappears.* With sufficient practice the reader may become very proficient in this analysis of musical tones. But *if he desires to derive musical pleasure, say from a horn tone, he had better make no effort to become an expert in its psychological analysis* Thus analyzed, a horn tone may cause him excruciating pain, while unanalyzed, it is probably the most soulful of all musical tones whose beauty cannot fail to attract attention. What holds of *tonal fusions* holds also of every other case of *fusions of sensations.* They undoubtedly occur, but all *can* be analyzed by attention. *Hence, the facts of tonal fusion cannot be used, as they have been used, to give a semblance of truth to certain metaphysical prepossessions in the explanation of conscious processes which transcend those of sensation.* We shall revert to this matter when discussing *thought* in detail.

The second thing to be noted in connection with the effect of "tonal fusion" is of importance in understanding certain matters of musical interest. We said that tonal fusion may be relatively "perfect" or "imperfect" and we pointed out that a musical "chord" (such as the major triad, for instance) is a case of imperfect fusion. Under certain conditions the effect of this "imperfect fusion" is like that of "perfect fusion." The overtones "perfectly" fused with the fundamental give this fundamental its peculiar timbre, say that of a violin tone. *The chords supplying the accompaniment to that violin tone give an additional "color" or "timber" to that violin tone.* One and the same violin tone sounds different according as it is accompanied by this chord or that. To the average listener the violin tone of a soloist is *the only thing which is really in the focus of attention.* The accompaniment is merely a setting in which that tone occurs. This setting, for the ordinary listener beyond analysis, gives to that tone a new "color" or "timbre" which cannot be described by him in more exact terms. To a musician, this setting determines *which one of the many possible harmonic relations that tone has here and now,* a relation which the violin tone itself merely suggests in a vague and equivocal sort of way.

8. Tones and Musical Tones. We had occasion to remark that "tone" and "musical tone" are not synonymous terms. *A "tone" is a sound of definite pitch. A "musical tone" is a tone of such a pitch that it bears definite harmonic relations to tones of a different pitch and which, as a result, can be combined with these other tones into harmonies and melodies.* Only about 85 of the 4,200 (or 11,000) tones which can be discriminated under laboratory conditions, answer the requirements of this definition. These 85 tones constitute the musical tone-system.

The 4,200 (or more) distinguishable tones can be accurately represented by *a simple straight line.* At one end of this line we place the tone of lowest ascertainable pitch, at the other, the tone of highest pitch. There is nothing in the tones of intermediate pitch to make any one more prominent than another. Accordingly, these intermediate tones find their places in regular succession of pitch discrimination between the two ends of the line. *But the 85 tones which constitute the musical tone-system cannot be thus represented.* Their graphical representation must indicate *the definite distances* or intervals by which these 85 tones are separated from one another. It must show, further, *the harmonic relations* which determine the intervals and which make the 85 tones available for harmonies and melodies. Figures 14 and 15 are attempts to represent the musical tone-system from two different points of view, as will be explained presently.

9. Harmony and Melody. Harmony is *the simultaneous combination of two or more tones of different pitch which is pleasing to the ear.* As a matter of empirical rule, only tones within the musical tone-system can be thus combined. All other combinations are distinctly offensive to the ear, whatever the why and

wherefore of this fact may be. All such offensive combinations
of tones are sometimes designated by the term "dissonance." It

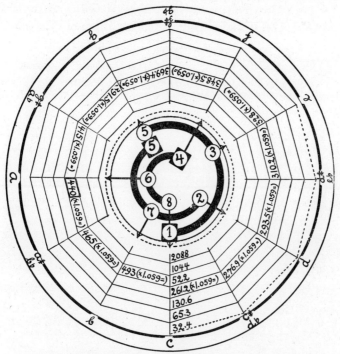

Fig. 14. A Musical Nomogram. A diagrammatic representation of the
musical tone-system as it is actually used by orchestral musicians today.
It indicates the fixed harmonic relations of all musical intervals and
(major) scales and their absolute pitch numbers as determined by
international agreement and the (ideal) requirements of equally
tempered intonation. The central diagram, included within the dotted
circle, is but another form of Figure 16 and indicates the structure of
every actual and possible major scale and the harmonic relations which
determine its seemingly irregular steps; hence *the central diagram may
be rotated at random.* Further explanations in the text.

should be noted, however, that here the term *dissonance* is taken
in the popular sense. Dissonance in *the technical sense,* as understood by the musician, means something totally different, as we
shall explain in due order.

A melody is a rhythmical succession of tones within the said tone-system which is perceived as a pleasing unit. The unitary character of a melody, not adequately accounted for by the enumeration of its successive parts or by the rhythm of their succes-

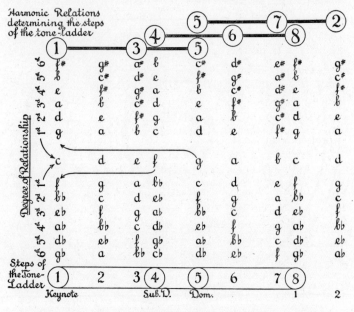

FIG. 15. The Constitution and the Family Relationship of All Major Scales. This diagram shows why a melody remains *"the same"* when transposed from one key to another. The reason is, because the harmonic relations which the single tones of the melody have to the keynote, are *identically the same* in all keys. In all keys these relations are *equally correct* and *equally incorrect,* that is, a compromise of equally tempered intonation.

sion, is *the classical example of what is discussed under the heading of "Gestalt,"* and a puzzling problem it is. In the experience of a musician many things are required to make a succession of tones a pleasing unit. But one of the most fundamental requirements of this unity is that the very tones thus combined — apart from the particular form which this combination takes in this or that melody — should *of themselves* belong together. The musician expresses this by saying that a melody must move in a definite *"key"* or, if it move successively in different keys, these different keys must have definite and recognizable family relationships to the principal key of the melody. This brings us to the consideration of scales and their family relationships For *a "key" is nothing else than a definite scale specified by its "keynote."* It is to this keynote that all the intervals or "steps" of the scale have a definite relation.

10. Scales and Intervals. A tone of any vibration frequency can become the keynote of a scale. It is only by international agreement that the choice of the keynote is limited to certain vibration frequencies. *Once the keynote is fixed, all the cardinal points of the corresponding scale are likewise fixed, namely, the octave, the fifth interval or dominant, and the fourth interval or subdominant.* These intervals in "just" intonation are determined by the simple ratios 1:2, 2:3, and 3:4. The other "steps" of the tone ladder are ascertained by erecting a "major triad" on the keynote, the dominant and the subdominant respectively. By a "major triad" the musician understands three tones which in "just" intonation are represented by the ratios 4:5:6 (see Fig. 16). The simultaneous combination of such tones is very pleasing, in fact, it is *the prototype of all pleasing combinations.* The great variety of "chords" used by the musician are but analogous imitations or inversions, further elaborations or mere suggestions of the "major triad." Even if these musical details be but dimly understood by the student, a mere glance at Figure 16 will show what a compact unit every scale is. From Figure 15 he will gather, further, that all *the scales of different keys form a unit of a higher order and that their family relationship is established through the cardinal points of each scale.* Every discussion of the *Gestalt* of a melody must begin with *this unitary character* of the very elements which enter into the composition of a melody and with the fact that this unitary character is recognized by a musician, not in terms of mathematical ratios, but in terms of *pleasing* *combinations* which each tone of a melody more or less clearly suggests The dimmer this suggestion is, the more readily will a melody fall apart into tones which no longer have any *Gestalt*.

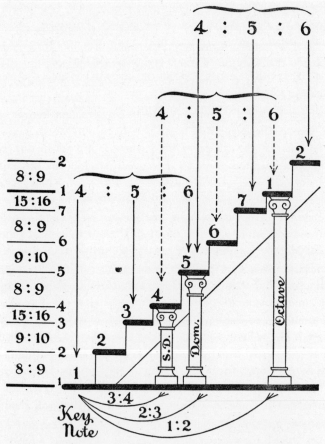

FIG. 16. Structure of the Major Scale. The seemingly irregular steps of the major scale are determined by the harmonic relation which each tone of the scale (or of a melody written in that scale) has to the keynote. This structure is the same for every major scale and is suggested by the melody in whatever key it is played: the first example of what modern psychologists mean by *Gestalt*. The minor scale (not diagramed) is an analogous imitation of the major scale. Also the ancient Greek scales and the modes of plain chant are (less perfect) analogous imitations of the major scale (or the ancient Ionian scale).

11. Consonance and dissonance are phenomena which present another problem of *Gestalt*. We have called attention to the fact that the difference between consonance and dissonance does not consist in this, that the former is a *pleasing* combination of musical tones, while the latter is a *displeasing* one. Modern music, even of the classics, *bristles with dissonances*. It need not be stated explicitly that they are not introduced by the masters in order to displease. On the contrary, *some of the most delightful combinations of musical tones in modern music are these very dissonances.* Thus, for instance, all the charming "embroideries" of melodies are essentially dissonances. *Take the dissonances away from the works of the masters and there is not much left to please.*

This premised, we divide all *pleasing* combinations, chords, and intervals into three classes; namely, *dissonant, consonant,* and *indifferent* combinations. *A dissonant chord or interval is a pleasing combination of tones which demands a "resolution," that is, a definite succession of chords or intervals.* Thus, for instance, the combination of tones having the ratios 4:5:6:7, and erected on the dominant, *peremptorily suggests the chord of the keynote.* This chord, accordingly, must follow the said dissonance at least eventually and in some form or other. The essential feature of a dissonance, then, is that it *creates a rather pleasing expectation or tension.* This tension must be relieved and it is relieved when the chord or interval expected follows. *This is what a musician means by a dissonance.* Plainly this is another problem of *Gestalt*

A consonant chord or interval, on the other hand, *is a pleasing combination of tones which does not demand a "resolution" but can stand by itself.* This is true in the most perfect sense only of the triad erected on the keynote. This chord, and only this chord, can be the final conclusion of a composition A triad erected on the dominant or subdominant is not so perfect a consonance. In the musician's language it can form only a "half conclusion." This again is not merely a matter of sensation but involves a problem of *Gestalt*.

An indifferent or neutral combination of musical tones is one which may be either a consonance or a dissonance according to the manner in which it is used. This very definition suggests a problem of *Gestalt*.

12. Some of the theories of consonance and dissonance which have been actually proposed, seem rather out of touch with the experiences of a musician. Thus, for instance, it has been said that when the vibration frequencies of two or more tones bear simple ratios to one another, their combination is a consonance. This would seem to fit the case of the major triad whose vibration frequencies have the simple ratios of 4:5:6. *But what about the ratio 3:4?* Surely it is a very simple one. The interval, however, thus designated is, in the experience of a musician, either a dissonance or a consonance. When this interval occurs in the combination 3:4:5, it is *decidedly a dissonance*. The interval, of course, remains the same whether it is expressed by the ratio 3:4 or by 6:8. *In the combination 4:5:6:8, this interval is part of the most perfect of perfect consonances.*

Moreover, it should be borne in mind that in *tempered* intonation *no chord of any kind can be expressed by ratios that are simple*. Thus, when listening to a piano recital, you will be perfectly delighted by a chord whose vibration frequencies are 261.2, 328, and 391.5, respectively. You cannot express the ratios of this "tempered" major triad with accuracy by any simpler numbers than those mentioned. But they roughly approach the ratios 4:5:6, and the musician likes the combination, unless perchance he be in a laboratory mood.

A similar criticism applies to the theory which holds that a dissonance is due to the fact that *the combination of certain tones is disturbed by beats of the upper partials*. These beats are due to the interference of waves. The result of this interference is that the whole mass of sound is broken up into pulses, and these pulses or throbs, if attended to, make the joint effect rough. If this account of dissonance were correct, then most, if not all, chords played on a piano or organ should be displeasing. All intervals of the piano and organ — except the octaves — are compromises of "equal temperament," as may be seen from Figure 14. Even the simple combination of two tones whose ratio in "just" intonation is 2:3, produces one beat per second, if the organ tuner has done his work properly. As a matter of fact, the organ tuner guides himself in tempering the intervals, not by mathematical considerations, but by the beats which are produced by the simul·taneous combination of the intervals. The result is that many chords played on the organ produce beats at an alarming rate. Happily a musician when playing on the piano or organ is in no laboratory mood; he simply pays no attention to the unavoidable beats. He has more pleasant things to think about.

Moreover, it is not true that all beats create the impression of roughness. Organ builders introduce such beats of set purpose even between the fundamental tones, as for instance, in devising the organ stop known as "Celeste." It is precisely because of the "celestial beauty" of these beats that this stop has received its name.

From all this it will be seen that the *phenomena of consonance and dissonance are not merely matters of sensation.* Like melody, they are phenomena of *Gestalt*.

13. The Musical Tone-System. Figure 14 is a diagram·matic representation of the musical tone-system as it is actually used by orchestral musicians today. It indicates the fixed relations of all musical intervals and scales and their absolute pitch num·bers as determined by international agreement and the require·ments of equally tempered intonation.

The constitution of every scale, explained on page 101, is dia·gramed in the center of the figure. The disk indicated by the dotted circle is to be detached from the rest of the diagram and is supposed to be *rotated* around its center.

In order to satisfy the requirements of equal temperament the distance from any keynote to its octave (1:2) is ideally divided into *12 geometrically equal steps.* These 12 steps are known as the "chromatic" scale. It contains not only the essential steps of the scale (indicated in the center of the figure by the numbers 1, 2, 3, etc.) but also its "accidental" steps, that is, steps which are *foreign* to the scale. The wave frequency of *a′* is fixed by inter·national agreement at 440 vibrations per second. From this the frequency of the next "chromatic" step is determined by multiply-ing 440 by the twelfth root of 2, which is 1.059+.

This premised, the details of the figure are sufficiently under-stood from what we have said in the preceding sections of this chapter. We wish now to call attention to some *remarkable prop-erties of the scales or octaves which constitute the musical tone-system.*

Note, first of all, the unique fact that *every scale of a definite key occurs seven times.* Thus, for instance, there are seven c major scales. They are indicated by the respective seven keynotes C_1, C, c, c^1, c^2, c^3, c^4. So similar are these scales that even a musi-cian may be altogether at a loss to tell in what particular c scale a melody, written in C major, is actually played. If a similar con-dition prevailed in the visible spectrum — which constitutes about one octave — we should have *seven spectra placed side by side.* When we have traveled from the red to the violet end, the red end begins over again, and so on, seven times.

The second fact, just as unique, is this: *Move the central disk in such a way that 1 points at d flat. The result is that you have now seven d flat scales.* The essential intervals of each are indicated by the numbers of the central disk. Most musicians are unable to tell whether a melody written in C major is actually played in that key or transposed to that of D flat major. If something sim-ilar were true in the case of the visible spectrum, *we should have to say that we can start the visible spectrum at any wave length* and thus get, in every instance, the same succession of colors from red to violet.

The third fact is *the remarkable family relationship of the scales of a different key.* Rotate the central disk counterclockwise exactly through the interval of a fifth so that 1 points at g instead of c. By means of the central disk you can ascertain the constitu-tive elements of the G major scale you thus get. In the experience of a musician the G major scale, if used *after* the C major scale, presents *a marked contrast* to the latter. And still *all the tones of the G major scale, except one, are identical with the tones of the C major scale.* It is only the harmonic relations of the tones which are changed and which are responsible for the contrast. When the musician says that he "modulates" from one scale to one of a different key, he means that *he "mistakes" the harmonic relations which a definite tone has in one scale for those it has in another scale.* In a similar manner you continue to rotate the central disk each time exactly through the interval of a fifth. Thus you arrive successively at all the scales of a different key *in the order of their degree of family relationship* as diagramed in Figure 15. After twelve rotations you arrive again at the scale with which you started out. *For this family relationship of scales we have no analogy* in the arrangement of colors or any other sensible qualities.

The fourth fact is still more unique than this. *Move the central disk in such a way that 1 points somewhere between c and d flat. The result is that you create a new tone-system.* As to its harmonic relations this new tone-system is identical with the present tone-system. But as to *absolute pitch numbers* it is so foreign to the present system that the two cannot be used together without offense to the ear. In a similar manner, you can create a great many — probably about 500 — different tone-systems. Quite a number of them have been in actual use. Händel and Mozart wrote for a tone-system which, in the sense explained, was altogether different from our present one. At the time of these great masters a' had 422 vibrations per second. And still we enjoy today identically the same masterpieces. In the light of this fourth fact the student will understand in what sense it is true that only 85 of the 4,200 distinguishable tones are "musical tones."

14. The Helmholtz Theory of Hearing. Many of the facts which we have ascertained in this chapter are plainly problems of *Gestalt*. The numerous theories of hearing which have been proposed are mainly concerned with *the analytic function of the organ of hearing* and with the problem how the hair cells of the organ of Corti are stimulated.

The organ of hearing, in sharp contrast to that of sight, is analytic in function. No matter how complex the air vibrations may be that impinge upon the eardrum, the organ of hearing answers each component of the air wave with a sound sensation which under appropriate conditions can be readily distinguished from the sensation aroused by any other component of this air wave.

The Helmholtz theory starts out from the fact that *the physical analysis of a compound air wave can be readily effected by a piano whose damper is raised*. When we sing into such a piano, each piano string whose vibration frequency corresponds to a

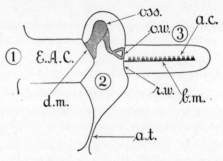

Fig. 17. Diagrammatic representation of the ear (after Dr. Pohlman). 1, external ear; E.A.C., external auditory canal; d.m., drum membrane (ear drum); 2, middle ear or tympanic cavity; oss., ossicles of the middle ear; a.t., auditory tube (Eustachian); 3, inner ear, the cochlear tube *uncoiled*, very schematic; o.w., oval window of the inner ear; r.w., round window; b.m., basilar membrane; a.c., auditory cells with cilia (hair cells of the organ of Corti), serially arranged.

frequency contained in the compound air wave, will begin to vibrate in unison with that frequency — a phenomenon of *res onance*. This premised, Helmholtz assumes that the basilar mem brane (see Fig. 17) on which the hair cells of the internal ear rest, is really a series of "piano strings." When a compound air wave strikes the eardrum, the latter begins to vibrate. By the mecha nism of the middle ear these vibrations are converted into similar vibrations in the liquid of the inner ear. This liquid is in direct contact with the basilar membrane. Each component of the com pound vibration will cause a definite "piano string" of the basilar membrane to vibrate, namely, that "piano string" which is at tuned to the frequency of that component. Thus the compound sound wave is physically analyzed into its components by the basilar membrane, just as it is by a piano whose damper is raised. Each "piano string" of the basilar membrane then stimulates the corresponding hair cells of the organ of Corti. The nerve-fiber connected with each hair cell conducts to the brain an impulse which is due to a definite component of the air wave impinging upon the eardrum. From this it will be seen why the theory of Helmholtz is also known as the *"piano theory"* or the *"resonance theory"* of hearing.

If the assumptions of this theory are correct, the analytic function of the ear is readily understood. There have been, however, *a great many objections* made against its assumptions. Suffice it here to say that *the "piano" which is supposed to exist in our inner ear, is of almost infinitesimal proportions.* The longest string of this "piano," supposed to vibrate in unison with the lowest note of the bass violin, is about half a millimeter or 1/50 of an inch long. *Whether such a "piano" can do the work it is supposed to do, may be seriously doubted.* For a more detailed discussion of the Helmholtz theory the reader is referred to Chapter VI of *The Foundations of Experimental Psychology,* edited by C. Murchison.[4]

15. The Sound-Pattern Theory of Hearing. When a metal plate covered with sand is appropriately clamped and then set into vibration by bowing or striking, beautiful patterns are formed in the sand. These patterns differ with the mode of vibration of the plate and are known as *sound patterns.* They are the starting point of the sound-pattern theory of hearing. According to this theory, air vibrations, after being converted into similar vibrations in the liquid of the inner ear, produce "sound patterns" on the basilar membrane on which the hair cells rest. This means that some parts of the basilar membrane are vibrating and others are at rest, and that some parts vibrate this way and others another way. It means, further, that some hair cells resting on the basilar membrane are stimulated and others are not, and that

---

[4]Pages 320 sqq.

some hair cells are stimulated one way and others another way. If such be the case, the neural current initiated by the hair cells would differ with every detail of the sound pattern. Accordingly, the neural current in the acoustic nerve would not be a "code message" to be deciphered by the brain, but each component of the sound wave would be represented separately by the neural current in some particular fiber of the acoustic nerve. In short, *according to this theory sound is physically analyzed into its components by means of the sound patterns on the basilar membrane.* This seems a plausible explanation of the analytic function of the organ of hearing.

In the opinion of the present writer *the principal objection against this theory is that its assumptions imply a variability in the function of each hair cell.* That is to say, the theory implies that the stimulation of one and the same hair cell results at one time in the sound sensation of one pitch, and at another in the sound sensation of a different pitch. Such a variability in the function of the hair cells seems unintelligible. It can be avoided only by assuming, further, that the sound patterns on the basilar membrane are so formed that a definite component of air-conducted sound stimulates invariably the same hair cells. *This further assumption is hardly called for by the known facts of sound patterns.*

Another objection that may be urged is that the sound patterns on the basilar membrane which are supposed to result from a symphony concert are not only very complex but must *change with astounding rapidity* in accordance with the rapid changes which occur in air-conducted sound during a symphony concert. *It may seriously be doubted whether the inertia of the basilar membrane would not interfere with such rapid changes in the extremely complex sound patterns.*

16. The Volume Theory of hearing starts out from a fact well known to everyone and popularly expressed by saying that low notes, like those of the bass violin, are "massive" and *"voluminous,"* while high notes, like those of the piccolo, are "thin." Hence we speak of differences in the *"volume"* of tones. Of

course, this is a mere figure of speech and must not be understood
to imply that tone sensations are spatial in character. Nor should
"volume" be identified with "intensity" or "loudness."

This premised, *the volume hypothesis assumes that the "volume" of a tone differs with its pitch and the latter differs with
the frequency of the air wave:* the greater the frequency of the
air wave, the smaller the volume of the tone. Each tone, then,
has a "specific volume" and it is inversely proportional to the
frequency of the air wave. The theory assumes, further, that
sounds of great volume affect *a large area of hair cells* resting on
the basilar membrane, and sounds of lesser volume affect a cor-
respondingly *smaller area* of hair cells. The more hair cells are
affected by the air wave, the greater is the number of nerve-fibers
which receive impulses from these cells. *The analytic function of
the ear, then, is intimately connected with the "specific volume"
of each sound.*

It is unnecessary to enter into further details of this hypothesis,
for the assumptions mentioned are not in accordance with facts.
Thus the statement that the "volume" of a tone differs with its
pitch and the frequency of the air wave, *needs a qualification
which is disastrous to the theory.* We have pointed out (p. 89)
that within the middle region of musical tones (that is, within
the octaves beginning with *c'* and *c"* respectively), the delicacy
of pitch discrimination of a musician is rather remarkable under
laboratory conditions. Thus within the octaves mentioned a practiced musician can discriminate *without fail* a difference of pitch
arising from half a vibration per second. But the ascertainable
difference in "volume" in the same region is almost negligible.
At the two ends of the tone realm, that is, in the case of very low
and very high notes, the difference in "volume" is remarkable
and plain to everyone, but the pitch discrimination in these two
end regions is remarkably poor even in the case of the best musician. *Whatever grain of truth may be contained in the volume
hypothesis, the theory as it stands is untenable.*

17. The Telephone Theory of hearing assumes that the
basilar membrane of the internal ear and the hair cells resting on

this membrane act just as *the carbon button of a microphone* does. Air vibrations impinging upon the telephone diaphragm produce variations in the pressure of the carbon particles in the microphone. These variations, in turn, produce variations in the electrical current passing through the carbon button. The pressure which exists at any given moment in the carbon particles is the compound result of the pressure exerted at that moment on the telephone diaphragm by all the components of the sound wave. Accordingly, the change which occurs at that moment in the electrical current is likewise the compound effect of all the components of the sound wave impinging upon the telephone diaphragm. In short, *a carbon button does not analyze a sound wave into its components*. If, then, the end-organ of hearing acts like a carbon button, there occurs no physical analysis of sound in this end-organ. This analysis, we are told, takes place *in the central station of the brain, but we get no information as to how the analysis is effected in the central station.*

From this it will be seen that the telephone theory of hearing *merely restates the fact to be explained,* namely, that the organ of hearing is analytic in function. Accordingly, we know as much about the analytic function of the organ of hearing as we did before the theory was proposed, except for the statement that the analysis does not occur in the peripheral end-organ.

18. A Modified Resonance Theory of Hearing. Dr. A. Pohlman, of Saint Louis University, proposes what may be called a modified resonance theory of hearing. He insists that *there is no visible structure in the inner ear that can be correlated with pitch analysis.* There is no "piano" in the inner ear as postulated by Helmholtz. Neither is there any need of assuming "sound patterns" on the basilar membrane as they have been postulated by others, or, if such sound patterns exist, they have nothing to do with pitch analysis. Dr Pohlman assumes that *each hair cell resting (indirectly) on the basilar membrane is, in virtue of its ultramicroscopic constitution, a resonator delicately attuned to a definite vibration frequency.* Accordingly, the true end-organ of hearing is a series of resonators in which all the pitches that can be discriminated under the most favorable conditions are represented. The number of hair cells resting (indirectly) on the basilar membrane is so great that it amply suffices for all the facts of the most delicate pitch discrimination. When, therefore, the compound air wave impinging upon the eardrum has been converted into a similar compound wave in the liquid of the inner ear, every resonator attuned to a definite component of that wave is stimulated *directly* by that component and sets up a neural current in the nerve-fiber to which that resonator is attached. From this it will be seen that the neural current in the acoustic nerve is not a code message to be deciphered in the brain, as is postulated by the telephone theory, but the message is deciphered in the "action current" of the acoustic nerve. That is to say, *each component of the compound air wave striking the eardrum sends a separate message to the brain,* because each component has been picked up separately by some particular resonator.

There is nothing incongruous in the assumption that the tuning of each resonator is not manifested by any visible structure but is due to an ultramicroscopic arrangement of it. Thus the "temperature organs" in the skin, namely, the "cold spots" and the "heat spots," can be definitely ascertained experimentally. Evidently the two organs are differently attuned. But on excising them and putting them under the microscope, we find nothing that would suggest why one organ is attuned to "cold" and the other to "heat": *their tuning is a matter of ultramicroscopic structure.*

Similarly in the hypothesis of Hering we are supposed to have three kinds of cones in the retina, each specifically attuned to certain light waves. If we examine the cones under the microscope, we find absolutely nothing that would suggest any difference in their tuning. The theory of Hering, as far as the present writer is aware, has never been rejected just because the microscope reveals nothing to corroborate his assumptions. The reasons why Hering's theory is considered unsatisfactory are of a totally different nature. Hence, if Dr. Pohlman's hypothesis fits the facts of hearing, it should not be rejected just because the series of resonators postulated show no visible adaptations for pitch analysis.

It may be asked: What, then, is the purpose of all the complicated visible arrangements of the internal ear, if they have nothing to do with pitch analysis? Dr. Pohlman answers that *all these arrangements have to do with intensity control.* He points out the curious fact that the end-organ of hearing is *immersed in a liquid.* If a physicist meant to construct a device that is specifically attuned to air waves, he would surely not immerse this device in water. For by doing so, he would *reduce the efficiency* of the device considerably. And the human inner ear, considered apart from the structures of the middle and outer ear, must be said to be rather poorly adapted to air-conducted sound. It is only because the eardrum comes in direct contact with the air and because the vibrations of the eardrum are communicated by the ossicles of the middle ear to the membrane of the oval window and to the liquid of the inner ear, that the true end-organ of hearing can be stimulated *effectively* by air-conducted sound. As a matter of fact, the inner ear is far from being "soundproof," but it is proof against any other form of mechanical stimulation. In view of the extreme delicacy of the inner ear, this arrangement is very teleological. According to Dr. Pohlman, then, *all the visible arrangements of the inner ear are intended to make it "shockproof"* and have nothing to do with pitch analysis. What enables the inner ear to analyze sound waves is the series of resonators resting securely on the basilar membrane and embedded in the liquid of the inner ear. Thus protected, these resonators are stimulated *directly* each by some component of the vibration in the liquid, but *their tuning is a matter of ultramicroscopic constitution.*

The present writer is rather favorably inclined toward the hypothesis of Dr. Pohlman. It should be emphasized, however, that the *positive information* we get from this theory is only *the general statement that there occurs a physical sound analysis in the in-*

ternal ear. As to details, the theory of Dr. Pohlman leaves us in the dark just as the sound-pattern theory or the carbon-button theory does. *We are still looking for a detailed theory of hearing just as we are still looking for a satisfactory theory of color-vision.*

References for Further Reading

J. Froebes, S.J., *Lehrbuch der Experimentellen Psychologie* (1923), Vol. I, pp. 95–122.

H. v. Helmholtz, *Sensations of Tone,* translated by A. J. Ellis.

D. C. Miller, *The Science of Musical Sound.*

Chapter VI

THE MONOCULAR PERCEPTION OF SPACE

1. The Problem Before Us. From the very outset it must be borne in mind that in this and the following two chapters we are not concerned with the reality of the spatial attributes of bodies, but with *the manner in which we become aware of them.* This problem is a rather intricate one, and that for various reasons.

First of all, various senses contribute to our perception of space and their data are inextricably interwoven in our adult experience. We must artificially separate these various data, especially those furnished by the senses of *touch* and *sight,* for theirs is undoubtedly the lion's share. *For the present we are exclusively concerned with our visual perception of space.*

In the second place, we perceive the spatial attributes of bodies both *monocularly* and *binocularly,* but the manner in which we become aware of them is very different in the two cases. Hence, monocular and binocular perception of space must be treated separately.

In the third place, the very nature of the subject under discussion demands that we distinguish the problem concerning *the direction* of objects seen from that concerning *their distance.* The two problems here distinguished can also be expressed thus: How do we become aware of the extended surface of a body seen? and how do we perceive its third dimension?

We shall proceed in our discussion as follows: In the present chapter we shall consider first *the monocular perception of the direction of objects,* and then *the monocular perception of their distance and third dimension.* In the next two chapters we shall deal with *the binocular perception of space in all its aspects.* In concluding this difficult subject we shall add a short discussion concerning *the contribution of the sense of touch to our perception of space.*

I. The Monocular Perception of Direction

2. **The direction in which we see objects with one eye depends directly on the points of the retina stimulated. The line of visual direction is the straight line connecting the retinal point stimulated with the optical center of the eye and prolonged into outer space. Under normal conditions the line of visual direction coincides with that of the unbroken ray which causes the retinal impression.**

The accompanying diagram (Fig. 18) will assist the student to understand the empirical rule stated. Light coming from different points (*a, b, c*) of an object reaches different points (*a', b', c'*) of the retina. The straight lines connecting these corresponding points of the object and the retina *pass through the optical center (o) of the eye.* These lines represent those pencils (or rays) of light which pass *unbroken* through the refractive media of the eye. There are indeed other rays of light coming from the same points (*a, b, c*) in nature which in their passage through the refractive media of the eye are *broken.* But whenever we see a definite point of an object clearly, *the broken rays coming from that point reach identically the same retinal point as the unbroken ray.* This was explained more fully in the second chapter and diagramed in Figure 5 (p. 31).

These preliminaries being clearly understood, we may express the aforementioned empirical rule by saying that the direction in which we see *a, b,* and *c,* does not depend on the manner in which the eye is stimulated but *only on the retinal points stimulated.* It makes no difference whether the rays of light which stimulate the retinal points *a', b',* and *c'* are actually broken or not, or whether they are broken in this manner or that, as by a reading glass, mirror, or microscope: *In all instances the lines of visual direction are the straight lines connecting the retinal points stimulated with the optical center (o) of the eye and prolonged into outer space.* This is the first part of the empirical rule.

The second part is that under normal conditions every line of visual direction described in the first part of the rule, coincides with the path of that ray of light which comes from the point of the object seen and passes unbroken through the refractive media of the eye. In other words, if we prolong the straight line connecting the retinal point stimulated with the optical center of the eye, this prolonged line will meet the objective point which under normal conditions stimulates the eye. Hence, we can also

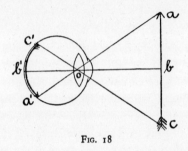

Fig. 18

say that *under normal conditions the lines of visual direction are represented by the unbroken rays which cause the retinal impressions.*

If it be asked, therefore, why we see objects in one direction rather than another, the answer is: *In normal monocular vision the reason for this lies both in the objects seen and in the retinal impression they make upon the eye.* Various objects occupy different positions in space, they really lie in different directions with reference to one eye: and the impression they make upon the retina corresponds point for point to these actual directions. It is this correspondence between the points of the retina stimulated and the actual directions which objects have with reference to one eye, which is the basis for the monocular perception of the direction of objects.

3. **The Nativistic Explanation of the Monocular Perception of Direction.** The impression which an object makes upon one eye takes the form of an inverted retinal image, as will

be seen from Figure 18. Hence we may also say that the inverted retinal image of an object is the basis for seeing its parts in different directions. But if such is the case, the question may be asked — and it has been proposed as a serious problem — *Why do we not see things upside down?* The answer is that this problem simply does not exist for an unsophisticated person and has nothing to do with his monocular perception of direction. For *from internal experience we know nothing of this inverted retinal image.* We acquire this knowledge from books or more directly in the anatomical dissecting room. Examining an excised eye of man we find that it is constructed after the manner of a photographic camera, and that the retina in particular is for the eye what the sensitive plate is for the photographic camera. Knowing the physics of light we can construct the formation of the image of an object on the retina. We thus find that the image must be inverted, and under appropriate conditions we can actually observe such an inverted image on the retina of an excised eye. All such knowledge, however, is not only far removed from our internal experience, but even after we have gained this knowledge in the manner stated, it helps us not at all in the cognition of the direction of objects seen in space.

Hence, when we say that the inverted retinal image of an object is the basis for seeing its parts in different directions, this statement must not be construed to mean that we first cognize this inverted image and from it construct, as it were, the topography of our retina, and on the basis of the knowledge thus gained project the impression made on point a' in the direction of point a in space, and the impression made on point b', in the direction of point b, and so forth. *There occurs no such eccentric projection of our retinal impressions* or of the corresponding impressions in the brain, as we have insisted in the chapter on sensation in general.

In a word, then, the inverted retinal image and the topography of the retina are *no criteria* for us by which we are guided when perceiving the direction of objects in space. *We need no such criteria.* We externalize an impression made upon a definite retinal point in the direction of a definite point in space, because this is the *innate* and *constitutional* property of this point of the retina. And when we call this property *"innate,"* we do not imply thereby what goes in philosophy by the name of *"innate ideas"* or *"Kantian forms"* or anything of the sort. What is meant by the whole phrase is simply this: *the direction of objects seen monocularly is an immediate datum of our visual experience.* It is in this sense that we accept what is known as the "nativistic contention."

4. The Local-Sign Theory. A number of psychologists deny the nativistic contention and maintain that our monocular perception of direction is in no sense immediate but gradually acquired by processes of association. In other words, the visual perception of direction does not depend *directly* on the retinal points stimulated but *indirectly* only. This theory is known as "empiricism" or more specifically as the "local-sign theory."

Suppose we are looking directly at object F (in Fig. 19). While we do so, a number of other objects (or other parts of the same object) form their respective images on peripheral portions of the retina. Such is, for instance, object X. If the latter attracts our attention, we instinctively move the eye in such a way that its image falls on the central portion (*f*) of the retina. It is only thus that we can get a clear view of it. In other words, *in order to see X clearly, we must rotate the eye through the arc FX (or fx).* If object Y had attracted our attention, we should have had to move the eye through the arc FY (or *fy*).

Though these fixation movements occur as a rule altogether involuntarily and automatically, we become aware of them, when they occur, just as, with closed eyes, we become aware of the movements of our arms, no matter whether they are voluntary or involuntary. Such sensations of movements of our body are known as "kinesthetic sensations."

It is these "kinesthetic sensations," arising from the movements of the eye, on which — it is claimed — our monocular perception of direction depends. They become *clues, criteria,* or *local signs* by which we judge the direction of objects seen. For just as we can judge the position of, say, the right arm from the extent of the movement necessary to reach this position, so from the extent of the eye movement, necessary to fixate a definite object, we are able to judge its direction. Plainly it requires less of an effort to rotate the eye through arc FY than through arc FX.

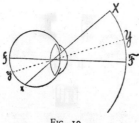

Fig. 19

Hence the difference in our judgment. It is thus that our perception of direction is originally acquired.

Once this association is firmly established, that is, in adult life, we judge the direction of objects seen even in the absence of the actual eye movements. *The mere stimulation of the retinal point x arouses the memory-image of the corresponding fixation movement.* That is to say, we imagine this movement and remember the effort needed to execute it, and *in virtue of this association we localize x in the direction of X.* "To see anything 'to the right' or 'to the left' of the line of vision (*fF* in our diagram) means nothing more than this, to be conscious of the magnitude of the achievement which would be necessary to bring the object into this line."[1]

5. The facts of visual acuity are irreconcilable with the local-sign theory. The accompanying figure (Fig. 20)

[1]Lotze, *Outline of Psychology* (translated by Ladd) p. 57.

contains some of Snellen's test letters used by an oculist before he prescribes a pair of spectacles. If the eyesight of the reader is normal, he should be able to recognize the upper two letters at a distance of 5 meters (about 16 feet). Those of the second and

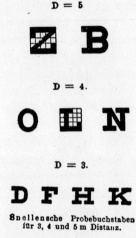

D = 5.

D = 4.

D = 3.

Snellensche   Probebuchstaben
für 3, 4 und 5 m Distanz.

Fig. 20. Snellen's Test Letters (from Nagel's *Handbuch*).

third rows should be legible at a distance of 4 and 3 meters respectively. The eyesight of many, even when they use properly adjusted glasses, falls below this standard, but that of others is considerably above this standard. We shall return to this presently.

Now note carefully what normal eyesight means in more exact terms. The letter B (of Fig. 20) seen from a distance of 16 feet, subtends a visual angle of 5 minutes and its every single line, a visual angle of 1 minute. To understand this, look again at the diagram (Fig. 19) with which we illustrated the local-sign theory. Magnify this diagram, that is, imagine one of your eyes to be the center of a circle whose radius is 16 feet. This circle is divided into 360 degrees (°), each degree into 60 further parts, known as minutes ('), each minute into 60 further parts, known as seconds ("). When the letter B (of Fig. 20) is placed at the circumference of this circle, it occupies an arc of 5 minutes and its single lines occupy each an arc of 1 minute. It has been estimated that the retinal area stimulated by each line of letter B is about 0.004 mm. wide.[2]

We said that the eyesight of some persons is keener. The most remarkable records are those of some illiterate persons. (The latter are tested by means of printed hooks, resembling the letter E and pointing in different directions.) Thus an Egyptian boy recognized the direction of the hooks correctly at a distance of 48 meters (about 156 feet). The single test objects, thus seen, occupied less than an arc of 8 seconds (7.5") or about one eighth of a minute arc.[3]

Let us see now whether the local-sign theory can account for these facts of visual acuity. If we recognize the standard test letters under the normal conditions mentioned, we localize their component parts each in its proper direction. If in doing so we are guided by the sensations arising from the fixation movements, we must rotate the eye through an arc of 1 minute, in order to fixate each recognizable part.

In other words, we must shift the retina an infinitesimal fraction of a millimeter (0.004 mm.). We must, moreover, become conscious of each fixation movement and of the effort needed to execute it. In the absence of these actual movements we must imagine them and remember the effort needed to execute them. And the Egyptian boy, whose visual acuity was eight times above the normal, had to execute fixation movements which are eight times more delicate, or else remember the effort needed to execute them.

The plain fact is that the kinesthetic sensations arising from eye movements are very dull so that even considerable movements of this kind may pass unnoticed. All investigators are agreed on this point. Therefore, the kinesthetic sensations arising

---

[2]Cf. Howell, *Physiology*, p. 337.
[3]Cf. Nagel's *Handbuch*, III, p. 350.

from the extremely delicate eye movements described in the foregoing cannot possibly play the part assigned to them in the local-
sign theory.

Everyone who has ever performed *experiments on negative
after-images* knows from his own experience how dull the sensations are that arise from eye movements. In these experiments
the instruction is, for instance, to fixate a red square on a neutral
gray background, and to maintain this fixation for 20 seconds.
It is very difficult to do this unless there is an ink dot on the red
square and we fixate this dot. Involuntary slips of fixation occur.
We become aware of them, not by the kinesthetic sensations
arising from the slips, but by inference from their visual results.
Every now and then the red square appears surrounded by a
bluish-green border. And when we readjust the eye we are again
guided by the visual results of the eye movements. *In these simple experiments we undoubtedly localize the different parts of
the red square in different directions. But in doing so we are not
guided by the sensations arising from the eye movements. On the
contrary, we infer the fact that we have moved the eye from the
visual results of these movements.*

It must be emphasized, moreover, that *eye movements, such
as are postulated in the local-sign theory, are not necessary* in
order to see each line of a test letter (of Fig. 20) distinctly at the
prescribed distance. For, each test letter at that distance is what
is known in the psychological laboratory as a fixation "point."
At reading distance an ink dot, a small cross, or any of the letters
printed on this page is a fixation "point." And when we observe
a church on the distant horizon, the whole church is a fixation
"point." And this leads us to a more fundamental consideration.

All this talk about "points" in space and retinal "points" stimulated, as understood in the local-sign theory, is based on a metaphysical abstraction which is far removed from the facts as they
occur. *A mathematical point in space cannot be seen nor is the
retina ever stimulated in a mathematical point.* It has been estimated that the diameter of a "retinal point" is about 0.0035 mm.[4]

---

[4]Cf. Howell, *op. cit.,* p. 338.

Accordingly, "points" in space and retinal "points" are always understood to be "areas," small areas, it is true, but true areas. When we fixate a "point" in space as steadily as we can, this "point" has recognizable parts which are situated in different directions and are actually localized in different directions. The conditions for this localization are given in the retinal "point," that is, the small area stimulated. This localization occurs independently of any fixation movements or the sensations arising from them. In the light of these facts the local-sign theory is untenable.

6. The movements of the eye in following the contours of an object are altogether too jerky and inaccurate to form the basis of our monocular perception of direction. Various methods have been devised for observing the movements of one eye when following the contours of an object. A very simple method is this: Look steadily for some time at a luminous point, say an incandescent filament, and thus obtain a very strong after-image of the luminous point. Such an after-image persists for quite a time and moves with the eye. While the after-image lasts, try to follow with the eye thus affected the contours of a circle drawn on a piece of white paper. By observing, then, the successive positions of the after-image, you can tell how jerky and inaccurate the movements of the eye are when it follows the contours of an object.

By means of a very elaborate arrangement, which need not detain us here, a similar movement of the eye "around" a circle has been actually photographed. Figure 21 is a reproduction of the result.[5]

If the monocular perception of the direction of objects depended really on such fixation movements and the sensations arising from them, we would construct for ourselves a rather crooked universe. Plainly the local-sign theory is out of joint with facts.

7. Artificial conditions can readily be created under which the retinal impressions of one eye are localized in

---

[5] Cf. *Philos. Studien.*, Vol. 20, p. 342.

accordance with the law of visual direction above stated, and this localization is altogether independent of all eye movements. Of the many experimental arrangements which could be cited we choose the following which is just as instructive as it is simple.

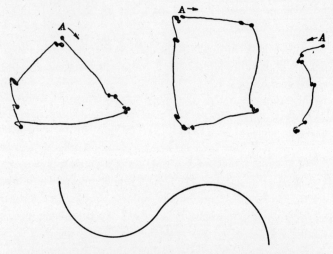

Fig. 21. Eye movements photographed by G. M. Stratton. The upper left-hand figure shows how the eye moves "around" a circle; the next figure, how it follows the contours of a rectangle; the right-hand figure, how it follows the curve indicated below. (From *Phil. Studien,* Vol. 20, p. 342.)

Look at this page through a reading glass, holding the latter in front of one eye. When you can see the print clearly, move the lens up and down. Note that the print moves apparently in the opposite direction. The following three diagrams (Figs. 22, 23, and 24) will help us to understand the reason for this phenomenon and that it is in accordance with the law stated.

When we see an object clearly through a convex lens, the former must be at or near the focus of the latter. Under these conditions the rays of light which are reflected from the object are rendered parallel by the lens. *If both the object and the eye are stationary,* the direction of these parallel rays will differ according as we move the lens up or down, that is, according as we look through the center of the lens (Fig. 22), or through its upper or lower edge (Figs. 23 and 24). In each figure, three pencils of such parallel rays are indicated by three lines, marked 1, 2, and 3. Not all of them will actually reach the eye, as the pupil is very small.

When we look through the center of the lens, the narrow pencil 2 will pass through the pupil and stimulate the central portion (F) of the retina. As a result we see the object (say, a definite letter of the print) in the direction of this unbroken ray, that is, in its true direction.

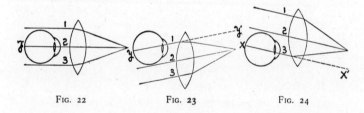

FIG. 22   FIG. 23   FIG. 24

When we look through the upper edge of the lens, the narrow pencil 1 will pass through the pupil and stimulate a lower, peripheral portion of the retina (y). Again we see the object in the direction of this unbroken ray, namely in the direction of y' In other words, when we move the lens downward, the object will apparently move upward.

When we look through the lower edge of the lens, the narrow pencil 3 will pass through the pupil and stimulate an upper, peripheral portion (x) of the retina. We see the object again in the direction of the unbroken ray which caused the sensation, that is, in the direction of x'. In other words, when we move the lens upward, the object will have an apparent movement downward.

In a similar manner the object will apparently move to the left, if we move the lens to the right, and vice versa. This is clear from the same diagram and in accord with the law stated. *The localization of the different impressions is independent of any fixation movements, because the eye must be kept steady Otherwise the phenomenon will not occur.*

8. A Modified Form of the Local-Sign Theory. For the reasons which we have advanced against the local-sign theory, many of its present-day defenders admit that the monocular perception of direction cannot have been acquired by the *individual.* They insist, however, that it was acquired gradually by the *race* and then transmitted through heredity. *Thus the task which a trained psychologist cannot perform is put on the shoulders of our "less developed ancestors," possibly of the monkey tribe.* We leave it to the good common sense of the reader to judge whether this is an improvement upon the theory. And as to the monkey, we had better keep him out of the psychological laboratory. He is really out of place there.

II. The Monocular Perception of Distance

9. In our adult experience we perceive also the distance of objects in space monocularly. But this perception, unlike that of mere direction, is not immediate. It is based upon a number of criteria which previous experience has furnished us and is thus the result of various processes of association and sometimes of an explicit reasoning process.

The impression which an object makes upon the retina of one eye differs indeed with its distance. There is, however, nothing in this retinal impression which could be the basis for the immediate perception of the distance of the object seen. But the differences in the visual experiences, thus aroused, may be, and are, as a matter of fact, *criteria* by which we judge the distance of the object seen. All this will become clear as we proceed.

10. The first and main criterion of the distance of an object seen is its apparent size.

The size of the retinal image is inversely proportional to the distance of the object which causes it. This will be seen from the accompanying diagram (Fig. 25). One and the same object (*ab*) at one distance (from the optical center *n* of the eye) causes a retinal image of the (linear) size $a'\,b'$; at twice that distance, an image of half that size, namely, $a''\,b''$.

But this difference in the size of the retinal image is of itself no sufficient basis for the immediate perception of distance, as will become clear from the next diagram (Fig. 26). Here objects of different size *(ab, cd, ef),* but situated at different distances, cause a retinal image of the same size *($a'\,b'$)*.

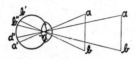

FIG. 25

Our visual experience, too, changes with the distance of the object seen. *Other conditions being equal,* an object appears bigger or smaller according as it is nearer to, or farther away from, the eye. Consequently we may also say that, *other conditions being equal, the apparent size of an object depends on the size of its retinal image.* When two men of equal height stand 10 feet away from us, both cause retinal images of the same size and

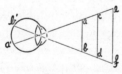

FIG. 26

both appear equally tall. When one of them moves to a distance of 20 feet away from us, we find he looks considerably shorter than his companion From this it will be seen that *the apparent size of objects, seen monocularly, may become for us a criterion of their distance.*

11. It is only in the light of many experiences that the apparent size of objects is a criterion of their distance, and then only of their relative distance.

We said above "other conditions being equal." For it would be far from correct to say that the apparent size of an object depends exclusively on the size of its retinal image. As a matter of fact, an object may have the same apparent size, though its retinal image varies considerably; and, vice versa, an object may vary considerably in apparent size, though its retinal image remains unchanged. No laboratory equipment is required to prove the first part of this proposition.

Simply hold your right hand at reading distance and look at it with one eye. Then move your hand away from you as far as you can. Figure 25 will convince you that the retinal image of the hand is considerably larger in the first case than in the second. In spite of that, your hand appears no larger at reading distance than at arm's length.

How large the retinal image of your hand is you can find out readily by looking out of the window at a row of houses and then holding your right hand again at reading distance. The latter now covers actually a great number of houses. This means that the retinal image of the houses coincides with that of your hand. In spite of that, your hand never looks as big as the houses.

From these simple experiences it is clear that the apparent size of an object is not an immediate datum of our sensory experience but it is a matter of judgment. And this judgment is based on a great many previous experiences. It is for this reason that familiar objects situated in our immediate neighborhood appear to us of "constant" size, no matter what the size of their retinal images may be.

A simple experiment will prove that also the second part of our above proposition is true, namely, that an object may vary considerably in apparent size, though its retinal image remains unchanged. Make an ink dot in the center of a red square and place it on a large sheet of white or gray paper. Hold the latter at reading distance and focus the ink dot long enough to secure a good negative after-image of the square. Project the after-image on some other part of the white sheet, marked previously by an ink dot or a small cross. You will find that the bluish-green after-image is of the same apparent size as the red square.

Now move the sheet of paper gradually away from you. Note that the after-image increases continually in apparent size. Bring the paper nearer and at last to less than reading distance. Note how the after-image shrinks. Now project the same after-image upon a distant wall or on the white clouds of the sky and note that its apparent size is considerable. This simple experiment again shows that the apparent size of an object is not an immediate datum of monocular vision but a matter of judgment, and this judgment is based on many previous experiences.

It is by no means easy to indicate those former experiences on which our judgment concerning the apparent size of a definite object is based and to analyze the process by which we arrive at such a judgment. The apparent size of the sun and the moon has been discussed from the time of Aristotle and many explanations have been offered for the changes in their apparent size No one has failed to notice how large the moon, for instance, looks when it is at the horizon and how it seems to shrink when it rises higher and higher. But no one has ever offered a satisfactory explanation of this phenomenon. Nor is this explanation any concern of ours in this chapter. The important thing for us to note is that *the apparent size of objects is far from being an immediate datum of our monocular vision.*

A subtle reader may ask how this statement concerning the apparent size of bodies tallies with what we said in the first part of this chapter concerning the immediate perception of direction. For the latter, after all, means that the extension of an object in two dimensions is an immediate datum of monocular vision.

The answer is that the extension of an object in two dimensions is one thing, and its apparent size quite another. Our visual experience of the former depends exclusively on the retinal area stimulated, our judgment concerning the latter depends on a definite standard of comparison. A simple illustration will make this clear. No matter at what distance from us a man may be, if we see him at all, we cannot but see him extended in two dimensions For he cannot possibly stimulate a mere mathematical point of the retina but only an area, and this area is the basis for our immediate perception of this extension in two dimensions. But does he appear large or small? That depends on our standard of comparison. Compared to a spaniel at his feet he is large; compared to a house in front of which he stands he is small. Similarly, as seen from a certain distance, he appears large or small, according as we compare him to himself, as seen from a greater or a shorter distance.

From all this it is also clear that the apparent size of an object cannot be a criterion of its distance, *unless we know beforehand what distance or extension in the third dimension is. We must know, moreover, how the object looks at a certain distance so that this appearance may serve as a standard of comparison.* In the case of an unfamiliar object, a familiar one placed side by side with it must serve as such a standard of comparison. Accordingly, it is only the relative distance of an object which we determine with more or less accuracy by its apparent size under definite given circumstances. *Many experiences, therefore, must have preceded before we can make use of this criterion.*

12. The second criterion of the distance of objects seen with one eye is their apparent lateral displacement which results from the change in our standpoint, that is, from the fact that either we ourselves or the objects seen move in space.

We have an exaggerated instance of this criterion when we are riding in a fast train. Looking out of the window we see the telegraph poles near the track move rapidly across our field of vision; one pole follows the other in quick succession. A conspicuous distant object, such as the steeple of a church on the horizon, remains practically stationary for quite a time, while trees and houses in the intervening space seem to move faster or slower according as they are nearer to, or farther away from us.

Something similar happens, only to a less degree, whenever we change our standpoint, that is, whenever we move about in space. If our movement is voluntary and the objects viewed are stationary, we are fully aware that the lateral displacement of the latter is merely apparent. It is due to the successive changes in our lines of visual direction. The degree of this apparent displacement, however, becomes for us a criterion by which we can estimate the relative distance of the objects thus seen.

When our standpoint is stationary and the objects seen are actually displaced in space, that is, when they are in motion, then the change in the lines of visual direction is more rapid in the case of nearer objects than in the case of objects farther away from us. The degree of this change becomes again a criterion of the relative distance of the objects seen.

It need not be stated explicitly that the facts here described cannot possibly be a basis for the immediate perception of distance.

13. Other criteria of the distance of objects in space are: the degree of distinctness with which we see familiar objects or their parts; the distribution of light and shade; the relative vividness of colors and other color effects, due to the distance of objects.

The various factors of the monocular perception of distance, here indicated, are made use of to great advantage by painters. All of them, except the changes in the natural colors of objects, can be readily ascertained by examining a good photograph of a landscape. In nature, however, they are not always unequivocal signs of the relative distance of objects. For they may also be due to the condition of the atmosphere. In a valley the latter has, as a rule, a dimming effect. On a clear day distant objects seen from a mountain or any elevated standpoint seem to be much nearer than on hazy days. Just such miscalculations show that our monocular perception of distance is far from being immediate.

14. Within very narrow limits also, the effort which we experience in actively accommodating the eye for near objects can become an additional criterion of their relative distance.

Several times we had occasion to state that the eye is constructed after the manner of a photographic camera. The phenomena of accommodation are best understood by means of this analogy. A camera must be focused. When its lens is set in such a way that it gives a clear picture of a definite near object, all objects still nearer are out of focus, that is, they produce a blurred image on the plate. To focus the latter properly, one of two things must be done. Either we must change the lens to one of greater refracting power, that is, we must use a more convex lens, or we must rack the lens farther away from the plate. In photography the latter method is the more common. It is interesting to add that certain animals do the same thing: they instinctively move the lens of the eye forward or backward according as they fixate an object at one distance or another.

The human eye has the marvelous capacity of changing its lens by changing the curvature of the latter. This, too, is done instinctively and automatically by the appropriate contraction or relaxation of the ciliary muscle in the eye. The whole contrivance is somewhat complicated and need not be explained here.[6] Suffice it to say that objects which are about 10 meters or farther away from us are properly focused — as well as they can be focused in proportion to their size — when the ciliary muscle is at rest. In psychological terms, this means that no effort is needed to focus such distant objects: we are *passively accommodated*.

For objects, however, which are situated within the distance of about 10 meters and 16 centimeters from the eye we must *actively accommodate* the eye. That is to say, we must change the curvature of its lens by a suitable contraction of the ciliary muscle. Though this is done instinctively, we may become aware of the effort needed in doing so. Hence, the degree of this effort may become a criterion for estimating the distance of the object clearly seen.

Though a marvel of teleology and of the utmost importance for clear vision, *active accommodation is practically a negligible fac-*

---

[6] Cf. W. H. Luedde, *The Mechanism of Accommodation*, Archives of Ophthalmology, Vol. VII (1932), pp. 40–70.

tor of our monocular perception of distance. For distances beyond that of a large room it does not come into play at all. Within the limits of a large room it is almost entirely neglected by most persons. In fact, it would require a rare appreciation of differences in muscular effort to base even a roughly accurate judgment of the distance of objects on this criterion.

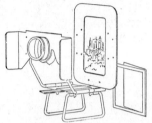

FIG. 27   The Verant (from one of the publications of Carl Zeiss Optical Works, Jena, Germany).

15. The remarkable plastic effect of the optical instrument known as "the verant," is entirely due to the fact that it enables us to view photographs with one eye from that standpoint from which alone objects in nature have that appearance which they have on the photograph, namely, from the standpoint of the camera which took the picture. Consequently the various criteria of distance in monocular vision can be made use of to an advantage which it is impossible to reach in viewing photographs without the verant.

Any picture, drawn in true linear perspective, gives us the impression of relief. This is due principally to the first criterion of distance. For *linear perspective is but another name for the effect of distance on the apparent size of objects.* In the case of photographs this impression of relief is enhanced in a most remarkable degree when they are viewed through an optical instrument known as the verant. It is shown in the accompanying illustration.

To understand the reason for the remarkable plastic effect of this instrument, it is important to note that it is only from a definite standpoint and only as seen with one eye that objects in nature have that apparent size which they have on the photograph. To a certain extent the same is true of the other effects of distance upon the appearance of objects. Hence, the familiar fact that paintings of an art gallery — in fact, all pictures of sufficient size — are better viewed monocularly and from a definite standpoint. The main reason why small pictures, even photographs, fall far short of the plastic effect which we get in monocular vision of the objects themselves is that it is impossible to get the necessary standpoint. The knowledge that we really handle a flat piece of paper is irresistibly forced upon us, even in monocular vision.

Of course, the linear perspective of a small photograph is mathematically exact. But it must necessarily be held at the distance of distinct vision, that is, about 8 to 10 inches away from the eye. At this distance, however, the apparent size of any particular object depicted is far from coinciding with that which it has when we view the object in nature. To effect this, the photograph would have to be magnified, and that to a definite size. It is just such a magnification of the photograph — or more correctly, the corresponding increase in the size of the retinal images of the objects photographed — that is effected by the verant lens. The latter is, moreover, so constructed that also the objects, depicted in the marginal portions of the photograph, cause no distorted retinal images. As a result, we forget almost entirely that we handle a flat piece of paper and can see each object in turn under the identical visual angle which it has when we travel with the eye from object to object in nature without changing our standpoint.

If both the photograph and the verant lens are correctly chosen, then the impression of relief is really surprising. Though strictly monocular relief, it rivals the effect of the well-known stereoscope which depends on a different factor altogether.

References for Further Reading

J. Froebes, S.J., *Lehrbuch der Experimentellen Psychologie*, Vol. I (1923), pp. 258-299, 317-326.

H. v. Helmholtz, *Phys. Optik* (2d ed.), pp. 669–841. Engl. Transl. ed. by J. P. C. Southall, Vol. III, pp. 154–232, 281–369.

Chapter VII

THE BINOCULAR PERCEPTION OF SPACE

1. The binocular perception of distance depends primarily on the slight disparity of the twin retinal images caused by objects situated at different distances and by parts of the same object extending in the third dimension.

Normally we see objects simultaneously from two slightly different points of view, namely, that of the right eye and that of the left eye. It is owing to this fundamental fact that objects situated at different distances and parts of the same object extending in the third dimension, cause twin retinal images which are partly alike and partly different from each other. Their difference is technically known by the name of disparity. The details of this disparity are somewhat complicated and may be waived for the present. But no elaborate arrangements are necessary to ascertain the main fact that the twin retinal images under the conditions mentioned are partly alike and partly different.

Simply look into the opening of a small box held at arm's length straight before the eyes. Close the left eye (or preferably have an assistant cover it with a piece of cardboard) and note that the box, as seen with the right eye alone, looks like R in the accompanying diagram (Fig. 28). When the right eye is closed (or covered) in turn, the view which we get with the left eye alone looks something like L in the same figure. In other words, when we look at the box with the right eye alone, its distant wall seems shifted to the right; and shifted to the left, when we look at the box with the left eye alone. The retinal images we do not experience. But from what we know of the eye as an optical instrument we infer that the two retinal images are reversals of the two views. They are diagramed at r and l, respectively.

When you have ascertained these facts experimentally you may begin to wonder how we ever succeed in combining two such views into one act of single vision. Well, the fact is that *under certain conditions we fail to combine them, namely, whenever the disparity of the two retinal images exceeds a certain limit.* But within these limits we combine the two views most readily, and when we do, the very disparity of the twin retinal images is the primary factor of our binocular perception of distance.

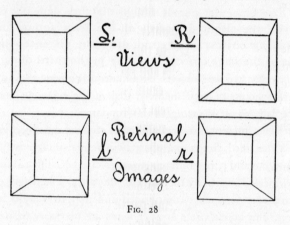

Views
Retinal Images

FIG. 28

We say *the primary factor,* for the binocular perception of distance depends on a great many factors All of them except the slight disparity of the twin retinal images, are undoubtedly derived from previous experiences of various kinds. They are the same in binocular as in monocular vision, namely, the various *criteria* discussed in the last chapter. *The slight disparity of the twin retinal images, on the other hand, is no criterion of distance,* for the simple reason that in our unsophisticated experience we know nothing of this disparity That of which we are totally ignorant cannot be a criterion for us. The question can only be whether the disparity of the retinal images is an independent factor of the binocular perception of distance or whether it derives its effectiveness precisely from the criteria of distance. The former is our contention.

This premised, it is a matter of terminology whether we shall call the disparity of the retinal images the primary factor or not. The remarkable perfection of our binocular perception of distance as we get it in our adult experience is undoubtedly due to the various criteria of distance. If this perfection, then, is the measure of the relative importance of the various factors, then these criteria are decidedly the primary factors. If, however, we call that factor the most important which of itself renders possible the purely visual perception of distance, even though it be very limited and imperfect, then the disparity of the retinal images must be called the primary factor and the criteria of distance are secondary factors. And this is the terminology which we adopt.

For, of the two considerations this is the more important, namely, how we come to see objects as extending in the third dimension or as situated at different distances at all. This problem looks puzzling enough. For the retinal images of objects are of only two dimensions. If this problem can be solved satisfactorily without recourse to criteria derived from previous experience, then the important conclusion is that the binocular perception of distance is, within definite narrow limits, as immediate as the monocular perception of direction. It is, however, only after a careful consideration of all the facts bearing on the disparity of the retinal images, that we can establish this important conclusion.

2. Whenever an object in our field of vision attracts our attention, we move both eyes in such a way that they have normally the same fixation point.

In the absence of a visible object to attract our attention, that is, in the dark, it is very difficult, if not impossible, to control the movements of our eyes. There is nothing to guide us in the execution of these movements except the kinesthetic sensations arising from the movements themselves, and these kinesthetic sensations are at best very dull. We shall return to this matter when discussing the local-sign theory as applied to the binocular perception of distance.

When, however, an object in our field of vision attracts our attention, we normally move our eyes in such a way that the image of the object attended to falls on the central area of each retina — the area of clearest vision. Whatever the details of these movements are — they may be, and frequently are, very jerky — the end-result is invariably the same: both eyes have the same fixation point.

The possible points of fixation are many as are also the possible eye movements. The coördination of these movements necessary to secure a common fixation point is, physiologically considered, a matter of great complexity. The empirical determination of the actual eye movements and the validity of the various laws which govern their coördination are no direct concern of ours: we leave all these matters to physiologists. What interests us as psychologists is, how we are guided in the execution of these complicated movements. Of the neuromuscular mechanism which renders their coördination possible we know nothing in our everyday experience. Even after we have become acquainted with this mechanism from what physiologists tell us about its arrangement and working, this knowledge does not help us in the least to bring these movements about. Of the movements themselves we are at best only dimly aware. As stated repeatedly, the kinesthetic sensations arising from these movements are very dull and frequently escape our attention altogether. These sensations, therefore, are at best a very poor guide. What, then, guides us in executing these movements with such precision?

The answer is: *We are guided by the visual sensations arising from the two retinal impressions made by the object attended to.* Thus, the psychological account of the coördinated eye movements is very simple: An object attracts our attention. As long as the two eyes are not set properly, the object will appear blurred. We endeavor to see it as distinctly as possible. These psychological conditions given, the two eyes move automatically until we see distinctly the object attended to, and when we do, both eyes have the same fixation point.

It should be added that in the case of most persons the two eyes are not equally good. Just as most people are congenitally,

or by force of habit, right-handed or left-handed — few persons
are ambidextrous — so most people are either right-eyed or left-
eyed. In fixating the object attended to, *the better eye generally
takes the lead* and the other eye follows until the object is seen
distinctly. Further details concerning this dominance of one eye
are of no interest in our present discussion.

**3. When the two eyes are set for a definite fixation point,
light coming from the fixation point stimulates the very
center of each fovea centralis; every point in our field of
vision nearer than the fixation point stimulates twin retinal points which are disparate; the same is true of every
point situated behind the fixation point, provided the fixation point itself is sufficiently near.**

We must now consider the disparity of the two retinal images
a little more in detail. For this purpose we must examine the relative positions of any twin retinal points which are stimulated by
light coming from the same point in space. (We need not remind
the reader explicitly that whenever we use in the following discussion the term "point," we always understand it in the sense
of a "real point" in accordance with what we said in the last
chapter.) Such twin retinal points* are either corresponding or
disparate. They are defined differently by different psychologists
in accordance with each one's particular theory of binocular
vision. *We shall define them independently of all theories* simply
in terms of a geometrical construction. This can be done with
precision. *For once the position of the two eyes is fixed by a
common fixation point, the system of twin points stimulated by
any particular point in space, is likewise fixed and is simply a
matter of geometrical construction.*

Fovea centralis is a little pit in the yellow spot or area of clearest vision in each retina, situated opposite the pupil of the eye. It
is the center of this little pit which is stimulated by light coming from the fixation point.

---

*A retinal "point," also known as a "physiological point." is an area of about
.0035 mm according to Howell. *op. cit.* 11 ed., p 346. This applies only to the
fovea. In the peripheral portions of the retina a physiological point is greater.

Corresponding points are any twin points of the two retinas which are situated at the same distance and in the same direction from the two foveal centers, so that if the two retinas were super-imposed, the twin points would cover each other.

Disparate points are any twin points, which do not thus corres-pond.

In Figures 29 and 30, f_1 and f_2 represent the foveal centers of the two retinas stimulated by the common fixation point F; n_1

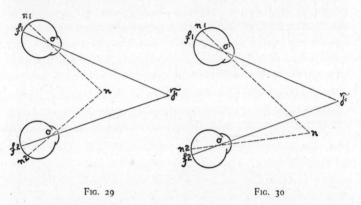

Fig. 29   Fig. 30

and n_2 indicate the twin retinal points stimulated by an object (n) situated nearer than the fixation point. These twin points are, in Figure 29, situated at equal distances from the foveal cen-ters but not in the same direction, n_1 being to the left, n_2 to the right of the respective foveal center. In Figure 30, n_1 and n_2 are situated at different distances from the respective foveal center though in the same direction with regard to it. In both cases the twin retinal points are disparate. The same is true in the case of every other point in space nearer than the fixation point.

In Figure 31, F represents a near fixation point and the eyes converge upon it. A point in space farther distant (d) than the fixation point stimulates twin retinal points (d_1 and d_2) which are plainly disparate.

If the common fixation point is far away, say near the horizon, then the eyes will not converge but assume a parallel position.

For the pencils of light coming from such a distant point, though ideally diverging, are practically parallel when they reach the two eyes. The same is true of every object which is still farther distant than the fixation point. Hence, such distant objects — no matter what their distance from one another and from the fixation point may be — cause retinal images which correspond in every detail.

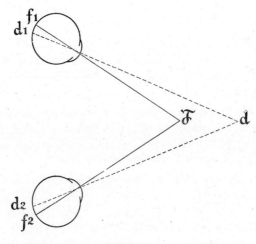

FIG. 31

4. An object attended to and directly looked at with both eyes cannot by any effort of ours be seen double. The same is true of all objects within the normal range of attention and distinct vision, that is, within the immediate neighborhood of the fixation point. All these objects stimulate corresponding points of the two retinas or points whose disparity is slight.

All objects which are outside the range of distinct vision are normally also outside the range of attention. If, however, such objects are attended to, many of them are seen double. All objects seen double stimulate twin retinal points whose disparity is considerable.

If it were not for the sense of touch by which we can feel our two eyes, or for the fact that sometimes one of our eyes becomes unserviceable because of an intruding cinder, or for other similar experiences which force the knowledge upon us that we have two eyes, from the mere fact that we see objects about us, we would never even suspect that we see with two eyes, just as we would never suspect that we hear with two ears and smell with two nostrils.

The famous problem why we do not see things double, though we see them with two eyes, simply does not exist for an unsophisticated person, any more than the other problem, equally famous, why we do not see things inverted, though their retinal images are inverted. For these very problems and all attempts that have been made to solve them in terms of previous experience, suppose knowledge which an unsophisticated person simply does not possess and which is of no use to him in binocular vision when he has acquired it. We shall return to this matter when discussing the local-sign theory.

Nor can we solve these problems any more than we can answer the question why we do not see with our ears or hear with our eyes. We may say, of course, that such is the nature of the ear that it hears, and of the eye that it sees. But this is really no explanation of these facts: it is only another way of stating them, an acknowledgment that they are ultimate and irreducible facts of our experience. In the same way *it is an ultimate and irreducible fact of experience that we normally see single with two eyes.*

While we cannot give an explanation of this fact, we can inquire into its conditions as well as into the conditions of double vision, if such a thing is possible. Now we find that an object attended to and directly looked at with both eyes cannot by any effort of ours be seen double. The same is true of all objects within the normal range of attention and distinct vision, that is, within the immediate neighborhood of the fixation point. The images of all these objects fall on the central area of each retina, the area of clearest vision. With the aid of geometrical constructions like those diagramed in Figures 32 and 33, we find further that all these objects stimulate corresponding points of the two retinas or points whose disparity is slight. *Single vision, therefore, is not restricted to vision with corresponding retinal points, but the disparity of retinal points must not exceed certain limits These limits are accurately defined by the range of distinct vision.* Objects attended to and seen with such slight disparity cannot by any effort of ours be seen double.

Objects so situated that their images fall on peripheral portions of the two retinas, constitute the dim portion of our field of vision, and it is difficult to explore it with eyes unmoved. It is within this dim portion of our field of vision that certain objects appear double, provided we pay attention to them. But normally we see them double, as if we saw them not: we neglect them. With the aid of geometrical constructions we find that all such objects stimulate retinal points whose disparity is considerable.

The accurate verification of the conditions of single and double vision here described requires rather elaborate experimental arrangements. But a fairly good idea of these conditions may be gathered from a very simple experiment. Simply hold a pencil at arm's length with the left hand and look at it directly with both eyes, but pay attention to the forefinger of your right hand held at reading distance. *This requires some effort, as we normally pay attention to the object fixated.* Under these conditions you will see the finger double. As seen with your left eye, the finger will appear to your right, and as seen with the right eye, it will appear to your left. In technical language this is expressed by saying that you see the finger double with *crossed disparity.*

Now fixate the near finger but pay attention to the distant pencil. Under these conditions the pencil will double. As seen with the right eye the pencil will appear to your right, and as seen with the left eye, the pencil will appear to your left. In technical language this is expressed by saying that you see the pencil double with *uncrossed disparity.*

Lastly, bring the pencil and the finger near together. It makes no difference whether these two objects are in the same plane or one of them slightly before or behind the other. Nor does it make any difference which of the two objects you fixate; you will not succeed in seeing either of them double. Both, however, will double if you stare vacantly at infinity, but then you artificially separate attention and fixation. The point to be verified is that all objects attended to and situated within the immediate neighborhood of the fixation point cannot by any effort of ours be seen double.

5. All objects or parts of objects which stimulate slightly disparate points of the twin areas of clearest vision, are not only seen single but are localized just where they are, namely, before or behind the fixation point, according as the slight disparity of twin points stimulated is crossed or uncrossed. This localization in the third dimension is in perfect accord with the law of visual direction which is valid for each eye singly.

That the empirical rule here stated is an accurate description of facts as they occur, may be shown very readily. For the conditions described occur frequently in our everyday experience, as is clear from what has been said in the last section; and we localize, as a matter of fact, in the manner stated, as is admitted by all. But in our everyday experience the conditions specified are inextricably interwoven with other conditions, namely, those described in the last chapter under the heading of criteria of distance. Hence, *from the facts of our everyday experience no inference can be drawn as to the part which the slight disparity of the retinal images plays in this localization.* For this purpose we must artificially isolate its various factors, if such a thing is possible, or at least devise means for ascertaining the influence of each. We shall do so in the subsequent sections of this chapter.

In the present section we mean only to emphasize that the empirical rule stated is in perfect accord with all the facts of both monocular and binocular vision so far ascertained. So perfect is this accord that it is possible (for a psychologist) to deduce the binocular vision of the third dimension from the facts so far ascertained. The accompanying diagrams (Figs. 32 and 33) will assist the student in following the argument. The dotted circle in both figures denotes the immediate neighborhood of the fixation point (F); n and d are objects situated within this neighborhood; n is nearer to the observer than the fixation point and it stimulates slightly disparate retinal points (n_1 and n_2). The disparity of the latter is crossed. Object d is farther distant than the fixation point and it stimulates likewise slightly disparate

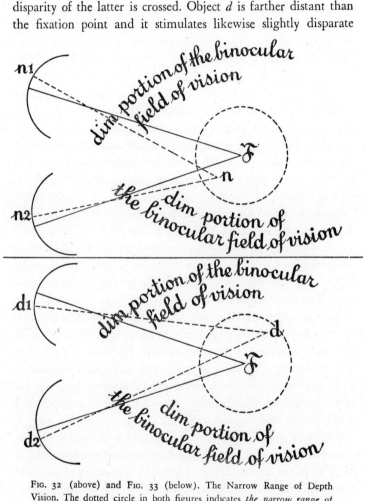

FIG. 32 (above) and FIG. 33 (below). The Narrow Range of Depth Vision. The dotted circle in both figures indicates *the narrow range of distinct vision and normal attention.* All objects within this range are *seen* where the twin lines of visual direction meet and just where the objects are, namely, at, before, or behind the common fixation point.

retinal points, namely, d_1 and d_2. The disparity of the latter is uncrossed.

These preliminaries being clearly understood, the argument may be formulated as follows: Two facts are definitely known concerning objects n and d situated within the immediate neighborhood of F. The first is that *both objects are seen single with two eyes*. The second is that *the direction in which each of the two objects is seen with each eye separately, is unalterably determined by the retinal points stimulated*. Thus, object n in Figure 32 is seen with the right eye in the direction n_2 n, and with the left eye in the direction n_1 n. These are the lines of visual direction as we ascertained them for each eye separately in Chapter VI (p. 117). The lines of visual direction for object d (in Fig. 33) are likewise determined by the retinal points stimulated. The right eye sees d in the direction d_2 d, and the left eye in the direction d_1 d.

From these two facts the localization of n and b in the third dimension can be determined. For n (in Fig. 32) can be seen single with two eyes only where the twin lines of visual direction meet, namely, before the fixation point and exactly where n really is. *No other point in space has the required direction with reference to both eyes.* Similarly, object d in Figure 33 can be seen single only where the twin lines of visual direction meet, namely, behind the fixation point and exactly where d is. *No other point in space has the required direction with reference to both eyes.*

Accordingly, when an object is seen with slight disparity, crossed or uncrossed, the localization of this object before or behind the fixation point is simply a *corollary* of the said two facts of monocular and binocular vision.

It follows further that, if the said two facts of monocular and binocular vision must be explained in the nativistic sense, as set forth on pages 120 and 143, then *the binocular vision of the third dimension must be likewise explained in the nativistic sense*. Figure 37 (which deals directly only with anatomical facts) *is a diagrammatic representation of our nativistic contention*.

If this theoretic interpretation of Figure 37 is correct, we should expect, further, that the *acuity of binocular depth-vision should be the same as the acuity of vision is for the single eye*. In other words, if the acuity of binocular depth-vision, as due to the slight disparity of the retinal images, be tested, the results should tally with the results obtained with Snellen's test letters. Now such is, as a matter of fact, the case, as we shall explain more fully later.

We shall not rest our nativistic contention on these arguments. Those who defend the local-sign theory, as applied to binocular depth-vision, deny or explain away our premises. We shall base our claim on experimental evidence in favor of the nativistic contention and against the local-sign theory.

One point, however, is abundantly clear from the aforementioned arguments and we mean to emphasize it, namely, that *the law of visual direction which holds for each eye singly holds also in the binocular perception of distance*. If we restrict our discussion to the facts of *normal* vision, *there are no discrepancies between the monocular and the binocular perception of direction or between space as it is and space as it appears in our binocular vision* All such discrepancies sometimes claimed to exist, concern oddities of binocular vision which are normally outside the range of our attention just like the double images aforementioned. These oddities are discussed under the headings of the *"Cyclopean Eye"* and the so-called law of *"identical visual directions"* and can be verified experimentally under abnormal conditions of attention. The facts thus ascertained are indeed very amusing but have nothing whatever to do with our normal perception of space. The reader who desires more information concerning these oddities and their bearing on normal depth-vision is referred to Chapter XII of the writer's *Introductory Course in Experimental Psychology.*

References for Further Reading

J. Froebes, S.J., *Lehrbuch der Experimentellen Psychologie,* Vol. I (1923), pp. 300–316.

H. v. Helmholtz, *Handbuch der Physiologischen Optik* (2d ed., 1859), pp. 841 sqq.; Engl. Transl. ed. by J P. C. Southall, Vol. III, pp. 281–488.

Chapter VIII

THE BINOCULAR PERCEPTION OF SPACE
(Concluded)

1. The Local-Sign Theory of the Empiricists. The empiricists contend that our binocular perception of distance is in its entirety gradually acquired. In other words, it does not depend *directly* on the slight disparity of the retinal images but *indirectly* only. Our eyes are normally in constant movement, thus changing their common fixation point continually. If it were not for these eye movements, we would not avoid double vision. For all objects, it is claimed, whose images fall on disparate points of the two retinas are seen double. Normally we ignore all objects thus seen double, precisely because of the continual eye movements. *When, however, an object thus seen attracts our attention, we instinctively converge our eyes upon it* and then we see it single. If this object is *nearer* to us than the former fixation point, we must *increase the convergence* of our eyes, and more so in proportion as that object is nearer to us. If the object which attracts our attention is *farther away* than the first fixation point, we must *relax* the eye muscles so as to *lessen the convergence* of the eyes.

Though these movements occur instinctively, we become aware of them, when they occur, that is, we experience kinesthetic sensations. We become also aware of the relative extent of these movements which are necessary to avoid double vision, that is, we discriminate between the various kinesthetic sensations. *Thus the movements of convergence (and accommodation) and the sensations which arise from them become criteria or "signs" for us by which we judge the distance of the object seen.* It is thus, according to the local-sign theory, that the perception of distance is originally acquired. In one word: *these eye movements are gradually worked out into a system of "local signs."*

Once this system of "local signs" is firmly established, that is, in adult life, we judge the distance of objects even in the absence of the actual movements of convergence. *The mere stimulation of definite twin retinal points arouses the memory-image of the corresponding movement and we remember the effort needed to execute it, and in virtue of this association we localize the object before or behind the fixation point.*

2. **The acuity of binocular depth-vision is altogether too delicate to be accounted for by the sensations arising from the eye movements. In the light of these facts the local-sign theory is untenable.**

The acuity of binocular depth-vision may be tested in various ways. One mode of procedure is as follows: Three needles are fastened vertically each on a small block of wood. They are then placed on a table in such a way that every needle is well within the range of clear vision. Precautions are taken that the observer cannot be guided in his judgments of distance by the movements of the blocks or by any of the criteria of distance discussed in the last chapter. When the observer now views the three needles with one eye, it is impossible for him to tell whether they are in the same plane or not; there is nothing to guide him in these judgments. He is then told to fixate the central needle with both eyes. If the other two needles are not in the fixation plane, slight disparity of the retinal images will be the result and it is possible to measure the accuracy of binocular depth-vision under these conditions.

Helmholtz experimenting in this manner obtained rather remarkable results. When the needles were at a distance of 34 cm. from the observer, it sufficed to move one of them half a millimeter before or behind the plane of the others to be thus appreciated without fail.[1] Other experimentalists using the same method obtained results which substantially agree with those of Helmholtz.

It is interesting to note that *the acuity of binocular depth-vision*

---

[1] Helmholtz, *Phys. Opt.* (2d. ed.), p. 790.

thus ascertained is about the same as the acuity of the monocular perception of direction. That is to say: with both eyes (under the conditions of retinal disparity) we can discriminate between objects situated in the third dimension just as accurately as we can discriminate with one eye between objects situated in different directions. With one eye we can discriminate two needles placed side by side in the same plane when the distance between the two needles subtends a visual angle of about 1 minute. We have explained the meaning of this statement in Chapter VI (see p. 122). On the retina this angle corresponds to an area of about 0.004 mm. in diameter, the area occupied by about two cones. When the retinal area is smaller than this, we can no longer tell the two needles apart. Helmholtz calculated from the data of his experiments that the disparity of the twin retinal points required to appreciate the distance of a needle before or behind the fixation plane corresponds likewise to a visual angle of about one minute. In simpler terms this means that, *if the two retinas were superimposed, the two points in question would not coincide but their distance from each other would be about 0.004 mm.* From this it will be seen that the acuity of binocular depth-vision is about the same as the acuity of the monocular perception of direction.

Now let us see whether we can account for these facts in terms of the local-sign theory In localizing a needle before or behind the fixation plane we are supposed to be guided by the sensations arising from the movements of convergence. If the needle fixated is moved forward or backward half a millimeter, we must increase the contraction of the eye muscles slightly in order to change from one fixation point to the next. In practical terms this means we must shift the position of the two retinas an infinitesimal fraction of a millimeter (0.004 mm.) and we must be able to tell the extent of the shift by the muscular effort needed to execute it. Accordingly, the local-sign theory supposes that the sensations arising from the movements of convergence are of extreme delicacy. The fact, however, is that these sensations are particularly dull so that frequently they escape our attention altogether even if they are relatively considerable and we try our best to discover them. All investigators who have made the sensations arising from these eye movements the subject of their special inquiry, are agreed on one point: These sensations are particularly dull.

We have already stated in the last chapter (p. 140) that the coördination of the movements of the two eyes in fixating an object attended to is, physiologically considered, a matter of great complexity. The contractions of the antagonistic muscles attached to each eye must be delicately balanced to secure a common fixation point, and, as stated before, we are guided in these fixation movements by the visual results of them. After we have secured a common fixation point, we cannot maintain this fixation for a long time. Everyone who has ever tried experiments on negative after-images knows this from his own experience. Involuntary slips of fixation occur frequently and we become aware of them, not by the kinesthetic sensations arising from these slips, but from their visual results, and in readjusting our eyes we are again guided by the visual results. This is true of all persons.

It should be noted further that *some persons have greater difficulty than others in maintaining a definite fixation.* This is due to the fact that the antagonistic muscles attached to each eyeball are not equally strong, a condition which is remedied by oculists by prescribing prismatic lenses. Persons of this kind can ascertain very readily how dull the kinesthetic sensations are which arise from eye movements. The present writer, whose eyes are in this condition, finds that if he looks with both eyes at a distant object and then tries to maintain this fixation while covering one eye, *considerable slips* of fixation occur in the covered eye without his even being aware of them. That is to say, the kinesthetic sensations arising from these slips give him no information whatever of the fact that the slips have occurred. He becomes aware of these slips *post factum,* namely, when he again uncovers the eye. For then the object formerly fixated now appears double: plain evidence that the kinesthetic sensations arising from these movements are particularly dull even when the movements are considerable.

3. Binocular depth-vision can be obtained with the two eyes completely at rest, that is, set for a definite fixation point, provided the disparity of the retinal images is slight. No further fixation movements such as are postulated by the local-sign theory are necessary for binocular depth-vision.

The local-sign theory supposes that all objects stimulating disparate points of the two retinas are always seen double, even when the disparity is slight. It is only by the successive fixation of such objects that we are supposed to avoid double images and acquire binocular depth-vision. That such successive fixation movements are unnecessary for binocular depth-vision, whenever the disparity of the retinal images is slight, can be shown in various ways. One of the experimental arrangements devised for this purpose is, in substance, as follows:

The observer is instructed to fixate with both eyes a silk thread seen against a uniform background. While he does so, a small bullet is dropped by the experimenter a little before or behind, and a little to the right or the left of the thread. This means that slightly disparate points of the two retinas are stimulated by the falling bullet for a small fraction of a second, altogether too small for a new fixation movement to occur. The observer simply has no time to do what according to the local-sign theory he is supposed to do, namely, to fixate the bullet while falling. Precautions are taken that the observer cannot guide himself in his judgments of distance by any of the criteria of distance. There remains, then, only the slight disparity of the retinal images to account for his binocular depth-vision, if he experiences it. And all observers experience it without fail whenever the conditions specified in the aforementioned empirical rule are verified; they can tell with accuracy whether the bullet is dropped before or behind, to the right or to the left of the fixation point. In other words, *all observers experience binocular depth-vision with the two eyes com-*

pletely at rest, that is, set for a definite fixation point. Hence, the local-sign theory does not agree with facts.

The real function of fixation movements in the light of facts is this: they secure for us a common fixation point. This secured, the slight disparity of the retinal images is *directly* responsible for binocular depth-vision but only *within the narrow range of clear vision and attention.* It is, however, impossible to maintain a definite fixation for any length of time. Accordingly, we secure soon a new fixation point, but here again we have within a narrow range binocular depth-vision due directly to the slight disparity of the retinal images. It is thus that *we piece together one snapshot of binocular depth-vision with the next in regular succession until we have viewed all that interests us in a large scene.*

4. Under artificial conditions all criteria of distance may be excluded, and slightly disparate images in the two retinas can be produced in the absence of all normal eye movements, even with the two eyes completely at rest in a position of actual divergence. Whenever these conditions are created — with or without the stereoscope — binocular depth-vision is the result and it is due directly and exclusively to the slight disparity of the retinal images.

The stereoscope is an optical instrument so devised as to facilitate the abnormal eye movements required for the artificial production of slightly disparate images of a tridimensional object in the two retinas and thus to facilitate the artificial binocular depth-vision of that object. This instrument may be used to great advantage in the decisive experiments against the local-sign theory but it can also be dispensed with. Hence, no detailed description of its various forms is called for here, especially as the commercial form of it, usually supplied by dealers, is well known.

Outside the psychological laboratory the stereoscope is merely used for the enhancement of the plastic effect which is obtained by viewing a *photograph* of a tridimensional object. For this purpose two photographs are taken of the same object or sets of objects, one from the standpoint of the right eye, the other from that of the left eye. These two slightly different views, known collectively as a *stereogram,* are usually mounted in such a way that the distance between the same object in the two photographs is about 80 mm. This distance is considerably greater than the average distance between the pupils of the two eyes, which is about 64 mm. Accordingly, if two such photographs are to be combined binocularly without the stereoscope — and this can be done readily with sufficient practice — *the observer must actually diverge his eyes.* Under normal conditions of everyday life, such eye movements never occur. If the distance between the two photographs is exactly that of the two eyes of the observer, he has to view these photographs *at reading distance* with *parallel* eyes. But in our normal experience our eyes are never in a parallel position when we view an object at reading distance. If the distance between the two photographs is less than that of the two eyes, the observer must *converge* his eyes, but to a *considerably less* extent than is required when he simply looks at the stereogram in the ordinary way. In all three positions of the eyes, moreover, *the observer must dissociate the accommodation movements* (p. 134) *from those of fixation: he must accommodate for reading distance but execute fixation movements as they are normally required for viewing an object at a great distance.* And this is true whether he uses the stereoscope or not. Accordingly, the eye movements necessary for the binocular combination of stereograms are under all circumstances very unusual. Their difficulty is only lessened by the stereoscope.

In the psychological laboratory and for the purposes of our present discussion, rather unusual stereograms are used, such as those shown in Figures 34, 35, and 36. In the stereogram of Figure 34 all criteria of distance are eliminated except that of linear perspective. When these two diagrams are combined binocularly with or without the stereoscope, a remarkable impression of relief is the result. How much of this result is due to the linear perspective, the reader can find out very readily by simply examining either of the two diagrams of Figure 34. In all probability he will see nothing but a flat pattern of lines and still the tridimensional object represented is a rather familiar one and its perspective is mathematically exact. If, therefore, the reader succeeds in the binocular combination of these two diagrams, *the impression of relief is not due to this linear perspective.*

In the stereograms of Figures 35 and 36 *there is absolutely nothing even to suggest linear perspective or any other criterion of distance. By focusing the bold-type letter of the combined print we exclude all eye movements.* Only the slight disparity of the twin retinal images is left to account for the impression of relief.

Fig. 34. Stereogram (from Martius-Matzdorff, *Die interess. Erscheinungen der Stereoskopie;* Winckelmann u. Söhne, Berlin).

In order to exclude *the very possibility of eye movements* we proceed as follows: We make a pinhole in the very center of the central letter E on each side of stereogram 35 or 36. Then we place either stereogram in the rear wall of a dark box in such a way that light enters the box only through these holes and we combine these holes binocularly. Thus the position of the two eyes is fixed before we see the letters of the stereogram and it makes no difference whether the eyes are convergent, parallel, or even divergent. Then the stereogram is illuminated by an electric spark. The duration of this illumination is so infinitesimal that *no change of fixation can possibly occur while the illumination lasts.* Under these conditions absolutely all criteria of distance are excluded; slightly disparate images in the two retinas are produced in the absence of all normal eye movements; the eyes are completely at rest in the position of either convergence, parallelism, or even divergence. And the result is the vivid impression of relief and this impression of relief is due directly and exclusively to the slight disparity of the two retinal images. *In the light of this crucial experiment the local-sign theory is untenable.*

It has been said that in these experimental tests we exclude indeed the actual eye movements but we do not exclude "the motor dispositions" of the eyes; and these, in the local-sign theory, may

WHERE?	WHERE?
WHERE?	WHERE?
WHERE?	WHERE?
WHERE?	WHERE?
WHERE?	WHERE?

Fig. 35. A very unusual stereogram.

WHERE?	WHERE?
WHERE?	WHERE?
WHERE?	WHERE?
WHERE?	WHERE?
WHERE?	WHERE?

Fig. 36. A very unusual stereogram.

take the place of the actual movements themselves. Hence, we really do not exclude all criteria of distance; to which the answer is that these "motor dispositions," if they exist, surely cannot be a better criterion of distance than the sensations arising from the actual eye movements themselves. But these sensations, as we have seen (p. 153), are altogether too dull to account for the acuity of binocular depth-vision of which we are capable and of which these very tests are a remarkable illustration. Hence, the local-sign theory cannot be sustained by an appeal to "motor dispositions" of the eyes or to "memory-images of these movements" or anything of that sort, even if we grant the existence of these problematical things.

5. The effect of practice, expectation, and "good will" on stereoscopic vision are no proof against the nativistic explanation of binocular depth-vision.

Some persons, in spite of repeated trials, do not succeed in seeing the stereograms of Figures 35 and 36 plastically even when
they use the stereoscope. To such persons the only advice that
can be given is: Try again and do so persistently! for in this, as
in all other useful accomplishments, the old adage holds: "Practice
makes perfect."

While this may be a bit of practical advice, what about the
value of our experiments with the stereoscope as tests of the nativistic contention? If plastic vision may be acquired by practice,
how can it be said that it is due to the congenital coördination of
the twin retinal points stimulated? *What is congenital is not acquired by practice, and conversely, what is acquired by practice
is thereby proved not to be congenital.*

Moreover, it would really seem as if *our "good will" helped us
considerably to see what we did not see before.* When we viewed
less difficult stereograms by means of the stereoscope, we saw
them plastically, and other observers say that they see also the
stereogram of Figures 35 and 36 plastically. They describe to us
the different distances at which the single lines and letters appear.
*Accordingly, we expect to see the lines and letters at the same
distances, and our imagination does the rest.*

Now there is a good deal of truth in all this but it is far from
invalidating our argument. *Practice is necessary for a beginner to
secure the artificial conditions of our experiments.* He must learn
to coördinate the movements of fixation with those of accommodation in a rather unusual manner. Hence the fact that at first
when the binocular combination takes place, the object viewed
looks anything but distinct. The eyes are not yet sufficiently
accommodated for reading distance. Of course, a stereogram will
be seen plastically only when the unusual coördination of fixation movements and accommodation movements is effected. *This
coördination of eye movements must be learned and it can be
learned only by practice.*

But if the effect is immediate, why should our plastic vision
improve with practice so that we now see the zigzag arrangement of the single letters which we failed to see before? *The an-*

*swer is that in the performance of this experiment we experience
what occurs to us a thousand times over in daily life.* Details of
a new object which are at first overlooked — not explicitly attended to — are appreciated gradually. If the object is a rather unusual
one, we frequently need someone else to call our attention to
such details, and then we wonder how we could have missed
them. *Here, as in the case of neglected double vision, we have to
do with the curious fact of attention,* which dominates our whole
conscious life.

Our imagination and expectation, too, help us to see what
otherwise would pass unnoticed. *This again is but another phase
of the curious fact of attention. Our memory-images, expectations,
and previous knowledge of all kinds are universally of paramount
importance in determining the direction of our attention.* An expert geologist and an ordinary traveler see the same embankment
which they happen to pass. The latter has seen nothing of what
the geologist has seen, and vice versa. Each, however, has seen
what is most in conformity with his previous knowledge, interests, and expectations. We shall revert to this topic in a later
chapter.

*Moreover, there is such a thing as ignoring one eye, though
both eyes are kept open.* Many squinters habitually ignore one
eye. For they cannot execute the proper eye movements to avoid
double vision. Those who work a good deal with the microscope
in the orthodox way — that is, who observe with one eye, while
the other is left open — acquire a similar habit. And we all occasionally do the same thing, namely, whenever one eye is rather
in the way of seeing clearly what we are interested in, or when
one eye is notably weaker than the other. Now *the same thing
may happen to a beginner, when he uses the stereoscope,* particularly if he is called upon to view such unusual stereograms as
those of Figures 35 and 36. The difficulties which he experiences
in the use of the stereoscope may result in his simply ignoring
one eye. If he does, of course, the stereograms will look flat. *Here
again we have to do with one of the curiosities of attention.*

No one will deny that color qualities are immediate data of our visual experience and yet practice has a great deal to do with our sensitiveness to colors. Without considerable experience and practice no one is able to make the fine discriminations between various color tones, tints, and shades, which are made by an expert worker in mosaic. *Practice sharpens not so much our senses as our attention.*

These answers suffice to assign the proper rôle to practice, good will, and imagination in the performance of our test-experiments. The difficulty based on these factors leaves our argument for the nativistic contention untouched.

6. The Limitations of Our Immediate Perception of Distance. Our normal perception of distance, insofar as it is due directly to the slight disparity of the retinal images, is immediate, but it is limited. Its limitations arise from the narrow range of clear vision and attention and from the fact that only a limited number of objects in nature can at any given time cause twin retinal images whose disparity is neither too great nor too small for binocular depth-vision. Only the immediate neighborhood of the fixation point can satisfy these conditions and this fixation point itself cannot be far away from us. Accordingly, there is ample room for the further development of our binocular perception of distance and this is accomplished gradually on the basis of the various criteria of distance discussed in Chapter VI. In this sense the most ardent defender of the nativistic contention must be an empiricist. *All we insist on is that we start with a capital, however small this may be. And this capital is furnished by the binocular depth-vision as due to the slight disparity of the retinal images.*

7. The Organ of Depth-Vision and the Real Meaning of "Nativism." It is unfortunate that our doctrine is designated by the term "nativism," because this term suggests something analogous to Kant's innate forms of cognition. As a matter of fact, our doctrine is diametrically opposed to that of Kant. We insist that we have in literal strictness *an immediate experience of the third dimension when we use both eyes,* just as we have an immediate experience of two dimensions of an object when we see it with one eye. Within the narrow limits just specified, our experience of the third dimension is a matter of *sensation* and not of perception.

The organ of depth-vision consists of the two foveas and their central connections. We may indeed use either of the two foveas separately, namely, by closing one eye; we may also artificially dissociate the two foveas by pushing one eyeball and thus interfering with the movements by which we secure a common fixation point; we may also be unable to execute the movements necessary for securing a common fixation point, because the muscles attached to the two eyeballs are not properly balanced, that is, we may be squinters. But in the absence of these artificial or pathological conditions and under normal conditions of attention, *the two foveas are not two organs of vision but two parts of one organ of single vision: and this is the organ of depth-vision.*

The central connections of the two foveas are diagramed in Figure 37. Only objects within the immediate neighborhood of the fixation point (or within the dotted circle of Figures 32 and 33) stimulate *twin foveal points,* and the latter are in every instance either corresponding or slightly disparate. *It is the congenital coördination of all such twin foveal points which is the physiological basis for the fact that we see all objects within the immediate neighborhood of the fixation point single with two eyes and that we localize them in the third dimension just where they are, namely, at, before, or behind the fixation point.*

It should be noted carefully that Figure 37 deals directly only with anatomical facts and that these facts have been ascertained independently of any theory of depth-vision. But as these anatomical facts are in perfect agreement with the data obtained in the psychological laboratory and with our theoretic interpretation of the latter, we may also say that *Figure 37 is a diagrammatic representation of our nativistic interpretation of normal depth-vision.* From this it will be seen that the only justification for designating our doctrine "nativism" is the physiological basis of our doctrine, namely, the congenital coördination of the two foveas to act as one organ of single vision.

All objects situated within the dim portion of our binocular field of vision stimulate *twin extra-foveal points,* and most of such

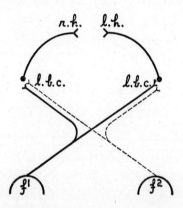

FIG. 37. Diagram to illustrate *the congenital coördination of the two foveas to act as one organ of single vision.* Let *f1* and *f2* be twin foveal points actually used in normal single vision. These two points are *doubly* connected with the brain through fibers of the optic tract; namely, (1) with the same center in the left hemisphere (*l.h.*) and (2) with the same center in the right hemisphere (*r.h.*). All twin foveal points which are normally used for single vision have a similar *double* connection with the brain. The result of this is that, *even if one hemisphere were eliminated,* the two foveas would remain coördinated to act as one organ of single vision. The lower brain centers which serve as relay stations are indicated by *l. b. c.* For further details the reader is referred to F. Schiek u. A. Bruekner, *K. Handbuch d Ophthalmologie,* Vol. I, pp. 398 sqq. and to A. T. Rasmussen, *The Principal Nervous Pathways,* Figs. 11 and 12, pp. 28–30.

points are disparate and their disparity is considerable. Under these conditions we see objects double. There are, however, also some objects within the dim portion of our binocular field of vision which stimulate corresponding points and may be seen single, provided we pay attention to them. *The physiological basis for such abnormal single vision with two eyes is diagramed in Figure 38.*

It is a matter of historic interest that the sum total of objective points in the entire field of vision which *may* be seen single with two eyes is known by the name of *horopter*. The discussion

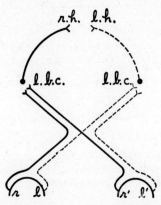

FIG. 38. Central Connections of Twin Extra-Foveal Points. Twin extra-foveal points (*l* and *l'*, *r* and *r'*) which *may* be used for single vision, namely, under unusual conditions of attention, are *not doubly* connected with the brain. Thus *l* and *l'* are connected only with the same center in the left hemisphere (*l.h.*); *r* and *r'* only with the same center in the right hemisphere (*r.h.*). If the left hemisphere is out of commission, the result is *partial blindness* (*hemianopsia*), namely, for that peripheral portion of the field of vision which corresponds to *l* and *l'*: if the right hemisphere is out of commission, the result is blindness for that peripheral portion of the field of vision which corresponds to *r* and *r'*. Persons thus afflicted have no "*watchdog.*"

of the horopter has never led to any results that are of service in the explanation of normal binocular vision. For normally we neglect all objects situated within the dim portion of our binocular field of vision, no matter whether they are seen single or double. If any of these objects attracts our attention, we turn our eyes in such a way as to make it the common fixation point. *Accordingly, the extra-foveal points of the two retinas serve the function of a "watchdog."* Under abnormal conditions of attention, however, a great many oddities can be observed in the dim portion of our binocular field of vision and they are discussed under the headings of the *"Cyclopean Eye"* and the so-called law of *"identical visual directions"* and sometimes even under the heading of *"discrepancies between space as it is and space as it appears in binocular vision."* All these phenomena are indeed very amusing but *have nothing whatever to do with our normal binocular vision.*

We said that the term "nativism" by which our doctrine is commonly designated is, strictly speaking, a misnomer. So is the term "empiricism," the name by which the local-sign theory generally goes. For this theory teaches precisely the opposite of what its name suggests. The defenders of this doctrine precisely deny that we have an immediate sensory experience of the third dimension, in fact, of any dimension. They create our whole perception of space out of nothing. The oddity of the term "empiricism" is further emphasized by the fact that some defenders of this doctrine postulate "innate associations" for localizing objects in space very much à la Kant. It is only by this supplementary hypothesis that they can extricate themselves from the difficulties which naturally arise when we try to create our whole perception of space without a capital in our sensory experience to start with.

Unfortunate though the terms "nativism" and "empiricism" are, they are in actual use, and we insist that we are in a limited sense "nativists" and for the rest decidedly "empiricists."

8. The Acquisition and the Development of Space Perception in One-Eyed Persons and Squinters. One of the famous difficulties against our nativistic contention is that one-eyed persons and squinters acquire and develop to great perfection their perception of distance. They surely are not in the possession of the capital which according to us is the starting point. The answer is that we have also another capital which may furnish the starting point for our space perception in all its aspects. This other capital — perhaps a little more limited than the first — is derived from our tactual experience of space. One-eyed persons and squinters have this starting point and it is thus that they acquire their perception of distance. The congenitally blind must build their entire space perception on this foundation. Hence, a few words are here in place concerning this second capital.

The surface of our whole body is furnished with end-organs of touch which are stimulated by bodies coming in contact with these end-organs. The stimulation thus set up in each end-organ is propagated separately by corresponding nerve-fibers to the central nervous system and at last to the brain. Hence, *the very juxtaposition of the end-organs of touch furnishes a physiological basis for the immediate tactual experience of the surface of an object which comes in contact with our body.* We have no explanation whatever to offer for this tactual experience of an extended surface: it is a primitive fact of our experience not analyzable into further facts which would make it intelligible. Here again we take the stand of "nativism."

In connection with these sensations of touch or as a result of other causes a baby performs a number of reflex, instinctive, and random movements with his limbs. In fact, from the moment of birth, when not actually asleep, he moves his arms, legs, head, and whole body almost continually. These movements, in turn, stimulate a number of end-organs especially in the muscles, tendons, and joints of the members moved and, as a result, *the baby acquires a sensory awareness of the successive positions of the member moved:* in short, he becomes aware of the movements themselves. However dim the sensory awareness of these movements may be at first — we can speak of these matters only in terms of inference — gradually he discriminates them from one another more and more perfectly by the kinesthetic sensations they arouse.

These kinesthetic sensations, in turn, become the cue for the voluntary performance of these movements, as we have explained already in the chapter on sensations in general (p. 17). *The visual impressions made by the movements are an additional cue.* Hence the accuracy in the performance of these voluntary movements is increased considerably when we see these movements. It is thus that we gradually acquire voluntary control over our body.

In proportion as we improve in the voluntary control over our body we are enabled to touch bodies actively and to explore all their surfaces with the fingers, which may be called the touch organs *par excellence. It is by thus manipulating bodies that we acquire a sensory awareness of their tridimensional properties.* Of course, only bodies in our immediate neighborhood can be thus explored. Hence, the sense of touch has been called a "near sense" while the eye can reach objects at a great distance.

The congenitally blind have no other capital to start with than the spatial data of the sense of touch. But this capital suffices as a foundation for the gradual acquisition not only of great skill which supposes fine spatial discriminations but also of considerable knowledge of mathematics. Since the congenitally blind have never associated the data of the sense of touch with those of sight, *it is natural to expect that they should at first be positively hampered by visual impressions when they are cured of their blindness.* Hence, from the results of these cures no valid argument can be drawn against our nativistic explanation of visual space perception.

One-eyed persons and squinters, on the other hand, associate their tactual data from the beginning with the visual impressions simultaneously received. When in childhood they manipulate objects, they also see these objects: when they build with blocks or clay, crawl or walk from spot to spot, they see the results of their movements. Hence it is that *one-eyed persons and squinters have a considerable advantage over the congenitally blind.* No wonder that their perception of space is gradually built up to that degree of perfection which they actually possess in adult life. From this it will be seen that *our nativistic account of the binocular perception of space is not weakened in the very least by the experiences of one-eyed persons and squinters.*

References for Further Reading

J. Froebes, S.J., *Lehrbuch der Experimentellen Psychologie*, Vol. I (1923), pp. 337–343; 362–375.

H. Gruender, S.J., *Introductory Course in Experimental Psychology*, Chap. XII.

C. S. Myers, *Text-Book of Experimental Psychology*, Chap. XX.

Chapter IX

IMAGINATION

1. **The Popular and the Technical Use of the Term "Imagination."** In our everyday language the term "imagination" is employed rather loosely. Even in scientific and philosophic discussions we are wont to follow this common usage, whenever there is no danger of misconstruing the term into something which we never meant to express. Thus, for instance, we say that we cannot "imagine" what causal connection there may be between two ascertained facts of experience, and we declare our "imagination" bankrupt to conceive the infinity of God. We ought to say instead that we cannot "conceive" or "reason out" the causal connection of the two facts, and we ought to declare our imagination bankrupt to deal with anything whatever that has not at some time or other been an immediate datum of our sensory experience. What we really mean is that we cannot form an intellectual representation of this or any other attribute of God in proper terms but only by means of analogous concepts derived from creatures.

Technically employed, an act of imagination or "an image" is nothing else than *the revival and the association of former sensory experiences of an object which is not now actually present to our senses*. It has also been defined briefly as *"centrally aroused sensations,"* that is, internal sensations, not initiated by the excitation of a peripheral sense-organ, but by some internal excitation of a brain center and thence propagated to other centers, as happens, for instance, in many dreams.

2. **Image and Sense-Perception.** From the logician's point of view the difference between a sense-perception and an image is this, that an object perceived is present, whereas an object imagined is absent. The two processes, however, are very much akin

168

if we compare them merely psychologically, that is, merely as
facts of internal experience. The main psychological difference
between them is that an image is, as a rule, much less vivid than
a sense-perception. But this difference is far from being universal
and thoroughgoing, as we shall see presently. Hence the possibility of mistaking one for the other.

In cases of doubt we rely on criteria which logical considerations furnish us. The principal criterion is that pointed out by
Aristotle, namely, that it is not in our power to have a sense-perception when we will. To perceive an apple, an apple must be
present. In its absence no effort of my will suffices to bring about
the perception of an apple or an experience which under normal
conditions could be mistaken for such a perception. The image
of an apple, however, depends, at least to a great extent, on our
will. I can make up my mind to imagine an apple.

Under ordinary conditions the application of this criterion is
easy enough. There are, however, cases in which its application is
very puzzling.

When images are usually vivid, and the voluntary control of
our mental life is in abeyance, they are easily mistaken for sense-
perceptions. This occurs regularly to all of us in ordinary dreams
and not unfrequently in the transitional states between waking
and dreaming. This fact is familiar to everyone. The hallucina-
tions of patients in fever delirium and of drug victims under the
influence of opium, hashish, or belladonna, are the most striking
illustrations of this kind.

A similar difficulty arises when the actual sensory stimulus, ini-
tiating a sense-perception, is so faint as to be near the threshold
of sensation. It has probably occurred to many readers that, on
awakening at night, they began to count the strokes of a distant
tower clock, and continued to do so, really not knowing any
longer whether they actually heard the clock or only imagined it.
Similar experiences could easily be multiplied.

A remarkable series of experiments was carried out in the Cor-
nell laboratory in demonstration of the same difficulty. The experimental arrangement used is altogether too elaborate to be

described in detail here.[1] Suffice it to say that many of the observers employed had considerable practice in laboratory work. Each observer was seated in a large, well-lighted laboratory and opposite the ground-glass window of a darkroom which was situated in the middle of the laboratory. He was instructed to fixate a definite white spot on the ground-glass window and to make a deliberate effort to imagine a familiar object indicated by the stimulus word, say *a tomato,* and to keep fixating said white spot while producing the image.

Simultaneously with the presentation of the stimulus word the experimenter signaled to two other experimenters, hidden in the darkroom. The latter then exposed and very gradually illuminated a transparency which exhibited the color and form of the object signified by the stimulus word. In other words, the two hidden operators presented to the observer an actual faint stimulus, such as would have been made by the object itself, say a tomato. The electrical signaling apparatus was so carefully concealed and handled so skillfully that the observers did not suspect anything of this elaborate arrangement. In a similar manner each observer was asked to imagine a book, a banana, a lemon, a leaf, and an orange, and corresponding transparencies were simultaneously exhibited and gradually illuminated.

Because of an error in the technique some observers became aware of the experimental arrangement, and they were promptly eliminated. In all the other observers the result was uniformly the same: *they all mistook the actual sense-perception for an image,* and this in spite of the fact that the actual stimulus was appreciably above the threshold-value.

It is worthy of note that in some observers imagery and sense-perceptions were peculiarly intermingled. Thus one, who had had long experience in the laboratory, reported that he imagined the tomato, as painted on a can; the book as a particular one, whose title he could read; the lemon was lying on a table; the

---

[1] Cf. *American Journal of Psychology* (1910), pp. 428 sqq.

leaf was a pressed one with red markings on it. Some saw an elm leaf, when they had been trying for a maple leaf.[2]

When at the end of the experiments each observer was asked whether he was "quite sure that he had imagined all these things," the question almost always aroused surprise and at times indignation. On the other hand, after the experimental arrangement was explained to a number of the observers — they were graduate students — "they invariably recognized the appearance of the stimulus at or before the point, at which they had previously reported an image."[3] They, as well as some competent visitors, could hardly believe that stimuli so "ridiculously real" had been mistaken for images.[4]

These experiments confirm what we stated above, namely, that *psychologically there is no thoroughgoing difference between an image and a sense-perception,* and that the latter can be easily mistaken for the former, when the actual stimulus is near the threshold-value of sensation.

3. Reproductive and Creative Imagination. When imagining an object, we at times merely reproduce the sensations which that object has produced in us in the past on the same or on different occasions. Then we have what is known as an image of sensory memory or simply a memory-image. (It is well to add that a memory-image is by no means identical with that complex experience which we shall discuss in a later chapter under the heading of memory.) The image of sensory memory, then, is a faithful copy of the object as actually sensed — a second edition, as it were, of our original sensory experience of that object. This statement, however, must not be construed to mean that we always reproduce every detail of the object sensed, nor that the revival of past sensations is peculiarly vivid. If this were required, few persons could boast of memory-images. But no sensory ex-

---

[2]*Op. cit.,* p. 432.
[3]*Op. cit.,* p. 430.
[4]*Op. cit.,* p. 450.

perience derived from other objects, may be incorporated into the image. Only in this sense is a memory-image a faithful copy of our former sensory experiences.[5]

Frequently, however, we combine in various ways the sensations produced in the past by different objects. This occurs — to use the traditional and somewhat grotesque example — when we combine the visual impression made by the head, arms, and chest of a man with that made by the body and legs of a horse, thus creating the appearance of an object which does not exist in nature, namely, the image of a centaur. This is known as an image of fancy, and our ability to form images of this kind is known as creative imagination.

It is well to add that the grotesqueness of the illustration used is a very unessential feature of an image of fancy. Whenever we are not faithful, as explained above, in copying sensory impressions of an object in nature, as when we "idealize" natural objects for artistic purposes, we make use of creative imagination.

From this description of creative imagination it will be seen that this term does not imply the arousal, by the mere *fiat* of the will, of internal sensations which have never occurred in our past experience as actual sensations. Such a thing is simply impossible. If we have never heard an oboe, we cannot, by a mere *fiat* of the will, imagine a melody as played by an oboe. And still we can with more or less success "create" such an image, provided we have had auditory experiences enough and are capable of recalling and combining them, that is, provided we have auditory imagery at all.

When a familiar tune is played on a violin, you may be able to reproduce this auditory experience. Then you have an auditory memory-image of it. The melody, as played by an oboe, is the same, as far as the pitch of each tone (say c'') and its loudness (say mf) is concerned. The distinctive character or clang tint of each note, however, is different from that of a violin tone, in fact, from that of every other instrument. The tone of an oboe

---

[5]*Op. cit.*

is remarkably mellow, somewhat nasal and penetrating, plaintive and idyllic. This description may recall sensory impressions of other sounds in your past experience which in part, at least, answer this description. Putting all these sensory experiences together you may make a fair approach at "creating" an image of a melody as played by an oboe. It is the *facility* in thus recalling and appropriately combining various sensory experiences of the past, which constitutes the talent of a musical composer, poet, painter, and all other artists, and enables them to "create" their works of art.

4. The Machinery of Sensory Association: One of the Factors of Reproductive and Creative Imagination. Undoubtedly one of the factors which determine both the faithful recall and the fanciful combination of former sensations, is the machinery of sensory association. Sensationalists, in fact, recognize no other factor, as we had occasion to point out briefly in former chapters. We must now give this matter a more detailed consideration. For in this sensationalistic explanation of imagination — in fact, of our whole conscious life — facts and theories are peculiarly intermingled; some facts are unduly emphasized, others are glided over with a remarkable ease and unconcern. As the very simplicity of an explanation makes it irresistibly attractive, the student should realize clearly what in the explanation is fact and what is theory, and he should ask himself whether all the pertinent facts have been duly considered. We shall begin with some fundamental facts of nerve-physiology and their bearing on the problems of sense-perception and imagination.

Actual sensations leave traces or records of themselves in the nervous system. Once a sensory center in the brain of a newborn babe has been acted upon by a sensory stimulus, this center is in a different condition from what it was in before. The neural excitement into which it was thrown ceases indeed when the stimulus is withdrawn, but it can be thrown more readily into the same excitement the second time, and still more readily the third time, and with the greatest ease the hundredth time.

This item of nerve-physiology is undoubtedly correct and it is because of such a record, left in the brain centers, that former sensations can be aroused again even in the absence of their actual stimuli. At least this is one of the factors of the revival of former sensations and is known by the name of "the perseveration of sensory experiences."

Moreover, *when different sensory experiences have occurred together or in immediate succession, any one of them, on recurring, tends to revive the others also*. This is the principle of sensory association, which — as here stated — is undoubtedly correct. The physiological basis of it is this. The brain centers of all the senses are connected not only with the peripheral sense-organs but also among themselves. The result is that the physiological excitement created in one brain center — say in the visual center — can be propagated to all other centers. The fibers connecting the various centers with the peripheral organs are known as "projection fibers," those connecting the centers among themselves, as "association fibers." When two sensations occur together or in immediate succession, the neural current will actually flow from one center to the other and thus a definite path is established. Once this has taken place, the neural current passes through it more easily the second time. The more frequently two actual sensations occur together, the deeper will the neural groove be and the more readily will the neural current pass along this groove, even in the absence of external stimuli. Thus it is that out of millions of possible paths definite ones gradually become firmly established.

Let A, B, C, and D represent four sensations, associated at some time in our past experience either simultaneously or in immediate succession. If now any one of them, say B, occurs again as an actual sensation, it will *tend* to revive also its former associates: A, C, and D. We say it *tends* to do so. For the actual revival of A, C, and D, may encounter difficulties. When revived, they constitute a sensory-image or a combination of such images.

If other sensations also, say E, F, G, and H, have been associated at some time with the sensation B, which one of its former associates (A, C, D, E, F, G, H,) will be here and now revived? This, we are told, will depend *exclusively* on the relative depth of their respective traces in the brain and on the relative strength of their interconnection. Some tracts are more pervious than others. The neural current follows the line of least resistance, that is, along the more pervious tracts. The revival of sensations depends on the neural currents. As a result, the actual sensation B will arouse C, F, and H, on one occasion; A, D, and G, on another occasion, and so forth, in accordance with the concrete neural conditions on each occasion. This sweeping generalization means in plain and outspoken terms that *voluntary control over our images — in fact over our whole mental life — is categorically ruled out.* If such voluntary control is referred to, as is done at times by sensationalists themselves, this term is understood to be strictly a misnomer.

The law of sensory association is, in its last analysis, but *a law of neural habit* and can, therefore, be expressed *in purely physiological terms.* In its broadest outline it may be stated as follows: *"When two elementary brain processes have been active together or in immediate succession, one of them, on reoccurring, tends to propagate its excitement into the other."*[6]

5. Voluntary Control as a Factor of Reproductive and Creative Imagination. At times, no doubt, the perseveration of sensory experiences and the machinery of association are the only factors which determine the occurrence and flow of our images. Who has not experienced images of both reproductive and creative imagination coming to him unbidden, and he knows not whence — in fact, in spite of himself? If you have worked all day in the laboratory with the color wheel, you will find in all probability that at the fag-end of the day you see nothing but disks, and that with a surprising vividness. You need not be an accomplished musician to experience snatches of this or that air of an opera you have just listened to, running through your head, now as faithful copies of what you have heard, now combined

---

[6]James. *Psychology,* p. 256.

into strange medleys. Willy-nilly you must listen to these haunt-
ing melodies.

Likewise after laboratory exercises in memory you may find
that fragments of this or that series of nonsense syllables, intermingled with disconnected portions of various poems, return to
your mind irresistibly and in parrotlike succession, just as you
compose yourself to sleep. On such occasions, with sleep so near
and yet so far away, one would wish that the psychologist, who
has set the machinery of association agoing and has imprinted
the brain records according to the most improved methods, could
also stop the annoying machinery. You may feel like saying with
Goethe: *"Die ich rief, die Geister, werd' ich nun nicht los."* (*The
spirits whom I called I cannot quell.*) In such a predicament the
best advice is to make up our minds deliberately, neither to
further nor to hinder the spontaneous flow of images and to be,
as it were, inert spectators and listeners until the excitement is
spent. This is the only remnant of voluntary control which then
remains practicable.

A similar condition prevails when we are under the influence
of strong emotions. Then the machinery of association fairly runs
away with us. If no effort to divert our attention from the images
is successful, the same advice will be of service to accomplish the
desired result.

The most absolute and uncontrolled sway of the machinery of
association, just as it is described by sensationalists, obtains in
fever delirium and in the brain storms of drug victims.

It is, however, only fair to say that we are not always in the
same condition as at the fag-end of the day, nor always under
the influence of strong emotions. Even in the drug victims the
brain storm subsides some time and they have lucid moments,
when the normal control of their mental faculties returns. And
under such normal conditions voluntary control is an unmistakable factor, determining the appearance and course of our imagery.

If it were not for this control which we exercise over our images, it would be absurd for me to expect the reader or the members of the class to follow me in the present discussion. For to

do so, they must suppress many an irrelevant image, aroused by
the machinery of association, and call up many other images
which do not lie along the line of least resistance.

*Every laboratory experiment on memory-images or those of
fancy is an experimental demonstration of that factor of imagery
which sensationalists wish to see ruled out in the interest of their
pet metaphysical theories.* If the subject of a psychological experiment does not want to carry out instructions, when told to call
up an image, say of a house, a banana, or anything else, according
as the experimenter may direct — or if he resists the appearance
in his mind of images, called up by the machinery of association,
by deliberately directing his attention to other things — we can
do nothing with him in the psychological laboratory, or in fact
in any kind of laboratory.

*The most conspicuous mark that distinguishes laboratory ob-
servations from those of ordinary life is that they are controlled
by the arbitrary choice of the experimenter,* and in the case of
psychological experiments, *by the arbitrary choice of both the experimenter and the subject,* each in his own sphere. It is simply
suicidal for a psychological experimentalist to deny voluntary control over our imagery in the interest of his pet metaphysical
theories.

No doubt, such voluntary control is mysterious. So are a thousand other facts in psychology and in all other sciences. But it
will not do to deny a fact because it is mysterious. We had better
take facts just as they actually occur. If they do not agree with
our pet metaphysical speculations of how facts ought to be, so
much the worse for these speculations. Accordingly, taking experience for our guide, we recognize voluntary control as a most
important factor of both memory-images and those of fancy.

6. **Images and Voluntary Movements.** The subject of voluntary control over our images leads us naturally to another aspect of imagination, namely, the part it plays in the acquisition of
voluntary control over our body In Chapter II, when discussing
kinesthetic sensations (or sensations of movement), we pointed
out the importance of these sensations in this regard. What holds

of the kinesthetic sensations themselves, holds also of their revivals: kinesthetic images.

Images of movement have been called *"kinesthetic equivalents."* The same is expressed by saying that images of movement
have "motor power." What is meant by the two phrases is simply
this: When we imagine a movement of our body, that is, when
we recall how such a movement feels, or how it looks, or how
it sounds, these images tend to produce the movement itself.
Thus, the image of a movement is the necessary link between
the act of the will and the actual movement itself so that without
an image of the movement the voluntary performance of that
movement is impossible.

We say an image of a movement "tends" to produce the movement itself. For by an act of the will we can inhibit the gross
movement. But the initial movement — the first beginnings of
the movement — will occur in spite of ourselves. These initial
movements are so slight that they cannot be detected by an ordinary observer. Under laboratory conditions, however, they can
be detected with precision. All that is necessary is to magnify
these slight movements by some suitable device. Some of these
devices are too elaborate to be explained here. The simple experimental arrangement which we shall describe presently amply
suffices to demonstrate that such initial movements occur under
the conditions mentioned.

Place the accompanying diagram (Fig. 39) flat on the table.
The lines of which the diagram consists indicate various possible
movements which you are to imagine. Then attach a plumb bob
at the end of a string, which should be about a foot long. Take
the other end of the string tightly between the thumb and forefinger of the right hand and hold the bob vertically over the center (O) of the diagram. When the bob is at rest, make up your
mind that you will not move the bob. At the same time, however,
imagine that the bob moves to and fro along the straight line AB.
Thus, for instance, you may recall how it would feel if you were
to swing the bob in that direction. You may succeed even better
if you swing the bob first voluntarily in the direction AB and

look attentively at the operation. Then, after bringing the bob to rest again, recall as vividly as possible how the operation looks Or again, you may place one tumbler at A and another at B and recall how it would sound if the swinging bob were to strike the two tumblers in turn. If you carry out these instructions accurately, you will find that before long the bob will actually begin to swing in the direction thought of. You will

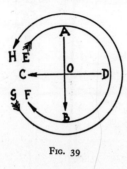

FIG. 39

find, moreover, that you are powerless to check the movements by any effort of your will — provided you persist in imagining the movements.

Now change your image of the movement. Imagine that the bob swings in the direction CD. The first beginnings of the new movement will be apparent as soon as you change the image of the movement, and at last the bob will swing plainly in the new direction.

Next try to impart a circular movement to the bob by imagining that it moves clockwise (EF) or counterclockwise (GH). The result will be again in accord with your image of the movement.

Figure 40 will help you to understand the physiological reason for these phenomena. When you swing the bob voluntarily and look at the operation, an impression is made on the eye. This impression is carried to the visual center (V) of the brain by means of the optic nerve. This nerve is indicated by the dotted line connecting the eye with V. When you hear a sound made by the

swinging bob, the impression thus made on the ear reaches the
auditory center (A) of the brain by means of the auditory nerve.
This nerve is indicated by the dotted line connecting the ear with

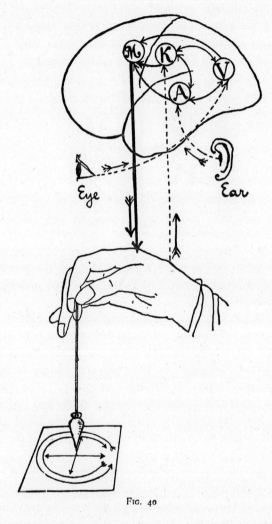

Fig. 40

A. You also feel the movement in the muscles, tendons, and
joints of the hand. Really the movement makes a record of itself
in the kinesthetic center (K) of the brain. This is done by means

of ingoing nerve-fibers which lead from the muscles, tendons, and joints of the hand to K. These ingoing fibers, subservient to the feeling of movement, are indicated by the dotted line connecting the hand with K.

All these sensory centers of the brain (V, A, and K) are connected with one another by means of fibers, known as "association fibers." They are indicated by the curved lines connecting V, A, and K among themselves. Moreover, every sensory center is connected by similar association fibers with the motor area (M) of the brain, as will be seen from the diagram. This means that every sensory center is connected with those outgoing nerve-fibers which lead from M to the muscles of the hand. Such outgoing brain fibers are known as "motor tracts." They are indicated in the diagram by the heavy straight line connecting M with the hand. It is by means of these "motor tracts" that the muscles of our body must be aroused to action when we want to carry out a definite voluntary movement.

Though a *voluntary* movement, say of the hand, does not occur without the intervention of an act of the will, the mere act of the will does not suffice to bring about the movement. Unless we know how a movement looks, or how it sounds, or how it feels, our will is powerless to execute the movement.

This premised, then, we say: When you imagine that the bob swings in a definite direction, you revive the record which the movement has left in the sensory centers of the brain: V, A, and K. *The physiological excitement thus created in any one of these sensory centers tends to discharge by way of the said association fibers into the appropriate motor tracts.* This will be particularly the case, if you have executed the movement frequently in the past. For the more frequently the neural current has passed along definite association fibers, the more readily will it pass there again. A neural groove, as it were, is formed and this groove is deepened with every repetition of the movement.

From all this it will be seen that images of our bodily movements are important factors of our actual voluntary movements. Acquisition of skill in the performance of these movements means in physiological terms the gradual formation of definite neural grooves in our brain.

7. **Images and Thought.** That images are in some way connected with thought has been known from time immemorial. So intimate is this connection that the popular use of the term "imagination" has its root here. And the hypothesis of sensationalism could never have been proposed with even a semblance of foundation in fact were it not for this connection. We shall discuss the hypothesis of sensationalism more fully in our chapters on Thought; here we wish to call attention briefly to two facts which modern experimental methods have brought to light and which will serve as a foundation for our discussion of thought. These two facts, however, are also of interest for the purposes of our present chapter. For they bring home to us the individual differences which exist with regard to imagination.

The first fact is that *different persons differ considerably with regard to the images which they experience when thinking of one and the same object*. On the basis of these individual differences persons have been arranged into groups, each said to possess a peculiar "type of imagination." This aspect of the first fact will be dealt with in the next section of this chapter.

The second fact is this. *In one and the same individual images vary considerably with the concrete conditions in which he finds himself*. The result is that there is hardly anyone who experiences on two successive occasions identically the same images when thinking of one and the same object.

Various methods may be employed by the student to ascertain these two facts for himself. Memory experiments furnish excellent material in this regard. Another method is to make a statistical inquiry like that begun by Galton in 1880. He addressed a circular to a great number of persons, requesting them to describe accurately the visual imagery they experienced when thinking of their breakfast table on a definite morning. The individual differences which the answers revealed were astonishing. Other investigators have prepared detailed questionnaires concerning images, namely with a view to determine the so-called type of imagination to which each individual belongs.

8. The So-Called Types of Imagination. Though no individual agrees perfectly with any other one as to the images he experiences when thinking of one and the same object, still certain regularities are discovered in the introspective reports of different persons. It can be said that, in general at least, *a certain kind of imagery preponderates in each one's experience.* According as the preponderating images are of the visual, auditory, or tactual and kinesthetic kind, we speak of the subjects as belonging to the visual, auditory, or kinesthetic type of imagination. They have also been called visualizers or visils, audils, and tactils, respectively. Gustatory and olfactory images are very rare.

The line of demarcation between the said types is far from being a sharp one. There are some, to begin with, who have equal facility in arousing *all* the various kinds of images, and they are said to belong to the *"mixed type."* This, of course, is but another way of saying that they belong to *no distinctive type.* And, what is more important, the kind of imagery which a person experiences depends not only on his *native constitution,* as the term "types of imagination" leads us to suppose, but also on his *acquired habits,* as well as on *the manner in which any particular sensible object most forcibly presents itself,* and last, but not least, on the *direction of voluntary or involuntary attention* in every individual case.

What complicates the matter still further is the fact that there are a good many persons who, on introspection, cannot discover either visual or auditory or tactual kinesthetic images, worthy of the name, at least of the sensible objects themselves of which they are thinking. This is particularly true of such as are given to scientific or philosophic pursuits. The only images they can trace are of the words by which they would outwardly express their thoughts. They are said to belong to the *word-type* of imagination in opposition to the *object-type,* and according as their word-images are visual, auditory, or kinesthetic in character, *verbal sub-*

types of imagination have been distinguished: *auditory, visual,* and *kinesthetic.* Also the distinction between these verbal sub-types is far from being clearly marked. Even that between the object-type and the word-type of imagination is anything but thoroughgoing, as there is hardly anyone in whose ordinary experience word-images do not play an important rôle. James quotes the report of an extraordinary object-visualizer, whose word-images are just as remarkable.[7] *This subject could look down the mentally seen page and see the words that commence all the lines, and from any one of these words he was able to continue the line.* As a proof, he copied a page of La Fontaine, 8, IV, from memory, thus:

Etant fait...............	Céres ....
Tous	Avec ....
A des...................	Un fleur...............
Que fit.................	Comme ....

9. Musical Imagination. Musical imagination is a special form of auditory imagination. It deserves special consideration because of the extraordinary development which it has received in modern times.

In its creative form it is especially astonishing in modern composers, particularly those who created their immortal works under peculiarly distressing circumstances. Beethoven, it is well known, wrote his greatest works at a time when he was deaf. Schubert, though not deaf, never heard the most remarkable of his orchestral compositions, except in his imagination: an accomplishment and a misfortune which many of the lesser stars in the musical firmament share with him. Mozart carried all the details of his compositions so accurately in his imagination that "the committing to paper (as he himself testifies) is done easily enough; for everything is, as I said before, already finished; and it rarely differs on paper from what it was in my imagination. At this occupation I can therefore suffer myself to be disturbed; for whatever may be going on around me, I write and even talk, but

---

[1] *Psychology,* p. 304.

only of fowls and geese, or of Gretel or Barbel or some such matters."[8]

In its reproductive form musical imagination is just as marvelous in virtuosi and orchestra directors. When the famous pianist Hans von Bülow began in the middle of the nineteenth century to play from memory in all his recitals and concerts — a thing not dreamt of until then — he created a veritable sensation. At present no soloist of repute would think of playing from a copy during a recital or concert. It was, however, as an orchestra director that the same Hans von Bülow capped the climax For he directed not only the comparatively simple orchestral works of the classical period by heart, but he did the same thing in the case of the music dramas of Wagner. Even musicians that can boast of a good musical memory cannot help wondering at such a feat. *How can a man carry all the details of the stupendously complex scores of Wagner so perfectly in his imagination that he can direct his attention to any one of these details, as an orchestra director must be able to do?* This prodigious feat of Bülow has since been imitated by a number of other orchestra directors.

To musicians who are thus gifted — or rather, who have developed their natural endowment in this regard by a deliberate effort and constant practice — *the reading of a musical score means their hearing it, so that they can have a concert whenever they like, and any program they like.* Such a thing is unintelligible not only to visualizers, but also to those "audils" whose highest achievement in this regard has been to experience a familiar tune running through their heads.

References for Further Reading

J. Froebes, S.J., *Lehrbuch der Experimentellen Psychologie,* Vol. I (1923), pp 204–237.

J. Lindworsky, S.J., *Experimentelle Psychologie* (1921), pp. 102–106.

C. S. Myers, *Text-Book of Experimental Psychology,* pp. 136–142.

---

[8]Quoted by Carpenter, *Ment. Physiol.,* p. 272.

Chapter X

MEMORY

1. Memory Proper and Immediate Memory. What the memory of an animal may be we can know only by inference and by a process of reconstruction from the objective data which animal behavior furnishes us. To be successful in such a process of reconstruction we must begin with memory as it occurs in man and we must beware of the danger of humanizing the animal. Accordingly, it is not the memory of animals with which we are directly concerned in this chapter. We speak of memory as it occurs in man.

But even in man widely different things are sometimes designated by the term "memory." Thus we speak of *immediate* memory; of *sensory, logical* and *rote* memory. Also the term *mechanical* memory is sometimes used. Some authors speak even of *organic* memory. All these various meanings of the term "memory" will be discussed in order. We begin with the distinction between memory proper and immediate memory.

Memory proper may be defined as the power which we have to retain, recall, and recognize the contents of a past experience. Accordingly, memory proper involves three distinct elements; namely, (1) the *retention* of a past experience of ours, (2) its *actual recall,* and (3) its *recognition.* We shall first describe these three elements in empirical terms and note the problems which each suggests. Only when these problems are clearly understood can we consider the various attempts that have been made to explain memory proper.

In order to understand the meaning of *immediate memory* it is important to note that no conscious experience of ours is strictly instantaneous. *The contents of every experience remain consciously present to us together with the contents of the next experience.* Simply repeat by heart the sentence here italicized, and you have an experimental demonstration of the fact stated in that sentence. Clearly you have understood the instruction of this little experiment. While the instruction is thus in the focus of your attention, the sentence italicized still lingers in your mind. *The conscious retention of a past experience side by side with the contents of the next experience which is here and now in the focus of attention, is known as immediate memory.*

We make use of immediate memory whenever we answer a question, carry out an instruction, write from dictation, read a book, or follow a discussion. Immediate memory, in short, is the *sine qua non* of every complex conscious process and of our whole rational life as it actually occurs. If by the time you arrive at the end of this sentence you have forgotten its beginning, you simply do not understand this sentence. Such failure to understand a sentence will actually occur whenever that sentence is too long or too involved. Then the number of units of which that sentence is composed exceeds your span of attention. The later units of the sentence will crowd its earlier units out of your mind. To understand such a sentence you must study and memorize it. Hence, the common-sense rule for all who write to be understood: Do not write sentences which exceed the average span of attention.

From this it will be seen that *the experimental investigation of immediate memory really belongs to the chapter on Attention.* What interests us here is the fact that the later occupants of the focus of attention tend to crowd out its previous occupants, a fact known under the name of *"retroactive inhibition."* Hence the necessity of memory proper, if we are to make use of those former experiences of ours which are beyond the limits of immediate memory. And this brings us to the first element of memory proper, namely:

2. The Retention of Past Experiences. Only an infinitesimal portion of our mental possessions is at any given moment consciously present to us. A mathematician, for instance, may rightly say that he "knows" plane geometry. But he does not mean thereby that every theorem of that science is consciously present to him and that he actually thinks of every link in the proof of every or any particular theorem. Such a thing would be simply impossible. It is incompatible with the most fundamental characteristic of our conscious life: *the narrowness of consciousness.* There is standing room for only a limited number of objects in the ever-shifting focus of attention. Sooner or later every experience drops out of our mind. Some of these experiences, however, are said to be "retained" in our mind. A favored few, in fact, are retained so perfectly as to constitute our permanent mental possessions. This "retention" in our mind of past experiences *which have actually dropped out of our mind,* is the first characteristic of memory proper.

It sounds paradoxical enough to say that we retain in our mind what has dropped out of it. What is really meant is this: The contents of a past experience which are no longer consciously present to us, *can be revived again.* And this is all we know about the first characteristic of memory proper in purely empirical terms. Whatever else, therefore, "retention" may mean, it signifies *potential recall* or the capacity we have of recalling the contents of a past experience. The greater this capacity, that is, the more readily we can recall the contents of a past experience, the more firmly is this experience "retained" and, in so far, the better our memory.

3. The Fact of Retention and the Hypothesis of Sensationalism. The fact of retention of past experiences presents two important problems which must be clearly understood and faced fairly and squarely. We shall propose the first of these problems in connection with a difficulty which has been raised against our ability to recall past experiences. *It has been said that our ability to revive an experience after it has ceased to be, can signify no more than our ability to create an experience which is more or less similar to that we had before.* If this statement in its sweeping generality were true, then memory would be *untrustworthy* and our ability to recall past experiences would be an accomplishment altogether *useless* for scientific purposes.

When in the final examination at the end of the school year

you are quizzed about a definite theorem in geometry, you are expected to be able to recall not a theorem which is more or less similar to that you had during the year, but *identically the same theorem*. It will make no difference whether you substitute arbitrary symbols, such as *m* and *n,* for those you used during the year, namely *a* and *b,* nor will it make any difference whether you use red chalk in drawing your figures whereas during the year you used white chalk or your lead pencil. Similarly you are not expected to repeat in parrotlike fashion the words of the textbook. You may change the construction of your sentences, and if your examiner knows German or French, you will satisfy him perfectly by recalling the theorem asked for in either of these two languages, whereas during the year it was presented to you in English. And if in speaking French you do not use the Parisian accent to which your examiner is accustomed, you will get your credits all the same. There is only one proviso for these credits and that is *your ability to recall identically the same theorem as that proposed to you during the year.*

From this the reader will see that the first characteristic of memory proper brings us face to face with the problem of sensationalism or the problem of the distinction between sensory experiences and thought. It is true that our ability to recall past sensory experiences is very imperfect, as we stated in the chapter on Imagination (p. 182). *Probably no one is able to revive identically the same sensory experience as he had on a former occasion.* Still less is he able to do so repeatedly on different subsequent occasions. The best that can be said of this ability is precisely what the above difficulty states, namely, that we are able to produce sensory experiences which are more or less similar to those we had before.

With regard to our ability, however, to recall thoughts, something very different is true. Every thought is specified by its *object.* We cannot distinguish one thought from another except by its object or content. If, therefore, we are able to recall identically *the same contents of thought* as on a former occasion, we revive *identically the same thought.* Such is actually the case when a mathematician, for instance, retains the knowledge of a definite theorem in geometry. *We now know with absolute precision what Euclid knew.* His theorems express necessary, eternal, and unchangeable truths, and they have become the permanent possession of mathematicians of all times. In the light of this fact the difficulty against our ability to revive former experiences needs a distinction, namely, between *the potential recall of sensory experiences and that of thought.* If this distinction does not fit into the hypothesis of sensationalism, so much the worse for this hypothesis.

To put the matter differently. There is such a thing as introducing refinements into experimental methods which are not only *irrelevant* but become *a positive hindrance to scientific research.* Introspectionists of the sensationalistic type have introduced such refinements into their methods of testing the ability to recall past experiences. *Suppose that a student has passed his examination in mathematics with first honors. If his ability to recall a definite theorem in geometry were tested in the laboratory of sensationalists, he would in all probability be told that it amounts to something next to zero.* That is to say, it amounts to zero, if the results are to be expressed in *"existential"* terms: such is the hallowed phrase of sensationalists. Of course, the student would be next dragged into the metaphysical darkroom of the psychology of "meaning." There matters would be patched up a little, that is, the discrepancies between the results of common-sense methods and those of the refined methods of sensationalists would be smoothed over. The student might be satisfied with this smoothing-over process. But men who have practical problems to solve -- and the behaviorists claim to be such -- will be dissatisfied. They insist that *there is something radically wrong with the refined methods of sensationalists.* Whatever else may be granted to behaviorists, in this they are right. The sooner we get rid of the refined methods of sensationalists in determining the *"existential"* aspect of our conscious processes and our ability to recall them, the better for the science of experimental psychology. It is much better off without the metaphysical dark-

room of the psychology of "meaning" and all the useless lumber
that has been collected here.

4. Retention and Its Physiological Explanation. We said
that retention, "whatever else it may mean," signifies "potential
recall." The question is irresistible: *What else* does retention signify? And this is the second of the important problems which are
suggested by the first characteristic of memory proper.

"Potential recall" is a term which reminds us forcibly of a well-
known term in physics, namely *"potential energy."* Undoubtedly there is some analogy between the two facts thus designated,
and the question is: How far does this analogy extend? When
the physicist speaks of "potential" energy, he does not mean a
mere logical possibility or something that exists only in the metaphysical order. He means *a physical condition of the body which
is said to have "potential" energy,* and this physical condition can
be described and measured with accuracy. When a body is raised
to a definite height it has, in virtue of that fact, potential energy
or the capacity to do work. This capacity is exactly equal to the
work spent upon that body in raising it to that height. When
the mass m of that body is raised to the height h against the local
accelerative effect of gravity g, then the potential energy or capacity of that body to do work is indicated by the formula mgh.
The student should note, then, that we thus measure the physical
condition of something that exists, namely, a body.

Similarly when we speak of "potential" recall we do not mean
a mere logical possibility or something that exists only in the
metaphysical order. We mean *the physical condition which I
have in virtue of the fact that I had a definite experience on a
former occasion.* It is in virtue of this fact that I am said to have
the ability to recall that experience. Those psychologists who have
faced this problem have said that the former experience leaves
a certain "disposition" or "trace." But where there is a disposition
or trace, *there is something real that has this disposition or trace.*
What within me is that real something that has the said disposition or trace?

In the case of our *sensory* experiences it is not difficult to indicate where within us the trace or disposition is which is the residue of that sensory experience. Plainly the trace exists in our nervous system and consists of *neural grooves*, as we explained in the chapter on Imagination. We can point out further that these neural grooves — much like the grooves left by a wagon on a soft country road — gradually disappear, unless the sensory experiences which left these grooves are frequently repeated and repeated in uniformly the same way. This would account for the fact that, frequently at least, we are able to recall sensory experiences only in a fragmentary and shadowy sort of way.

In the case of our intellectual experiences, however, it is not so plain that the trace left by these experiences consists of grooves in our nervous system. To begin with, *the absolute accuracy* with which we can recall former thoughts, is not thus accounted for. There are many other things in this recall which are not thus accounted for. We shall point them out when considering certain anomalies of memory, particularly those discussed under the heading of "aphasia." *An experimentalist may abstain from the philosophical considerations to which the careful analysis of these facts leads. But one thing he cannot do: he cannot say with even a semblance of truth that he has explained the potential recall of our intellectual experiences simply in terms of neural grooves.*

It is true that Aristotle insisted on the physiological explanation of retention, *even in the case of concepts.* But a short quotation from his "memory and recollection" will suffice to show what his position really was. He says: "Memory, even the memory of concepts, *does not take place without an image.* Consequently, memory concerns the faculty of thought accidentally and the primary power of sense intrinsically."[1]

5. The Second Characteristic of Memory Proper: Recall. By recall we mean *the actual revival* of the contents of a past experience. It may be *voluntary* or *involuntary, complete* or *incomplete, systematic* or *desultory.*

When we make a deliberate effort to bring back to our mind

---

[1]Cf. Hammond, *Aristotle's Psychology*, p. 198.

what we have seen, heard, known, said, or done, and succeed in the effort, we have an instance of *voluntary recall*. When these experiences come back to us without any effort on our part or even in spite of ourselves, recall is *involuntary*. Aristotle long ago called attention to this distinction in his treatise on "memory and recollection." He reserves the term "recollection" for voluntary recall and he points out the peculiar problem which it involves. How can we try to recall a thing when we do not know what that thing is? It is like looking for something in our room we know not what. The answer is that *we must know something about the experience* to be recalled and this furnishes *the starting point* for our search. Aristotle has described the process of recollection in a manner that cannot be improved upon and in doing so he incidentally hints at all the other distinctions of recall indicated in the foregoing. He says: "When a person wants to recall a thing, he will do the following: he will try to gain a starting point in the process, in sequence to which the desired experience was had. Consequently, recollections which are awakened from the starting point are most quickly and best effected. For just as things are mutually related in their order of succession, so also are the mental processes. And such things as have a fixed order are easily remembered, as, for example, mathematical truths. Other things are remembered poorly and with difficulty."[2]

The more details of a former experience are revived, the more *complete* is our recall; the more details drop out, the more *incomplete* is our recall. It is important to note that *most lapses of memory — in fact, all lapses of memory of which we become aware — are really cases of incomplete recall.* Thus, for instance, we may remember distinctly that we spoke to Mr. X but fail to recall just what we said to him. Or we may remember distinctly what we said to him but cannot recall whether we did so on this occasion or that, and so forth. If the detail not recalled is the all-important thing we are looking for here and now, then our incomplete recall is spoken of

---

[2]Cf. Hammond. *op. cit.*, p. 206

as *a lapse of memory*. If, however, the forgotten detail is here and now irrelevant, the same incomplete recall may be *an instance of a remarkably good memory*. If this fact be kept in mind, a good deal of quibbling will be avoided in the discussion of certain anomalies of memory spoken of as cases of "alternating personalities."

From what we have said it is clear that *neither completeness nor incompleteness of recall is, of itself, a desirable mark of memory*. What is desirable is that recall should be as complete as possible for all details that are *relevant*, and as incomplete as possible for all details that are *irrelevant*. Such recall is *systematic*. Of course, the things that we experience do not come to us with labels gummed to their backs. We must label them and thus create the system of which each experience forms a part. As we go along we must pigeonhole all those experiences which are relevant to our purposes and which we wish to remember. These pigeonholes will differ from person to person. A chemist has one set of pigeonholes and a biologist another. A scrapbook may be used but it must be indexed, else it is very much like a junk shop. When actually recalling an experience, we must be guided by our system. If recall is not thus guided, that is, if irrelevant details are revived with the same vividness and emphasis as the essential ones, we speak of *desultory* recall.

When we are not particularly busy, desultory recall is one of the most delightful foibles of human nature, and comic literature has made the best of this foible. But we want none of it in the classroom or in the business office. Whenever "efficiency" is the watchword, *forgetting is an essential feature of a good memory*. A specimen of a desultory recall will bring the truth of this seemingly paradoxical saying home to the student more forcibly than any learned disquisition can. We borrow the specimen just where James did, namely, from Miss Austen's "Emma." Suppose that in recalling a simple past event — say, on the witness stand — we were to redintegrate as impartially as the garrulous Miss Bates does:

" 'But where could you hear it?' cried Miss Bates. 'Where could you possibly hear it, Mr. Knightly? For it is not five minutes since I received Mrs. Cole's note — no, it cannot be more than five — or at least ten — for I had got my bonnet and spencer on, just ready to come out. I was only gone down to speak to Patty again about the pork. Jane was standing in the passage — were not you, Jane? — for my mother was so afraid that we had not any salting pan large enough. So I said I would go down and see, and Jane said: "Shall I go down instead? for I think you have a little cold, and Patty has been washing the kitchen." "Oh my dear," said I — well, and just then came the note. A Miss Hawkins — that's all I know — a Miss Hawkins, of Bath. But Mr. Knightly, how could you possibly have heard it? for the very moment Mr. Cole told Mrs. Cole of it, she sat down and wrote to me. A Miss Hawkins — ' "[3]

6. The Third Characteristic of Memory Proper: Recognition. The mere revival of a past experience does not constitute memory. I saw my typewriter yesterday; I see it again today; and I may see it again many a time before it is thrown on the scrap pile. In the meantime, therefore, whenever I see my typewriter, the contents of a past experience of mine are revived. But seeing again what I have seen before is, of itself, something very different from what we understand by remembering a past event.

Nor does the revival of the contents of a past experience become memory by the additional fact that the revival is due to this past experience. A scene which I witness may make such a deep impression upon my nervous system that its image recurs to me in season and out of season. This image is undoubtedly a revival of the contents of my past experience and it is due to this past experience. But imagining a scene and remembering a scene are two very different things. In other words, *a "memory-image" and memory proper are far from being synonymous terms*, as we pointed out in the chapter on Imagination. In fact, *a "memory-image" is not even a necessary ingredient of what we call memory proper.* When here and now I look at the typewriter before

---

[3] Quoted by James, *Psychology*, p. 261.

me, I remember distinctly that I used it yesterday. But I am not aware that I place a "memory-image" of the typewriter side by side with the object of my present sensory experience and that I compare the two. The most carefully conducted experiments have frequently failed to reveal such a "memory-image" under conditions similar to those described.[4]

What makes the revival of the contents of a past experience an act of memory, is the knowledge that I have experienced the contents of my present experience before. This knowledge is called "recognition" and it is the third characteristic of memory proper. When this knowledge is present it makes no difference how the revival of the contents of a past experience is effected: in terms of sensation, image, or thought. Whether I see again a landscape, or whether, in the absence of the landscape, I have a "memory-image" of it, or whether I think of it without any memory-image worthy of the name: in all three cases I remember the landscape, provided I have the additional knowledge that *I have seen the landscape before.*

It is this characteristic of memory which more than the other two must be explained, if we are to explain memory proper. Recognition presents problems the discussion of which leads us directly to the domain proper to the philosopher. *An experimentalist may avoid such problems. But if he does he cannot say that he has explained memory proper.* And if he faces the problem of recognition, he cannot be satisfied with explanations which merely restate the problem in another form. Most theories of recognition are of this kind. Hence the first thing to be done is to state clearly the psychological facts which are involved in recognition. It is these facts which must be explained in a satisfactory theory of recognition.

Recognition implies three facts: (1) *the knowledge of the past;* (2) *the knowledge of my past.* This means: the perception of the Ego as the subject of both the past and the present experience. To be more explicit, it means: *the perception of the identity of the*

[4]Cf. T. V. Moore, *The Process of Abstraction,* p. 134.

*Ego which was the subject of the past experience and of the Ego
which is the subject of the present experience.* Recognition involves (3) *the perception of the identity of the object of the past
experience and of the object of the present experience.* We become aware of this identity of the object when we perceive its
individual identity or its identity in *kind.* Even similarity suffices;
for *similarity is partial identity.* All three facts here enumerated
are plainly implied in the simple and unsophisticated statements
by which we express recognition: "I have seen this individual
typewriter before"; "I have seen a typewriter of this kind before";
"I have seen something similar before."

7. **"Localization in Time," "The Temporal-Sign Theory," and "The Familiarity Mark."** Some psychologists have
introduced a fourth element into the definition of memory proper and they have called it "localization in time." Others have
substituted this element for recognition. *By "localization in time"
they mean the fact that we are able to reproduce past experiences
of ours in the order in which they have occurred.* At times, no
doubt, we are able to do so, and when we do, this fact needs
explanation.

One of the theories which has been proposed in explanation of
this fact is analogous to the "local-sign theory," discussed in the
chapters on the perception of space, and it has been called the
"temporal-sign theory." The two theories are about on a par. At
any rate, as proposed by some psychologists, *the "temporal-sign
theory" is merely an effort to divert attention from the Ego-problem which is involved in the fact of recognition or an effort to
explain away the plain fact of the perception of the permanent
identity of the Ego.* These psychologists insist that we do not find
the Ego but that we construct it by a process of association. It is
in this effort that they always *merely restate in another form the
fact to be explained.* The reader who desires further details concerning these unsuccessful attempts to explain away the Ego, is
referred to the writer's monograph *Psychology Without a Soul.*

From what we have said in the preceding section of this chapter it is clear that every recognition involves some localization in time. But if it is understood to mean the reproduction of past experiences *in the order in which they have occurred,* such "localization in time" is *neither required nor sufficient* for memory proper.

It is not required. I may remember distinctly a definite past event in my history without being able to recall the events which immediately preceded or followed it. This is a mere detail of recall and, as stated before, recall is in most instances incomplete.

It is not sufficient. For the recall of past experiences in the order in which they have actually occurred, is no memory proper unless they are referred to *my* past. In short, besides retention and recall, memory proper involves the three facts implied in recognition, just as we explained them in the previous section. The Ego-problem and its implications cannot be eliminated from the problem of memory by the "temporal-sign theory" or any other attempt of associationists.

When we see an object that we have seen *frequently* before, there occurs *no exact localization in time.* We express the fact of recognition in such cases by saying that the object is *familiar* to us. We are told by psychologists of the associationist school that *"the familiarity mark"* which thus accrues to our present experience is the essential feature in the explanation of recognition. In detail, we are told that a friend, for instance, whom I meet and whom I have frequently met before, arouses not merely definite sensations and their associated processes but also feelings, say the feeling of pleasantness. Among these feelings is that of "familiarity." It is described as a glow of warmth, a feeling of intimacy, a sense of ownership, an "at-home" feeling, an "of-course" feeling, etc. *This feeling is said to be the essential feature of recognition.* We do not deny that on recognizing a friend we have a feeling of pleasantness. But no elaborate analysis is required to see that the said "familiarity mark" *is but another way of stating that "I have seen my friend frequently before."* This is the fact of recognition which must be explained and *the explanation but restates that fact.* Of course, we are next dragged into the metaphysical darkroom of the psychology of "meaning." There we are told that the sum total of processes which accrue by association to my present experience "means" recognition. This is the general formula which extricates sensationalists out of all their difficulties.

8. Direct and Indirect Recognition. No matter how we recall a past event, its recognition is either direct or indirect. *We call recognition direct when a past event is referred to my past, that is, attached to the Ego, in its own right and without the help of an associate with which that event was connected.* When, however, the only reason for referring an event to my past is, because this event is connected with *another event* which I recognize directly, then we speak of *indirect recognition.* Thus, for instance, when confronted with the statement that I did this or that on July 4, 1900, I may be simply unable either to affirm or deny the fact. Let us call this fact in question X. I am asked next whether I do not remember another fact in my history, namely, Y. Immediately and without further ado I recognize fact Y. Now this *fact Y, recognized in its own right, "reminds" me of fact X.* For — so I reason — Y could not possibly have occurred without X. From this I conclude that also X has occurred as an event in my history.

We may diagram the two forms of recognition by the formulas: Y + Ego, and X + (Y + Ego). The plus sign merely denotes conscious association. In direct recognition it is *the immediate association of Y with the Ego* that makes it possible for me to recognize Y. But in the case of indirect recognition it is *the association of Y with* (X + Ego) that brings about recognition. Many of our recognitions are of the indirect type. It is important to note, however, that every indirect recognition supposes a direct recognition. Hence *associationists derive no benefit from an appeal to indirect recognition when they attempt to explain away the Ego-problem.* Here again we are dragged into the metaphysical darkroom of the psychology of "meaning." There we are told that X + Y *"means"* Ego. In this instance the subterfuge is peculiarly odd as I became aware of the Ego before X appeared on the scene, namely, when I recognized Y.

9. Errors of Recognition — Paramnesia. If we relied exclusively on *direct* recognition when saying that we saw this or that before, and if we never said so unless this direct recognition was *clear,* there would never occur an error in recognition. But the trouble is that we frequently make use of indirect recognition and our direct recognition is sometimes far from clear. Thus *inference and dimness of direct recognition become fruitful sources of error.*

I argued "Y could not possibly have happened unless also X had occurred." If this is correct, also my inference is correct. But is it really *impossible* that Y could have occurred without X? Is there no other explanation? Then, again, Y, *which I see now, consists of definite elements, say a, b, c, D.* What I really experienced before consisted of the elements *a, b, c, E.* In other words, what I experience now is only *similar* to what I experienced before. There is only *partial identity* between my present experience and that which I had before. If I am careful, I state my recognition just in these terms. Instead of saying that I experienced Y before, I will say that I experienced *something similar* to Y before. But frequently we are not careful in our statements of recognition and thus *we mistake a, b. c, D, for a, b, c, E.* Hence all the discrepancies in the testimonies of different witnesses, all of whom may be perfectly sincere.

There is a curious experience which many persons have at times and which in popular literature is surrounded with a good deal of mystery. The facts are thus described by Dickens in his *David Copperfield:* "We have all some experience of a feeling that comes over us occasionally, of what we are saying and doing having been said and done before, in a remote age — of our having been surrounded, dim ages ago, by the same faces, objects and circumstances — of our knowing perfectly what will be said next, as if we suddenly remembered it." To explain such mysterious occurrences some recondite facts of brain physiology have been invoked. But really there is no mystery at all. *What happens in such instances is very much akin to what happens a hundred times over to habitual liars, especially of the cheerful variety: the*

story-tellers. Suppose they begin with a real incident, telling it
well and to their full satisfaction. Reviewing the story before the
next recital they find that they can improve upon it by this addition, this omission, this transposition or substitution. They do so
in their next recounting of it. Of course, they tell their stories
often; they will not be limited in the "once-a-month" rule. The
result is, that after some time they really do not know any more
which is which. *Thus they come to believe their own inventions:
a typical case of false recognition.* It has been said that such persons are really incapable of telling the truth even if they try to
do so now. And to a great extent this is correct. They may be
perfectly sincere when they say "This reminds me" — that's the
way they generally begin their stories.

Substantially the same thing occurs in the phenomenon of
"paramnesia" referred to. The present fact which "reminds them"
consists of the elements *a, b, c, D,* and the fact of which they are
reminded consisted of the elements *a, b, c, E.* The "reminding"
is *not very clear* and thus false recognition results. All cases of
this mysterious paramnesia which have been analyzed, can be
reduced to this general formula.[5]

10. Sensory Memory. The *mere retention and recall of past
sensations* is sometimes designated *sensory memory.* Its result is
the "memory-image" discussed in the chapter on Imagination.
When such a memory-image is accompanied by recognition, it is,
of course, a case of memory proper.

We have stated frequently that in our adult experience we
never have a mere sensation technically so called. It always occurs as a part of a more complex process. The same is true of
sensory memory as above defined. Whenever we recall past
sensations we normally recall also some of the thoughts which
were connected with these sensations.

*The nearest approach to sensory memory, as above defined, is
the retention and the recall of a series of nonsense syllables,* that is,
syllables which are not used as signs of anything beyond them-

[5] *American Journal of Psychology,* Vol. 24 (1913), pp. 56 sqq.

selves. Accordingly, nonsense syllables, such as riz, tas, wog, etc.,
have been extensively used in the experimental investigation of
sensory memory. The purpose of this experimental investigation is,
to *determine and measure the strength of purely sensory associations.* Also isolated letters or disconnected words may be used for
the same purpose. We say "isolated" and "disconnected." For the
proviso is that in learning a series of words we do not establish
rational connections between the members of the series. This is
important. For *rational associations are a most powerful factor of
retention and recall even of sensory material.* Accordingly, this
factor must be eliminated lest we ascribe to sensory association
what is really due to rational associations. A student who memorizes a poem or a portion of his textbook *verbatim,* with little or
no attention to the thoughts expressed, deprives himself of this
most powerful factor of retention and recall and relies almost exclusively on the strength of sensory associations. The same is true
of one who memorizes a series of foreign words together with
their English equivalents, but apart from the context in which
they occur. Hence, the fact that many students after several years
spent in the study of a foreign language know little more than
they did when starting their lessons.

Sensory memory, *as it actually occurs in our adult experience,*
may be more accurately defined as that form of memory in which
retention and recall are *mainly* dependent on sensory associations.
We say *mainly.* For the retention and the recall even of sensory
material depend on a number of other factors besides sensory
association. Apart from rational associations, which are never entirely eliminated in our normal adult experience, *voluntary control* is a most important factor, as we pointed out in the chapter
on Imagination. Laboratory findings have shown that *the intention to learn* has a great deal to do with the learning process.
Mere repetition is not as effective as repetition with the intention
to learn. Thus, for instance, a subject was made to repeat a series of
nonsense syllables in the usual manner. Being a foreigner, he had
not understood the instruction of the experimenter properly. He
read the series an unusual number of times. Then he was stopped

and asked whether he could not yet repeat it by heart. Surprised, he asked, "Am I supposed to learn this by heart?" Being told that this was the very purpose of the procedure, he secured the desired result by a few more repetitions. Even *the intention to "learn for good"* is more effective than the mere intention to learn. This, too, is one of the laboratory findings.[6] The obvious conclusion from all these data is, that *memory, even sensory memory, presents a problem which is far more complex than it is in the metaphysical speculations of sensationalists.*

Before leaving the subject of sensory memory, we must point out an abuse of nonsense syllables in the investigation of memory. It has been said that it is the nonsense syllables that have mainly helped us to our present knowledge of the mechanics of reproduction. An elementary rule of laboratory procedure will enable the student to judge about the truth of this generalization. If we want to study a phenomenon in the laboratory, we arbitrarily create, and vary systematically, the conditions under which that phenomenon is expected to occur and then observe and describe the phenomenon. *If, therefore, we eliminate of set purpose a definite phenomenon, say thought and its rational associations, we cannot say that our laboratory procedure has thrown light on the nature of rational associations or on the mechanism by which we reproduce thoughts.* From this it will be seen that the above statement concerning nonsense syllables is an unwarranted generalization. It is moreover, directly contradicted by facts as we shall point out presently.

11. Logical memory is that form of memory in which retention and recall are *mainly* dependent on intellectual associations. By intellectual associations we denote that fact that *we establish relations among the contents of simultaneous or successive experiences.* We say, we *establish* these relations. For the number of relations which exist and of which we may think is very great. Such are, for instance, the relations of similarity and difference, cause and effect, means and end, a whole and its parts, a genus

---

[6] Cf. Meumann. *Oekonomie u. Technik des Gedächtnisses* (3rd ed.), pp. 42–45.

and its species, a subject and its attributes, a general law and its particular applications, a thesis and its proof, and so forth and so on. It depends, of course, on the direction of the attention of each individual, which one of these relations reaches his focus of attention here and now. None of them may succeed in doing so. But if any particular relation is thus focalized, then this fact constitutes *a new psychological link* between the objects thought of in this relation, and becomes a new factor of their retention and recall. We say *a new psychological link*. That is to say, it is a link altogether distinct from that which arises from the fact that the contents of our experience have occurred simultaneously or in immediate succession. Laboratory findings have in this regard confirmed the data of our daily experience.

In establishing intellectual associations we may proceed in a haphazard and desultory way or systematically. According as we do the one thing or the other, recall will be *desultory* or *systematic,* as we have explained before.

Undoubtedly much of what we know is remembered as a result of intellectual associations of the desultory kind. Thus, to use the illustration of Aristotle, one may pass "from milk to the suggested idea of white, from white to air, from air to moist, and from this one recalls the late autumn, which is the season one was trying to think of." What is logically connected in such a series is not the series as a whole, but each individual pair of the series. Considered as a whole, the series may be a veritable hodge podge. This is the weak point of intellectual associations of the desultory kind. When the contingency arises that a series of heterogeneous material is to be learned, it may be useful deliberately to establish such desultory associations. But even then the time spent in artificially establishing them is in most instances more profitably spent by learning such a series after the manner of nonsense syllables.

The most powerful intellectual associations are those which connect all the units of a memory task into a system. A mathematical demonstration is an ideal instance of such a system Every

step in such a demonstration has a definite logical relation to
every other step. Once the fixed interrelations of these steps are
clearly grasped, any one of the steps will lead to the reconstruction of the whole system. Hence the notable fact, pointed out by
Aristotle, that "such things as have a fixed order are easily remembered, as for instance mathematical truths."

*We rely principally on logical memory in the study of all the
sciences.* For to study a scientific subject means to find out, and
to impress upon the mind, the logical arrangement of the thoughts
as presented, for instance, in an orderly discussion of that subject.
*It is the logical arrangement of the thoughts which keeps them
chained together when they are retained and which raises
them to the surface again when they are recalled.* From this it
will be seen that the cultivation of logical memory is the first
requisite of every successful college and university student.

12. Rote memory, in the ordinary acceptation of the term,
is that form of memory in which retention and recall are effected
by rote, that is, *the repetition of words with slight attention to
the thoughts that are expressed by them.* This repetition strengthens the sensory associations which connect the words into a
series. From this it will be seen that rote memory, as defined, is
really synonymous with sensory memory.

In a wider sense of the term rote memory is *a combination of
logical and sensory memory.* Whenever the memory task consists
of meaningful material — be it a poem, a speech, or anything else
— it is not wise to memorize *verbatim* before the thoughts expressed by the words, their grouping and logical connections, are
clearly understood. Once they are understood, the intellectual
associations are established and remain a factor of verbal memory. If entirely new material is to be learned, the first readings of
it are generally employed in familiarizing ourselves with the
thoughts expressed and with the *plan* according to which they
are grouped. From this it will be seen why *the piecemeal learning of a poem or speech is less effective than the memorizing of
the task as a whole.* It will be seen, further, that the successive

readings of a poem are of very *unequal* value. Hence, the number of readings required for memorizing a poem or for relearning it after it has been forgotten, are *not an exact measure* of the learning process. This leads us to the so-called "curve of forgetting."

13. The Curve of Forgetting. Many attempts have been made to *measure* the retention of material learned and to state the results in the form of a curve. From all we have said so far, it is clear that there cannot be *one* curve of forgetting. The ability of a person to recall *the exact words* by which thoughts are expressed is one thing, and his ability to recall *the thoughts themselves* independently of the wording is quite another. The curve of forgetting will differ considerably according as we test the one or the other. The curve will also differ with other factors of retention and recall — with *the method employed in first learning* a memory task, *the degree of mastery* attained in the initial learning, *the speed* with which the original learning was accomplished, the nature and amount of work in which the person was engaged *between the initial learning and the test applied,* the *method used in testing,* etc.

One factor of retention must be emphasized. It may be inferred from the experimental data obtained by Ebbinghaus and Radosavljevich. A glance at Figure 41 will reveal the surprising fact that after 24 hours considerably more was retained than after 8 hours. *These 24 hours include a period of sleep.* The main significance of sleep is that during this period our nervous system is thoroughly cleansed. The removal of the waste products of metabolism goes on all the time. But this removal, as it occurs during waking hours, is not thorough enough. Our brain may be likened to our living room. Dust accumulates and, if we are careful, we remove it every day. This, however, does not suffice. From time to time the room needs a more thorough cleaning. That is secured for our brain by a good night's rest. This is the only way in which we can explain the fact that more is retained after 24 hours than after 8 hours. Further data concerning the beneficial effect of sleep are contained in the article "Obliviscence during Sleep and Waking," by Jenkins and Dallenbach, in *American Journal of Psychology.*[7]

The mode of procedure in the experiments of Radosavljevich was this. A number of subjects learned a series of nonsense syl-

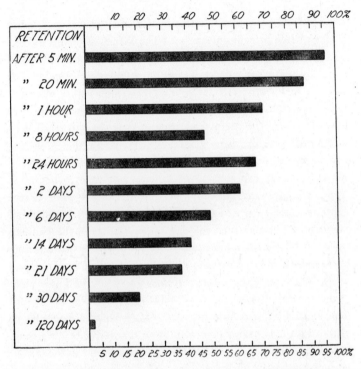

FIG. 41. Curve of Forgetting, based on experiments with nonsense syllables (cf. Meumann, *Oekonomie,* etc., p. 247).

lables or a poem *"completely,"* that is, until they were able to recite it faultlessly once. When this was accomplished the learning process was discontinued. After 5 minutes some of the subjects were requested to recite the memory task again. They had to relearn it. Retention was determined by the number of repetitions which were *saved* in relearning the task. Other subjects

[7]1924, 35:605-612.

were tested in a similar manner after 20 minutes, others again after an hour, and so on. In this way the curve of forgetting was made.

Ballard, in 1913, published the results of experiments on memory which differed considerably from those obtained by Ebbinghaus and his successors. The mode of procedure was as follows: A typewritten copy of a poem, say "The Wreck of the Hesperus," was given to each of a number of children. The poem was read aloud by the experimenter. Then the children were allowed 15 minutes to memorize it. After the typewritten copies were collected, the children were instructed to write down whatever they remembered of the poem. The amount thus actually recalled by any particular child was called 100 per cent for that child. As will be seen from this, *the first learning was not "complete"* as in the case of the experiments of Ebbinghaus, but *"incomplete."* The next day — without any previous warning — some of the children were requested to write down what they could recall now of the poem learned the day before. Others of the children were tested in a similar manner two days after the first learning of the poem; others again three days after the first learning, and so on *The remarkable result was that some children* knew more of the poem on the second, third, fourth, and even on the seventh day than they did on the first day. Other children knew about as much on these subsequent days as on the day of first learning. It was found that the younger children gained most in the second reproduction.

Ballard obtained similar results with children when the memory task consisted of nonsense material. It is to be noted, however, that he did not use nonsense syllables but nonsense verses. He gives the following specimen:

> "Inka rima rinka ro,
> Banim bokie salib so,
> Bick bock, sec sim,
> Thigger thogger, donner dim.

Billin fimpol en sol mun
Sarn il wotlip discol dun,
Flom flam, sen mol simp,
Disper bo rin sopper timp.

Som lep raccal nes lo tad,
Beslo delpit fixil nad.
Tamp rilk, lectom bish,
Entoc riplam in sal rish."

Plainly the sing-song, the jingle, the rhythm, the rimes, the alliterations interested the children. *And whatever interests is better retained.*

Other investigators experimenting with *children* in the same manner have confirmed the data of Ballard. Similar experiments with *adults* had not the same results. The reader who desires further details concerning these interesting experiments is referred to the monograph of Ballard,[8] or to the somewhat detailed summary of these experiments contained in *The Foundations of Experimental Psychology*,[9] edited by Carl Murchison.

Ballard tries to account for the increase in retention by assuming that there occurs a progressive consolidation in the neural processes involved in learning. That is to say, he supposes that the neural processes continue to "set" for an appreciable time after the period of first learning. This assumption seems very plausible but it hardly explains all the details of the experimental results. Only by further experimentation can we come to a fuller appreciation of all the factors involved. But one thing is abundantly clear from the experiments of Ballard and his successors, namely, that *it is not as simple to make a "curve of forgetting" even in the case of rote memory, as it was supposed after the first investigation of memory by Ebbinghaus.*

A similar remark applies to a problem which has been dis-

[8]Monograph Supplement No. 1, *British Journal of Psychology* (1913).
[9]Pp. 608 sqq.

cussed, namely, *What is the best method of memorizing?* To this question no answer can be given which is universally valid. It is like asking: Which is the best pair of shoes to wear? *That depends on the purpose* for which you want the pair of shoes. For tennis playing a different pair will be required than for organ playing, walking, dancing, etc. So it is with the best method of memorizing. But the experimental results described will bear out the statement that *"cramming" shortly before a test is very unsatisfactory, if the matter learned is to be a permanent possession.* What is called "intensive study" is mostly "intensive waste of time."

14. **Mechanical memory** is that form of memory in which recall is *automatic* and takes the form of *a series of coördinated movements.* We may "know" a poem so well that we can recite it without thinking either of the words as they follow one another or of the thoughts expressed by them. Recital in such a case is a purely neuromuscular transaction. All that our conscious processes — that is, those in the focus of attention — have to do with such a neuromuscular transaction is this: We must *start* the series of movements; we must make up our minds to recite the poem. This done, we may become inert listeners or we may even divert our attention to something very different. The recital takes care of itself. This will occur all the more accurately, the more completely we abstain from any attempt to recall voluntarily what word comes next. In fact, such an attempt may stop the working of the neuromuscular machinery altogether. The only assurance we then have of having recited correctly, is derived by *inference* from the fact that we have not interfered with the machinery. In other words, recognition, if present at all, comes to us only *post factum:* after recall and by inference from the fact of mechanical recall.

It is only in rare cases that an entire memory task — a whole poem or speech — can be recalled in a manner so thoroughly mechanical as is here described. But *portions* of almost anything that we know *verbatim* are thus recalled, or at least we are capable of thus reciting them. Once we are started on a phrase, a line, a paragraph, or a verse, one word gives the next so that we can, if we choose, go through that portion without thinking either of the words or of the thoughts expressed by them.

Mechanical memory, as a supplement to conscious memory, plays a rather important rôle in our whole life. A good deal of what we are said to "know" or to have "learned" or to "remember," resolves itself in scientific terms into neuromuscular habits. A pianist must rely as much on his *"finger memory"* as on his conscious memory. So must a telegrapher, a stenographer, and a typist. In all of us mechanical memory must frequently fill out the gaps of conscious memory. For details concerning practice curves the reader is referred to *Foundations in Experimental Psychology,* pp. 572 sqq.

The nature of this mechanical memory is not changed in the very least by the fact that the muscles involved are now those of the vocal organs, now those of the fingers, hands, arms, or feet. Thus, for instance, much of our "knowledge" of correct spelling is simply a matter of "finger memory." When asked how this or that word is spelled, we may be completely at a loss for an answer. Our conscious memory fails us. But let the same word occur in a sentence we are writing or typewriting, *our fingers will spell correctly, provided we do not hesitate or question.* And so it is in a thousand other cases in which we make use of what we are popularly said to "know" or to have "learned" or to "remember."

From this it will be seen that "learning" is far from being a univocal term. The discovery of new relations between objects by means of original research, the acquisition of scientific knowledge established by others, the formation of new sensory associations, the gradual formation of a neuromuscular habit: all these heterogeneous processes, and a few others besides, are denoted by one and the same term *learning. This equivocal usage is a fruitful source of quibbling.* Much of the "evidence" for animal intelligence, for instance, consists of verbal quibbles.

Analogous to mechanical memory is the term *organic memory.* It is used to denote *the periodic reappearance of conditions once created in the nervous system.* Of course, it is not memory proper. The fact, that certain nervous functions recur periodically, may account for some puzzling phenomena in the instinctive life of animals. Perhaps their "time-sense" is merely a matter of "organic memory."

15. Two Outstanding Problems of Memory. There are two problems suggested by the facts of memory which require a more detailed consideration than they have received in this chapter. They are (1) *the nature of thought* and its distinction from our sensory experiences, and (2) *the Ego-problem* or the problem of the unity of consciousness. We shall deal with the first problem at great length in later chapters. A thorough discussion of the second problem is impossible without entering the domain of philosophy. The reader is referred to the monograph published by the present writer under the title *Psychology Without a Soul.*

References for Further Reading

J. Froebes, S.J., *Lehrbuch der Experimentellen Psychologie,* Vol. II (1929), pp. 124 sqq.

E. Meumann. *Oekonomie u. Technik des Gedächtnisses,* 3rd ed. (1912).

W. S. Hunter, "Experimental Studies of Learning," (Chap. 15, in *Foundations of Experimental Psychology,* edited by C. Murchison (1929).

H. J. Watt, *The Economy and Training of Memory* (1909).

Chapter XI

ATTENTION

1. The Foreground and Background of Our Sensory Experience. Our account of sensation would be very incomplete, if we were simply to say that an object by its activity causes a definite change in a sense-organ and that the latter then responds to this change by a conscious sensation. For there are a great many objects which act simultaneously on one and the same sense-organ and all the other sense-organs are acted on at the same time by a host of other objects. If the great variety of changes thus brought about simultaneously in the various sense-organs were answered each by a conscious sensation, chaos would be the inevitable result. But, as a matter of fact, our normal sensory experience is far from being a chaos. Only a limited number of objects succeed at any given time in gaining an entrance into our conscious life. Their rivals are for the time being more or less rigidly excluded or, maybe, put on the waiting list. Now, the object, or the definite group of objects, which at any given time successfully enters into our conscious life is "attended to," the others are "not attended to"; they are ignored.

There are, then, to use a figure of speech, always a foreground and a background in our normal sensory experience, the foreground being occupied by the favored few, the background by those rejected or on the waiting list. For those rejected remain there and hammer away as vigorously as before at the gates of our senses and, what is more, they are actually heard, seen, and felt, though they are not attended to. As you read this page, the ticking of the clock in the room is not in the focus of attention. The rumble of the street cars and the rest of the city hubbub are not even on the waiting list. But if all these noises stopped suddenly, you would find out very soon that something would be lacking in your experience, namely, the background of rejected sensations, which belong as much to your normal experience as the foreground. Moreover, the next moment may bring a reversal of things: the present occupant of the foreground may change places with any one of those in the background.

2. **The Foreground and Background of Thought.** A similar condition prevails when we are thinking of some object not present to our senses or incapable of being thus presented, as when we are thinking of some scientific or philosophic problem. Then not only most objects of sense — possibly all of them — recede to the background, but with them also many objects of thought and fancy. For it is a well-known fact that none of us can think of any subject for a length of time without distractions. This means that the machinery of association introduces into our mind many an irrelevant thought and fancy which we are struggling to keep in the background, but which succeeds nevertheless — ever and anon — in actually occupying the foreground.

It would be far from an accurate description of our intellectual life, as it actually occurs, if we were simply to say that by some process of association the idea of a definite object arises in our mind, and this, in turn, by force of association, calls up the idea of another object, and thus, as one brain cell awakens another in regular succession, our ideas pass in Indian file before our mind. There are a great many things to be said against such a description of our rational life. Here it may suffice to point out that all objects of thought and fancy are interconnected in a thousand different ways and have been thus associated in our past experience. Hence, it would be very surprising indeed, if the thought of a definite object called up in our mind only that associate which fits here and now into the rational sequence of thought. If associations are effective, they must be effective in various directions. If, however, all of them were *equally* effective, then indeed no rational sequence of thought would be possible.

The finished product of our mental work as presented, for instance, in an orderly essay, is one thing, and the actual workshop conditions under which it arose are quite another. An orderly essay presents only the foreground of thought, and that considerably idealized. For many irrelevant intermezzos, breaking up the rational sequence of thought, are carefully eliminated. But there was also a background, and most writers would probably be mortified if it, too, were put on paper. And justly so. For thus equal emphasis would be given to the irrelevant thoughts and fancies and to the orderly sequence of thoughts. But this was not so. The irrelevant thoughts, though present, were not attended to, except during the pardonable intermezzos. The objects of the writer's attention were those presented in the orderly essay. He "minded" the latter; he "did not mind" the former.

3. **The Narrowness of Consciousness.** These familiar facts are not explained but only called by another name, when we refer to them as "the narrowness of consciousness." Why is our consciousness so narrow? Why are not the gates of our senses equally open to all comers, and why are not all processes of association equally effective?

Is it a question of strength among the rival claimants of attention, so that those who hammer hardest force their way into our conscious experience? This is indeed at times the case, but it is far from being universally true. We may pick out, for instance, a faint noise, the ticking of a watch, as the object of attention.

Or is it a question of voluntary choice among objects, so that we ourselves open the gates of our senses for one object and lock them against all others, and voluntarily direct the processes of thought into definite channels? This again is true at times, but not universally. For frequently we are simply overpowered by an object which "attracts" our attention, at least for the time being. In other words, we must recognize the fact that there are two kinds of attention, voluntary and involuntary.

Nor can it be said that those objects successfully enter into our conscious life which are "interesting," that is, appealing to our natural or acquired tendencies. For a repulsive object may force its way into our mind, although it cannot be brought or kept voluntarily, unless it derive some interest from some other object, inherently interesting. In other words, interest is indeed an important factor of attention, but attention itself is not interest.

Nor, again, can it be said that those objects occupy the foreground of our consciousness which are presented most clearly to the senses or the intellect. For we may select a vague and undefined object for attention. Clearness is rather an effect of attention, not an essential feature of attention itself, unless indeed by clearness of an object nothing else is meant than that here and now it occupies the foreground of consciousness. For thereby also a vague object acquires prominence over the neglected background.

Nor, finally, should attention be confounded with the characteristic bodily attitudes, which we assume — for the most part instinctively — when we attend to some object of sense or thought. These attitudes are rather accompaniments of attention: adjustments of the sense-organs and of the whole body for the favorable reception of helpful stimuli and the exclusion of distracting ones. As a result they become signs for us by which we judge whether others are attentive or not. In Scholastic terminology these bodily attitudes were aptly designated "external attention" in opposition to attention proper or "internal attention." By a voluntary effort, moreover, we can also attend to an object of sense for which the sense-organ is not adjusted. Such was, for instance, the case in our experiments on double images (p. 145).

4. What is Attention? Accordingly, neither voluntary choice nor interest nor bodily attitudes on our part, nor force nor clearness on the part of the object, are essential features of attention. What, then, is the essential feature present in all states of attention? What is attention?

We cannot define attention in any other way than by the use of some metaphor. Thus we say that we "direct" or "concentrate" or "focus" our mind on one object and not on others. Or we say that our mind is "occupied by," or "absorbed in," one object in preference to or to the entire exclusion of others. Or, again, we say that an object moves to the "foreground of consciousness," while others stay in its "background." Now, when we come to analyze these metaphors, and realize that they must fit both voluntary and involuntary attention, attention both to an "interesting" and to a "repulsive" object, to a "clear" as well as to a "vague and undefined" object, we find that we are only using circumlocutions for stating again the marvelous fact of the "narrowness of consciousness." In other words, we simply restate the fact that out of a multitude of stimuli simultaneously bombarding our senses, and out of several processes of association going on simultaneously, only one or a limited number is for the time being successful in gaining an entrance into our conscious life, and the others — well, they are not successful here and now. And this was the fact with which we started out.

In other words, attention is a primitive and irreducible fact of our experience which is none the less mysterious because it is so familiar to us. We do not mean to clarify this mystery, but simply to embody all the above facts in a shorthand phrase when we "define" attention as *the voluntary or involuntary direction of our mind toward one object of sense or thought, or a definite group of such objects, to the more or less complete exclusion of all others.*

5. Subconscious Sensations, Fancies, and Thoughts. Familiar phenomena, no matter how mysterious and wonderful they may be, come to us as a matter of course. But when the same phenomena are presented to us under unusual conditions, we are puzzled and liable to accept the most grotesque interpretations put upon them. So it is in the realm of physical phenomena, and so it is in the realm of psychology.

The phenomena of hypnotism, table-turning, Ouija-board writing and all other forms of automatic writing are so weird and extraordinary, that by some they are thought to be of their very nature outside the realm of psychological inquiry, while others see in them evidences of a most outlandish theory, namely, that of the "double Ego" or "double personality," the one conscious or normal, the other subconscious or abnormal. The truth here, as elsewhere, lies in the middle.

It is not our purpose at present to inquire into the real nature of these weird phenomena. Here it may suffice to say that hypnosis is a condition of unusual "narrow-mindedness" brought about by suggestion. The consciousness of a person in this condition is narrowed down to the hypnotizer and whatever he suggests. No other object has a ghost of a chance to come within the focus of his attention. Automatic writing in its *initial stage* is simply the result of the "motor power" of images explained in the chapter on Imagination. In its most *advanced stage* it supposes a condition substantially the same as hypnotic trance and this condition is brought about by autosuggestion. It is in this advanced stage that automatic writers are capable of recalling events which they could not possibly recall under normal conditions. This introduces us to two problems which are relevant to the subject matter of this chapter. The problems are: (1) Is there such a thing as a subconscious sensation or thought? And if so, (2) are we ever guided in our outward actions by subconscious cognitions?

The reader who has carefully followed our discussion in the previous paragraphs cannot be in doubt as to what the answer to the first question should be. Of course, there are subconscious sensations and thoughts, and not only by way of exception, but we are never without them. There are always a foreground and a background in our conscious life. Subconscious sensations and thoughts are but other names for this background.

There are certain curious facts of "immediate memory" which cannot be explained except in the hypothesis of subconscious cognitions *We sometimes become conscious of an experience only when it is recalled shortly after it has occurred*. Thus, for instance, when walking on the street, you may pass somebody without recognizing or even noticing him. Of course, if your eyes were not closed, he made an impression upon them. But absorbed as you are in your own thoughts, you have seen him as if you saw him not. When, however, he is two or three steps behind you, his features and manner of walking arise clearly in your mind. You recognize him as Mr. So-and-so. Promptly you turn around to address him. Or you may have an appointment for 4 p.m.

Busy as you are with your work you entirely fail to notice the clock striking that hour. Right after, however, you become aware of the fact. So distinctly are the past sounds recalled that you can count them with precision. How could you recall sounds which you never "heard"? But you have heard them as if you heard them not. Your experience reaches the focus of attention only when it is recalled.

In discussing a scientific subject *we may observe the rules of grammar and of style without paying explicit attention to them.* Our attention may be focused exclusively on the subject under discussion. However, the observance of the rules of grammar can never become as mechanical as the recital of a poem. For in constructing the sentences we accommodate ourselves to the requirements of each case. The rules, then, must in some way be present to our mind. And yet they are not in the focus of attention. Such thoughts are "subconscious thoughts." *All "implicit" knowledge is of this kind.*

6. Subconscious Activities. As to the second question, a little reflection will show that this, too, must be answered in the affirmative. You may be engaged in an animated discussion with your friend while walking up and down with him in the garden, avoiding obstacles as you go along, and turning at the right time. In addition, you may be playing with the button of your coat, slipping it alternately through its proper hole and back again, incidentally interrupting this operation by driving away a fly that insists on landing on your nose — and all this with your mind most intently focused on the subject of your discussion.

Now, you cannot avoid obstacles in walking and turn in the right place without being guided in these operations by some cognition of the obstacles and the place for turning. Yet none of these cognitions is here and now in the focus of attention. In walking, too, you feel the ground at every step. The contractions of your muscles cause likewise a number of sensations. You feel also the button and your coat. If your hands and feet became suddenly deprived of sensation, you could not perform any of these operations. The plain fact is that the various sensations mentioned are indispensable links in the chain of movements which make up the simple acts of walking and buttoning the coat.

What adds to the marvel of your performance is that the acts of walking and buttoning your coat are — physiologically considered — far from being as simple as we are liable to think. They require a great many coördinated movements, too complex to be explained here. And when these operations were performed for the first time in your life, they required a good deal of concentrated attention. There were, moreover, many attendants there to see that these feats were done right. Now as you are discussing a scientific problem with your friend, these operations and the various sensations with which they are linked, never come to the foreground of your attention *You are guided in these operations by subconscious sensations.*

Subconscious fancies and thoughts are no less effective in guiding outward actions. You may be absorbed in reading an interesting novel in the library and be not even aware that you are annoying your friend, who likewise is trying to read, while unwittingly you drum with your fingers a familiar tune that is running through your head. If you are a pianist, you may under the same conditions, and just as unwittingly, execute the complicated series of movements involved in playing on an imaginary keyboard the familiar piece of music that you hear in the background of your imagination. Such and a thousand other similar occurrences of our daily life leave no room for doubting that subconscious cognitions of all kinds may, and frequently do, guide us in performance of outward actions, and sometimes of highly complicated ones. The following quotation from the *American Journal of Psychology*[1] is pertinent.

"Helen Keller's well-known unconscious plagiarism at the age of twelve, which caused her so much unjust suffering, furnishes an excellent example of such a case in which the associations with the past having been lost, a story written by Miss Canby was reproduced as her own. The circumstances were as follows: The

---

[1] Vol. 24, p. 52. "Paramnesia in Daily Life," by T. L. Smith.

autumn after Helen had first learned to speak, she spent summer and fall at the summer home of her family in Alabama and Miss Sullivan described to her, in her usual vivid fashion, the beauties of the autumn foliage. Helen wrote a little story called the "Frost King" which she sent to Dr. Anagnos as a birthday present. The story was a remarkable production for any twelve-year-old child; and for a blind child, a marvel, abounding as it did in vivid descriptions of color. Dr. Anagnos was greatly pleased with it and published it in *The Mentor*. A few weeks later this story was discovered to be an almost *verbatim* reproduction of a story written years before by Margaret T. Canby and published in a book called *Birdie and His Friends*. Miss Sullivan had never seen this book and Helen, though finally convinced that she did not originate the story, could recall absolutely nothing of the way it had come to her. So far as she was concerned, the story, in spite of all her painful efforts to recall the circumstances by which it had come into her mind, still seemed to be her own creation. The explanation was finally found in the fact that four years before, Helen and Miss Sullivan had spent the summer at Brewster with a friend, Mrs. Hopkins, who possessed a copy of Miss Canby's book and who probably, though she could not definitely recall doing so, read it to Helen during Miss Sullivan's absence on a vacation. Helen had at that time been under Miss Sullivan's instruction scarcely a year and a half and had learned her first word after Miss Sullivan's arrival. The story was read to her by the only means of communication then possible, by spelling the words into her hand. It could have conveyed little or no meaning to her mind, but the spelling of strange words probably amused and interested her. It is little wonder that, when four years later the words came so readily to her pen, all previous associations with them should have been lost and they should seem her own."

7. **Expectant Attention.** We said that certain objects "are on the waiting list." This is more than a mere figure of speech. For our expectations, previous knowledge of all kinds, and ac-

quired mental tendencies are most important factors in determining whether a certain object will pass unnoticed or actually reach
the focus of attention. Hence we speak of expectant attention. Its
influence is to a great extent a matter of daily observation. A
popular adage has it that *the wish is father to the thought.* This
is true not only in the opprobrious sense in which the adage is
mostly used, but also in a very good one. As the matter is of
great theoretic and practical significance we shall describe a simple experiment which will reveal the effects of expectant attention.

On the harmonium hold down the key which corresponds to
c of the small octave (1 in Fig. 42). Be sure to use only one stop,

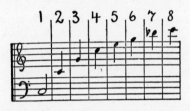

FIG. 42

namely, an 8-foot stop, so that only one tongue is vibrating when
you press the key. The tone produced by the vibrating tongue
seems simple and unitary. As a matter of fact, however, it is a
clang or compound tone, consisting of a number of partial tones,
of which the one indicated by the musical notation is only the
principal or fundamental one. We have explained this in the
chapter on Auditory Sensations.

Now suppose you get the instruction — and this is the instruction in the present experiment — to pay attention to the third
partial of the compound tone you hear, that is, to bring this partial from the background into the foreground of attention. How
are you ever going to carry out this instruction? It is like telling
you to look for Mr. Jones, when you do not know how Mr. Jones
looks nor where he might possibly be. You would not know
that you had found him, even if you came upon him accidentally.

If you are to be successful in your search you must have a pre-

monitory image of the object which you are looking for In the
present experiment you must know beforehand how the said
third partial sounds. It sounds like the tone marked 3 in the accompanying figure.

You insist that you are not a musician and are, therefore, incapable of carrying out the present experiment. The fact is, you
need not be a musician to carry out the experiment, nor does it
denote any hidden musical talent in you, if you are remarkably
successful. It is exclusively a matter of attention. The only thing
in which a good musician is ahead of you — for the purposes of
the present experiment — is this: Once the fundamental tone is
given, the musical notation of its third partial suffices for him to
call up the premonitory image of the sound he expects to single
out by attention. If you are not a musician, then have a musician
friend play for you on the harmonium first the fundamental (1)
and then its third partial (3). Now you know what the latter
sounds like.

Then proceed to the experiment proper. Press down the key
of the fundamental tone again, and at the same time sound, as
softly as possible, the third partial on the harmonium. Discon-
tinuing then the sounding of the partial, listen attentively whether
there is not a similar faint sound to be heard, when you press the
key for the fundamental alone With repeated trials you will be
successful. And when you are successful, you are not imagining a
sound which does not exist in nature, but your imagination and
expectant attention have helped you to single out an extremely
faint sound, which without expectant attention would surely have
passed unnoticed.[2]

It may be well to add that by means of a properly adjusted
Helmholtz resonator any partial tone can be detected with ease.
But this mode of procedure only proves the physical existence
of the partial vibration for which the resonator is adjusted. For
when you hold the resonator to the ear, you really do not hear

---

[2] Cf. Helmholtz, *Sensations of Tone* (translated by Ellis), pp. 49 sqq.

the faint partial of the vibrating tongue, but the comparatively strong sound, produced by resonance in the air column of the resonator.

We said in the chapter on Auditory Sensations that also a chord can be analyzed by attention into its component tone sensations. Proceed as follows: Strike on the harmonium the chord indicated below (2 in Fig. 43), using an 8-foot stop for the experiment. Though four notes are sounding simultaneously, they come to most people as a unit whose component parts are not separately attended to. But we can attend to any one of them in particular, and that with comparative ease, provided we have a

1. The melody you expect to hear. 2. The Chord to be analysed.

FIG. 43

premonitory image of the sound which we wish to single out. To secure this image, play one of the tones of the chord separately, say c'. Knowing now what you expect to hear, strike the chord again and hold it. Direct your attention to the tone whose memory-image you have in mind. *It will now sound louder* than the other tones of the chord, or more correctly, *it will now be in the foreground of attention,* while the other tones recede to the background.

In a similar manner we can single out successively every tone of the chord, so that we hear a sort of simple melody. To do this, play first the melody you expect to hear (1) but play it slowly; then strike the chord and hold it (2). Now pay attention successively to the notes as they follow one another in your memory-image of the melody. By means of expectant attention you thus single out successively the component parts of a chord, which without this expectant attention would have come to you as a unit.[3]

8. "Habitual Setting" of Attention or "Einstellung."
Very much akin to expectant attention is what German psychologist call *Einstellung*. A typical example will show what is meant by this term.

In the part of every orchestra performer the following musical notation (1 in Fig. 44) occurs time and again. Of course, it depends on the clef and the signature (2 and 3 in Fig. 44), placed at the beginning of the musical staff, which note is meant in the part of each performer. The result is that the same musical notation means one note for the violinist, another for the viola player,

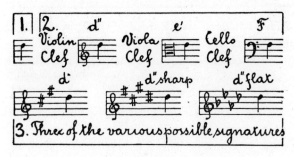

FIG. 44

again another for the cellist, etc. Even for the same performer it means one note in this piece of music, and another in another piece of music. Before starting to play, each performer notes his clef and the particular signature of this piece of music, and thus *sets his attention in a definite direction*. The result is that out of various possible interpretations of this musical notation only that one comes to his mind for which his attention is set and that without ever afterwards referring explicitly to the clef and signature which determine its meaning. As will be seen from this ex-

---

[3] Cf. Titchener, *Experimental Psychology*, p. 111, and Helmholtz, *op. cit.*, p. 59 sq.

ample, *Einstellung* is really nothing else than "habitual expectation" or "habitual setting of attention."

The same factor is present in the conscious life of every individual. The mental habits of men differ as widely as their occupations, and these habits limit each one's horizon and determine his point of view. The chemist lives in a world of his own, the physicist in another, the biologist, the mathematician, the farmer, the tailor, and so forth, each again in another. In other words, each one has acquired a definite turn of mind: his attention is set habitually in a definite direction. Hence it is that one and the same object of sense will be noticed by one and not by another, arouse a definite thought in one and a widely different one in another.

9. Sense-Illusions and Errors of Judgment Due to Expectant Attention. So strong are our expectations in determining the direction of our attention, that many sense-illusions and errors of judgment have their origin here. You may find out experimentally how sense-illusions of this kind arise. Fill a small box with shot. Then take a larger box of the same shape and material, and place enough shot in it that the two boxes are of exactly the same weight. This determination should be made by means of an accurate balance. Now ask someone, who does not know how these boxes were prepared, to lift one after the other and to tell which of the two seems the heavier. It will invariably be found that the smaller box is judged to be decidedly the heavier one. In lifting the small box we experience a certain effort. Seeing the other box of the same material and shape, but larger than the first, we expect to experience more of an effort in trying to raise it. The actual effort falls considerably below our expectation, and as a result we judge the larger box to be the lighter one.

That it is really the said expectation which is responsible for the illusion can be tested in the following manner. Prepare two additional boxes, larger than the first two, and of equal weight, shape, and size. Inclose the small box in one of the latter, the larger one in the other. Then no expectation influences us in testing the weights and the illusion is gone. There may indeed be errors, but just as well in favor of the one as the other box.[4]

Similar sense-illusions of all kinds are due to expectant attention. Children going out in the dark and with their minds filled with ghost stories, will actually "see" what they are only too afraid to see: a ghost. Anything, a white sheet moving in the wind, a shrub, or what not, will be interpreted in accordance with their expectant attention.

Errors of the gravest sort may be likewise due to expectant attention especially if they become habitual and take complete possession of the mind. We all know what bias can do. It blinds its victims to everything that does not agree with their bias, and makes them actually see things which exist only in their prepossessed minds. This is true not only in the realm of religion and politics, but also in the domain of experimental science. The same facts may be investigated by two observers, the one with unwarranted assumptions in his mind, the other without such assumptions and ready to let the facts speak for themselves. The two will differ not only in the interpretation of what they have observed, but in all probability even in the phenomenal description of the facts themselves. Take, for instance, the assumption of evolution. We do not speak here of that form of the theory of evolution, which is kept within the limits of a strictly scientific hypothesis but of that sweeping metaphysical dogma of evolution *which must be true, whatever else may be true.* Investigators who approach psychological facts in this frame of mind, will actually see evidences of the animal ancestry of man where other investigators see none.

10. The Span of Attention. To how many objects of sense or thought can we attend simultaneously? The story is told of Julius Cæsar that he actually dictated four letters, while writing a fifth. Similarly, expert chess players are reported to have played simultaneously five, ten, or even more games blindfolded. But

---

[4]Cf. Witmer, *Analytical Psychology,* p. 20.

here the word *simultaneously* is used in a rather loose sense. What really occurs in these and similar cases is a rapid "oscillation of attention." In other words, there are persons who are remarkable for their ability to turn rapidly from one subject to another. Hence their performances prove rather an extraordinary memory and an unusual flexibility of controlled attention but do not throw any light on our present question.

By way of digression it may be stated here that diametrically opposed to this unusual flexibility of controlled attention is that absolute rigidity of uncontrolled attention which occurs as a pathological condition, namely that of "fixed ideas." The mean between these two extremes is the normal condition which should be aimed at by all. We should never allow ourselves to become so engrossed by any one thing — be it study or play or anything else — that we cannot turn our mind to something else when duty calls.

To return, then, to our original question. It really amounts to this: How large can the "group of objects" be of which we spoke in the definition of attention? How many units may such a group contain, and yet allow us to give *equal* attention to all? Unless this equality in the distribution of attention is included in the question, we have answered it already, when speaking of the foreground and background of attention. For among the things in this background there may be some that are rather near to the foreground, that is, which are somewhat less attended to than the object in the foreground.

Several experimental arrangements — some of them rather elaborate — have been devised to answer the question stated. But the interpretation of some of the experimental data obtained has been justly criticized.[5] We shall not enter into any details but rest satisfied with recording the brief summary of results, as given by Ebbinghaus.

In the case of very simple mental tasks (such as the perception of simple objects of sense, or the making of easy and obvious con-

---

[5]Cf. Ebbinghaus, *Grundzuege der Psychologie,* pp. 591 sqq.

siderations, or the execution of simple routine movements) attention may be easily divided between two, possibly three, independent things.

The more complex, however, a mental task is, that is, the greater the number of parts which it involves, the more it becomes impossible to do justice at the same time to another task. Though attention may then be equally distributed among the different parts of such a complex task, these parts are not focused as independent units but precisely as interconnected parts of one and the same task.

All this, moreover, cannot be done with equal success by every individual nor by the same individual at all times. In other words, there are not only individual differences in this regard but success depends also on the actual condition of the subject at the time of the experiment, particularly as to whether he is fatigued or fresh.[6]

The practical conclusions from the experiments are: (1) In the case of trifling tasks you gain time (or, at least, you lose less), if you do two or three of them simultaneously. Thus, for instance, if you must listen to a twice-told tale, and must read the gossip column of the newspaper for the third time, you may profitably combine the two tasks. (2) If several serious tasks demand your "immediate" attention, the quickest way of doing justice to them all is to do strictly one at a time and each in its proper order. You gain time in this way even for your sports.

11. The Span of Immediate Memory. Another problem of the span of attention is this: How many objects can be presented successively so that all of them remain consciously present to us? In this sense the span of attention is synonymous with the span of immediate memory.

When nonsense syllables are presented for immediate recall, it has been found — and the reader can readily find out for himself — that six constitute about the limit of immediate memory.

---

[6]Cf. Ebbinghaus, *op. cit.*, p. 594.

When a seventh syllable is added, the series falls apart in the experience of most persons. Then retroactive inhibition sets in, as we have explained in the chapter on Memory. If, however, syllables are presented which form a sentence, the number of syllables that can be repeated immediately and without fail is considerably larger. *What keeps the successive syllables together in our mind is the thought expressed by the sentence.* When the thoughts expressed by three sentences are as systematically grouped as they are in a syllogism, an *enormous* number of syllables can come within the limits of immediate memory. Of course, *it is the systematic grouping of the thoughts which keeps these thoughts and even the sensory elements of a syllogism chained together.*

From this it will be seen that immediate memory is *immensely better for thoughts than for sensory experiences.* Thus the facts of immediate memory, just like those of memory proper, emphasize the problem concerning the distinction between thought and sensation.

12. Fluctuations of Voluntary Attention. The most important form of attention, that on which all success in the intellectual and moral advancement of every individual depends, is voluntary attention. If a student can be prevailed upon to concentrate his mind on the subject to be mastered; if one who tries to overcome an evil habit, in every temptation deliberately fixes his mind on the motives which prompted his resolve; if in any enterprise whatever we carry out consistently the golden maxim *Age quod agis,* "Do what you do," that is, do with undivided attention, whatever you do; then success will take care of itself. But the difficulty is in carrying out these precepts. Voluntary attention is difficult, and that for two reasons.

In the first place there are so many claimants to attention, and many of them appeal rather strongly to our natural tendencies. Unless we make an effort and renew this effort frequently, we shall find ourselves distracted and following the line of least resistance. We are only too keenly aware of these fluctuations of voluntary attention from our everyday experience. Unless we are on our guard, we shall find ourselves wool-gathering and dilly-dallying, before we make even the first effort in the right direction. "I know a person," says James, "who will poke the fire, set chairs straight, pick dust specks from the floor, arrange his table, snatch up the newspaper, take down any book which catches his eye, trim his nails, waste the morning *anyhow,* in short, and all without premeditation, simply because the only thing he *ought* to attend to is the preparation of a noonday lesson in formal logic which he detests. Anything but *that!*" Ebbinghaus, quoting this passage, wittily adds that in all probability the reader knows such a person too.

In the second place, though voluntary attention can be "sustained," even for hours together, if its object arouse our interest, it is, strictly speaking, not true that we in such a case pay uninterrupted attention to the same identical and unchanging object. We simply cannot do this except for very brief periods at a time. The most deliberate effort will not carry us further. The object will, in spite of ourselves, periodically drop out of our mind.

Common experience would seem to be against us, for we know that by an effort we are capable of "sustained attention to one and the same object." But there is an ambiguity here in using the term "object." A topic is an object, and its various phases or aspects are objects. If we get interested in anything, it will grow and develop in our mind, and branch out in various directions. In other words, its various phases or aspects will be presented successively to our mind, and thus it will hold our attention. When this takes place, a great multitude of thoughts pass through our mind, each with its own object. But these objects are all phases of one and the same topic. Though thus the direction of our attention is continually changing, we call it "sustained" attention, as long as we revolve the same topic in our mind. As soon as the interest in the topic flags, it ceases to develop and drops out of our mind: we pass to something irrelevant and are "distracted."

From this it will be seen what an important rôle interest

plays in attention. It makes voluntary attention easier and sustained attention possible. Voluntary attention, sustained by interest, gradually shades off into involuntary attention. Once we have launched ourselves on a definite topic with a deliberate effort, we are carried along by the stream of thought it provokes, and this stream of thought can be called voluntary only because it depends on the deliberate effort by which we launched ourselves on this stream. Either the object must be thought-provok-

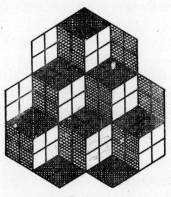

FIG. 45

ing or we must provoke the thought, and it is the continual alternations of these two processes that constitute the fluctuations of voluntary attention.[7]

All this is but an analysis of our common experience in this regard. We may study the matter also experimentally. The accompanying figure (Fig. 45) is an equivocal one, admitting of several spatial interpretations. It is not drawn in true perspective, nor is the shading what it ought to be if the figure were meant to represent solid objects in relief. There are, however, strong suggestions, both as to perspective and shading, of a number of cubical blocks.

---

[7] Cf. James, *Psychology*, pp. 224 sqq.

If we go simply by the data of our immediate experience, prescinding entirely from the criteria of relief which previous experience has furnished us, we can interpret the figure to be just what it is: a geometrical pattern, consisting of 96 diamond-shaped quadrangles, all of the same size, 32 white, 32 light gray, 32 dark gray, juxtaposed in a definite order on a flat surface. *Looking at the figure,* can you really prescind from the criteria of relief, and thus interpret the figure as a flat geometrical pattern? If so, how long? It requires an heroic effort to do this even for a brief period of time. The immediate data of your present experience have been associated a thousand times in the past with the third dimension, with relief. It is extremely difficult to prevent these habitual associates from entering your mind together with the immediate data of your experience.

The experiment is very instructive. We experience here just what happens, whenever we try to direct our mind to any definite object and to keep the latter uninterruptedly in the focus of attention. If the object has had associates in the past — presto! they are called up too. If they are relevant, belonging to the same topic — well, we are not yet distracted. The object only grows and develops in our mind. If, however, the associates are irrelevant, our mind begins to wander after the first effort. Happily the associations which most objects have formed in our past experience are not so deeply rooted as those which we have to contend with in the present experiment. We rarely meet such irrepressible associates.

Yielding to the suggestion of relief, you will interpret the figure as a representation of a number of cubical blocks. Count the blocks! Are there six or seven? As the figure is not drawn in true relief, the suggestion it contains of six blocks is just as strong as that of seven. Which of these two interpretations will come to you first, no one can foretell, at least when you see the figure for the first time and without any definite expectation. But once you have a definite interpretation in your mind, try to keep it voluntarily in your mind as long as possible! How long do you succeed? Possibly even before you have finished counting the blocks, as directed, the aspect of the figure is changed entirely. Instead of six blocks you now see seven, or vice versa. Now try to hold this second interpretation steadily before your mind! Presto, the figure turns over again.

You can study here experimentally, how far an effort of your will can carry you in contending with rival associations. In studying your lesson in logic, or physics, or biology you will come upon many objects which have been associated in the past with other objects. If you are intensely interested in your lesson, the struggle will not be so hard, especially as many of these past associations help to develop the topic which you revolve now in your mind. But you will not succeed in holding an unchanging object in your mind except for very brief periods at a time.

The obvious practical conclusion from these experiments is: Get interested in whatever you study, and try to connect whatever new things you learn with the things you know already, not only with those you have learned in the classroom but with anything and everything that has interested you before. The contagion of interest will spread from one object to another, and thus you make allies of those very associates which might prove your greatest adversaries.[8]

View the following "stereogram" (Fig. 46) by means of the stereoscope. Of course, you cannot possibly combine the right-hand view with the left-hand one, nor are you to attempt this. The instruction in this experiment is, simply to ignore one eye, first the right eye, then the left one. This you can do with more or less success, provided you go at the task with a deliberate effort. The sincerity of this effort, however, will be put to a most severe test.

In the beginning the two columns of print will become hopelessly mixed. After that, one of them will periodically replace the other. This is known as "binocular rivalry." If you want to be successful in reading the text from the beginning to the end with

---

[8] Cf. James, *Talks to Teachers*, pp. 91 sqq.

"I find that I am able to attend voluntarily, now to one and now to the other system of lines; and that then this system remains visible alone for a certain time, while the other completely vanishes. This happens, for example, whenever I try to count the lines first of one and then of the other system. . . . But it is extremely hard to chain the attention down to one of the systems for long, unless we associate with our looking some distinct purpose which keeps the activity of the attention perpetually renewed. Such a one is counting the lines, comparing their intervals, or the like. An equilibrium of the attention, persistent for any length of time, is under no circumstances attainable. The natural tendency of attention when left to itself is to wander to ever new things; and so soon as the interest of its object is over, so soon as nothing new is to be noticed there, it passes, in spite of our will, to something else. *If we wish to keep it upon one and the same object, we must seek constantly to find out something new about the latter,* especially if other impressions attract us away."[9]

Fig. 46. A very unusual "stereogram."

as few interruptions as possible, you must be methodical in the experiment. Thus, for instance, you may profitably read the whole text, before using the stereoscope. Then your expectant attention will help you greatly in carrying out your resolve. Other means to success are indicated in the text of the "stereogram" itself. The latter is really the comment of Helmholtz on an experiment which he performed with the stereogram indicated in Figure 47.

Now perform the same experiment as Helmholtz did. You are to combine binocularly the two systems of lines in Figure 47. In doing so, profit by the preceding comment of Helmholtz. You thus find out experimentally what you must do, if you are in earnest about studying under powerful external distractions. You can find out, too, how to go about thinking or meditating on a

[9]James, *Psychology*, p. 226.

definite topic so as to avoid distractions. If you take no precautions, but simply present the object of thought to your mind, the object will go out in a short time. But if you revolve it in your mind, ask different questions about it (such as "who, what, where, with what aids, why, how, when") you will succeed, that is, more or less. There is no other road to success.

13. Voluntary Attention and the Threshold of Sensation. When discussing Weber's law we said that the threshold of sensation is not a fixed minimal amount of energy which must be

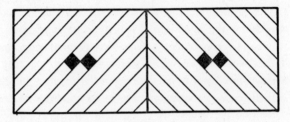

Fig. 47. A "stereogram" from Helmholtz.

applied to a sense-organ in order to arouse a conscious sensation. The amount needed differs with the multifarious conditions under which the stimulus is applied. Among other things, voluntary attention and its fluctuations are of great importance in determining the threshold of sensation. The following experiments can be readily performed and are very instructive.

In a quiet room have an assistant hold a watch at such a distance from your ear that you can just hear its ticking. When this distance has been ascertained, close the eyes so as to exclude all disturbing visual stimuli, and being seated comfortably, listen as attentively as possible to the ticking of the watch. The faint sound you hear is near the threshold of audibility and thus very favorable for the observation of fluctuations of attention. It would be best to employ a continuous sound of medium pitch and just as soft as the ticking of the watch. But this is difficult. Though the ticking of the watch is, strictly speaking, not an unchanging object of attention, the succession of faint sounds, of which it consists, is monotonous and thus equivalently an unchanging object. It is easy, moreover, to prescind from all associations which the ticking might arouse; such associations, if there be any, are not liable to be very obtrusive, so that you can direct your attention exclusively to what is immediately given in your sensory experience.

These conditions secured, we find that the ticking of the watch will periodically grow still fainter and drop entirely out of our mind There will be fluctuations of voluntary attention which can be recorded in the form of a curve.

Similar experiments have been devised for ascertaining and recording the fluctuations of voluntary attention when it is directed to visual and tactual stimuli. The results are, in general, the same as previously described. It may be well to add that these results are complicated by the fact that the organs of sight and touch readily become fatigued. This shows itself, for instance, in troublesome visual after-images and in a general blur and confusion, resulting from so steady and unchanged an application of the eyes. Hence we really do not know any longer whether we are studying the effects of sensory adaptation or the problem proper, namely, how far a voluntary effort will carry us.[10]

14. The Physiological Theory of Attention. Many theories of attention have been proposed. Commenting on them, Titchener says that "attention offers itself as an admirable touchstone by which the views of modern psychology may be tested."[11] This is undoubtedly correct. The student who has carefully followed our empirical description of the facts of attention, will see that in trying to explain them we must distinguish attention to *sensory* experiences and attention to objects of *thought—voluntary* and *involuntary* attention. There is no general formula which will do justice to all the facts. *We insist that the different forms of attention must be explained separately.* Accordingly, we are forced to wait for a full explanation of attention until we have

---

[10]Cf. E. A. Pace, in *Philosophische Studien*, Vol. 20, pp. 232 sqq.

[11]*Text-Book*, p. 267, quoted by permission of the Macmillan Co., publishers.

settled the further problems it involves. Prominent among these
are: *the distinction between sensory experiences and thought,
free will* and all it implies, and last, but not least, *the problem
of the Ego.* Here we wish to review briefly a theory which tries
to explain all the facts of attention by an appeal to their *physiological* conditions. We quote Titchener:

"Neurologists are agreed that one nervous excitation may influence another in two opposite ways: by helping and by hinder-
ing, or, in technical terms, by facilitation and by inhibition. . . .
It seems plain that the conditions of the attentive consciousness
are of these two kinds. The clear processes, at the crest of the
attention wave, are processes whose underlying excitations have
been facilitated. Similarly, the obscure processes, at the lower
level of consciousness, are processes whose underlying excitations
have been inhibited. The attentive consciousness is thus condi-
tioned upon the interplay of cortical facilitation and cortical
inhibition."[12]

Prof. W. McDougall says substantially the same thing in his
Physiological Psychology when explaining his "drainage theory"
of attention. We quote:

"In an earlier chapter we have provisionally adopted the hypothesis that inhibition is effected by drainage of energy from
the inhibited to the inhibiting tract, through the inhibiting tract
becoming the path of lower resistance."[13] "Whether, then, we
regard the process of the turning of the attention from one object
to another from the point of view of the inhibition of one neural
system by the other, or from the point of view of the establishment of a path of low resistance between them, the formation
of a neural association, we arrive at the same conclusion — the
one system drains the other."[14]

We do not deny that in our purely sensory processes inhibition
occurs and that it may take some such form as is here described.

---

[12]*Op. cit.,* p. 300, quoted by permission of the Macmillan Co., publishers.
[13]Page 131.
[14]Page 134.

When explaining the phenomena of simultaneous contrast we said that all the profound modifications in our color sensations which occur under these conditions are best understood if they are considered as phenomena of total or partial inhibition. But there are more things to be explained in psychology than the phenomena of simultaneous contrast. Attention dominates our whole conscious life and it is a leap into the metaphysical dark to say that all the facts of our conscious life are best understood if they are considered as phenomena of total or partial neural inhibition. Prof. McDougall himself is not so sure about that. For he modifies the view expressed in the text by the following footnote: "If this view should be found untenable we should be compelled to look for an explanation in some psychical guidance of the neural discharge."[15] Recent research decidedly points in the direction indicated in this footnote. We refer to *The Measurement of Conation, An Enquiry Into Volitional Processes* by R. C McCarthy, S.J., Ph.D. The experimental results of this careful research will be summarized in a later chapter.

References for Further Reading
J. Froebes, S.J., *Lehrbuch der Experimentellen Psychologie*, Vol. II, pp. 67–99.
J. Lindworsky, S.J., *Experimentelle Psychologie* (1921), pp. 240–251.
C. S. Myers, *Text-Book of Experimental Psychology* (1911), Chap. XXV.

---

[15]*Loc. cit.*

Chapter XII

INSTINCT

1. The Anti-Instinctive Attitude of Modern Psychology.
The growing tendency in modern psychology is to discard instinct altogether. Some authors retain the term "instinctive reactions" and define them as *native reactions of the more complex kind,* but they insist on eliminating the term "instinct." It has been said that this term is not only ambiguous but useless, and so does more harm than good in psychological discussions. Of course, if everything in psychology is to be explained in purely physiological terms, the term "instinct" is a useless one; but so are a great many other terms, such as will, choice purpose, etc. In fact, all psychological terms should be eliminated.

Before the advent of the behaviorists this elimination of instinct — and all other conscious realities — took the form of an inconsistent camouflage generally discussed under the heading of "psychophysical parallelism." The real name of this theory, as far as explanations are concerned, is *the automaton theory,* as James correctly called it. If man and animal are but automata whose bodily reactions are neither helped nor hindered by the conscious processes which are said to run parallel with these bodily reactions, why not be consistent and simply say with the extreme behaviorists that the "psycho" part of parallelism does not exist? Then only the automaton represented by the "physical" part of parallelism remains. The problem which really concerns the behaviorists is: What can the human or animal machine do from the beginning in response to changes in its environment and what new reactions can be elicited from it by the variations of native reactions? The most consistent way of handling this problem would seem to be that of Watson. Begin with physiological reflexes and show how by conditioning them all the complex reactions of the adult human machine can be built up.

Potent realities, however, cannot be thus summarily eliminated. Parallelists in trying to do so were *sadly out of touch with facts as they actually occur.* And behaviorists, if they are consistent, are in the same predicament, their claims to the contrary notwithstanding. But consistency is a jewel and is frequently conspicuous by its absence. Thus it is that instinct, though refused entrance at the front door of psychology, has been smuggled in again by some behaviorists through the back door. Some half-hearted behaviorists, in fact, have in this shame-faced way made perfect restitution of what they have taken away. This shows that the uselessness of instinct is simply a matter of theory, if not a mere matter of fad. You must talk that way whether you believe it or not, else you cannot be a behaviorist. Unless you use at least once in a while the recognized jargon of behaviorists, you lose caste and are ostracized from the ranks of scientific psychologists.

So much for the *uselessness* of instinct. The *ambiguity* of the term is a more serious matter. But this can be remedied by taking facts for our guides. The great variety of meanings which have been actually attached to the term "instinct" are due partly to theoretic considerations, partly to the complexity of the facts to be investigated and partly — in fact, to a large extent — to the manner in which the investigation of these facts has been approached and conducted. Hence, the first thing to be done is to state the problem in such a way that all these sources of ambiguity are eliminated.

2. The problem which we mean to discuss in this chapter may be formulated as follows: *How are we to account for those complex activities of animals which are common to all individuals of the same species and by which the welfare of the individual and the preservation of the species are secured?* The problem thus stated makes no theoretic assumptions of any kind. It contains *a merely preliminary and noncommittal description of "instinctive activities"* such as might be admitted by the most radical behaviorist and by the most ardent defender of animal intelligence. The three elements which enter into this preliminary definition are plain facts. The first is that *the reactions in ques-*

*tion secure the welfare of the individual and the preservation of
the species.* Such are all the activities of animals by which they
provide themselves with appropriate food; similarly, those connected with their defense against enemies; and lastly all the activities which come under the general headings of mating, hatching, and caring for their offspring.

The second fact is that instinctive activities are *common to all
the individuals of the same species.* This must be understood in
the same sense as we say that all individuals of a species have
the same anatomical structure: it is *specifically* the same, though
it varies *individually.* Similarly, instinctive activities have certain
features which are common to all individuals of the same species, though they vary individually. No animal is fully described
unless the specific way in which it performs the actions in question is indicated. Plainly the second characteristic of instinctive
activities presents a problem of heredity. But it is complicated
considerably by the individual variations of these activities.

The third fact is that these activities are *complex.* By this we
mean that they *constitute a whole chain of reactions* so that the
welfare of the individual and the preservation of the species are
not secured unless these reactions follow one another in regular
succession and form a system. Thus, when a bird picks up a piece
of straw, this reaction is only part of the process of nest building,
and the building of the nest, in turn, is only part of the sum total
of reactions by which the preservation of the species is secured.
Of course, we are also interested in the relatively simple reactions
which form the links in the chain, and the explanation of each
link may, at least in principle, be the same as that of the whole
chain of reactions. But the fact that the reactions in question form
a *system,* alters the problem considerably. An explanation which
may be sufficient when applied to a single reaction considered
by itself, may be hopelessly inadequate when applied to the whole
system. What adds to the complexity of instinctive actions is that
the units of which they are made up are sometimes widely separated from one another both in time and in space.

The three characteristics by which we have defined instinctive activities of animals are expressed *in purely objective and noncommittal terms.* Our problem, then, is: *How are we to account for those animal activities which have these three characteristics?* Are we to suppose, for instance, that the bird when picking up a piece of straw does so with foresight and knows that it provides for the generation to come? Or are we to say that this and similar actions of animals are simply neuromuscular transactions which occur independently of all conscious processes? What, in short, is the driving force, conscious or unconscious, back of these activities? If we can describe this driving force in empirical terms that can be verified, then we have an empirical definition of instinct and we have solved our problem. For the present we must be satisfied with a preliminary definition of instinct which is just as noncommittal as our definition of instinctive activities. *We define instinct as the driving force, conscious or unconscious, which is back of the activities above described.*

3. The Starting Point in Our Investigation. Of the conscious life of animals we have no immediate knowledge whatever. We cannot observe it directly, and animals cannot give us an introspective report of it. Whether or not, therefore, animals are guided in their instinctive activities by conscious processes, and if so, what these are in detail, we can know only by *inference.* We must construct the conscious antecedents of their instinctive activities and *the starting point in this process of construction is the investigation and analysis of our own instinctive activities.* It is after the analogy of our own instinctive activities that we must explain those of animals, and in doing so we must beware of humanizing the brute. This brings us to a new difficulty in the solution of our problem.

It has been said that man really has no instincts at all; he is endowed with reason. Hence, by observing the conscious antecedents of our behavior we shall never arrive at an empirical description of the driving force back of instinctive activities. We should have to describe the conscious processes which prompted us to activity in early childhood and this we cannot do in empirical terms any more than in the case of animals. Hence, we really have no starting point at all for our investigation. The answer is that our starting point is the analysis of our adult experience. But our task is complicated by the fact that in our adult life we rarely, if ever, perform purely instinctive actions. We experience, indeed, that driving force which everybody designates by the name of instinct, but we also have direct experience of other incentives to action, and can discover yet others by inference. The result is that in our adult life our instinctive activities are complicated not only by habits but also by rational considerations and by the voice of conscience which insists that we control our instincts in conformity with the law of God. What complicates matters still further is the fact that one and the same activity may have very different antecedents on different occasions. Hence we can arrive at those conscious antecedents which we call instinct only by artificially separating them from other incentives to action, conscious or unconscious, without which they never occur.

From this it will be seen that the interpretation of the instinctive activities of animals after the analogy of those in man, is peculiarly difficult. It will not do simply to describe the antecedents of human activities which are rightly or wrongly designated as instinctive and then to say that the same antecedents occur in animals. The simple fact is that in our adult experience there are no purely instinctive actions any more than there are purely rational activities, mere physiological habits, etc., save by way of exception or under artificial conditions. Ordinarily, all the various incentives to action are inextricably interwoven in our activities. Instincts, in particular, are factors even of those external activities which in ethics are described as specifically "human acts." Accordingly, we shall never arrive at a satisfactory solution of our problem, if we begin with *classifying human activities* as purely instinctive, purely rational, purely emotional, etc. Instead, we must rather *classify the various incentives to action,* both conscious and unconscious, as they actually occur in our adult experience or are known by legitimate inference. When we have made such a list of these various incentives to action, our task is to determine which of them are *required* and *sufficient* to account for those animal activities which we have defined in non-committal terms as instinctive.

It has been said that the problem of animal instinct can only be decided by *experiments* with animals. The answer is that such experiments cannot help us in deciding our problem unless *we have the proper starting point for the interpretation of animal behavior*. The principal benefit we derive from such experiments is, that we thus obtain reliable data of animal activities. As a matter of fact, many such data have been obtained by a number of investigators, and the experimental methods which have been employed in gathering them, and are still used on a large scale, are very ingenious. But the interpretation of these data has been radically different in the case of different investigators. Each investigator has interpreted his data in accordance with his starting point. In this regard the experimental method, as actually used today, is no improvement on the anecdotal method by which a host of observers some decades ago tried to prove or disprove animal intelligence and man's animal descent; hence, the importance of settling first of all the starting point of our investigation. Unless we want to write animal eulogies in experimental or anecdotal form, or merely air our mechanistic conception of all life, there can be no other starting point than the one which we have outlined. In other words, experiments with animals, no matter how devised, can never settle *directly* the point of issue, namely, the antecedents of animal instinctive activities; these antecedents will ever remain a matter of *theoretic interpretation*. Accordingly, our problem naturally breaks up into several part-problems. They deal with the various theories which can be proposed and have been proposed in explanation of the instinctive activities of animals. The principal ones are: (1) *the reflex theory* of instinct; (2) *the intelligence theory;* (3) *the lapsed-intelligence theory;* (4) *the sensitive-impulse theory.* We shall consider each theory in turn in the light of what we have said concerning our starting point.

4. The reflex theory of instinct holds that the animal activities described are purely neuromuscular transactions after the manner of reflex actions. The latter may be defined as *stereotype responses of the neuromuscular organism to objective stimuli which occur independently of any conscious processes and are carried out by an innately determined mechanism known as the "reflex arc."* The structural elements of the reflex arc (s.s. I, II, III, *m*) may be seen in a simplified and diagrammatic form from Figure 4 (p. 26). The stock example of a reflex action is the involuntary withdrawal of the hand when we inadvertently touch a flame. We feel, indeed, the pain caused by the flame and we become also aware of the movement when it occurs. But all these conscious processes have nothing to do with the withdrawal of the hand. Similar reflex actions are obtained from decerebrated or decapitated frogs. In fact, they are executed all the more vigorously and with greater mechanical precision when the brain is removed or disconnected from the rest of the organism. They occur also in man when he is asleep, and have been obtained from decapitated criminals. Accordingly, there can be no doubt that such activities occur independently of all conscious processes. What really happens in our stock example is this: The flame comes in contact with the nervous end-organs of the skin (s.s. in Figure 4) and produces in them a change to which they are specifically attuned. Thus a nervous impulse is started in an afferent fiber (I) connecting the end-organ with the spinal cord. Before the nerve current ever reaches the sensory centers of the brain, it is "short-circuited" *via* a reflex-collateral (*r. c.*), and by means of a correlation neuron (II) is shunted into an appropriate efferent fiber (III). The result is that an appropriate muscle (*m*) contracts and we are protected from harm.

From this it will be seen that *reflex actions are just as purposive in character as instinctive actions of animals,* and the defenders of the reflex theory have made capital out of this fact. To an unsophisticated observer nothing is more startling than to watch a decerebrated frog "defend" itself against obnoxious stimuli applied to its skin. When the breast of the suspended animal is touched with acetic acid, both forepaws will promptly come forward and rub it off. If the elbow is irritated in a similar manner, the hindfoot on the same side will move with precision to that spot and remove the acid. If the irritant is placed on the back of the animal, the hind foot on the same side will reach also that spot without fumbling and thus relieve the situation. If this foot is now cut off and the acid applied to the back as before, a most surprising thing happens. At first the animal tries to remove the acid with the stump. Of course, it does not succeed and after some time gives up the attempt. It looks as if the decapitated frog realized its predicament and bethought itself of another way of relieving the situation. The other foot might come to the rescue, and *so it does*. What really happens, however, is only this. The nerve-current which before was short-circuited *via* a reflex collateral and shunted by a correlation neuron into an appropriate efferent fiber on the same side of the body, is now shunted by a similar neural arrangement into an appropriate efferent fiber on the other side of the body. *What appears as intelligent adaptation of the animal's behavior to the changed conditions of its defense, is merely a "crossed" reflex.*

It has been said that "the conception of reflex action is surely one of the best conquests of physiological theory; why not be radical with it? Why not say that just as the spinal cord is a machine with few reflexes, so the hemispheres are a machine with many, and that that is all the difference?"[1] If conscious processes are unnecessary for the performance of instinctive actions, why postulate them? And thus we arrive at the reflex theory of instinct.

According to this theory, then, the driving force back of instinctive activities of animals is an innate mechanism. The difference between instinctive actions and reflexes is only one of complexity. In instinctive actions many reflex arcs are coördinated and they involve also paths in the brain. They are, moreover, chained together into a series: they constitute a chain of reflexes. Let S_1 stand for an objective stimulus, and R_1 for the muscular contraction or glandular secretion which occurs as its response.

---

[1] James, *Principles of Psychology*, I, p. 129.

This very contraction or glandular secretion constitutes a new stimulus, S2, which is responded to by a second contraction or glandular secretion, R2, and so on, in regular succession until the complex series of reactions known as instinctive is performed. In this manner the spider, for instance, is said to construct its web: the operation is a chain of reflexes.

5. The answer is that the reflex theory of instinct squares indeed with the facts of neurology but is *hopelessly out of touch with those facts which constitute the starting point in the interpretation of animal behavior.* We begin with the knowledge we have of the driving force back of our own instinctive activities.

$$S_1 \rightarrow R_1 \qquad S_3 \rightarrow R_3$$
$$S_2 \rightarrow R_2 \qquad S_4 \rightarrow R_4 \, etc$$

Fig. 48. A Chain of Reflexes.

A behaviorist observing my outward actions when taking my breakfast, may rightly insist that these actions, physiologically considered, differ only in complexity from physiological reflexes. But he would be wrong in concluding from this that all these activities of mine occur independently of all conscious antecedents. For I know from direct experience that I am guided in these activities by sensations and a number of other conscious processes supplementing these sensations. *Whatever else, then, may have to be said about the reflex theory of instinct, it surely does not apply to my own instinctive activities.* The mechanistic speculations of behaviorists cannot undo the facts known to me by direct internal experience.

With this knowledge as a starting point we are able to construct the conscious antecedents of the instinctive activities of at least *many* animals, and at least *some* of these conscious antecedents we can construct with *certainty.* For many animals have *sense-organs similar to ours and they exhibit behavior similar to ours when we are guided by sensations.* From this we conclude that these animals likewise have sensations and are guided by them in their outward actions. We may justly doubt whether animals have all those conscious processes which *supplement our sensations*. For these supplemental processes differ in our experience from one occasion to another, and the outward behavior of animal and man is frequently *an equivocal sign of these supplemental processes*. It is in the interpretation of such equivocal signs that the argument from analogy is apt to be misleading. Thus, when I see a dog run for a bone, his behavior does not justify any inference as to what he thinks about that bone or about bones in general. *But I cannot doubt that he sees the bone.* I may not know whether he is principally guided by the sense of sight or by the sense of smell in his outward behavior, but I cannot deny that *he has those conscious processes which are essentially bound up with the stimulation of sense-organs similar to mine, namely, sensations.* There is nothing equivocal in the dog's behavior when I merely infer from it that he is guided by sensations. *And this suffices to make the reflex theory of instinct untenable.*

It is true that instinctive activities of animals, viewed exclusively from the neurologist's point of view, differ only in complexity from physiological reflexes. But this is true also of the *highest type of human activities,* voluntary actions. Viewed exclusively from the neurologist's point of view, they too are neuromuscular transactions which differ only in complexity from physiological reflexes. A glance at Figure 4 (p. 26) will show this. In this diagram all the facts of internal experience are precisely left out of consideration. Hence, if the reflex theory is correctly applied to instinctive actions of animals, it is just as correctly applied to voluntary actions of man, in fact, to all his outward activities. Thus *the reflex theory of instinct leads us logically to the general automaton theory* with all the absurdities it contains. James has expressed the logical consequences of the reflex theory in a manner that cannot be improved upon. We quote: "The movements of our tongues and pens, the flashings of our eyes in conversation, are, of course, events of a physiological order, and as such, their causal antecedents may be exclusively mechanical. If we knew thoroughly the nervous system of Shakespeare, and as thoroughly all his environing conditions, we should be able, according to the theory of automatism, to show why at a given period of his life his hand came to trace on certain sheets of paper those crabbed little black marks which for shortness' sake we call the manuscript of Hamlet. We should understand the rationale of every erasure and alteration therein, and we should understand all this without in the slightest degree acknowledging the existence of the thoughts in Shakespeare's mind. The words and sentences would be taken, not as signs of anything beyond themselves, but as little outward facts, pure and simple. In like manner, the automaton theory affirms, we might exhaustively write the biography of those two hundred pounds, more or less, of warmish albuminoid matter called Martin Luther, without ever implying that it felt."[2] Of course, all this is against common sense and thus we have reached the *reductio ad absurdum* of the reflex theory of instinct. It is a one-sided and distorted view of instinctive activities of animals.

Before dismissing the reflex theory of instinct we must briefly answer the question, *"How can we tell the difference between physiological reflexes and those activities which result from conscious antecedents?"* The answer is that *in my own case* the data of internal experience furnish a clear dividing line. When I reflexly withdraw my hand from a flame, I simply find myself doing so, and I am fully aware that neither my will nor any other conscious process had anything to do with the performance. When somebody flashes a light into my eye, I am not even aware of the fact that the pupil of that eye contracts, unless I watch the eye in a mirror. When, however, I go to dinner or to the lecture hall, I know that I am guided in these activities by definite purposes.

In the case of animals we know the dividing line only by inference. Physiological reflexes are *stereotype* in character and occur with *machinelike* precision whenever a definite stimulus

---

[2]*Psychology,* p. 102.

is applied. Flash a light into a dog's eye and the pupil of that
eye will contract. It will contract a thousand times over, provided you flash a light a thousand times over into the dog's eye,
just as an electrical bell will ring a thousand times over, provided
you press an appropriate button a thousand times over. *Instinctive activities of animals are far removed from this machinelike
precision.* Thus we know, for instance, that the taking of food
is not a physiological reflex. The dog does not snap at food whenever it is presented. His mode of action resembles unmistakably
our mode of action when we are guided by sensations, feelings
of comfort or discomfort, likes and dislikes. It is very teleological
that the dog does not snap at food with machinelike precision
whenever it is presented. For if he did so, he would soon die
from overeating. This shows that sensations, feelings of comfort
or discomfort, likes and dislikes, are far from being such useless
things as they are supposed to be in the behavioristic account of
instinctive activities.

There is, however, *a grain of truth in the reflex theory of instinct* It is this: Sometimes our data of observation are insufficient
to decide whether a definite reaction occurs with machinelike precision, and must therefore be classed as a physiological reflex, or
whether it belongs to some other category of behavior. This is
simply a matter of *detail,* and it makes little difference whether
we interpret this detail of animal behavior one way or the other.
But such an admission is far removed from the general statement
that animals act *universally* as mere reflex machines.

It must be granted, further, that true physiological reflexes are
sometimes *links* of that complex chain of reactions which we call
instinctive, and that without these reflexes the welfare of the
individual and the preservation of the species would not be
secured. Thus, though the taking of food is not a physiological
reflex, it will not secure the welfare of the individual unless it
be *swallowed,* and swallowing is a true physiological reflex. Similarly in the series of reactions which lead to the preservation of
the species, certain links are true physiological reflexes. The only
thing we deny is that *all* the reactions of animals which occur in

the processes of mating, hatching, and caring for their offspring, are of the reflex type. What Loeb, for instance, says concerning certain reactions of bees, may be perfectly correct. In fact, it is a matter of utter indifference to us whether these reactions can be thus explained or not. But one thing Loeb has not proved, namely, that his "tropism theory" — a variation of the reflex theory — can be applied to *all* the links in the chain of reactions which are known collectively as instinctive.

6. The intelligence theory of instinct maintains that the purposive character of instinctive activities forces us to assume that animals are guided in them by *intelligence*. Not only do animals *adapt* means to an end but they *learn to do so*. Most instinctive activities of animals, as we actually find them, are modified by a process of learning. Such learning, however, it is claimed, is impossible without intelligence. Hence, at least those instinctive activities which are modified by learning are considered evidence of animal intelligence.

This theory has received a new impetus of late years from the results which Dr. Koehler has obtained in a series of experiments with anthropoid apes. Many psychologists are of the opinion that these experiments have put the problem of instinct and intelligence on a new basis. At present, no one can discuss this problem without taking into consideration the data of Dr. Koehler. His supporters insist that he has removed all the inaccuracies which obscured the theory of animal intelligence as long as it was discussed on the basis of anecdotal material. More than that, he is said to have reversed the verdict which Dr. Thorndike had arrived at by his experiments with animals. Such are the claims made for the work which Dr. Koehler embodied in his book *The Mentality of Apes.* It should be added, however, that there are a number of psychologists, particularly in Europe, whom Dr. Koehler has failed to convince. Also in this country several protests have been voiced against the above exaggerated claims. The present writer is of the opinion that Dr. Koehler's experimental data leave the problem of animal intelligence about where it was when the anecdotal method was used to prove or disprove animal intelligence.

The great difficulty in discussing this subject has always been *the vagueness of the terms "intelligence" and "learning"* as employed by the defenders of animal intelligence. The difficulty *Dr. Koehler has not removed,* as will become clear when we shall let him speak for himself.

Outside of the Würzburg school — the followers of Kuelpe and Buehler — there are few, if any, psychologists who admit an essential distinction between thoughts and images. According to *the current doctrine of associationists* the whole mental life of man, the most abstract reasoning included, is the result of the combination, liberation, and substitution of mental elements, and these elements are *sensations,* to which some have added the vague elements of *"feeling."* Associationists insist that thought processes differ only in complexity from those images which can be readily analyzed into their sensation elements.

If this fundamental doctrine is admitted even as a working hypothesis, the intelligence theory of instinct must be likewise admitted as a working hypothesis. Unquestionably, many animals furnish evidence by their behavior not only of actual sensations but also of their revivals and associations. No one can deny that horses and dogs are guided in their behavior by memory-images. If, therefore, images *are* thought, then horses and dogs think. We may admit that they are less intelligent than man, but they have all the essentials of intelligence. *To an associationist it must be a matter of course that animals can be arranged, according to their degree of "intelligence," into a definite series.* The dogma of man's animal descent is additional "evidence" of such an ascending series of "intelligence." Man, of course, is at the top of the ladder. But his first cousin, the anthropoid ape, is naturally expected to rank next to man in degree of "intelligence." From this it will be seen why the experiments of Dr. Koehler with anthropoid apes are claimed to be of such importance.

7. Dr. Koehler's Statement of His Problem. On page 1 of

The Mentality of Apes (second edition, revised and reset, 1927) we are told that anthropoid apes "in many ways are nearer to man than to the other ape species; in particular it has been shown that the chemistry of their bodies, insofar as it may be perceived in the quality of the blood, and the structure of their most highly developed organ, the brain, are more closely related to the chem- istry of the human body and human brain structure than to the chemical nature of the lower apes and *their* brain development." The instructed reader will know that the blood tests and the similarity in anatomical structure, to which Dr. Koehler here refers, loom large in popular literature as *"circumstantial evi- dence" of man's animal descent.* It would lead us too far afield to discuss these biological matters here. We refer the reader to Wassmann's *Biology and the Theory of Evolution,* where the value of this "evidence" is examined in detail. For the purposes of our psychological discussion it is more important to point out that *the theory of man's animal descent implies the theory of mental evolution, and this, in turn, involves the hypothesis of sensation- alism and associationism.* Only on this supposition can man's rational life have been evolved from the conscious life of animals. In fact, the theory of mental evolution is but another phase of the theory of sensationalism. The two theories are really two aspects of one and the same problem: they stand and fall together.

This brings us to *the vagueness of the problem* which Dr. Koehler meant to solve by his experiments with anthropoid apes. On page 2 of his book he says: "One might say that the question whether intelligent behavior exists among anthropoid apes can be discussed only after recognizing the theoretical necessity of distinguishing between intelligent behavior and behavior of any other kind; and that, since association psychology, in particular, claims to derive from one single principle all behavior which would come under consideration here, up to the highest level, even that attained by human beings, a theoretical point of view is already assumed by the formulation of problem I; and one which is antagonistic to association psychology." In answering this difficulty, Dr. Koehler insists that "this is a misconception. There is probably no association psychologist who does not, in his own unprejudiced observations, distinguish, and, to a certain extent, contrast unintelligent and intelligent behavior. For what is association psychology but the theory that one can trace back to the phenomena of a generally known, simple association type even those occurrences which, to unbiased observation, do not at first seem corresponding to that type, most of all the so-called intelligent performances?"[3]

We interpret this passage to mean that even associationists are sometimes unprejudiced and then they can tell the difference between thoughts and images readily enough. Unless they did, the problem of animal intelligence could not arise. But when they are biased, they explain this difference away. Dr. Koehler should have told *how* an association psychologist in his unprejudiced observations distinguishes and contrasts unintelligent and intelligent behavior. In this manner he would have given us *a descriptive and noncommittal definition of "intelligent behavior"* which might have sufficed for the purposes of his discussion, and then he could have waived the discussion of the association theory. But *Dr. Koehler gives us no such description of "intelligent behavior" and thus his problem remains vague,* and he is fully aware that it is vague. He says:

"Accordingly, if we are to inquire whether the anthropoid ape behaves intelligently, this problem can for the present be treated quite independently of theoretical assumptions, particularly those for or against the association theory. It is true that it then becomes somewhat indefinite; *we are not to inquire whether anthropoid apes show something well defined, but whether their behavior approximates to a type rather superficially known by experience, and which we call 'intelligent'* in contrast to other behavior, especially in animals. But in proceeding thus, we are only dealing according to the nature of the subject; for clear definitions have no place at the beginning of sciences founded on

---
[3]*Op. cit.,* p. 2.

experience; it is only as we advance toward results that we can
mark our progress by the formulation of definitions."[4]

The answer is that *Dr. Koehler here confounds essential definitions with merely preliminary and descriptive definitions.* It is
true that essential definitions have no place at the beginning of
sciences founded on experience; they rather embody the results
of experimental investigations. But the same is not true of merely
preliminary and descriptive definitions. Even a problematical
phenomenon can be thus defined. What is problematical in anthropoid apes, namely "intelligence," is a plain fact in the case
of man, and different men show it in different degrees of perfection. Even the lowest degree of true intelligence such as Dr.
Koehler might expect to find in anthropoid apes, can be described
with accuracy in terms of human experience. And it should be
thus described, for only then can we know what we are looking
for.

There are many preliminary descriptions of intelligence which
Dr. Koehler could have embodied in the formulation of his problem. Thus, for instance, he might have said: *The question is
whether anthropoid apes under the conditions to be described are
aware that pulling a string or using a stick or piling one box on
top of another is a means of reaching a definite end, namely,
getting a banana.* If there were *unequivocal* evidence that apes
thus perceived the relation of means to an end, Dr. Koehler could
have said definitely that they have intelligence. His preliminary
description of it would have been just as *clear* as *noncommittal;*
for the perception of relations is acknowledged even by associationists to be a thought process. If the existence of such a perception in anthropoid apes had been demonstrated experimentally, Titchener could have dealt with it in accordance with his theoretic assumptions. He could have taken the anthropoid ape into
his metaphysical darkroom of "meaning." There he would have
said that "in existential terms" what happened to the ape was
this: an image of a banana or anything else "passed swiftly down

his visual field from northwest to southeast" pretty much as happened in his own case when he had a "feeling of relation," as for instance, the "feeling of but" or "the feelings of if, and why, and nevertheless, and therefore." Accordingly, the excuse which Dr. Koehler offers for not defining intelligence in the beginning of his experimental investigation is invalid. The inevitable result is that his problem is vague.

When, however, Dr. Koehler comes to the *conclusions* which he draws from his experiments, he becomes *remarkably clear.* On page 219 he states explicitly that there is experimental evidence that anthropoid apes become aware of *relations* and that association psychology must deal with this fact. He explains that by "relation" he means an *"interconnection based on the properties of these things themselves,* not a 'frequent following each other' or 'occurring together.' This problem is the first that should be solved, because such 'relations' represent the most elementary function participating in specifically intelligent behavior, and there is no doubt at all that these relations, among other factors, continually determine the chimpanzee's behavior. They are not facts merely of the type 'sensations,' and the like, merely further associable elements, but it can quite definitely be proved (and quantitatively proved) that they determine in a very marked degree the chimpanzee's behavior, i.e., his inner processes, by their functional properties. Either the association theory is capable of clearly explaining the 'smaller than,' 'farther away than,' 'pointing straight toward,' etc., according to their true meaning as mere associations from experience, and then all is well; or else the theory cannot be used as a complete explanation, because it cannot account for those factors primarily effective for the chimpanzees (as for man)."[5]

Such language is clear and unmistakable. *We naturally wonder on what experimental data he bases such a remarkable conclusion.* In a footnote we are referred to the *Abhandl. d. Preuss. Akad. d. Wiss.* (1918), Phys.-Math. Section, N. 2. If this publica-

---

[5] *Op. cit.*, pp. 219 sqq.

tion contains proofs not embodied in his book *The Mentality of Apes,* then Dr. Koehler has left out the principal thing. We take it, then, that the experimental data on which the above conclusion is based, are at least substantially contained in his book. Accordingly, we must examine these data and the rule which guided him in their interpretation.

8. Dr. Koehler's Rule for the Interpretation of Animal Behavior. In his Introduction, Dr. Koehler indicates this rule. He says: "As experience shows, we do not speak of behavior as being intelligent, when human beings or animals attain their objective by a direct unquestionable route which clearly arises naturally out of their organization. But we tend to speak of 'intelligence' when, circumstances having blocked the obvious course, the human being or animal takes a roundabout path, so meeting the situation."[6]

This rule consists of two parts. The first is claimed to be derived from experience but its meaning and application seem far from clear. We shall return to this presently. As to the second, Dr. Koehler says that it is accepted by "unexpressed agreement." For he continues: "In unexpressed agreement with this, nearly all those observers who heretofore have sought to solve the problem of animal intelligence, have done so by watching animals in just such predicaments."[7]

Coming to his own experiments he describes them in general terms as follows: "All the experiments described in the following pages are of one and the same kind: the experimenter sets up a situation in which the direct path to the objective is blocked, but a roundabout way left open. The animal is introduced into this situation, which can, potentially, be wholly surveyed. So we can see of what levels of behavior it is capable, and, particularly, whether it can solve the problem in the possible 'roundabout' way."[8]

As to the first part of Dr. Koehler's rule. Suppose that at break-

---

[6]*Op. cit.,* pp. 3 and 4.
[7]*Ibid.,* p. 4.
[8]*Loc. cit.*

fast I find an apple right before me. I can "attain my objective —
the apple — by a direct unquestionable route," by simply reaching for it. Suppose that I do so. Would an outside observer be
justified in concluding from this that my action "without doubt
arose naturally out of my organization"? If, while taking my
breakfast, I philosophize about some abstruse problem of metaphysics, the apple before me may never reach the focus of my
attention and I may take it in an impulsive or semireflex way.
But many a man in such a situation has philosophized: "One
apple a day keeps the doctor away." If I philosophize likewise,
I perceive the taking of the apple as a means of keeping the doctor away. Accordingly, my action comes plainly under the heading of "intelligent behavior," and it does so according to the explanations which Dr. Koehler himself gives on page 219. From
which we conclude that the first part of the rule which he gives
on page 3 is not a safe guide in the interpretation of human behavior. If it is derived from experience, as Dr. Koehler claims,
he has not worded it in such a way that its meaning and application are clear: it is equivocal.

The second part of the rule on page 3 is just as equivocal. With
the exception of some privileged poodles and other animal pets,
animals do not, as a rule, find their breakfast neatly prepared so
that they can "attain their objective by a direct unquestionable
route." Most animals in nature must "take a roundabout path,"
and many have a hard time of it, particularly in winter. Even if
their objective — the prospective breakfast — should be plainly
in view, many "circumstances block the obvious path." Their
enemies are likewise looking for a breakfast, and men place many
a barrier in the way of marauding animals. Still, somehow or
another, when spring comes, not all animals have been snuffed
out of existence. From which we conclude that many of these
animals have "met the situation successfully in a roundabout
way." According to the second part of Dr. Koehler's rule, these
animals behave intelligently. *If we accept this rule, the intelligence of animals presents no serious problem at all. It is settled
by an obvious inference from obvious facts.*

Neither can this inference be evaded by saying that it is based on facts ascertained by "the anecdotal method." Such is not the case. We need neither anecdotes nor the experimental data of Dr. Koehler to convince us that animals in nature are frequently placed in predicaments, and that many of them meet the situation successfully in a roundabout way. His experimental data furnish us at best only *details* concerning the *obvious* fact that such animal behavior exists. The persistent problem of animal intelligence is not so much a question concerning such *details of fact*, it is rather *a question of principle,* namely, concerning the rule which is to guide us in the interpretation of such animal behavior. And the rule of Dr. Koehler is equivocal.

9. Dr. Koehler's Distinction Between a "Genuine Achievement" and a "Successful Chance Solution." Dr. Koehler is fully aware that his rule is equivocal, for on page 16 he qualifies it in order to meet the obvious objection that it may be a matter of chance that the animals attain their objective in a roundabout way. He distinguishes between a "genuine achievement" due to intelligence or insight and a "successful chance solution" and gives us a criterion by which we can tell the two apart. We quote: "The genuine achievement takes place as a single continuous occurrence, a unity, as it were, in space as well as in time; in our example as one continuous run, without a second's stop, right up to the objective. A successful chance solution consists of an agglomeration of separate movements, which start, finish, start again, remain independent of one another in direction and speed, and only in a geometrical summation start at the starting point, and finish at the objective."[9]

The criterion, then, by which we can tell whether a "roundabout" solution is due to intelligence, is this: the detour of the animal must be "a *unity,* as it were, in space as well as in time." If the detour is no such "*unity,* as it were," well, then there is no intelligence.

To begin with, this new rule seems to be somewhat hard to

---

[9] *Op. cit.,* pp. 16 and 17.

follow. The decision as to whether a given detour of an animal has the required "unity" or not, depends a good deal on the subjective estimate of the observer. Dr. Koehler claims that "no one who has performed similar experiments on animals (or children) will be able to disregard this difference."[10] For the sake of the argument let us suppose this to be true. But even then his criterion of intelligence or "insight" is equivocal.

The most obvious conclusion which can be drawn from the fact that a given detour of an animal is performed unhesitatingly as a "unity," is, that *the neural organization of that animal is very perfect.* No complex activity of any kind can be performed unhesitatingly by either animal or man without such a neural organization. As far as the smoothness of the performance is concerned, it makes no difference whether the neural organization is *inherited* or *acquired,* whether it is *acquired this way or that.* One way of acquiring such a neural organization is the process of "learning" of the sensori-motor type explained in the chapter on Memory under the heading of "Mechanical Memory." The neural organization thus acquired will be just as effective in producing a "unity" of action as that acquired with the additional guidance of intellectual considerations. *How, then, does Dr. Koehler know that the "unity" of a detour implies something over and above the neural organization of the sensori-motor type?*

The situation into which Dr. Koehler introduces his animal is *not an entirely new one.* It has many elements in common with predicaments in which that animal has frequently been before. Similarly, the detour by which the animal extricates itself from the present predicament has many sensori-motor elements in common with detours by which the same animal extricated itself from similar past predicaments. Accordingly, the situation which the animal meets here and now by a successful detour may, for the purposes of our discussion, be resolved into a series of situations, S_1, S_2, S_3, etc. By the mere fact that the animal reacts in any manner whatever to S_1, it finds itself in the next situ-

[10] *Op. cit.,* p. 16.

ation, S2, and so on. Similarly, the successful detour of the animal may be resolved into a series of reactions, R1, R2, R3, etc. The piecing together of these reactions into a "unity" is a matter of neural organization. All we have to suppose in this explanation is, that among the numerous associations acquired in the past, there is one sufficiently strong for the present association between S1 and R1 to arise promptly, and so of all the other associations, S2 + R2, S3 + R3, etc. In popular terms the explanation amounts to this: When the animal is introduced into a definite situation it has definite sensations (S1), and it reacts to them impulsively with a definite movement (R1). As a result of this movement the animal has other sensations (S2), and it reacts to them just as impulsively with a second movement (R2), and so on, until the objective is reached (R5). Accordingly, we may diagram a successful detour as follows:

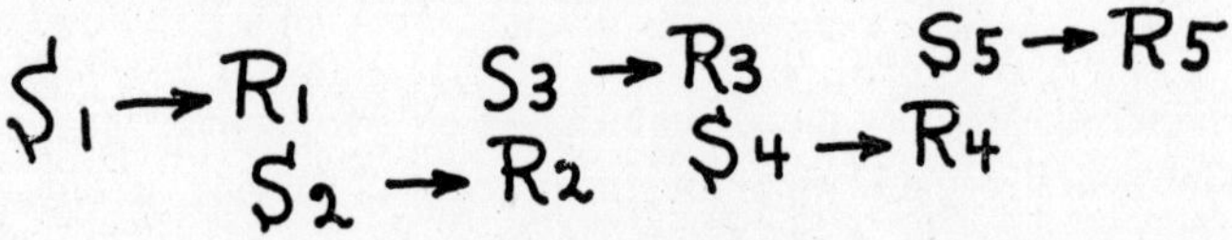

$$ S_1 \rightarrow R_1 \qquad S_3 \rightarrow R_3 \qquad S_5 \rightarrow R_5 $$
$$ S_2 \rightarrow R_2 \qquad S_4 \rightarrow R_4 $$

FIG. 49. A Successful Detour.

It cannot be objected that this explanation of a successful detour is fanciful and that it has nothing to do with the real world in which we live. Far from it. An acquired neural organization such as we suppose here is the *sine qua non* of a "successful detour" on a football or baseball field. If the player had to reason out what in a given situation must be the first move, and what the second, third, and so on, he would never reach his objective, whatever that may be in a particular case. Of course, he plays by rule and this raises his performance essentially above that of any animal. But without considerable practice no one can play by rule and make a "successful detour" on the football field. The effect of practice is precisely the gradual formation of a neural organization and the gradual dropping out of intellectual considerations which were required in the beginning to apply a rule to a given situation. The more a player can rely on his neural organization and the less he requires by way of actual reasoning here and now, the more successful will he be in doing the right thing in every contingency, no matter what the details of the "detour" may be which are required to do it. And if he fails, it is not because he does not understand the rule or its application to the present case, but because his neural organization is not sufficiently perfect.

We emphasized in the foregoing that, as far as the smoothness or the "unity" of a complex reaction is concerned, it makes no difference how the neural organization for that reaction is acquired. Another consideration is just as important for our present discussion. It is this: *Once the neural organization for a complex reaction, say, of a football player, is acquired, it makes no difference how that complex reaction is touched off, whether by a flash of intellectual insight or by the mere sensation aroused by the football "signal."* No doubt, flashes of insight occur on the football field. But from the mere "unity" of a player's reaction even a trained psychologist cannot tell how the reaction is touched off here and now. Bias in favor of *Alma Mater* may lead an enthusiastic spectator to decide that the player has solved his problem by a flash of intellectual insight. It is, however, only by an introspective report of the successful player that this matter can be settled definitely. In the absence of such an introspective report an unbiased spectator — if he philosophizes about such matters at all — must say in cool reasoning that neither of the two modes of reaction is proved. *How, then, does Dr. Koehler know that a definite detour of an animal is due to intellectual "insight"?* Evolutionary bias may lead an observer to make such a decision. But there is no objective proof for it. Neither the "detour" nor its "unity" is such a proof. *The criterion by which Dr. Koehler guides himself in the interpretation of his experimental data, is equivocal.*

10. **A Special Feature of Dr. Koehler's Experimental Arrangements.** There is one feature of Dr. Koehler's experimental arrangements on which he insists very much. We have

indeed supposed it all along in our discussion. But it deserves special consideration as it constitutes an essential element in his experimental demonstration of animal "intelligence." The animal, he says, is introduced into a situation *"which can, potentially, be wholly surveyed"* by the animal.[11] This feature, he claims, was absent in Dr. Thorndike's experiments. Hence, the conclusion based on these experiments is in Dr. Koehler's opinion invalid. We quote: "Regarding their principle, I must make a further objection to Thorndike's experiments. They were designed as *intelligence tests* of the same type as our own (insight or not?), and ought, therefore, to have conformed to the same general conditions, and, above all, to have been arranged so as to be completely *visible* to the animals. For, if essential portions of the experimental apparatus cannot be seen by the animals, how can they use their intelligence faculties in tackling the situation?"[12]

We are not concerned here how far this criticism of Dr. Thorndike's experiments may be justified. The point on which we here insist is, that the complete visibility of the experimental apparatus does not change the fact that Dr. Koehler's criterion of "insight" is equivocal. By "insight" we mean here the perception of relations as Dr. Koehler himself does in a later section of his book (p. 219). Of course, no one can perceive the relations which objects have to one another, if the objects themselves are not perceived in any manner whatever. In this Dr. Koehler is perfectly correct. But it does not follow that an animal *perceives these relations* because these *objects are completely visible* to the animal. Nor does it follow that these relations are *actually* perceived, even by man, because they *can* be perceived. Such an inference would be against an elementary rule of logic. No matter, then, how Dr. Koehler understands the phrase that a situation "can, potentially, be wholly surveyed," *the feature thus expressed adds nothing to the value of his experimental demonstration of animal intelligence.* The complete visibility of the experimental appara-

---

[11] *Op. cit.,* p. 4.
[12] *Op. cit.,* p. 22.

tus is indeed an important point in the phenomenal description of facts, but *the question of animal intelligence cannot be settled by a phenomenal description of facts.* It can be settled only by the theoretic interpretation of the facts observed. And the value of this theoretic interpretation depends entirely on the value of the criterion which guides us in this interpretation. In spite of the complete visibility of his experimental apparatus *the criterion of Dr. Koehler is and remains equivocal.*

What makes Dr. Koehler's criterion even more ambiguous is that in applying it he does not distinguish sharply between facts and theory. He seems to think that he is describing plain facts when he says, for instance, that animals "begin with something very like an inventory of the situation"; that their conduct "from the very beginning arises out of a consideration of the characteristics of a situation" and that "this survey then gives rise to the behavior required for the solution." In short, *the question whether animals intelligently survey a situation, would seem to be settled, in Dr. Koehler's opinion, by a mere description of the phenomenal facts.* For he makes such a survey the *criterion* of "insight." We quote: "Chimpanzees, whose behavior is incomparably more expressive than that of hens, show by their careful looking around that they really begin with something very like an inventory of the situation. And this survey then gives rise to the behavior required for the solution."[13] Explaining this further, Dr. Koehler says: "We can, in our own experience, distinguish sharply between the kind of behavior which from the very beginning arises out of a consideration of the structure of a situation, and one that does not. Only in the former case do we speak of insight, and only that behavior of animals definitely appears to us intelligent which takes account from the beginning of the lay of the land, and proceeds to deal with it in a single, continuous, and definite course. Hence follows this criterion of insight: *the appearance of a complete solution with reference to the whole*

[13]*Op. cit.,* p. 190.

layout of the field."[14] What Dr. Koehler here sets down as the *criterion* of "insight" in animals is just as *hypothetical* as animal *"insight"* itself. In a word, *he is begging the question.*

11. Details of a Typical Experiment. It will be best to describe an actual experiment. This will enable the student to judge for himself what Dr. Koehler's experimental demonstration of animal intelligence amounts to. The subject of the experiment was Sultan, one of the chimpanzees. Dr. Koehler considers the achievement of the animal in this experiment so important that he has actually photographed "Sultan making a double stick." The photograph may be found in Plate III facing page 128. Two sticks were thrown to the animal and the problem was: "Are the two sticks ever combined so as to become technically useful? . . . His sticks are two hollow, but firm, bamboo rods, such as the animals often use for pulling along fruit. The one is so much smaller than the other, that it can be pushed in at either end of the other quite easily. Beyond the bars lies the objective, just so far away that the animal cannot reach it with either rod."[15] The animal played with the sticks for a long time but did not get his objective, namely, the fruit beyond the bars. In fact, Sultan even committed what Dr. Koehler calls "a 'bad error,' or, more clearly, a great stupidity."[16] After more than an hour the experiment was stopped as hopeless but "Sultan is left in possession of his sticks; the keeper is left there to watch him."[17] What follows is taken from the keeper's report. Sultan after some time "gets up, picks up the two sticks, sits down again on the box and plays carelessly with them. While doing this, it happens that he finds himself holding one rod in either hand in such a way that they lie in a straight line; he pushes the thinner one a little way into the opening of the thicker, jumps up and is already on the run toward the railings, to which he has up to now half turned his back, and begins to draw a banana toward

[14]*Loc. cit.*

[15]*Op. cit.*, p. 125.

[16]*Ibid.*, p. 126.

[17]*Ibid.*, p. 127.

him with the double stick. I call the master: meanwhile, one of
the animal's rods has fallen out of the other, as he has pushed
one of them only a little way into the other; whereupon he connects them again."[18] After Dr. Koehler was called, he observed
for himself that the animal combined the sticks and thus secured
the bananas.

12. Two Theoretic Interpretations. These, then, are the
facts. We shall not try to explain them *in globo* but shall consider separately the chimpanzee's behavior (A) before the accident reported by the keeper, (B) during this accident, and (C)
after the accident. To enable the student to estimate the relative
value of our explanation and that of Dr. Koehler, we shall put
them side by side.

A. The Chimpanzee's Behavior Before the Accident.
Our explanation is that the chimpanzee acted merely impulsively. When an animal sees food and tries to reach it, there is
nothing in this action that calls for intelligence. At best, such "trying" is an equivocal sign of intelligence; it is explained perfectly
by the sensory impulses arising from the situation and by the
hereditary and acquired equipment of the animals. The use of
sticks in such impulsive trials is, at best, an equivocal sign of intelligence. The chimpanzee is by its organization equipped for grasp-
ing anything, be it a banana or a stick. An impulse to use an organ
goes with the presence of that organ. Hence, neither scientific nor
popular nor even the most elementary *knowledge of levers* is
required for the learning of the use of sticks in reaching for
food. It would be a hard thing to prove that a human baby makes
use of his intelligence when manipulating a spoon or other im-
plements in reaching for food. Accordingly, the use of sticks in
reaching for a banana is adequately accounted for in terms of
purely impulsive action. Such an action, moreover, has frequently
occurred in the past experience of the chimpanzee which was the
subject of Dr. Koehler's experiment. The sticks which are here
and now within the reach of the chimpanzee are too short and

---

[18]*Op. cit.,* p. 127.

hence useless in its present predicament. The animal knows nothing about their uselessness in the present situation, just as it knew nothing about their usefulness in past situations. Accordingly, "trying around" with the sticks is not an attempt at a rational solution of a problem which is as yet only "half understood" by the chimpanzee. There is no evidence whatever for such an interpretation of the animal's behavior. *The animal just fumbles impulsively in a situation of which it understands nothing.* This is our explanation of the chimpanzee's behavior before the accident.

Dr. Koehler's explanation of the same behavior is contained in the following general remarks: "It may happen that the animal will attempt a solution which, while it may not result in success, yet has some meaning in regard to the situation. 'Trying around' then consists in attempts at solution in the *half-understood* situation; and the real solution may easily arise by some chance outcome of it, i.e., it will not arise from chance impulses, but from actions, which, because they are *au fond* sensible, are great aids to chance."[19]

B. The Chimpanzee's Behavior During the Accident. **Our explanation** is that the chimpanzee "learned" a useful reaction by what is known as the "hit-and-miss" or trial-and-error" method. It is true that the behavior of the animal as reported by the keeper, is *per se* equivocal, that is, it admits *per se* of two explanations. It might be a case of learning by accident *and* insight, or one by accident *without* insight. Man has learned a great many things by accident *and* insight. A classical example of such a mode of learning is that known in the history of physics as "Oerstedt's experiment." Oerstedt knew nothing about the relation between a magnet and a current, but recognized it immediately when he stumbled upon it by accident. It is thus that electromagnetism was discovered. Explaining the chimpanzee's behavior in the light and after the manner of Oerstedt's experience, we should say: The animal merely stumbled upon the

[19] *Op. cit.,* p. 193.

combination of the two sticks but immediately recognized that
now the stick was long enough and could serve as a means of
securing the bananas. Accordingly, the chimpanzee promptly
makes use of the knowledge thus acquired, "jumps up and is
already on the run toward the railings . . . and begins to draw
a banana toward him with the double stick." *This explanation
is known in the history of psychology as "humanizing the brute,"*
one of the greatest dangers of the injudicious use of the "argument from analogy." The mere fact that the chimpanzee "jumps
up and is already on the run toward the railings" is no objective
proof for the correctness of this explanation. There is an alternate
explanation which is in accord with what we said in an earlier
section of this chapter on the starting point in the interpretation
of animal behavior. It runs as follows: After the accidental combination of the two sticks the impulse to get the bananas revived
and was promptly acted upon. The animal did exactly what it
did during the hour before the accident. But now the stick happened to be long enough and thus by "accident without insight"
secured the bananas.

Dr. Koehler's explanation of the same behavior is as
follows: "A lucky accident may occur in some action, which has
nothing to do with the objective. Here again, there is no question
of a meaningless impulse — the chimpanzee only gives way to
these, as already remarked, when driven to it — but of some kind
of intelligent activity, even if with no reference to the objective.
This is what probably occurs, when Sultan discovers the way to
combine two sticks; only a Philistine would call his playing with
these sticks 'meaningless impulses,' because it follows no practical
purpose. That an accident helped him is not the most important
fact in either case; the important thing is how the experiment
then proceeds. For we know from Man that even an accident
may lead to *intelligent* further work (or intelligent repetition),
especially in scientific discoveries (compare Oerstedt: *Current
and Magnet*). Thus Sultan's behavior, when he has once carried
out his usual play, 'put stick in hole,' with both the bamboo

rods, is exactly the same as if he had discovered the new procedure in a genuine solution."[20]

C. The Chimpanzee's Behavior After the Accident.
Our explanation is that the chimpanzee's behavior after the accident was exactly of the same type as before and during the accident. The only difference is that a new association of the sensori-
motor type (acquired during the accident) became an additional
factor of his impulsive behavior. The mere fact that the chimpanzee after the accident acted without hesitation in combining the
sticks does not prove his insight in the usefulness of the combined stick. The details of our explanation are exactly as given
in the foregoing when we discussed Dr. Koehler's "unity" of a
"detour" as a criterion of "insight."

Dr. Koehler's explanation of the same behavior is this:
"After this there is no doubt that he makes use of the double-stick
technique intelligently, and the accident seems merely to have
acted as an aid — fairly strong it is true — which led at once to
'insight.' "[21]

**13. Dr. Koehler has not furnished an experimental proof
of animal intelligence.** There are, then, two explanations of
the chimpanzee's behavior just as there are at times two explanations of the behavior of a player on the football field. From
the mere fact that a player successfully extricates himself from a
difficult situation, we have no right to conclude that, in this particular instance, he solved his problem by the *actual use* of his
intelligence, for the alternate explanation, namely, that he acted
impulsively and as a result of his training, remains possible. If
our doubt on this point is to be settled by an appeal to *direct
experience,* this can be done only by the player himself, namely,
by giving us *an introspective report* as to the actual antecedents
of his behavior in this particular instance. In the absence of such
an introspective report neither explanation can be said to be
proved experimentally. An enthusiastic spectator of the game,

---

[20]*Op. cit.,* p. 193 sq.
[21]*Ibid.,* p. 194.

biased in favor of *Alma Mater* and of the intelligence hypothesis, may insist that the actions of the player speak louder than his words. The answer is that the actions of the player may speak louder than his words, but they are not as intelligible as his words. No matter how accurately the actions of the players may be observed and described, and no matter how astonishing they may be, they are, of themselves, *only equivocal signs of the actual use of the intelligence of the player*.

If the chimpanzee could give an introspective report concerning the conscious antecedents of his behavior, the correctness of Dr. Koehler's explanation could be settled on the basis of direct experience. But this the chimpanzee cannot do. Hence, the correctness of Dr. Koehler's explanation cannot be settled on the basis of *direct* experience. As long as our explanation is sufficient to account for the chimpanzee's behavior, the explanation of Dr. Koehler remains unproved. No matter how accurately the behavior of the chimpanzee on a definite occasion was observed and described by Dr. Koehler, and no matter how astonishing this behavior was to Dr. Koehler, the data observed and described by him contain no experimental proof of the chimpanzee's intelligence. At best, we can say that Dr. Koehler has accurately observed and described equivocal signs of the animal's intelligence. And we have had such equivocal evidence in abundance prior to, and independently of, the elaborate experiments of Dr. Koehler. These experiments, then, have done nothing to further the solution of the problem of animal intelligence.

There is no need of discussing any further details of Dr. Koehler's experiments. *The data which we have chosen and analyzed are typical* of Dr. Koehler's work with chimpanzees and *his explanations quoted in the foregoing are typical* Hence, further quotations would bring us nothing new. We say this with one qualification. The theory of *Gestalt,* precisely as understood by Dr. Koehler, also enters into the discussion. Here, however, the present writer must confess that he is confronted by an enigma and he makes no pretense of solving it. One of the enigmatical features of Dr. Koehler's *Gestalt hypothesis,* as explained incidentally in his book *The Mentality of Apes,* and more fully in his book *Gestalt Psychology* is this: Dr. Koehler seems to think that when we observe the behavior of other men or of animals or of chimpanzees in particular, "insight" is not a matter of interpretation but of *direct experience.* If such be the meaning of Dr. Koehler's statements, *they must be met with a simple denial.*

14. The Lack of Conceptual Language in Animals and its Significance. As experimentalists, we might be satisfied with the verdict at which we have arrived in the last paragraph and rest our case here. Behaviorists have insisted that we cannot go any further and that a *positive* proof either for or against animal intelligence is impossible. The answer is that, though we have no direct experimental proof either for or against animal intelligence, as we have insisted in the last paragraph, we have *circumstantial evidence* which points *unequivocally* to the lack of intelligence in animals. It is the argument on which Fr. Wasmann relied in his explanation of all animal behavior, namely, the argument from the lack of conceptual language in animals If the argument is conclusive, we reach a definite stand with regard to animal intelligence and we make use of this stand whenever we are confronted with equivocal evidence for animal intelligence. Thus the explanation of Dr. Koehler and all defenders of animal intelligence is *positively* ruled out as incompatible with our circumstantial evidence.

Suppose that two phenomena, A and B, always occur together in our experience. That is to say, whenever we have *unequivocal* evidence of A, and we have likewise *unequivocal* evidence of B. Suppose, further, that A, as we know it from our experience, necessarily leads to B so that B is the necessary complement of A. These suppositions granted, *the very absence of B is circumstantial evidence which points unequivocally to the absence of A.* Thus we reach a definite stand with regard to the absence of A and we make use of this stand whenever we are confronted with equivocal evidence for the presence of A.

In this schematic form of our argument, A stands for intelligence, and B for conceptual language in some form. *By conceptual language we mean not only its most developed form, namely, oral speech, but any system of conventional signs by which we are enabled to communicate our thoughts, ideas, and judgments with others.* This involves three distinct elements. *The first* and most fundamental is *the ability to think,* that is, the ability to form concepts and judgments even of the most elementary kind. Every animal that has any of the internal experiences comprehended by Dr. Koehler under the heading of "insight," has the first requisite for language: he has something to say, and the more "insight" he has, the more he has to say. And every animal that lacks "insight," lacks the fundamental requisite for language: he has nothing to say; hence, it is no wonder that he says nothing.

The second requisite may be called the *material* part of language and consists in *the ability to acquire what are technically known as "nonsense movements."* By this term we mean any movement that can be seen, heard, or felt by other sentient beings, but has, of itself, no connection whatever with a definite idea or judgment and hence, of itself, cannot lead any other being to form that idea or judgment. Every word of every language is, of itself, a "nonsense syllable," a "nonsense movement" of the vocal muscles or a combination of such movements. Similarly, every signal of every sign language or code message is, of itself, a "nonsense movement." The material part of the telegrapher's language may be resolved into two movements pure and simple, one corresponding to the dot, the other to the dash. Neither the dot nor the dash, nor any combination of them has, of itself, any connection whatever with a definite idea or judgment. It should be noted that *all animals endowed with a neuromuscular system have in virtue of that very fact the second requirement of language.* And the chimpanzee, whose neuromuscular system is not so very much different from that of man, has the second requirement of language practically in the same degree of perfection as man. There would be nothing surprising in the fact if somebody succeeded in training a young chimpanzee to articulate English words or sentences. Parrots and other animals with a less perfect neuromuscular system have been thus trained.

The third requisite may be called the *formal* element of language and consists in *the ability to associate a definite idea or judgment with a definite "nonsense movement" and to transform that movement into a conventional sign of that idea or judgment.* This transformation has been investigated experimentally even in the case of aphasics, that is, individuals who through some brain lesion have lost the power of speech. We shall return to this important topic in a later chapter. Here it must suffice to state that the transformation of a nonsense movement into a conventional sign of a definite idea can be accomplished only by the coöperation of at least two intelligent individuals.

The essential feature of this coöperation consists in this, that both individuals on some previous occasion have formed identically the same idea and have associated it with identically the same nonsense movement. It makes no difference whether this association arises by force of environment or as a result of deliberate design. The first occurs when a child acquires the very rudiments of his mother tongue; the second occurs when an adult deliberately memorizes a list of foreign words and their equivalents in his mother tongue, thus associating his ideas with the sounds or written symbols of a foreign language. The most elaborate form of deliberate design occurs when scientists come to an explicit agreement as to the meaning of their technical terms. Without such an explicit agreement scientists would not understand each other, and others who are not parties to this agreement will actually fail to understand the language of the scientist. For in no case is the word the father of the thought but, *vice versa,* the thought is in every instance the father of the word, that is, of a conventional sign of that thought. It is only when an idea previously formed by a number of intelligent individuals is associated by all of these individuals with identically the same nonsense movement, that this nonsense movement becomes a "name" of a definite object and arouses in virtue of this association the idea of that object in the mind of any one of these individuals.

For the purposes of our discussion it is important to note that the transformation of nonsense movements into conventional signs of definite ideas and judgments is simply *a social necessity for any group of sentient beings endowed with intelligence* Whoever has ideas or judgments ever so elementary concerning the nature of the objects he sees, hears, or feels, or concerning the purposes they can serve, *has something to say* and, what is more, *he has the impulse to say it* when his needs require it. But he cannot say it without some system of conventional signs of his ideas. As stated in the foregoing, his actions may speak louder than his words, but they are not as *intelligible* to others as his words. And it is the intelligibility of conceptual language in any form which constitutes its social function. Hence, the social needs of an intelligent being are not satisfied by any form of outward behavior, be it ever so intelligent in the sense of Dr. Koehler, but only by some system of conventional signs of definite objects and their corresponding ideas.

Which of the many possible systems is actually acquired by the human child is simply *determined by his social environment.* When a baby babbles with delight and imitates instinctively the sounds that occur in his social environment, *a great many random and instinctive movements become associated in the most haphazard manner with the ideas he gradually acquires.* Of these movements, some become fixed by habit, namely, those which constitute the particular language of his environment and *which, when repeated by him, satisfy his needs.* Thus the little thinker comes gradually to use these movements *deliberately* in order to *indicate* his needs. With this important step the transformation of nonsense movements into conventional signs of ideas is begun. The more ideas the child acquires and the more his social needs grow, the more complex will his system of conventional signs become.

That conceptual language in some form is simply *a social necessity* for intelligent beings as we know them from experience, is further evidenced by the fact that no tribe of men has ever been found without conceptual language in some form. The experiences of deaf-mutes and particularly of some persons born blind and deaf or who became so in earliest infancy, point to the same conclusion. The case of Helen Keller is too well known to need description.

This premised, we are in a position to formulate the argument which *positively* excludes the intelligence hypothesis of Dr. Koehler as an explanation of the behavior of his chimpanzees. Conceptual language in some form is simply a social necessity for a tribe of sentient beings that are endowed with intelligence. If, therefore, the chimpanzees had intelligence, they could not be without conceptual language in some form. But chimpanzees are without conceptual language in any form. They have indeed what we have called the mechanical or material part of language, that is, a great variety of random and nonsense movements and the neuromuscular equipment for acquiring articulate sounds substantially like those of human speech. They have also numerous movements which are signs of their internal experiences. But all these movements are of the instinctive kind known as "expressive movements," or natural signs of their emotions and instinctive impulses. Similar movements, even when they occur in man, are at best only equivocal signs of ideas and judgments. *Such equivocal signs do not satisfy the social needs of intelligent beings.* They may be called a "language of emotion" but do not satisfy our empirical description of conceptual language in any form. From the very fact, then, that chimpanzees and all other animals lack the necessary complement of intelligence, namely, conceptual language in some form, we conclude that they have no intelligence. If it be asked, therefore, why chimpanzees, though endowed with a neuromuscular equipment and a brain almost like those of man, never say anything, our answer is, because they have nothing to say, that is, because they lack intelligence.

15. Clever Hans. Before dismissing the intelligence theory of instinct, it may be well to state briefly that another experimental demonstration of animal intelligence was once attempted, which, in its day, was even more sensational than that of Dr. Koehler. We refer to the wonderful doings of Clever Hans, the horse owned and "instructed" (not "trained") by Herr von Osten. The latter was a teacher of mathematics, and his horse became a mathematical genius. The story went like wildfire all over the world, and Clever Hans became a trade name pretty much like Babe Ruth is today. The *dénouement* came when the psychological department of the University of Berlin examined the horse.

The experimental arrangements used in discomfiting Clever Hans were devised by Dr. Pfungst and are described by him in a monograph entitled *Clever Hans*. The data obtained in this investigation showed clearly that *the performances of Clever Hans were substantially on a par with those of every other animal that has been trained to associate definite movements with definite signals of the trainer*. The principal difference was that the trainer of Clever Hans, Herr von Osten, had *no intention* to *"train"* the animal, and *gave his signals without even being aware of the fact*. These signals arose naturally from the very *expectations* of von Osten. When he *expected* a tap of the horse, he nodded his head, and he made an upward jerk with his head, when he *expected* the horse to stop tapping. Though these movements were unintentional on the part of Herr von Osten, and though they became gradually very slight, they were nevertheless the signals which guided the animal in his performances. Accordingly, the horse knew exactly as much mathematics as his questioner knew, that is, he tapped exactly as his questioner *expected* him to tap. When a questioner *expected* the answer 17 to the question "How much is twice two?" the horse answered without fail "17."

Clever Hans is dead. But his successors "the Elberfeld horses" seem to live to this day, at least in popular magazines. After the remarkable work of Dr. Pfungst with Clever Hans there is no reason why his successors should receive a detailed discussion in a text of psychology.

References for Further Reading

E. Wasmann, S.J., *Instinct and Intelligence in the Animal Kingdom* (1903).
E. Wasmann, S.J., *Psychology of Ants and of Higher Animals* (1905).
J. Lindworsky, S.J., in *Stimmen der Zeit*, Vol. 95 (1918), pp. 886 sqq.
E. L. Thorndike, *Animal Intelligence: An Experimental Study, etc.* (1911).

Chapter XIII

INSTINCT
(Concluded)

1. **The lapsed-intelligence or racial-habit theory of instinct** is an attempt to explain the origin of instinctive activities by the combination of three theories, namely, (1) a modified form of the reflex theory, (2) a modified form of the intelligence theory, and (3) the Darwinian theory of natural selection. There are some instinctive activities, we are told, that show the marks of skill so plainly that it is impossible to explain their origin without attributing to animals some degree of intelligence. It is straining belief to suppose, for instance, that the extremely complex operations required for nest building are determined by a neural organization which is entirely inherited. If it is not entirely inherited, it has been in part acquired. But it could not possibly have been acquired except by *the intelligent adaptation of the animal to its environment.*

The real point of the argument is that animals have thus acquired something which is *without comparison more complex than anything that Dr. Koehler has observed in his experiments with chimpanzees.* If Dr Koehler, for instance, had observed that a chimpanzee gradually acquires the skill necessary for building a structure such as beavers erect, we could not possibly deny that there is an intelligence at work. In other words, what Dr Koehler has actually observed are the merest trifles in comparison with what animals in nature must have done in the acquisition of their skill. Hence even though our explanation of Dr. Koehler's experimental data is admitted as perfectly adequate, it is hopelessly inadequate when applied to the facts which must have occurred in the gradual acquisition of animal skill.

What adds to the force of the argument is this: If the skill of the beaver is gradually acquired, there have been many generations of beavers whose neural equipment was insufficient to deal with their building problem successfully. But *of what use is an insufficient neural equipment?* If all beavers in the past had fumbled, there would be no beavers today. But there are. Hence the evident conclusion that not all beavers in the past have fumbled. Some indeed have, and they — we are told by Darwin — were snuffed out of existence by "natural selection." But those that have survived have not fumbled, or at least they have not fumbled all the time. And this means that the beavers of the past generations had intelligence.

According to this theory, then, *instinctive activities of animals are conceived as "racial habits."* This means that successive generations of animals have acquired their skill pretty much the same way as man in the course of his individual lifetime acquires skill, namely, by *the gradual mechanization of intelligent actions.* It is a plain fact of experience that such a gradual mechanization of intelligent actions occurs during the lifetime of every individual man. The result of this process of mechanization is the formation of a neural habit. When you began to play the piano, every movement had to be considered and was performed intelligently. As you kept on practicing a piece of music, you paid less and less attention to the thoughts that guided you in the beginning. When you "know" your piece perfectly, you pay no further attention to the thoughts that guided you in the beginning. The whole series of complex movements may now be touched off by one thought, namely, to play a definite piece of music. Your nervous system takes care of all the rest. The skill you show now is, at least to a great extent, simply a matter of neural habit. *By hypothesis now a similar process of mechanization is assumed to have occurred in the successive generations of animals,* say beavers. As long as their inherited neural organization was insufficient to deal with their building problem, it had to be supplemented by intellectual considerations. That is why not all beavers are snuffed out of existence. What was acquired by the intelligent activity of any successful beaver was *transmitted to its offspring.* Thus the neural organization of successive generations of beavers gradually improved until it reached the perfection it has in beavers today. *But each genera-tion of beavers had to supplement the deficiencies of its neural organization by intelligent adaptation.* The further we go back in the history of beavers, the more intelligence we must assume in them. Beavers today are but bundles of "racial habits," and very little, if any, intelligence is required in them for the success-ful solution of their building problem. But primeval beavers re-quired a good deal of it. From this it will be seen why this ex-planation of instinctive activities of animals is called the "lapsed-intelligence" theory.

2. **The first and most obvious objection to the lapsed-intelligence theory is that it ascribes to animals of past generations a kind of knowledge for which no human in-telligence suffices.** To convince ourselves of this, we have only to apply the theory to some instinctive activities which have been most carefully observed and described by a number of naturalists. Thus, for instance, many insects never see their progeny and hence cannot possibly know from experience what becomes of the eggs they deposit.[1] Yet they have the peculiar habit of plac-ing next to each egg, food materials such as are best suited to the needs of the larva which develops from the egg. What adds to the marvel of the performance of these insects is that this food differs from their own and in some instances would be utterly useless for themselves. Now what sort of reasoning can possibly guide the insects in the performance of these acts? *A naturalist who observes these operations and has identically the same data as are within the reach of the hypothetical intelligence of the in-sect, could not possibly reason out what the insect of a past gen-eration is supposed to have reasoned out.* If this insect really knew what it is supposed to have known concerning the useful-ness of its operation, then it has sources of knowledge not within the reach of man: *its intelligence is superhuman.* Thus we have

[1] For details, we refer the reader to a publication which is readily accessible, namely, *Science and Scientists*, by J. Gerard, S.J.

reached the *reductio ad absurdum* of the lapsed-intelligence theory.

Another consideration leads us to the same conclusion. All instinctive actions are complex, that is, they consist of a series of part-operations. *The single links of this series are sometimes widely separated from one another both in time and in space.* They are not useful for the preservation of the individual or the species unless they follow one another in regular order and are joined into a system. Moreover, at times *the usefulness of any particular action depends on future contingencies* which are beyond the control of the animal performing that action. Consequently the animal could not possibly know the usefulness of a present action unless it foresaw these future contingencies and unless it correlated facts widely separated from one another both in time and space. Naturalists with all the resources of modern science at their command have as yet not succeeded in correlating all these facts in every instance. Far from it. At any rate, *no naturalist could determine the usefulness of any particular action of an animal from the data which are within the reach of the hypothetical intelligence of that animal.* If, in spite of all that, the animal knows the usefulness of that action, it knows what human intelligence could not know; *its intelligence is superhuman.*

3. The second serious objection to the lapsed-intelligence theory is that it makes assumptions concerning the hereditary transmission of acquired characters which cannot stand the test of a scientific theory. No doubt, the instinctive accomplishments of animals present a problem of heredity and probably also one of development in the animal kingdom. It would lead us too far afield to discuss these biological matters here in detail. Nor is this necessary for the purposes of our present discussion. For it can be shown quite readily that of all the theories dealing with these matters the lapsed-intelligence theory is the least satisfactory. We need only point out some plain facts concerning the most marvelous instincts known to see that these instincts could not possibly have arisen by an hereditary transmission such as is postulated by the lapsed-intelligence theory.

The instincts referred to are those of *neuter insects.* Working bees are the best-known example of this class of animals. They are really undeveloped females which never reproduce their kind. Reproduction is taken care of by the queen bee and one of the drones who have different habits altogether. *The workers, then, are descended from parents who never did a stroke of work for the community and were not equipped to do it.* All such work devolves on the neuter bees and they have, marvelously enough, special organs and special instincts to do it successfully. Whatever intricacies of Mendelian heredity may be required to explain the origin of their equipment, one thing is abundantly clear, and that is, that *these instincts could not possibly have been inherited from their parents after the manner stated in the lapsed-intelligence theory.* And the workers themselves never have any offspring. Hence, even if they acquired new accomplishments by intelligent adaptation, *they could not possibly transmit them to the next generation.* Thus, the lapsed-intelligence theory breaks down completely when applied to a concrete example of those very animal activities which are invoked to prove it, namely, activities which bear unmistakably the imprint of intelligence.

It is well to add, however, that ruling out the lapsed-intelligence theory of instinct is one thing, and a *positive* explanation of the origin of the peculiar instincts of neuter insects is quite another. In our present state of knowledge concerning the facts of heredity and variation, we are simply not able to give such a positive explanation. We refer the interested reader to the excellent treatment of these biological matters in Wasmann's *Biology and the Theory of Evolution.* And as to the theory of evolution, we must be satisfied here with stating that *evolution and Darwinism are far from being synonymous terms.* If evolution has occurred in the animal kingdom — and it seems probable that it has – it cannot have occurred along Darwinian lines. *The work of Abbot Mendel and his followers is more likely to lead us to a truly scientific conception of evolution in the animal kingdom than the speculations of Darwin concerning the function of natural selection.* If Darwin had known the epoch-making discoveries of his contemporary, Abbot Mendel, he could not possibly have said what he did say concerning the subjects of heredity and variation, and *the whole discussion of evolution would have taken a different turn.* But these epoch-making discoveries lay buried and forgotten in the archives of a local scientific society, while everybody was speculating on the wonderful things that natural selection could do. Fr. Wasmann's book, previously referred to, will supply all the details merely hinted at in our general remarks. In this book the reader will also find a thorough discussion of the comprehensive dogma of materialistic evolution which includes the mental endowments of man in its scheme concerning the origin of everything in this sublunary world of ours. There is no evidence whatever for such a conception, if evidence be understood in its accepted scientific meaning.

For a more detailed discussion of the moot question concerning *the heredity transmission of acquired mental traits* we refer the reader to the first chapter in *The Foundations of Experimental Psychology* edited by Carl Murchison.

4. **There is a grain of truth both in the intelligence and the lapsed-intelligence theory** and it is this: It is true that many instinctive activities of animals bear so *unmistakably* the imprint of design that it is impossible to deny that there is an intelligence at work. The design, moreover, thus manifested is so *intricate, constant,* and *universal* that *no human intelligence* could originate or execute it, as we have pointed out in the foregoing. Where there is design, there is a designer, and where there is a superhuman design, there is a superhuman designer. But it does not follow that the animal is a superhuman designer. The whole difficulty vanishes if we assume that the Maker of the animal is the designer. The only thing which then remains to be explained is, *what part the animal plays in the execution of the Divine design.* We shall deal with this when examining the sensitive-impulse theory of instinct.

It has been said that modern science has outgrown the view that God is the designer of the animals and their instinctive activities. "Apart from the older view," says Baldwin, "which saw in animal instinct simply a matter of original created endowment, whereby each animal was made once for all 'after his kind,' and according to which there is no further reason that the instincts are what they are than that they were made so; apart from this 'special creation' view, two different ideas have had currency, both based upon the theory of evolution."[2] The answer is that our doctrine just stated is not necessarily bound up with the "special creation" view and does not exclude a scientific theory of evolution in the animal kingdom. All it excludes is the materialistic form of evolution. Whether our present animals are the unchanged descendants of those created immediately by Almighty God, or whether God in creating the great diversity of animal forms made use of secondary agents such as are postulated in a scientific theory of evolution, *in either case God is the designer of animals and of all their instinctive activities.* In fact, humanly speaking, the Divine design appears even *grander* and *more comprehensive* if it includes laws of development imprinted upon the primitive types of animals which proceeded immediately from the hand of Almighty God.

Another consideration is just as important in this connection. When we say that God is the designer of the instinctive activities of animals, this does not imply that animals are merely extrinsically directed by God pretty much as a machine is directed by an engineer. *A naïve anthropomorphism like this is as little in keeping with the dignity of Almighty God as it is far removed from the facts of instinct as we know them.* The facts of instinct postulate that *there is a driving force within the animal itself which in ordinary contingencies guides it unerringly to the attainment of definite ends but under unusual conditions fails to do so.* If we admit that God has endowed each animal with a driving force such as will be explained presently in the sensitive-impulse theory

---

[2] *The Story of the Mind,* pp. 29 sqq.

of instinct, we not only avoid all anthropomorphism but we do justice to all the facts of animal instinct. Then it can be said in a true, though imperfect, sense that *the animal directs itself and tends toward ends of which it knows nothing,* these ends being known and willed only by Almighty God. Then and then only will *the seeming inconsistencies, antinomies, and paradoxes of animal activities disappear.* We understand why animals show forth such superhuman intelligence side by side with unspeakable stupidities. Thus, in general outline at least, the enigma of animal instinct is solved, and in our present state of knowledge we cannot accomplish more. For *with regard to many details of animal instinct we are and, in all probability, shall ever remain in the dark.* In order, then, to complete our account of this difficult subject it remains for us to examine the sensitive-impulse theory of instinct.

5. The sensitive-impulse theory of instinct maintains that *the driving force back of instinctive activities of animals is neither more nor less than a sensitive impulse aroused by pleasant or unpleasant sensory experiences, and that the animal in doing what is pleasant or avoiding what is unpleasant reaches what is useful for the individual and the species and thus coöperates in the execution of the Divine design.* This hypothesis is not only sufficient but also required to account for the facts of animal instinct in accordance with what we said concerning the starting point in explaining animal behavior.

It is sufficient. For we experience in ourselves sensitive impulses such as are postulated in our hypothesis and they guide us effectively in the performance of operations which are of vital importance for the welfare of the individual and the species. Hence such impulses, if present in animals, are, of themselves, sufficient to account for similar activities of animals.

Our hypothesis is also required. For only thus do we avoid the incongruities of all rival theories (the reflex, the intelligence, and the lapsed-intelligence theories) and retain all the grains of truth contained in them. In a word, only by the sensitive-impulse theory do we satisfy the demands of a legitimate argument from analogy. This is sufficiently clear from what we have said before. To clinch our argument, then, we must show *from our own experience* that sensitive impulses such as are postulated in our hypothesis, suffice to explain all the facts of animal instinct.

6. An Empirical Description of Instinct in Terms of Our Own Experience. Of course, in our adult life we never experience sensitive impulses pure and simple. They are always interwoven with other incentives to action. Prominent among them are rational considerations of various kinds, considerations of propriety, expediency, politeness, and the obligations we have toward God and our fellow men, etc. These considerations give rise to rational impulses which may reënforce or inhibit our sensitive impulses. Thus our conduct becomes, frequently at least, one of free choice, even though we actually yield to the promptings of our sensitive nature. It is not difficult, however, to distinguish these sensitive impulses from the rational incentives to action. We can observe how these sensitive impulses arise and how they guide us in our actions. *Thus we are enabled to describe instinct — the driving force back of instinctive activities of animals — in terms that can be verified in our own experience.* We shall describe in turn (1) the food instinct, (2) the play instinct, (3) the sexual instinct.

The Food Instinct

When after a hard day's work you come home, you must still perform a series of operations which are of the greatest importance for your welfare. You must furnish your body with a number of calories sufficient for your physiological combustion. Physiologists have calculated exactly how many you need. They have also calculated what percentage of the combustible materials you take must be in the form of proteids, carbohydrates, and fats, respectively. They insist also that over and above these materials you require certain peculiar substances known by the name of "vitamins," and that some of them must be water-soluble and others fat-soluble. If you have ever read a treatise on the physiology of nutrition, you will realize that the task which confronts you at the fag-end of the day is really the hardest of all. How are you ever going to solve this difficult problem?

Now God in His infinite wisdom has arranged it in such a way that the difficult task ahead of you becomes a pleasure, and that by doing what is pleasant you reach what is useful and of vital importance for you. What happens is something like this: The food spread on the dinner table is rather pleasant to look at and it smells good. Cooks call it "appetizing" and a psychologist could not express it better. The pleasant sensory experience you have arouses what in ordinary parlance goes by the name of "appetite." *You experience an impulse to put things that look like this and smell like this, right into your mouth, and if you do so, they taste like more.* Ill-smelling and ugly-looking things do not arouse such an impulse; they rather arouse an opposite impulse, to get away from them. *Thus food is distinguished from nonfood,* not in terms of physiological requirements, but *in terms of pleasant sensory experiences and the sensitive impulses arising from them.* This is what "food" means to the vast majority of mankind and to the physiologist as well when he is outside his laboratory. Thus the perplexing problem of nutrition is solved practically by the God-given "food instinct": the sensitive impulses arising from certain pleasant or unpleasant sensory experiences.

A qualification is in place here. What we said a little while ago of all instincts of animals, holds also of the "food instinct" of man. In ordinary contingencies instinct guides both man and animal unerringly to the attainment of the end intended by God, but under extraordinary conditions it fails to do so. When a fish snaps at a worm, it follows its instinct and thus procures its own welfare. But sometimes there happens to be a hook in the worm and the fish in snapping at the worm gets caught on the hook. Something similar may happen to man. His superiority over the animal consists in this that he can, and is supposed to, make use of his reason and detect the danger which *per accidens* lurks in the things that arouse his appetite. It has been said that many men dig their graves with their teeth. This is true. But it is not the God-given "food instinct" itself which is at fault, but rather the abuse of it which leads to destruction. It is not the intention of God that man should be guided exclusively by his instincts. He is to be what no animal can be, the master of his animal cravings. He is supposed to control them in conformity with the dictates of right reason. The notable fact is that man, by his free choice, acquired habits, and theoretic prepossessions of all kinds, can and does sometimes, interfere with the designs of Divine Providence. If it were not for this fact and for the further fact that the problem of nutrition is in part also one of the pocket-book, the investigations of the physiologists would be only of academic interest. Things being as they are, man had better take into consideration the warnings of the physiologist, particularly in the case of sickness. The physiologist, on the other hand, would be wide of the mark if, in prescribing a balanced diet, he did not take the facts of instinct here described into consideration. In short, *man is a rational animal and his place in nature is unique.*

The Play Instinct

We must, moreover, take a certain amount of exercise every day in order to remain in a healthy condition. Setting-up exercises have been devised which are in accord with the particular requirements, say, of a growing boy. Preach to that boy about the physiological basis of such exercises and about the neural organization he will thus acquire, and tell him that his work in manhood will depend on such a neural organization; add to this what psychologists have to say about the advantages to be derived from such exercises: the boy may not even understand what you are saying. The problem thus put to him from the scientific point of view, appeals to him very little. It will be at best a task as irksome as a problem in arithmetic that must be solved before he goes back to school the next day. But give that boy a ball, and that task will become a pleasure for him. *He just likes to play with the ball. By doing what he likes, he gets what is useful and necessary for him.* Even physical setting-up exercises will be performed all the better, if they take the form of rhythmic play. Thus the God-given "play instinct" does for the boy what no rational considerations could do. And the "play instinct" resolves itself into the sensitive impulses arising from pleasant sensations.

The Sexual Instinct

The problem of the propagation of the human race takes, in each instance, the form of a love story and it does so according to the design of Almighty God Himself. It is, however, not the intention of God that man should be guided in this important matter *exclusively* by his instincts, as irrational animals are. Man is supposed to *control* the sexual instinct in accordance with the dictates of right reason. Most of the evils resulting from this instinct would be avoided if man acted in a manner befitting his rational nature and in obedience to the law of God. In short, *it is not the God-given instinct as such that leads to disaster, but the "ingenuity" of man in devising means for frustrating the designs of God* Of itself, this instinct has a most important function to perform. For without it the human race would soon become extinct. It is not the thought of the future generation that insures the propagation of the human species; it is the God-given instinct that does so.

7. Limitations in the Application of Our Hypothesis to the Individual Activities of Animals. If animals are guided in their instinctive activities by sensitive impulses arising from pleasant or unpleasant sensory experiences, as our hypothesis postulates, the question naturally presents itself, *"Why do animals do such strange things?"* What thrill, for instance, can there be for the hen in incubating a nestful of eggs? Or what fascination can there be in a putrifying carcass that a fly should select it out of all the world for depositing its eggs there?

The answer is that these things seem strange *to us,* for we have no such instincts. But to the animals that have these instincts there is nothing strange whatever in the actions which they feel impelled to perform. If these animals could philosophize about their doings, they would say what a boy would say when

asked why he likes to play with a ball. *Of course,* he likes to play
with a ball. To him it is simply absurd to ask any *further reason*
why he likes to do so. Similarly it is a *matter of course* that animals like to do just what they do, and to them — if they could
reason — it must seem simply absurd to ask why they like to do
so. *As James has put it "to the broody hen the notion would
probably seem monstrous that there should be a creature in the
world to whom a nestful of eggs was not the utterly fascinating
and precious and never-to-be-too-much-sat-upon object which it
is to her."* In short, there is no disputing about tastes. This is
true not only of those human tastes that are plainly acquired and
change with the fashions or habits that give rise to them, but it
is particularly true of those tastes which are essentially bound
up with the inherited constitution of each species of animal.
Such tastes and the impulses arising from them of necessity differ
from animal to animal just as their inherited organizations differ.
And, what is more important for our discussion, all the tastes and
impulses of brute animals differ, of course, from human tastes
and impulses.

This brings us to a limitation in the application of the argument from analogy. *This argument does not justify us in attributing to animals human tastes and impulses even of the purely sensory kind.* Far from it. All we are justified in concluding
from certain modes of behavior in animals is contained in this
general statement: Just as we experience sensory impulses to do or
to avoid certain things, so animals experience sensory impulses to
do or to avoid just what they do or avoid. And just as our sensitive
impulses arise from pleasant or unpleasant sensory experiences, so
do the impulses of animals. What these pleasant or unpleasant
sensory experiences are in detail we cannot tell. It would seem
probable, however, that *the sensations of smell and taste and the
various organic sensations due to changes within the animal body
itself, are the principal sources of animal pleasures and displeas-
ures and the corresponding impulses to action.* In short, in the
absence of an introspective report, we can reconstruct the psychic

antecedents of instinctive actions only in *general* terms. And this, to a certain extent at least, is one of the reasons why many of the things that animals do seem so strange to us.

There is another limitation in the application of the sensitive-impulse theory to the *individual* actions of animals. We said that instinctive actions consist of a whole series of reactions and we have admitted all along that some links in this series may be true physiological reflexes. At times the analogy between animal and human behavior is not sufficient for us to decide whether a particular reaction of an animal is due to a sensitive impulse and pleasurable sensations or whether it belongs to some other category of reactions. In other words, *we admit the grains of truth contained in all the rival theories of instinct,* as we have pointed out before. If this be kept in mind, a good deal of the strangeness of animal reactions will disappear. In short, we emphasize again that our sensitive-impulse theory is couched in general terms. We recognize the fact that *with regard to details of animal instinct we know very little.*

8. Instinct and Experience. Perfect and Imperfect Instincts. Without a suitable neural organization no sensitive impulse would arise in the animal and no instinctive action would be performed. This neural organization may be *entirely inherited* or *partly acquired* by the various forms of "learning" of which the animal is capable. In the first case we speak of *perfect instincts,* in the second, of *imperfect instincts.*

There are certain actions of animals which are *performed only once in their individual lifetime.* They must be performed successfully when the time for action comes or the animal will be snuffed out of existence. The conditions under which the actions occur are such that the animal cannot be guided either by its own past experience or by its instinct of imitation. In short, all modes of "learning" of which the animal is capable are excluded. In such instances, then, the animal must have an inherited neural organization perfectly sufficient to perform the act without fumbling. Thus, for instance, a bird frees itself only once in its lifetime from the shell in which it develops. And the operation is complex, so much so that considerable time is required to perform it. To be successful, the animal must coördinate two series of movements. While pecking at the shell it must so turn in the shell that it makes an opening large enough to slip through. Undoubtedly the neural organization required for doing this must be inherited in its entirety. *If,* therefore, these operations of the bird are not merely a chain of reflexes, but are due to sensitive impulses or instinct proper, this instinct is a *perfect* one. We express the same thing by saying that the instinct is *innate.* This, however, must not be construed to mean that the animal has any innate cognitions. *What is innate, is only the neural organizatio*n. The sensory experiences are aroused by the stimuli present, and give rise to feelings of pleasure or displeasure. These emotional experiences, in turn, arouse sensory impulses to action. *The three elements, then, into which instinct proper is resolved, namely, sensory experiences, emotions, and impulses, are indeed intimately bound up with the inherited organization, but none of these psychic elements is innate as the neural organization is.* At least there is no evidence that anything beyond the neural organization is innate in the case of a perfect instinct.

The vast majority of instincts are imperfect. In the case of these the inherited neural organization is not sufficient for a perfect performance of the actions to which they lead. Thus, for instance, even so simple an operation as the chick's pecking at a grain of seed has been found under experimental conditions to be far from perfect in the beginning. The improvement which comes with practice has been accurately recorded. The same is particularly true with regard to more complicated actions. Thus, for instance, canaries have from the beginning only the organs necessary for their peculiar song and an impulse to use these organs. If young canaries are kept in isolation, they will acquire a different song or they may not sing at all. If they are kept from the beginning in the company of shouting sparrows, they will develop a very disagreeable song. The original canary from the Canary Islands is not worth having. *The singing canary is in every single instance an artificial product, the result of instinct and training.*

Master birds are used, and other devices are employed in training them. Among these devices is an instrument known as a bird organ, so constructed as to produce liquid trills. Besides, if one of the youngsters begins to sing harshly, he is promptly removed from the company of the others. Thus the young birds are given perfect models to imitate. The instinct of imitation supplements the original instinct to use the vocal organs, and practice does the rest.

9. The Principal Causes of the Variations of Instinct. The variations which occur in the case of imperfect instincts are due to a number of causes. The first is *the engrafting of a habit on an instinct*. Once an instinct is acted on in a definite way, something by way of a trace is left in the nervous system and this means a change in the neural organization. When a habit is formed by the frequent repetition of the same act, the neural organization thus created is just as strong as one that is inherited and perfect from the beginning. And, what is more important, *the habit thus formed will be an incentive to action quite distinct from the original instinct on which the habit is grafted*. Hence, even if the original instinct should gradually fade out — and some do, as we shall explain when speaking of the transitoriness of certain instincts — the action to which the instinct gave rise, will still be performed simply by force of habit. It is thus that numerous variations in instinctive actions of animals of the same species arise. As stated in the beginning, such actions are only *specifically the same* for all individuals of the same species: *individually they differ*.

Another cause of the variation in instinctive activities of animals is the *supplementing of one instinct by another*. Thus, as explained previously, many imperfect instincts are supplemented by the instinct of imitation, which is present in all higher animals and in some to a marked degree.

A third cause is *the inhibition of one instinct by another*. Some objects arouse opposite instincts either simultaneously or on different occasions. We know this from our own experience. Thus a dog may arouse the impulse of fondling or that of fear. If a child acts on the impulse of patting the dog, and gets bitten, this impulse may die out entirely. At any rate, the instinct of fear will exert an inhibiting influence when the impulse of fondling arises again. In animals the matter is settled by the line of least resistance. The method of "learning" known as "the trial-and-error" method, similarly that known as the "formation of a new association" are really cases of the inhibition of one instinct by another.

Still another cause of the variation in instinctive activities of animals are the facts known under the headings of the maturation and the transitoriness of instinct.

10. The Maturation and the Transitoriness of Instincts. We said that all instincts suppose a neural organization which at least in part is inherited. This needs an explanation, let it be misunderstood. *When we say that a neural organization is inherited, this does not necessarily mean that it is ready at the birth of the animal.* The nervous system of the animal is not yet fully finished at birth, and this is particularly true in the case of man. All we mean by calling a neural organization inherited is, that *it is not acquired dependently on the experience of the animal or of man.* There occurs a post-embryonic development of the animal body which, in part at least, is independent of any process of "learning." The result is that some instincts arise normally only at a definite period of the individual's life. Thus, for instance, the sexual instinct normally does not arise before the age of puberty. Internal secretions — that is, secretions which arise in ductless glands and are poured directly into the blood stream — are additional factors of the neural organization and the impulses connected therewith. Though the fact is well established, the manner in which internal secretions contribute to the maturation of "delayed instincts" is as yet little understood.

If through some cause or other an impulse is not acted upon at the time when the instinct is mature, the instinct may die out. This is what is meant by the transitoriness of instincts Even if an instinct does not completely die out, it makes a great difference whether or not it is acted on at the time of its maturity. It is thus that some variations in instinctive activities of animals arise which.

at first sight, are somewhat puzzling, as we shall explain presently. The facts here referred to throw light, also, on what really takes place when animals are said to *"recognize"* their parents, offspring, friends, and enemies. This "recognition" is a most important element in the driving force back of instinctive activities. By describing it in the light of all the pertinent facts we get information as to the part which memory plays in the instinctive operations of animals.

11. How Animals "Recognize" Their Parents, Offspring, Friends, and Enemies. Animals give undoubted evidence not only of sensations, emotions, and sensory impulses, but also of *memory.* Now memory, as we explained in a previous chapter, involves three essential elements; namely, (1) *retention* (2) *recall,* and (3) *recognition.* There can be no difficulty about retention and recall in the case of animal memory. They can be expressed readily in terms of association psychology. But what about the third element? We have explained what recognition really implies in terms of our own experience. It involves the perception of time, the perception of the Ego, the perception of the identity of the present Ego with the Ego of the past, and the perception of the identity of the object of the present experience with that experienced on a past occasion. All this is implied in the simple, unsophisticated statement by which we express recognition, as for instance, "I have seen this before." Without these perceptions we simply have no memory as we understand that term in ordinary parlance, and all of these perceptions are of the intellectual kind. *If animals have such perceptions, undoubtedly they have intellect. And if these perceptions be absent, as we are bound to say according to the sensitive-impulse theory, how can it be said that animals have memory at all?*

The answer is that animals have purely sensory memory and this involves, of course, also some form of recognition. But *this recognition is merely an analogous imitation of recognition as defined in the chapter on Memory* In that chapter we dealt exclusively with human memory. It would be an unwarranted use of the argument from analogy if we ascribed all our experiences without qualification to animals. If we call recognition as defined in the chapter on Memory *"formal recognition,"* we deny that animals have "formal recognition." Instead of this, animals have *a practical equivalent of formal recognition,* that is, they have *sensory experiences, emotions, and impulses which guide them just as effectively in their actions as formal recognition would.* Only in this sense do animals "recognize" their parents, offspring, friends, and enemies. Some facts concerning the maturation and the transitoriness of certain instincts will show that this explanation suffices perfectly to account for all the phenomena of "recognition" in animal life.

Most higher animals immediately after birth show no instinct of fear but rather that of attachment, and allow themselves to be handled very freely. If the animal at this stage of its life be introduced to its "natural enemy," equally young, and if both be watched carefully by a trainer, as is done in menageries, each may "recognize" the other for life as his "friend." If, however, such animals are born in the wilderness and are introduced to each other at a later stage, when the instinct of attachment has died out, and that of fear is mature, each will "recognize" the other as his "enemy." Chicks are said to "recognize" their mother, and hens are said to "recognize" their young and tell them from those of other broods. If the objective data thus interpreted be carefully observed and recorded in laboratory fashion, *this "recognition" resolves itself into something very prosaic indeed.* James quotes the observations made and recorded by Spalding on this subject. If a chick is born in the absence of the hen, it "will follow any moving object. And when guided by sight alone, they seem to have no more disposition to follow a hen than to follow a duck or a human being. Unreflecting lookers-on, when they saw chickens a day old running after me," says Mr. Spalding, "and older ones following me for miles, and answering to my whistle, imagined that I must have some occult power over the creatures: whereas I had simply allowed them to follow me from the first.

There is the instinct to follow; and the ear, prior to experience, attaches them to the right object."[3]

The instinct to follow, mature at the birth of a chick, fades out in a few days. If, therefore, chicks are kept hooded during the first days of their life, no habit to follow the hen will be engrafted on their early instinct. Instead, another instinct has matured in the meantime, namely that of flight. Speaking of chicks that had been kept hooded for a number of days, Spalding reports as follows: "A chicken that has not heard the call of the mother until eight or ten days old then hears it as if it heard it not. I regret to find that on this point my notes are not so full as I could wish, or as they might have been. There is however, an account of one chicken that could not be returned to the mother when ten days old. The hen followed it, and tried to entice it in every way; still, it continually left her and ran to the house or to any person of whom it caught sight. This it persisted in doing, though beaten back with a small branch dozens of times, and, indeed, cruelly maltreated. It was also placed under the mother at night, but it again left her in the morning."[4]

What holds of "recognition" holds equally of "insight," "judgment," and all other mental acts of undoubted intellectual character. If we call judgment, as we know it from our internal experience, "formal judgment" — and we shall analyze and define it carefully in the chapter on Thought — then we deny that animals have "formal judgment." Instead of this *they have a practical equivalent of formal judgment,* that is, they have *sensory experiences emotions, and impulses which guide them just as effectively in their actions as formal judgment would.* Only in this sense do animals "judge." Only in this sense are they "sagacious," "clever," "cunning," "economical" and so through the whole list of analogous imitations of human intelligence in the instinctive life of animals.

12. **Summing up,** then, our lengthy discussion, we note, first

---

[3]Quoted by James, *Psychology,* pp. 400 sqq.
[4]Quoted by James, *op. cit ,* pp. 402 sqq.

of all, that the nature of instinct — the driving force back of instinctive activities of animals — can be determined only by inference from the purely objective data that animal behavior furnishes. A merely phenomenal description of the facts as observed
either inside or outside the laboratory contains nothing of "insight," *Gestalt* or any other mental fact, not even the simplest
sensation of an animal. All such mental facts are a matter of interpretation. And all such interpretation to be legitimate must
take the form of the argument from analogy, the analogy,
namely, between human and animal behavior, and we must
not state more by way of conclusion than is required and sufficient to account for the facts observed. Behaviorists by denying
all psychic antecedents of animal behavior go too far in one
direction and the defenders of the intelligence and lapsed-intelligence theories go too far in the opposite direction. The
truth lies in the middle. All that is required and sufficient to
account for instinctive actions of animals are sensory experiences, actual or revived, emotions and sensory impulses, together with corresponding neural organizations which are
either totally inherited or partly acquired. Our explanation,
however, is couched in general terms, for with regard to details
very little is known. In fact, sometimes it is very difficult to decide whether any particular reaction of an animal is a physiological reflex or due to those mental factors which are postulated in
the sensitive-impulse theory.

The science of psychology has gained nothing by the numerous
attempts made in the past and in recent times to humanize the
brute and the chimpanzee in particular. Though these attempts
may satisfy those biased in favor of man's animal descent, they
have in reality only emphasized the inconsistencies, antinomies,
and paradoxes of animal life. In our sensitive-impulse theory
all of these inconsistencies, antinomies, and paradoxes disappear
and all the facts of animal life are harmoniously explained. Of
course, our doctrine supposes the existence of an All-wise
Creator Who directs all His creatures in accordance with each
one's peculiar nature and to ends which fit into the compre-

hensive plan of Divine Providence. And our doctrine safeguards man's unique place in nature as king of the visible creation. These aspects of our doctrine are probably the real reasons why our simple explanation of animal instinct is not acceptable to many.

References for Further Reading

J. Froebes, S.J., *Lehrbuch der Experimentellen Psychologie*, Vol. II (1929), pp. 408 sqq.

E. Wasmann, S.J., *Instinct and Intelligence* (1903).

E. Wasmann, S.J., *Modern Biology and the Theory of Evolution* (1910).

J. Gerard, S.J., *Science and Scientists*.

Chapter XIV

THOUGHT

1. A Preliminary Description of Thought or Intelligence; Our Problem. Opinions of modern psychologists differ widely as to the nature of thought. Hence, we cannot begin with an essential definition of thought. We should be thus anticipating the conclusions which we shall arrive at as a result of our empirical inquiry. However, in order to have a starting point, we must give a preliminary and noncommittal description of thought or intelligence.

When we discussed animal intelligence we were confronted with a similar task: we had to give a preliminary description of intelligence. But there our mode of procedure was dictated by the requirements of the subject in hand. The description of any particular thought process was sufficient. At present our preliminary description of intelligence must not only be accurate and noncommittal, but it should, if possible, be comprehensive: it should fit all and only those conscious processes with which our conclusions deal. Lastly, our preliminary definition should recede as little as possible from the common usage of the term intelligence. Science gains nothing by getting out of touch with the problems of everyday life. What description of intelligence satisfies all these requirements?

Some descriptions of intelligence that have been proposed are too narrow, others are too wide. Thus, for instance, intelligence has been described as *the ability to advance knowledge by original research.* According to this definition a college freshman who appropriates and reproduces knowledge that has been acquired by others, shows no intelligence. The definition is evidently too narrow and recedes unnecessarily from the common usage of the term. Not only a college freshman but also children in the grade school show a good deal of what is ordinarily designated by the term "intelligence." Even a child in the kindergarten gives unequivocal evidence of that characteristic which according to our account of instinct, separates man by an impassable gulf from all animals.

Intelligence has also been described as *the critical attitude of a student in acquiring knowledge* so that he looks for reasons before giving his assent to what is proposed to him. This definition, again, is too narrow. It describes that degree of intelligence which is expected of every college student.

Altogether too wide is the definition of intelligence which is given by some behaviorists. They describe it as *flexibility of behavior*. It is true that the extraordinary flexibility of man's behavior is due principally to his intelligence, but it is not true that all flexibility of behavior is due to intelligence. *The behavior of many higher animals is rather flexible* and far from the stereotype character of physiological reflexes, but, as we have seen, these animals give no evidence of intelligence. In fact, *even a purely physiological process such as embryonic development shows a good deal of adaptation* to the varying conditions under which it takes place. Hans Driesch has observed and described some remarkable adaptations which occur in this and other organic processes, particularly when they are artificially interfered with. He finds in these phenomena the principal argument against the machine theory of life. Adaptation occurs even under normal conditions of development and nutrition and can thus be called a general characteristic of all life. Hence, if such adaptation or flexibility of behavior is called intelligence then intelligence is coextensive with life.

There is a grain of truth in this. For where there is adaptation of means to an end, there is someone that knows the end and designs the means to that end. But it does not follow that the animals or plants which manifest such adaptation, know the end and design the means to that end. Only a superhuman intelligence suffices to do so. *No biologist has sufficient knowledge of the process of embryonic development, for instance, to supervise this most remarkable of all building processes.* The only architect that can erect the extremely complex structure of an adult organism is the developing organism itself. And it does so without knowing anything about the plan of construction. *God is the designer. The developing organism merely executes the Divine design It is enabled to do so by that plastic tendency which God has imprinted on the developing organism itself.* In short, all flexibility of behavior supposes intelligence, but there is no evidence that the animal or plant organism which manifests flexibility of behavior, has intelligence. Thus the behavioristic description of intelligence is wide of the mark.

Intelligence has also been defined as *conscious adaptation to varying conditions.* This definition, again, is too wide, since animals also show conscious adaptation to their surroundings, namely, by the various forms of "learning" of which they are capable. For the same reason it is unsatisfactory to define intelligence as the *profiting by experience.* Most, if not all, higher animals give unmistakable evidence that they profit by their experience. The same has been shown to occur to a certain extent even among the lowest forms of animals, namely, protozoa.

Some psychologists when using the term "intelligence" merely mean any conscious process of any kind, such as sensation. In this sense all animals have intelligence. We have simply no problem before us if we accept this definition of intelligence. Nor does this definition agree with the common usage of the term "intelligence." From time immemorial the term "intelligence" and its equivalents in other languages have been used to denote *conscious processes which are in some way opposed to sensations.* Our problem begins only when we thus oppose in some preliminary sort of way thought to sensation. We have indeed no right to assume that this opposition is an essential one. Nor have we any right to assume that the distinction is only one of complexity. Even the most radical sensationalist opposes thought to sensation. Unless he did, his very contention that every thought is reducible to sensations as its constitutive elements, would have no intelligible meaning. *The problem in our present chapter is whether the sensationalistic account of thought processes is acceptable or not.*

Accordingly, we define thought processes as *those conscious processes which from time immemorial have been called "intellectual" and have been opposed to purely sensory experiences, namely, ideas, judgments, and reasoning processes.* Our problem in the present chapter thus breaks up naturally into three part-problems. The first deals with the sensationalistic account of ideas; the second, with that of judgment; the third, with that of reasoning processes.

2. A Preliminary Description of an Idea. We have described all thought processes by their opposition to sensations, whatever the nature of this opposition may be. Following out this mode of procedure more in detail, we shall arrive at a preliminary description of the simplest and most fundamental of all thought processes, namely, ideas. Waiving all theoretic considerations, we shall describe ideas by indicating in purely empirical terms their opposition to sensations, on the one hand, and their distinction from judgments and reasoning processes, on the other. We shall deal with the latter distinction after we have settled in a preliminary fashion the distinction between ideas and sensations.

The nature of sensations in general and of the various sensations in particular has been dealt with at considerable length in Chapters II to V, and, to a certain extent, even in the chapters on Visual Space Perception The reader will recall that our awareness of the spatial attributes of bodies is, within definite narrow limits — clearly indicated in the chapters on Visual Space Perception — a matter of sensation and not of perception. On the basis of these empirical inquiries *we define sensations as those conscious processes which are the immediate results of objects affecting our sense-organs and by which we become aware of these very objects according to their sensible qualities, that is. as they appear to our senses here and now, namely, white or gray, red or green, hot or cold, small or large, etc.*

In virtue of a sensation, then, aroused by a sensible present object, I have no information concerning the nature of this object or of its sensible qualities. *I merely experience that object as it appears to my senses here and now* and this appearance changes with the multifarious conditions under which the sensation is aroused. Thus a star in the firmament appears as a small luminous speck surrounded by radiating lines, very much like an asterisk (*) A tree when seen from a great distance appears as a small blurred patch of dark gray; when seen from near by, it looks very different. A mountain peak at sunrise may look flaming red; on a cloudy day it appears jet black. The neck of a pigeon seen from one angle appears green, seen from another angle, red, from a third, dark gray, etc. We *know* full well that a star is not a luminous speck shaped like an asterisk but an immense body containing elements at incandescent heat. We *know,* too, that a mountain peak has the same nature and even the same power of absorbing and reflecting sunlight, whether it looks flaming red or jet black. But it can absorb or reflect only the light it gets, and it gets very different amounts and kinds of sunlight at sunrise and on a cloudy day. The atmosphere, too, absorbs a good deal of this light before it reaches the eye. There occur, moreover, numerous variations in the other factors which determine the peculiar *appearance* of the mountain peak on a particular occasion. Something similar we know to be true of a tree and the neck of a pigeon and the *changes in their appearance.* As to the feathers of a pigeon's neck, in particular, we know in addition, that the physical structure of their reflecting surfaces resemble that of a refraction grating. The result of this is that the reflection of light from the surface of the feather is interfered with, certain wave lengths being thus eliminated in one direction, other wave lengths in another direction. Consequently very different light reaches the eye according as we look at the feather from one angle or another. This is for us the *rationale* of the peculiar changes in the appearance of a pigeon's neck. We express this knowledge by saying that it has irridescent colors.

In short, we *know* a good deal about *the nature of objects we sense* and about *the nature of their sensible qualities.* But all this knowledge is not the immediate effect of these sensible objects acting on our sense-organs; it is not a matter of sensation but of intellectual interpretation.

We *know,* moreover, a good deal about *the nature of many things that cannot be seen, heard, felt, or sensed in any manner whatever for the simple reason that these things have no sensible qualities.* The reader can readily find this out for himself even without going into the psychological laboratory. Thus, for instance, he *knows,* and is supposed to know, *the nature of a straight line* and *the nature of the relation* between the hypotenuse and the other two sides of a right-angled triangle. And this leads us to a preliminary description of an idea, a description which is sufficient, at least, to distinguish an idea from a sensation.

We define, then, an idea as a conscious process by which we become aware of the nature of any object whatever. Thus, when we become aware of the nature of a star, or a tree, or a feather, we have an idea of the star, or the tree, or the feather. Similarly, when we become aware of the nature of a straight line or of the relation between the hypotenuse and the other two sides of a right-angled triangle, we have ideas concerning these mathematical things.

When we say that we become aware of the *nature* of a thing, we mean nothing mysterious and unexampled. No special training in metaphysics is needed to understand what is meant by the phrase Aristotle by a master stroke of common sense has defined the *nature* of a thing in purely empirical terms that can be understood by everyone. He calls it the *"to ti en einai"* which has been translated by "quiddity" or "whatness." *In plain English the Aristotelian phrase means "anything that answers the question, what a thing is."* We become aware of the nature of a tree, for instance, when we become aware of anything that answers, completely or incompletely, vaguely or clearly, popularly or scientifically, the question what the tree is. *According as we can answer this question one way or the other, we have a complete or incomplete, vague or clear, popular or scientific idea of the tree.*

3. Watson's Scathing Criticism. In order, then, to find out, inside or outside the psychological laboratory, whether any particular conscious process is an idea or a sensation, *we need not* *have recourse to the alchemistic practices of the structuralists* which have brought disrepute on the introspective method. We make use of introspection, but we do not incur the scathing criticism of Watson when he says: "One is supposed to need several years' training in a psychological laboratory in the observation of the kaleidoscopic changes that go on every moment in states of consciousness before one's introspection takes on a scientific character. This training supposedly gives one facility to take one's own states of consciousness and subject them to analysis. In other words, the introspectionist claims to become adept in reducing complex states to still simpler states until finally he reaches irreducible data called sensations and affecting tones."[1] None of all this is needed. All we have to do is this: We examine carefully the *object* of which we are aware and which is in the focus of attention. Suppose that I look at a star in the firmament. When I become aware of *the star as it appears* to my senses here and now, I have *a sensation* aroused by that star. When in addition, I become aware of anything that answers in any manner whatever the question *what the star is,* I have, so far forth, *an idea* of the star.

It comes to identically the same empirical distinction when German psychologists of the Würzburg school distinguish between *Wissen* and *Empfinden,* that is, between *knowing* and *sensing.* We *know* a thing when we become aware of anything that answers the question *what that thing is.* We sense an object when we merely experience *an object as it appears* to our senses here and now. The object as it appears to our senses is frequently indicated in the German laboratory reports by the term *Erscheinung* (literally *appearance*). When, therefore, the subjects of the Würzburg experiments state, for instance. that they were guided in the solution of a task by what they *know* about the object and not by its *appearance* (*Erscheinung*), the distinction thus made *involves no theoretic consideration* of any kind but it is one of a purely empirical kind. The conditions under which the facts

---

[1]*Psychology* (2d ed.), p. 2.

and regularities reported occurred, are accurately described. Anybody can reproduce the conditions described and can observe the facts and regularities for himself and compare his data with those of the Würzburg school. *In this regard the work done in the Würzburg laboratories does not differ from that done in the laboratory of the physicist, chemist, or physiologist.*

There is still another way in which we can, in many cases at least, tell an idea from a sensation, and that, again, without becoming guilty of the alchemistic practices of the structuralists. This mode of procedure, too, is suggested by our preliminary description of an idea. We said that by an idea we become aware of the nature of *any object whatever,* while by a sensation we become aware only of *a sensible object as it appears* to our senses here and now. When, therefore, we become aware of an object which has no sensible qualities, *we know by that very fact that we have an idea and not a sensation.*

Suppose, then, that you are in the psychological laboratory of the Würzburg school and are instructed to describe the conscious processes which occur at a given time. A practical example will show what is required of you. Suppose that at a given signal the experimenter presents the word *karyokinesis* to you and you are required to observe and describe the conscious processes that occurred while you heard or saw the word. Your introspective report may be something like this: "I do not understand the word. The only thing at the focus of my attention was the sound of the word or the printed letters. If there is such an object as is designated by the word presented to me, I surely do not know what it is." By this very report the experimenter knows that the conscious process at the focus of your attention at the specified time was a sensation and not an idea. Suppose you anwer: "I not only heard the word but understood without further ado *the object designated by the word."* The experimenter can find out very readily whether you understood the word or not There are thousand of ways in which that can be found out: every teacher knows how to go about it. *So far, then, there is nothing cloudy or alchemistic about the methods of the thought experiments.*

The observers describe their conscious processes by simply describing the objects which at the specified time were in the focus of their attention and which are still perfectly fresh in their immediate memory. There is no other way of describing conscious processes and distinguishing them from one another. Suppose now that the object which at the specified time was in the focus of your attention is the relation between the hypotenuse and the other two sides of a right-angled triangle. Both you and the experimenter know by this very description that the conscious process reported is an idea and not a sensation. For the said relation — the object at the focus of your attention — is neither hot nor cold, neither black nor yellow, etc.: it simply has no sensible qualities.

It is worthy of note that *this criterion of distinguishing ideas from sensations occurs frequently in the introspective reports of the Würzburg school*. German psychologists describe sensations, or rather their objects, as *anschaulich* and ideas, or rather their objects, as *unanschaulich*. In plain English this means that in one case the observer became aware of *an object that has sensible qualities,* in the other, *one that has no sensible qualities.* Thus, for instance, the investigation of Lillien J. Martin reported in the *Z. f. Psych.*[2] is entitled — we translate — "Quantitative researches concerning the relation between *anschauliche* and *unanschauliche* contents of conscious processes." The present writer acted as one of the observers when this investigation was carried on in the University of Bonn. From his personal experience he can testify that nothing was done in this investigation that resembled those practices of Titchener which have brought such disrepute on the introspective method. What was done required no more than *common sense* and *can be repeated in any laboratory.* The same is true of all the important researches of the Würzburg school, that is, *those on which the conclusions of the Würzburg school really rest.* At present we are not concerned with these conclusions but only with the mode of procedure em-

---

[2] Vol. 65, pp. 417 sqq.

ployed in these researches. This is entirely based on the preliminary and noncommittal description of ideas which we have given.

Before proceeding in our discussion we wish to emphasize that our preliminary description of an idea suffices only to distinguish it from a sensation. This and no more. But an idea is also distinguished from other thought processes, namely, *judgment* and *reasoning*. This distinction is *not* indicated in our definition and will be dealt with later.

4. The Process of Abstraction and Its Result, the Universal Idea. Several experimental researches of the Würzburg school deal with the process of abstraction and its result, the universal idea. It may suffice to mention here the investigation of Kuelpe (*Versuche über Abstraktion*) reported at the German Psychological Congress which met at Giessen in the summer of 1904; that of Dr. T. V. Moore (*The Process of Abstraction*) published in 1910; and that of Dr. A. Willwoll (*Begriffsbildung*) which appeared in 1926 as the first of a series of Psychological Monographs edited by Dr. Buehler. Further references to the extensive literature on the subject may be found in the two last-named publications.

It has been denied that the process of abstraction which results in the formation of a universal idea, occurs in our experience. "Whether others," Berkeley says, "have this wonderful faculty of abstracting their ideas, they can best tell; for myself I dare be confident I have it not." For one who shares the theoretic prepossessions of Berkeley in favor of sensationalism, the process of abstraction must be something "wonderful" and extraordinary. But for those not thus biased there is nothing "wonderful" or extraordinary about it. The process is a fact of internal experience with which we are perfectly familiar. It is only a special form of the familiar fact of attention: this and no more.

When dealing with the fact of attention (Chapter XI) we said that only a limited number of objects succeed at any given time in gaining an entrance into our conscious life. Their rivals are for the time being more or less rigidly excluded or, maybe, put on the waiting list. The object, or that characteristic of an object, or that group of objects, which at any given time successfully enters our conscious life, is said to be "attended to" or to be "in the focus of attention" or in the "foreground of consciousness." All other objects or characteristics of an object recede *thereby* to "the margin of attention" or to the "background of consciousness," or are entirely eliminated from our conscious life. Of all these objects or characteristics of an object we say that they are "not attended to." With all this we are perfectly familiar, and this leads us naturally to *that form of attention which is known as the process of abstraction* and which results in the formation of a universal idea.

Many of the objects which we meet in our everyday experience have plainly some characteristics in common, and others by which they differ from one another. We may "concentrate our attention" on any object whatever and on any characteristic of an object. Suppose, then, that we concentrate our attention, voluntarily or involuntarily, on a characteristic of an object which it has in common with other objects. *By that very fact* all those characteristics by which this object differs from other objects, recede into the background of consciousness or are entirely eliminated from our conscious life. *This form of attention is known as (generalizing) abstraction.* As a result of this mode of attention, then, *we retain in the focus of attention only that characteristic of an object which it has in common with other objects.* No one can deny the existence of the conscious process which under these conditions constitutes the very focus of attention, and this conscious process is *a universal idea.* This and nothing else is meant by a universal idea. It may be defined in purely empirical terms as *that conscious process by which we become aware of what is common to several individuals and can be predicated of these individuals singly and in exactly the same sense.*

We have described here the universal idea by describing the process of its formation. This process of formation has been observed frequently in the experimental researches of the Würzburg school. German psychologists have distinguished clearly the *two phases* of the process of abstraction, and they call them *positive* and *negative* abstraction, respectively. By positive abstraction they mean the concentration of attention on that characteristic of an object which it has in common with other individuals. By negative abstraction they mean the fact that all other characteristics of the object, namely, those by which it differs from other individuals, tend to recede to the background of consciousness or are entirely lost sight of. It should be noted that *the positive abstraction of the German psychologists is really nothing else than the universal idea in the process of formation.*

It should be noted, further, that some ideas thus formed are *more* universal than others. The more characteristics of a particular object are positively abstracted from its other characteristics, the fewer are the individuals to which the idea can be applied, and the less universal is the idea. And *vice versa,* the fewer characteristics of a particular object are positively abstracted, the greater is the number of individuals to which they can be applied, and the greater is their universality. Thus, the idea of a white man is evidently less universal than the idea of man, and the idea of an animal is plainly more universal than the idea of a rational animal. *When we thus try to ascertain to how many individuals a universal idea can be applied, we become explicitly aware of its universality,* and we can group different ideas into a system according to their degree of universality. This systematization of universal concepts is not a task that interests only the logician for the purposes of speculation. On the contrary, it is an eminently practical task with which every scientist is perfectly familiar. The grouping of observed facts into classes is a task which is mentioned in the introduction to every natural science. Now, such a grouping of facts forces the process of generalizing abstraction on the attention of every scientist. That is to say, under these conditions a scientist *not only makes use of universal ideas but he is explicitly aware of their universality.* A practical example of a system of universal ideas created for eminently practical purposes is that of the systematic biologist who arranges all animals and plants into species, genera, families, orders, classes, and phyla. What guides him in this important task is the process of generalizing abstraction.

It is of interest to add that in this process of classification the characteristics of an individual by which it differs from other individuals are indeed, for the time being, forced into the background of consciousness. But they are, as a rule, not so entirely eliminated from our consciousness that they never return to the focus of attention But when they thus return, they do not interfere with the result of positive abstraction, that is, with the universal idea, *provided we remain aware of the fact that these characteristics (the individual differences) are irrelevant* as far as the *common nature* of several individuals is concerned. As long as we distinguish between what is relevant and what is irrelevant to the common nature of several individuals, we have a true universal idea and we are, moreover, fully aware that we have a universal idea.

When, therefore, Berkeley and his followers ask us to point out the exact time when we go through that "wonderful" process of abstracting ideas, we answer with two formulas which denote two distinct stages in the formation of a universal idea. *The first stage* is this: We abstract a universal idea *whenever we concentrate our attention on some characteristics of an individual which, as a matter of fact, are common to several individuals,* and ignore all those characteristics of that individual by which it differs from others. *By this very fact* we separate the characteristics in the focus of attention from those not in the focus. The characteristics thus retained in the focus are, as a matter of fact, common to several individuals, whether we are aware of this fact or not, whether we apply them to several individuals or not. Accordingly, we have by the mere fact of our peculiar mode of attention a universal idea, even though we are not yet aware of its universality. *The second stage* is this: We not only abstract universal ideas but are explicitly aware of doing so, *whenever we classify objects or any observed facts for the purposes of scientific discussion.* We do this at times. But we cannot do so without becoming explicitly aware of what is relevant and irrelevant to the common nature of individuals belonging to the same class.

In many of the experiments of the Würzburg school conditions were created which are similar to those which confront the biologist when attempting to classify animals and plants. Of course, the task which the observers in the Würzburg experiments had to solve, was much simpler than that of the biologist. Thus, for instance, the subject of the experiment was requested to find an idea more universal than that presented to him, or one subordinated to it, and then to describe what guided him in solving the problem. Many variations of this mode of procedure were used.[3] *All of these experimental arrangements forced the fact of generalizing abstraction on the observer.* Accordingly, there can be no doubt concerning the fact of generalizing abstraction. The fact, however, thus plainly established, does not settle the sensationalistic controversy concerning the intimate nature of the universal idea and its relation to the image. With this we shall deal later.

To complete our account of the process of abstraction we must briefly mention another form of it. It is known by the name of *isolating abstraction* and its result is the *abstract idea*. Sometimes the term *abstract idea* is treated as synonymous with universal idea. Strictly speaking, however, this usage is incorrect. *The universal idea is the result of generalizing abstraction* which we have described. We focus our attention on some characteristic of an individual which it has in common with other individuals and we thus separate it from the individual differences. *The abstract idea is the result of isolating abstraction* which may be described as that mode of attention by which we focus it on any characteristic of an individual and *separate it from the subject* which has that characteristic. Of course, we know full well that that characteristic does not exist thus separated, but we represent it as if it were. Thus the idea of man is universal, the idea of *humanity* is not only *universal* but also *abstract*. Many of the

---

[3]Cf. T. V. Moore, *op. cit.,* p. 96.

words in common use are abstract, as is too well known to need further exemplification. Thus our ordinary vocabulary shows unmistakably the traces of isolating abstraction. Also this form of abstraction has been dealt with experimentally. It is, however, not of that absorbing interest which attaches to generalizing abstraction. Whenever we speak in the sequel of abstraction without qualification, we always mean the process of generalizing abstraction.

5. The Finished Product of Abstraction and Its Association with Other Ideas and with the Common Vocable. Thus far we have observed and described the universal idea in the process of formation. We must now consider the use we make of the finished product of abstraction, its connection with other ideas and in particular its association with the common vocable. *It is this aspect of the universal idea which is liable to obscure the process of its original formation,* and has led to theories of certain modern psychologists concerning the nature of universal ideas. The reader should know the facts which guide us in our later discussion of these theories.

Once a universal idea is formed, it is retained. In this regard the universal idea does not differ from any other conscious process. We are not concerned here with the question of what the retention of a universal idea may mean in theoretic terms. In purely empirical terms it means that a universal idea *can be recalled.* This is sufficiently clear from what we have said in the chapter on Memory concerning retention in general. There we explained, too, how recall is effected. Ideas, or rather their objects, are interrelated in many ways. Once we become aware of these relations, *the rational associations thus established are the most powerful means of recalling an idea once formed.* This is particularly true when ideas become incorporated in judgments and these judgments, in turn, are grouped into a system known by the name "science." Leaving the discussion of judgment to a later chapter, we are satisfied here with emphasizing the fact that *the finished product of abstraction tends to become an integral part of our intellectual possessions* and is a constitutive element of a system of ideas. This system differs from person to person: the biologist has one system, the chemist another, a merchant still another, and so forth.

Besides the rational associations of the systematic kind, founded as they are on the very nature of things, associations of a looser and haphazard kind are also established between one idea and another and, in particular, between a universal idea on the one hand, and purely sensory processes on the other. *By these haphazard associations we mean that, as a matter of fact, several ideas, or an idea and a sensory process have occurred simultaneously or in immediate succession in our experience.* This is another means of recall, as was explained in the chapter on Memory.

Prominent among these haphazard associations is the connection which is established between the finished product of abstraction, say, the universal idea of a horse, and the sound of the word which is used as the conventional sign of this idea and its object. *This connection is of all haphazard associations the most haphazard.* It is a mere accident of birth. If you had been born and reared in Germany, the sound of the word *Pferd* would recall the universal idea of a horse and bring its object again into the focus of your attention. But those among whom you live never use this odd sound as the conventional sign of the object of your idea. They always use the sound designated by the letters *h, o, r, s, e* The sound of the English word is, *of itself,* just as odd as the sound of the German word. Both are, of themselves, just nonsense syllables. As a matter of fact, however, the sound of the English word has been so frequently connected with the finished product of your previous abstraction that, by sheer force of repetition, *the sound of the word and the idea of a horse seem inseparable.* It suffices to mention the word *horse* and you recall without fail the universal idea of a horse.

It requires some artificial device to separate the sound from the idea of the object. The trick originally devised by James, I think. is very effective. Just repeat the word *horse* a dozen times over. *Under these conditions your attention becomes fixed on the sound itself* and is entirely withdrawn from the object whose conventional sign it is. As a result, you experience the sound pure and simple and you begin to wonder at the oddity of the sound. Then this common vocable becomes again what it was before its association with the universal idea of a horse, namely, a nonsense syllable exactly on a par with wug, tas, etc.

Under *normal* conditions something very different happens. *The sound of the word receives no more than passing attention.* Our attention is rather fixed on the object whose sign it is. This is true of the sound of a common vocable as it is of the sound of any other vocable. And the noteworthy fact is that most words of every language — most nouns, adjectives, and verbs — are common vocables, that is, they can be applied to different individuals singly and in exactly the same sense. This premised, we say that *a common vocable as used in everyday life, may be compared to a signpost which guides a traveler in finding his way to a definite city.* The signpost *is* not the city but it *points to* the city. Similarly, the common vocable *is* not the universal idea but it is a *sign* of the idea and its object: it *points to* that object. A traveler is not interested in the signpost itself but only in the city to which it points. As a result, the signpost no sooner reaches the focus of attention than it is replaced by the thought of the city of which it is the sign. So it is with the common vocable. *The sound of a common vocable no sooner reaches the focus of attention than it is replaced by the universal idea of the object of which it is the conventional sign.* Thus it is that the common vocable and the universal idea seem to merge into each other. As a matter of fact, *some philosophers and psychologists have identified the universal idea with the common vocable* and their doctrine is known as *nominalism.* We shall revert to this doctrine in the next section of this chapter.

For the present we wish to point out *the grain of truth which is contained in the statement of Berkeley that he was not aware of abstracting his ideas.* The grain of truth is this: When a universal idea formed on a previous occasion is recalled by the common vocable with which it has become associated, *we do not in every instance go through the process of generalizing abstraction again,* nor do we claim that we do so. As a rule, we simply recall what we have retained, and *in this recall the process of the original formation of the universal idea is lost sight of.* Only when the nature of the task before us demands it, do we again go through the process of positive abstraction, as for instance, *when we are confronted with a problem of classification.* Hence it is that a task of this latter type was used in the experimental arrangements of the Würzburg school in order to *force* the process of abstraction on the attention of the observer. But whether we again go through the process of its original formation or merely recall what we have retained, *in either case the universal idea is and remains the result of positive abstraction.*

The gradual association of the haphazard kind between the result of positive abstraction and the common vocable has been studied experimentally in the researches of the Würzburg school. Conditions were created under which the observers had to focus their attention on some characteristic or group of characteristics which an object has in common with other objects. *Together with the object that had definite characteristics a definite nonsense syllable was uniformly presented.* Thus the result of positive abstraction became attached by loose association to a definite nonsense syllable. This was frequently repeated and thus *the gradual transformation of a nonsense syllable into a "name of a thing" or a common vocable could be observed and described.* In short, artificial conditions were created which resemble those under which in early childhood mere sounds become gradually "names of things" or common vocables. The reader who desires further details concerning these and similar experimental researches of the Würzburg school is referred to Dr. Willwoll's monograph *Begriffsbildung.* Here the work of three investigators, N. Ach, S. Fischer, and D. Usnadze, is described at some length.[4] The experiments of N. Ach were repeated by Dr. Willwoll and the results obtained were compared with those of N. Ach.[5]

It is interesting to note that the associations formed in the lab-

---

[4] Pages 18–35.
[5] *Op. cit.,* pp. 43–59.

oratory between the results of positive abstraction and definite nonsense syllables were so effective that *the nonsense syllables were actually used by one of the subjects even in a business transaction.* An account of this amusing incident may be found on page 26 of Dr. Willwoll's monograph.

Another item of interest is worth recording in this connection. Among the persons experimented upon were two whose brains had been injured by bullet wounds and who in consequence had great difficulty in finding the words which by common usage are employed as signs of definite ideas. Such persons are known as aphasics and their condition is known as aphasia or inability to speak. It is important to note that such inability to speak does not arise from this that the aphasic has lost the power of abstraction nor does it consist in the loss of the ideas formed by previous abstraction. This was shown by the very results of the experiments. For, *the two aphasics mentioned went through the process of abstraction just like normal subjects and, like them, they learned to associate the ideas thus formed with definite nonsense syllables.* Thus these nonsense syllables were also for these aphasics gradually transformed into "names of things."[6]

6. The Logical and the Psychological Aspects of Universal Ideas. This seems to be the appropriate place to mention an objection that has been frequently made against the existence of universal ideas. *It has been said that we are really mixing up logical with psychological considerations, a thing to be deplored in psychology.* The experimental psychologist, it is claimed, has no evidence of universal ideas; they are the product of logical reasoning.

We might answer: Suppose, for the sake of argument, that it is only logical considerations which force us to admit universal ideas, what of it? *What is true in one science, is true in every other science.* When a chemist ventures to state something which is in plain contradiction of what is recognized as true in physics, it will not do for him to say: That is a matter of physics and the mixing up of a physical with chemical considerations is to be de-

---

[6]*Ibid.*

plored in chemistry. If a statement of a chemist does not fit known facts or plain inferences from facts treated in physics, then such a statement cannot be used by anyone even as a working hypothesis.

But there is no need of resting our case on this answer. For *it is not true that anywhere in the above account we have deduced the existence of universal ideas from logical considerations* Our discussion of universal ideas is totally different from that of logicians. Logicians (or rather, epistemologists) are concerned with *the objective reality* corresponding to universal ideas. This is no concern of ours. To show this, we must make a digression here into the field of major logic or epistemology. The charge made that we are really mixing up logic with psychology is our excuse for this digression.

A rough illustration will bring home to the reader what the problem of the epistemologist really is. *Suppose that the question at issue is what the stocks and bonds I have in my pocket are worth.* Some say they are worth millions; these correspond to the *ultra-realists* in epistemology who exaggerate the objective reality corresponding to universal ideas. Others say that the stocks and bonds in my pocket are just paper and that the proper place for this paper is the wastebasket. These correspond to the *conceptualists* in epistemology who admit the existence of universal ideas in our mind but claim that nothing whatever corresponds to them. Others again take a middle course and claim that the stocks and bonds in my pocket are indeed very valuable but only in a limited sense. These may be said to correspond to the *moderate realists,* provided it is understood that our illustration is a very rough one. For the purposes of our present discussion we need not explain the details of the important doctrine of moderate realism. Others, again, solve the problem in an altogether different way. *They deny the supposition of the whole discussion, that is, they deny that I have stocks and bonds in my pocket.* These correspond to the *nominalists* of ancient and modern times, who deny that we have such conscious processes in our mind as are described under the name of universal ideas. As soon as the discussion takes this form, we can dispense with all syllogizing and recondite argumentations. *I settle the question by simply turning out all my pockets.* Then everyone present can find out for himself whether I have stocks and bonds in my pocket or not. No logical considerations are needed to ascertain the fact. If we have in our mind such conscious processes as we have described under the name of universal ideas, *we can find out the fact by simple introspection, which corresponds to the turning out of my pockets. And this process of introspection is the peculiar task of the experimental psychologist.* We have used nothing but the data of introspection in ascertaining the "existential aspect" of universal ideas. Nor have the psychologists of the Würzburg school, at least in the researches mentioned, made use of logical considerations to ascertain the "existential aspect" of universal ideas. *Accordingly, it is not true that we are mixing up logical with psychological considerations when maintaining the "existential aspect" of universal ideas.*

7. **Ideas and Images.** That there is some connection between thought and imagination has been recognized from time immemorial "As without sensation," Aristotle says, "a man would not learn or understand anything, so at the very time when he is actually thinking he must have an image before him. For mental images are like present sensations, except that they are immaterial."[7] From the whole context it is clear that by this "immateriality" of images — the only difference Aristotle admits between images and sensations — he means exactly what we expressed in our technical definition of an image. In the chapter on Imagination we defined it as *the revival and the association of former sensory experiences of an object which is not actually present to our senses,* or briefly, as centrally aroused sensations. As, therefore, we depend on *sensations* in the acquisition of ideas, it is natural to expect that we should depend on *images* in the use of ideas In fact, the question is pertinent whether ideas differ at all from images. "It may be asked," says Aristotle, "How will the simplest

---

[7] *De Anima*, III, 8, Hick's translation, p. 145.

notions differ in character from mental images? I reply that neither these nor the rest of our notions are images, but that they cannot dispense with images."[8]

Aristotle, then, states *two* things concerning the relation between ideas and images. *The first is that ideas are not images. The second is that ideas never occur without images.* Both statements have been questioned by modern psychologists. Of the two the first is the more important and we mean to investigate its truth on the basis of experimental data that can be verified and reproduced by anyone as often as he likes. The second statement is synonymous with the claim that *imageless thought never occurs.* It is worthy of note that all experimentalists of the Würzburg school agree on the first statement of Aristotle, but some disagree with him as to the impossibility of imageless thought. They insist that the second statement of Aristotle is too sweeping a generalization and needs a qualification. *It makes little difference to us whether we ever have imageless thought or not.* This is one of the *minor* issues of the Würzburg school. What really interests us is the question whether thoughts *are* images. If, therefore, introspection reveals images, as it undoubtedly does in many cases of thinking, the important question for us is *whether these images are the only thing or even the principal thing* in our mind when we are thinking. If this question must be answered in the affirmative, then Aristotle's first proposition is wrong and the sensationalists are right when claiming that ideas are nothing but images.

8. The Method of the Structuralists in Solving the Problem of the Thought Processes. It has always been the boast of all natural sciences that their method is that of *refined common sense.* Special training in making observations is indeed valued highly, for it saves a good deal of time in solving a scientific problem. *But the work of observers who have no special training is not rejected.* Abbot Mendel never had any special training in the biological laboratory. Using his *common sense,* he devised a

---

[8] *Op. cit.*

number of experiments in order to solve the intricate problem of heredity. The convent garden was his laboratory. The results he obtained lay buried for a long time in the archives of a local scientific association. But once they became known *they were not rejected because they were obtained by one who lacked special training*. On the contrary, their unusual importance was immediately recognized and the data of Abbot Mendel became the starting point of a new science. Even mere chance observations are taken into consideration *whether they are made by a university professor like Oerstedt or by one who makes his living as a farm hand*. What counts is that observation be accurate and that others may repeat and *verify* the data obtained. Identically the same common-sense methods can also be applied to the problem which now engages our attention, namely, that of the relation between thoughts and images. We shall explain how this can be done when describing how the experimentalists of the Würzburg school arrived at their fundamental conclusions.

For the present we are interested in *the peculiar method introduced into experimental psychology by the structuralists* with Titchener as their leader. The structuralists started with a fundamental assumption which we have explained briefly in the second chapter. The assumption was that our whole conscious life — or "mind" as it was called — was made up of simple elements, all of the same general kind or class. On the very first page of a famous laboratory manual this fundamental assumption was applied to the thought processes. The student was told that if we take "a thought-consciousness, our mind as it is when we are arguing something out, and analyze it, we find that it reduces to a number of quite simple processes, all of the same general kind or class. These are called 'sensations.' The sensation, then, is the structural unit or structural element of these consciousnesses."[9] The student was told, further, that it would be wasting time to test such an hypothesis before accepting it at the very be-

---

[9] Titchener, *Experimental Psychology*, Part I, Student's Manual, p. 1, quoted by permission of the Macmillan Co., publishers.

ginning of laboratory work. For we have as yet no scientific knowledge of sensation. As a result "we should be struggling, ignorantly, to solve a difficult problem by 'common sense,' and neglecting the skilled work of those who have attacked the problem before us."[10]

Structuralists claimed to have this special skill in analyzing their "mind" as it is when they are thinking, into simple sensations (to which later "feelings" were added). Hence, when the problem of perception came up for experimental investigation, *the student was told with precision what he had to find,* namely, sensations. His task in the laboratory was described as a threefold one: *"the analysis of the constituent sensations; the tracing of the pattern, the mode of connection, imposed upon them; and the discovery of the substitutions and short cuts that have obscured the original formation."*[11] Knowing thus what he had to find, namely, sensations, the student did find what he was looking for. And if he did not, well, then he lacked the necessary skill. He had no sufficient training in analyzing his thought processes or he forgot that "the perceptions that we tease out from our present consciousness are of very ancient origin, far older than man."[12]

The student was aided in the analysis of thought processes into their constituent sensations by a special laboratory device created for this very purpose, namely, *the metaphysical darkroom of the psychology of "meaning."* It has been known from time immemorial that we have, frequently at least, images when we are thinking. These images can be analyzed into their constituent sensations. This done, all that was necessary for a laboratory proof of sensationalism was to end up with the flourish: And these images *mean* this or that. Thus, the experimental proof of sensationalism was accomplished. For further details of this experimental proof the reader is referred to the next chapter.

Of course, such methods of investigation *do not carry conviction.* The claim that *special training was needed* to accomplish

---

[10]*Op. cit.,* p. 2, quoted by permission of the Macmillan Co., publishers.

[11]*Op. cit.,* p. 129.

[12]*Op. cit.,* p. 128.

the work of the structuralists *created suspicion*. Watson came along and said that we are getting nowhere with such methods. *He ridiculed the special training required by the structuralists.* He insisted on a return to common-sense methods in psychology. All other sciences, he pointed out, are making advances with their common-sense methods, but psychology with its specially trained observers is in a condition of stagnation. *And in this Watson was perfectly correct.* His mistake, however, was, that he applied to the introspective method in general what was true only of *the peculiar methods of the structuralists.* Incidentally, he made another mistake in his scathing criticism of the introspective method in psychology. We shall point this out when discussing what Watson calls the "kaleidoscopic changes in the states of consciousness."

References for Further Reading

J. Froebes, S.J., *Lehrbuch der Experimentellen Psychologie,* Vol. I (1923), pp. 417 sqq.

A. Willwoll, *Begriffsbildung* (1926).

T. V. Moore, *The Process of Abstraction* (1910).

Chapter XV

THOUGHT
(Continued)

1. **"The Kaleidoscopic Changes in the States of Consciousness."** We pointed out in the chapter on Imagination that there are probably no two persons who have identically the same images when thinking of one and the same thing. Indeed, it is doubtful whether anyone, when thinking on two successive occasions of one and the same thing, experiences images alike in every detail. *This variability of images is a fact of the utmost importance in the experimental investigation of the thought processes.* Before discussing its bearing on the problem before us, we must settle a preliminary question.

Behaviorists have seized upon "the kaleidoscopic changes that go on every moment in the states of consciousness" to show that the common-sense methods of other sciences cannot be applied to introspective data and that "introspection" is of its very nature "a serious bar to progress." If this be the contention of Watson in the passage quoted in the last chapter (p. 307), the answer is that *"the kaleidoscopic changes that go on every moment in the states of consciousness" are paralleled by similar kaleidoscopic changes that go on every moment in the states of matter with which physical sciences deal.* The whole world of our immediate experience — external as well as internal — is one of continual change.

The objects of the physical world do not come to us with labels gummed to their backs: we must label them. We do so with more or less accuracy outside the physical laboratory and with scientific precision in the laboratory. If we are interested in a particular thing, we note those features of it which seem to remain *constant* throughout all changes and separate them from its *vari-*

able features. To have a starting point for further inquiry we express both the constant and the variable features of a thing in purely empirical and noncommittal terms. Thus by making use of our common sense we gradually bring order into the kaleidoscopic change which the physical world presents. Laboratory methods are but a refinement of this common sense. By the same methods of common sense and by the same refinement of common sense we bring order into the kaleidoscopic changes which go on every moment in our conscious states. Accordingly, *the mere fact that such a kaleidoscopic change occurs in our conscious states, is no proof that the common-sense methods of natural sciences cannot be applied to the problem of the thought processes.* How these methods were applied in detail by the experimentalists of the Würzburg school, we shall explain presently.

A practical example will show that the objects of the physical world as we get them in immediate experience, present a kaleidoscopic change. Thus, for instance, such a common object as water comes in a great variety of forms. The chemist, as a result of scientific inquiry, has labeled it H_2O. But water, as we meet it in rivers, lakes, oceans, wells, cisterns, and stagnant pools, presents a great many variable features not indicated by the label of the chemist. These variable features of water are described differently by an unsophisticated observer and by a chemist. An unsophisticated observer says, for instance, that some samples of water are hard, others soft; that some are fit for drinking, others are not, etc. The chemist says that the water of springs and cisterns, for instance, contains almost always some foreign ingredients such as carbonates, sulphates, chlorids of calcium, and sometimes also bicarbonate of magnesium. In the neighborhood of human dwellings it contains also ammonia, nitric acid, etc., and some organic substances. In short, one and the same object in nature, namely, water, occurs in a kaleidoscopic series of changes in its condition. And what is true of water, is true of every object in nature with which physical sciences deal.

From this it will be seen that *the kaleidoscopic changes of which Watson speaks are no peculiarity of the data of conscious-*

ness; they are common to the data of all natural sciences. Provided, then, that we make use of the same common-sense methods in dealing with the kaleidoscopic changes of the inner world as are used by the other sciences in dealing with the kaleidoscopic changes in the outer world, there can be no difficulty whatever in the scientific investigation of the thought processes. Only when we depart from these common-sense methods in the investigation of the thought processes, will our whole inner world remain forever just a series of kaleidoscopic changes in the states of consciousness.

2. The Four Steps in the Common-Sense Method of Science as Applied to the Problem of the Thought Processes. The inductive method of investigation which has been so successfully applied to the problems of the physical sciences, is perfectly familiar to every scientific investigator. If it be, therefore, a twice-told tale to explain even briefly the four steps of the inductive method in general, our excuse for telling this story is that we mean to show that every one of these steps can be applied to the problem of the thought processes and has been thus applied by the investigators of the Würzburg school.

The first step of scientific inquiry is preliminary observation. We simply gather facts concerning the thing in which we are interested. In this manner we arrive at a preliminary description of the subject of inquiry; we make purely empirical distinctions between the various facts observed and ascertain some empirical rules concerning them. It makes no difference whether this preliminary work be done inside or outside the laboratory. The important thing is that all the facts, distinctions, and empirical rules ascertained *can be verified by other investigators.*

If it be asked how this first step of the inductive method is applied to the problem of the thought processes, the answer is that *Chapter XIV is in its entirety devoted to these preliminaries:* there all our descriptions of thought, ideas, the process of abstraction, and universal ideas were of a purely empirical kind. The same is true of all our distinctions between ideas and sensations, between "*knowing*" and "*sensing*" (*Wissen* and *Empfinden*), be-

tween *anschauliche* and *unanschauliche* contents of conscious processes. Anyone can verify these distinctions for himself by simply
creating the conditions under which they were ascertained, and
describing what is in the very focus of his attention. Accordingly,
in gathering the facts concerning the thought processes the method of the Würzburg school in no way differs from that used in
all other sciences.

*The second step in the inductive method is the formulation of
a tentative hypothesis.* For the sake of argument we make a supposition which, if true, would render all the facts observed, and
all the empirical distinctions and rules ascertained, intelligible to
us. Such a supposition may be, and frequently is, suggested by
the work done in the first step or it may be a simple guess. Whatever the manner may be in which the assumption is arrived at, it
must be made only *for the sake of argument* and it must *explain*
the facts observed. "Explaining," in the full sense of the word,
means knowing a thing from its causes. In the case of a tentative
hypothesis the term means considerably less than that. The very
minimum, however, meant by "explaining" is that *the supposition should enable us to correlate all the known facts and thus
bring order into what otherwise must remain a kaleidoscopic
change of phenomena.* The atomic hypothesis is an excellent
illustration of what is meant by correlating facts. Without this
hypothesis all the chemical changes in nature would be but a
confused mass of facts. When, however, these facts are expressed
in terms and by the symbols of the atomic hypothesis, they are
reduced to a most orderly system.

This second step, too, has been taken by the experimentalists
of the Würzburg school in the investigation of the thought processes There are two hypotheses which can be made for the sake
of argument concerning the relation between thoughts and im
ages. The first is that the empirical distinctions between thoughts
and sensations, between ideas and images, as we ascertained them
in the first step, are only superficial and apparent. It is assumed,
then, that by analysis we shall succeed in reducing ideas and all
other thought processes to elemental processes which resist

further analysis, namely, sensations. *In practical terms this means that ideas really are images, although at first sight they do not seem to be.* It was with a view to test this hypothesis of sensationalists that the work of the Würzburg school began. The rival hypothesis is that all empirical distinctions between thoughts and sensations, between ideas and images, are *distinctions of kind and not of degree.* This hypothesis, if verified, suggests the further problem as to what really the function of images is in thinking.

The third step in the inductive method is deductive reasoning. No natural science has ever been able to dispense with deductive reasoning, all claims to the contrary notwithstanding.. If an assumption made is true, certain conclusions follow from it, and the very purpose of the third step is to realize these conclusions. If we are to proceed in an orderly manner in taking this step, we must make sure that our conclusions are warranted by their premises. But we can find this out only by the laws of deductive reasoning. It is only a change of label if we express this deductive reasoning by saying that from the assumption made we "expect" certain things to be true. If our "expectations" are not to be mere leaps into the metaphysical dark, we must test them first by the laws of Aristotle's logic.

A subtle reader may suggest that it is a much better plan to test our expectations in the laboratory. The answer is: Of course, we can test our expectations in the laboratory and we may succeed in verifying them; but this verification of our "expectations" is, of itself, no verification of our hypothesis. We must first show that our "expectations" are necessarily bound up with our hypothesis: that they are legitimate conclusions from our hypothesis. And this can be done only by the laws of logic. In short, laboratory work is no device for dispensing with accurate thinking. Deductive reasoning as described will not only save us a good deal of useless work in the laboratory, but it will eliminate effectively all quibbling about the experimental verification of our hypothesis. All the assumptions of the atomic hypothesis, for instance, were first subjected to deductive reasoning. *Far from be-*

ing a hindrance to scientific progress, this very deductive reason-
ing pointed out the direction which chemical research had to take
and gave the impetus to this research. Alchemists did not fail because they did not experiment; they failed because they did not
devise a logical plan of their experiments. They bungled along
because of the haziness of their deductive reasoning.

This important step, too, was taken by the investigators of the
Würzburg school and, like all other steps, can be reëxamined
by anyone who desires to do so. In this regard, again, the method
of the Würzburg school differs in nothing from the method employed by other scientists. We shall describe the third step in detail in subsequent sections of this chapter.

The fourth step in the inductive method is the verification
of the conclusions drawn from our hypothesis. This is done by
comparing these conclusions or "expectations" with the facts already collected in the first step. If the data there obtained are insufficient for a complete verification of our conclusions, we must
plan a new set of experiments and go back to the laboratory for
further research. Thus we may succeed in the complete verification of our hypothesis. It is well, however, not to be hasty in pro-
claiming our hypothesis established. The conclusions deduced
from rival hypotheses must also be tested in a similar manner.
On doing this, we may find that at least some facts agree just as
well with the hypothesis of others as with our own. This indicates the need for further research. The same is true when we
find that many of the facts are in agreement with our hypothesis
but others are not. Then some change in our hypothesis must be
made to meet these difficulties and thus we must again go over
the work of the second, third, and fourth steps. Only when all
the facts ascertained are in agreement with our hypothesis and
all rival hypotheses plainly fail to meet their difficulties, have we
assurance that our hypothesis plainly is the true explanation of
the facts observed *Then our hypothesis becomes an established*
law of nature, that is, a general proposition concerning the nature of the object which we have been investigating.

This fourth step, too, has been taken in the investigation of the thought processes and it can be reëxamined by anyone who cares to do so. We shall explain the details of this fourth step together with those of the third step in subsequent sections of this chapter.

3. Misconceptions Concerning the Work of the Würzburg School. From what we have said in the last section, it is clear that the common-sense methods of all natural sciences *can,* and *must,* be applied to the problem of the thought processes. We are in perfect agreement with Watson when he insists that we must base nothing on the testimony of psychological "experts." *What characterizes a truly scientific investigation is that its data are public property and that the interpretation of these data is likewise public property. If the investigation of the thought processes as carried out by the Würzburg school does not measure up to this standard, this investigation has no scientific value.*

This being clearly understood, we are in a position to remove certain misconceptions concerning the introspective reports of the observers in the Würzburg experiments. We wish to emphasize, then, that *we base nothing on the theoretic convictions of any observer for or against sensationalism.* If such convictions were ever expressed or asked for, they simply do not enter into our discussion. The observers in the Würzburg experiments did exactly what observers do in any other scientific investigation: they *furnished the facts* of the first step (p. 328) and those of the fourth (p. 331). Many objective means were used to secure the accuracy of their introspective reports. The single observers, moreover, disappeared behind the mass of facts that were ascertained by many under the same experimental conditions. The data thus obtained from all observers were correlated by the experimenter.

The influence of suggestion, which is a fruitful source of error even in the laboratory of the physicist, *was eliminated as effectively as this can be done.* The observers were designedly left in the dark as to the particular purpose of the experiments devised by the experimenter and as to the "expectations" of the latter. *This disposes of the objection sometimes made that the subjects of the Würzburg experiments were asked to decide a difficult theoretic problem.* Nothing of the sort was done. If this had been done, the work of the Würzburg school would be at best a *symposium* on the thought processes and not an experimental investigation of them.

We wish to emphasize, further, that *we need not, and do not, rely even on the theoretic verdict of the experimenter.* His conclusions are worth no more than his arguments, and they are open to the inspection of all.

Lastly, we wish to emphasize that *each particular research must be judged on its own merits.* As a matter of fact, the present writer is far from inclined to accept all conclusions arrived at by this or that experimenter. Anyone can come to his own decision for or against sensationalism. All he has to do, is to test the two rival hypotheses, that of sensationalists and that of the Würzburg school, by the facts ascertained. We shall proceed to do so now.

4. First Test of the Two Rival Hypotheses. *In the supposition of sensationalism and structuralism thoughts are and forever remain a mere kaleidoscopic change of states of consciousness. In the supposition of the Würzburg school the kaleidoscopic change of states of consciousness is reduced to a definite order.*

An hypothesis is invented to "explain" the facts observed. As stated before, *the very minimum that is meant by "explaining" facts is, that the hypothesis made should bring order into what otherwise would be a confused mass of facts.* We shall apply this criterion to each of the two rival hypotheses.

Anyone who examines critically the introspective reports of the Würzburg school or those obtained by a statistical inquiry like that made by Galton (see p. 182) or a similar inquiry which can be made readily in the form of simple class exercises[1] must be struck by a fact which stands out boldly from all the rest. The different observers disagree hopelessly as to the images which they had when thinking of one and the same thing, say, a horse.

---

[1]Cf. pp. 275 sqq. of the writer's *Introductory Course in Experimental Psychology.*

The introspective reports show undoubtedly a kaleidoscopic variety of conscious states aroused by one and the same word, *horse*.

The Würzburg hypothesis is that the empirical distinctions between thought and sensations, between ideas and images, as we ascertained them in Chapter XIV, are distinctions of kind and not of degree. Accordingly, the idea of a horse — the "knowledge" of what a horse is, or the ' knowledge" of what is common to all horses — is a conscious process altogether distinct from an image of a horse. *This supposed, we can say that there is one conscious process which is substantially the same in all observers, namely, the idea of a horse.* The very reports show that every observer, immediately upon hearing the word *horse,* became aware of the object of which this common vocable is the conventional sign. This is an accurate description in purely empirical terms of an idea of a horse, as we explained in Chapter XIV.

The observers really disagree only with regard to the images they experience. Many of the observers in Galton's inquiry were men of science. "To my astonishment," Galton says, "I found that the great majority of the men of science to whom I first applied protested that mental imagery was unknown to them."[2] They "knew," for instance, with absolute precision what objects were present on their breakfast table, but they had no image of any of these objects. Other observers, however, succeed in recalling the sensible appearance of the object of which they are thinking, say, a horse, or of sensible objects connected with the horse. Some recall visual sensations, others those of an auditory or kinesthetic kind, etc.: some recall these sensations completely, others in a very fragmentary manner; some recall them vividly, others dimly; some do so with ease, others with great difficulty. Each observer in describing what he actually recalls of the sensible appearance of a horse or of other sensible objects connected with the horse, gives an accurate description in purely empirical

---

[2]Quoted by James, *Principles of Psychology,* II, p. 52.

terms of his images, as is clear from what we said in the chapter on Imagination (p. 168).

In the Würzburg hypothesis these images are the variable accompaniments of one and the same thought. As Dr. Buehler rightly remarks, "that which enters into consciousness so fragmentarily, so sporadically, so altogether accidentally, as images do when we are thinking, cannot be looked upon as the carrier of the continuous and well-knit content of our thought."[3] Even in the experience of each observer these images create the immediate impression of being "unessential accessories" of a thought and might just as well be absent without any change in the clearness of that thought.[4] In other words, though these images vary not only from observer to observer but in each observer from one occasion to another, they never create a confusion of thought. For an unsophisticated observer they are just what they are in the hypothesis of the Würzburg school, namely, "unessential accessories" of one and the same thought. They correspond to the variable accompaniments or "foreign ingredients" of one and the same substance as the chemist meets it in nature, say, water.

From this it will be seen that the assumption of the Würzburg school brings perfect order into the kaleidoscopic variety of conscious states aroused in different observers by one and the same word, just as the assumption of the chemist brings perfect order into the kaleidoscopic variety of water as he meets it in rivers, lakes, cisterns, etc. This accomplished, the psychologist can inquire, just as the chemist does, into the why and wherefore of the presence of these "foreign ingredients." *Thus the Würzburg hypothesis has the additional advantage of a good working hypothesis: it suggests new problems and suggests them effectively.* Many of the researches of the Würzburg school were precisely concerned with the functions that images have in thinking. These functions can be expressed in the form of empirical rules just as

[3] *Arch. f. d. ges. Psych.,* IX (1907), p. 317.
[4] *Ibid.*

is done in the case of the "foreign ingredients" of water. We shall deal with these empirical rules at the end of the next chapter (p. 387).

We shall now apply the same test to the hypothesis of sensationalism. The images aroused by the word *horse* differ from observer to observer By hypothesis these images are not the variable accompaniments of one and the same thought: they *are* the thought aroused by the word *horse*. It is by analyzing these images into their constituent sensations that each observer comes to describe the "existential aspect" or the very constitution of his thought. In terms of the hypothesis, then, *the word "horse" aroused a thought whose "existential aspect" or constitution differs from observer to observer*. If the constitution of the thought thus aroused differs from observer to observer, the thought itself differs from observer to observer. *And this means in plain terms that words cannot be used as signs of definite thoughts;* it means that words can only create a confusion of thought; it means, in short, that language is impossible. Thus we reach the *reductio ad absurdum* of the hypothesis of sensationalism.

The only way to avoid this criticism is to say — and it has been said — that the different observers really have "substantially the same thought" though "the scenery of the one mind differs astonishingly from the scenery of the other." But this interpretation of the facts makes matters only worse for sensationalists. For now they must say *that one and the same thought is variable in its constitution, a proposition just as unintelligible as that of a chemist who would maintain that the very constitution of water differs from one sample of it to another*.

Sensationalists, then, in applying their hypothesis to the facts observed, are confronted by a dilemma, and it makes no difference which of its horns they choose. *Whether they grant that words can only create a confusion of thought or whether they assume that one and the same thought is variable in its constitution: in both cases our thought processes are a confused mass of facts*. The facts observed remain what they were before we made the hypothesis: just a kaleidoscopic change of states of consciousness. If sensationalism is right, we had better do just what Watson suggests, namely, throw all states of consciousness and their kaleidoscopic changes overboard. In one word, *the hypothesis of sensationalism fails when the first and crucial test of a working hypothesis is applied to it.*

What we have said here in criticism of the hypothesis of sensationalism applies equally to *the various modifications of the theory* that have been proposed. One modification is that thought consists in *internal speech,* that is, in the images of words. It has also been said that thought is not necessarily identified with actual images but it may consist in the *"reproductive tendencies"* to such images. Though, for instance, we do not recall an actual image of this or that horse we have seen in the past, still a tendency to such a reproduction exists. It is claimed, then, that the thought of a horse consists in the combined effect of all the reproductive tendencies which we have because of our numerous sensory experiences of horses in the past.

The answer is that *images of words, like all other images, are variable.* They may be auditory, visual, kinesthetic, or mixed, and differ in detail from person to person and in the same person from one occasion to another and from one language to another, while *the thought* of which the word (in any of its various forms) is the conventional sign, *is identically the same* in different observers and in the same person on different occasions. Hence, if images cannot be identified with thought, because they are variable, the same must be said of images of words. *It is, moreover, plain nominalism to identify thought with word-images, and nominalism is in contradiction with the facts explained in Chapter XIV.*

The *reproductive tendencies* to images are likewise *variable.* No two observers have had identically the same sensory experiences in the past. Hence, no two observers have the same "reproductive tendencies," while they have *identically the same thought.* Accordingly, when thought is identified with these tendencies, the very constitution of one and the same thought differs from person to person. In one word, what we said concerning the "image theory" of thought holds likewise of the "word-image theory" and the "reproductive-tendency theory" of thought.

5. Second Test of the Two Rival Hypotheses. *Thoughts expressed in the theoretic terms of sensationalism are useless oddities incapable of verification. Thoughts expressed in terms of the Würzburg hypothesis are common property just like all the data of natural sciences.*

It has always been the boast of every natural science that its data are common property. And a scientific theory must be such that it makes no difference whether these data are expressed *in purely empirical terms* of common sense or *in terms of a definite theory:* in either case the data expressed must be capable of verification. Thus the empirical data which are embodied by the chemist in his laws of definite and multiple proportions, *are not obscured when they are expressed in terms of the atomic theory.* On the contrary, they stand out even more boldly when expressed by the theoretic symbols and formulas of the atomic theory, as, for instance, by the pithy formula H_2O. The very minimum that is required of a scientific theory is that the data of experience which are readily understood when expressed in purely empirical terms of common sense, *should not be rendered unintelligible and incapable of verification when expressed in theoretic terms.* As long as science is but refined common sense, we have here a simple criterion by which we can judge the value of any scientific theory. Let us apply this criterion to the two rival hypotheses concerning the nature of thought processes.

When explaining the object with which psychology is directly concerned (p. 7) we insisted that the "privacy" of our conscious life must not be exaggerated as has been done by behaviorists. It depends on our method in dealing with the data of our conscious life whether they are useless oddities or potent realities capable of becoming public property just like the data of every other natural science. This brings us back to a fundamental consideration dealt with in the first chapter.

A conscious process is not a purely subjective fact, for it has an essential relation to an object: we become "aware of some-

thing" and this something is known as the content or object of
that conscious process. Hence, there is a very simple way of describing any particular conscious process and of distinguishing
it from every other conscious process: *we simply describe the object of which we are aware here and now*. Common sense knows
of no other way of describing conscious processes and this mode
of procedure was adopted by Aristotle and his followers. It was
adopted also by the investigators of the Würzburg school. The
observers in their experiments described the "existential aspect"
of a definite conscious process — that is, the subjective fact that
they have here and now a definite conscious process — *by simply
describing the object or the peculiar aspect of the object of which
they are aware*. Thus they arrived at the purely empirical distinction between conscious processes whose contents are *anschaulich*
and *unanschaulich,* as was explained in Chapter XIV (p. 309).
Images are designated as *anschaulich* and ideas as *unanschaulich*.[5]

In the Würzburg hypothesis this plain empirical distinction
is assumed to be one of kind. Accordingly, images, when present
side by side with a definite idea, are interpreted by the experimenter to be mere accessories of that idea. No attempt is made
by the experimenter or his subjects to arrive at a more accurate
description of this idea by analyzing its accessories, the images,
into their component sensations. No such work of psychological
"experts" is needed. Furthermore, just as ideas are distinguished
from images by their objects, so also one idea is distinguished
from every other idea in terms of the object of that idea. Hence,
it has always been an adage of the followers of Aristotle that
"an idea is specified by its formal object," that is, by that peculiar
aspect of an object of which I become aware here and now.

These fundamentals being clearly understood, it is not hard
to see that ideas can become public property and that they do not
cease to be public property when expressed in terms of the Würzburg hypothesis. For in this hypothesis the "existential aspect"
of a definite idea — the subjective fact that I have a definite idea

---

[5]Cf. F. E. O. Schultze, *Erscheinungen und Gedanken, Arch. f. d. ges. Psych.,*
VIII (1906), pp. 241 sqq., and pp. 256 sqq.

— is described *in terms of the object* of which I become aware. The objects of ideas can be described with precision by using the system of conventional signs of objects known as language, particularly the technical language peculiar to each science. *When ideas are thus defined, they lose their privacy and become common property. There is absolutely no idea, no matter how delicately it may differ from another idea, which cannot be defined and shared with everyone that uses the same system of conventional signs, that is, who knows the language of the country wherein he resides.*

It is true that for the purposes of everyday life the full accuracy with which we can manifest our ideas is rarely aimed at and, even if aimed at, is frequently not attained. We are frequently careless in the use of words. As a result we frequently misunderstand one another. Even scientists sometimes fail to make their ideas clear to others. The principal reason for this failure is that the technical usage of terms in designating definite objects is not adhered to or that there is as yet no agreement among scientists in using a definite term to designate a definite object. But whenever such an agreement is arrived at and adhered to, we know with precision the idea which a physicist, chemist, or any other scientist has when using the sign agreed upon for designating the object of that idea.

It is possible, then, to make an introspective report of our ideas and thus to render them public property. In fact, every scientist when lecturing on any topic whatever can be said in literal strictness to make an introspective report of his ideas concerning that topic. *He succeeds in doing so because he describes his ideas not in terms of their accessories but in terms of their objects.* In a word, every scientist succeeds in sharing his ideas with others because he describes them *in a manner which fits with precision the theory of the Würzburg school,* to wit: ideas must not be confounded with their accessories, namely images, but are conscious processes essentially different from these images. Accordingly, the Würzburg hypothesis concerning the relation between ideas and images, meets successfully the second test of a scientific hypothesis.

In the hypothesis of sensationalism and structuralism images are not accessories of ideas, but they *are* ideas. *Accordingly, sensationalists insist that the "existential aspect" of a definite idea —* the subjective fact that an observer has here and now a definite idea — *must not be described by him in terms of the object of that idea but in terms of the sensations into which his images can be resolved.* Thus expressed a definite idea of a definite observer becomes *a mere oddity which cannot be verified by anybody else for the simple reason that no two observers agree with regard to the images they experience when thinking of one and the same object.*

A practical example of the introspective data obtained in the laboratory of sensationalists will show the force of this criticism. Titchener quotes[6] the introspective data of three trained observers who describe the "existential aspect" of one and the same idea. We shall not indicate in terms of common sense what the idea was which is described, but invite the reader to find this out for himself from the very descriptions of it which are in accord with the theory of sensationalism and structuralism. One observer describes his idea *"as the blue-gray tip of a kind of scoop,"* etc.; a second *"as the mental unrolling of a white scroll,"* and a third as *"a horizontal line with two short verticals."* If we agree with sensationalists and structuralists that these three observers are *not describing mere accessories* of their idea but the very idea itself and *identically the same idea,* then the introspective data of sensationalists are *useless oddities devoid of all human interest.*

And the refinement of accuracy in the description of such useless oddities is sometimes unspeakably ludicrous. Suppose that while thinking of the relation which one object has to another, some odd imagery passes through my mind. We all know that this occurs at times, but men who have work to do pay no atten-

---

[6]*Lectures on the Experimental Psychology of the Thought Processes,* p. 19.

tion to such imagery. Now suppose that I not only pay attention to it but insist on describing with accuracy that this imagery is "passing swiftly down the visual field from northwest to southeast." The pattern of sensations thus indicated is indeed the all-important thing for structuralists. *But who cares whether this imagery is passing swiftly down the visual field from northwest to southeast or from northeast to southwest?* No wonder that the ire of Watson was aroused by the useless lumber that has accumulated in the laboratories of the structuralists.

Undoubtedly, also, sensationalists and structuralists succeed in expressing their ideas, but only when they express them as common sense has done from time immemorial, namely, in terms of their objects. And these are the terms of the Würzburg hypothesis. Expressed in the terms of sensationalism, these very ideas are not only obscured beyond recognition but become useless oddities that cannot be verified by anyone. From this it will be seen that the hypothesis of sensationalism and structuralism fails signally when the second test of a scientific hypothesis is applied to it.

6. Third Test of the Two Rival Hypotheses. *The empirical data which have been obtained in the investigation of the process of generalizing abstraction are irreconcilable with the hypothesis of sensationalism; they are in perfect accord with the hypothesis of the Würzburg school.*

As was stated in Chapter XIV (p. 311), generalizing abstraction is nothing else than a special form of attention. It consists in this, that we direct our attention to a feature of an individual which, as a matter of fact, is common to several individuals, thereby diverting our attention from all those features by which this individual differs from other individuals. Undoubtedly this form of attention occurs in our experience and it has been observed with accuracy under laboratory conditions (p. 310). We need not state explicitly that our mode of attention brings about no change in the *physical* condition of the individual. But as far as our experience is concerned, the common feature of this individual is "positively abstracted" from its individual differences, that is, *we represent the former without the latter.* As a result we have an idea which is universal. We become explicitly aware of the universality of our idea when we find that its contents can without any change be applied to each of several other individuals.

No one can deny that we have ideas whose contents can be applied without any change to each of several individuals, and such ideas have been called from time immemorial universal ideas. We make use of universal ideas whenever we classify objects, a process which no science can dispense with. Similarly, we make use of a universal idea whenever we define a common feature of several individuals. In this manner we *clarify* our universal ideas. This process, too, is perfectly familiar to every scientist. A scientific definition of a common feature, even if it be merely descriptive, leaves out all those features by which individuals differ from one another. In short, *a scientific definition indicates with precision the contents of the universal idea or category which a scientist has formed by a process of generalizing abstraction.* Thus, for instance, biologists have formed the universal idea or category of a four-footed animal or that of a four-footed mammal or that of a placental mammal or that of a rational animal. Whatever the scientific value of these four ideas may be, every one of them is a universal idea arrived at by a process of generalizing abstraction.

We have also explained how the process of the original formation of a universal idea becomes gradually obscured. We do not, and need not, go through the process of generalizing abstraction again every time we make use of a universal idea. Like every other conscious process, the universal idea, once formed, is retained and its contents become associated with those of other ideas either in a systematic or a haphazard way, as was explained in Chapter XIV. The contents of a universal idea become also associated with those of sensory experiences of various kinds. The most noteworthy of these associations is one which, of itself, is of all associations the most haphazard: we mean the association of a universal idea with a definite sound of the human voice or with a definite group of curious black marks traced on sheets of paper with pen and ink or, more efficiently, by the modern printing machine. Such sounds and marks are, of themselves, but nonsense syllables. They become, however, gradually transformed into common "names" of things, that is, arbitrary signs for the contents of universal ideas and for the ideas themselves. This process, too, has been studied experimentally (p. 318).

The question now arises whether the sensationalistic hypothesis is in agreement with the empirical data here set forth. Some sensationalists have answered this question by denying or explaining away the fact of generalizing abstraction. With these attempts at a solution of our present problem we are no longer concerned: they have been sufficiently dealt with in Chapter XIV. We are here concerned with *the image theory of universal ideas.* A little consideration will show that universal ideas as we know them from experience cannot be identified with images of any kind. *The peculiarity of a universal idea is that its contents can be applied without any change to each of several individuals. The contents of an image, however, cannot be thus applied to several individuals. Accordingly, a universal idea is not an image.* This argument occurs time and again in the discussions of the data of the Würzburg school and is really the classic argument of Aristotle. An illustration will show its force.

By a process of generalizing abstraction, precisely as explained above, we can undoubtedly arrive at the idea of a rational animal. The contents of this *idea* are in the focus of attention and can be examined carefully by anyone who cares to do so. No alchemistic practices are required to accomplish this examination nor is any special skill in introspection needed to find out what the contents of our idea really are. They are plainly two features of some individual man we have seen, namely, his animality and rationality. All the other features of this man have receded into the background of attention or are entirely forgotten. We find, further, that the two features thus retained in the focus of our attention can be applied without any change to each of a great many different individuals, no matter whether they are white, yellow or black, large or small, etc.

In a like manner and without recourse to any alchemistic practices we can also examine the contents of an *image* of man. When we actually see some particular man, we get a visual impression of him: we experience this man as he appears to our sense of sight here and now, namely, black or white, large or small, etc. Closing our eyes we can revive the visual experience we had and then we have an image of that man. This image may be vivid or faint, complete or very fragmentary. But its contents never exceed those of the sensation or sensations of which the image is the revival. We find, then, that our image of a man is always particular. If it is the image of a black man, its contents cannot be applied to a white man; and if our image is that of a small man, its contents cannot be applied to a large man, etc. In short, *we find that the contents of every image of man, no matter what its details may be, cannot be applied without change to every individual man.* From this we conclude that our *universal idea of man,* namely, that of a rational animal, *cannot be identified with any image of man.* This plain inference agrees perfectly with the Würzburg hypothesis but disagrees hopelessly with the theoretic assumption of sensationalists.

What holds of the universal idea of a rational animal, holds likewise of all the universal ideas which have been created by systematic biologists for purposes of classification. Thus *the contents of the idea of a four-footed animal can be applied without change to a great many different individuals,* to every cat, to every horse, to every dog, etc. An image of a four-footed animal must of necessity be that of a particular four-footed animal, say, of a particular cat. *The contents of this image cannot be applied without change to every four-footed animal.* Thus, for instance, they cannot be applied to a horse or a dog, etc. Accordingly, the universal idea or category of a four-footed animal, which guides the systematist in his work of classification, cannot be an image.

7. The "Composite Image" Theory of Universal Ideas. Many are the attempts made by sensationalists to evade the force of this argument. Thus, for instance, it has been said that what we call a universal idea of a cat is really *a blurred image of a* *great many cats, formed after the manner of a composite photograph.* Let us suppose that a photographic film requires ten seconds of exposure and that a composite photograph of ten cats is to be made. We put the first cat in a definite place and in a definite position before the camera and in photographing it we expose the film only for one second. Another cat is put in the same place and in approximately the same position before the camera and again only one second of exposure is allowed for taking the picture. In a similar manner all ten cats are photographed on the same film. When we develop such a film we get a rather *monstrous-looking picture:* a composite image of ten cats in which *their resemblances are emphasized and their differences are slurred.* In a like manner, it is claimed, we acquire what is called a universal idea of a cat. We get a definite visual impression of the first cat we see and the trace of this impression remains in our brain. This trace is the physical basis of the "reproductive tendency" of the image of this cat. The second cat we see leaves a slightly different impression on our brain, and so does the third, fourth, and every other cat we see. As a result, we have a great many traces of individual cats in our brain. But these traces fuse into one and constitute the "reproductive tendency" of a blurred image of a cat formed after the manner of a composite photograph of ten different cats. And this blurred image is what we call a universal idea of a cat.

We do not deny that many persons when thinking of a cat, have also a blurred image of a cat. We admit, too, with certain qualifications, that such an image may arise after the manner of a composite photograph of ten cats. If all cats we see were approximately of the same size, and if every cat were obliging enough to present itself to the photographic camera of our eye in approximately the same position and at about the same distance from the eye, we would undoubtedly succeed as well as a photographer does in making a composite image of ten or more cats. Since cats are, as a rule, not so obliging, the success of each person in this regard can be determined only by his own introspective report. He, and he alone, can tell us whether he has actually a blurred image of a cat that could be likened to a composite photograph of all the cats he has seen. One thing, however, is certain, namely, that many of us fail to detect by introspection a blurred image of this kind. So much for the composite image of all the cats we have seen.

It is well to add, however, that *the formation of a composite image of a "four-footed animal" would be a more problematical affair.* Probably no photographer would undertake to make a composite photograph of ten four-footed animals, say, a mouse, a lion, a dog, a horse, a cat, a full-grown chimpanzee, a giraffe, etc. Accordingly, the hypothesis of a composite image of all the individual four-footed animals we have seen, seems little in accord with the facts as we know them. The formation of *a composite image of a body in general,* the combined effect of all individual bodies we have seen, *would be worse than problematical.* Who is the photographer who would undertake to make a composite photograph of such objects as the following: a steam engine, a diamond, a pair of scissors, a coat, the Woolworth Building. It is safe to say that the most expert introspectionist of the sensationalistic school has never detected in himself the presence of such a composite image of a "body in general."

But all these discrepancies between theory and facts are of minor importance. The most important thing is that no blurred image that we detect by introspection, even if it be formed after the manner of a composite photograph, can possibly perform the function of a universal idea. A universal idea as, for instance, that of a four-footed animal, *guides the systematic biologist in classifying the individuals with which he deals. A blurred image of a four-footed animal, even if it be formed after the manner of a composite photograph cannot thus guide the biologist.* Hence, such a blurred image cannot be his universal idea of a four-footed animal. A systematic biologist may indeed have a blurred image of a four-footed animal side by side with the universal idea of it. And let us suppose, for the sake of argument, that such a blurred image is formed after the manner of a composite photograph. Such an image is, of itself, rather a *hindrance* than a help in accomplishing his work of classification. For this image forces upon the attention of the systematist features which are irrelevant for the purposes of his work of classification. Only when he realizes that these features are irrelevant and then turns his attention again to those features which are relevant, will he succeed in accomplishing his task. And these relevant features are the content of his universal idea of a four-footed animal arrived at by a process of generalizing abstraction.

8. The Typical-Image Theory. Another attempt that has been made to rehabilitate the image theory of the universal idea is that of Wundt.[7] He starts out with the plain fact that in the experience of most persons their images are rather blurred and frequently fragmentary and very fleeting. Such being the case, we select, he says, the image of a definite individual, say, that of a definite man, to serve as a type of man. Accordingly, we have what Wundt calls a "typical image" of man. But *with this typical image we combine, he says, the "peculiar feeling"* (*eigenthümliches Gefühl*) *that it serves a vicarious function.* That is to say, the individual man thus imaged typifies for us what holds of all men.

Suppose, for the sake of argument, that we always have a typical image of a definite man, when thinking of man in general. This supposed, it is clear from the very description of Wundt that over and above such an image we have also a true universal idea of man arrived at by a process of generalizing abstraction. *For a definite man, whom we imagine, cannot be for us a type of what is true of all men, unless we are aware of what holds of all men. But when we are aware of what holds of all men, we have by that very fact a universal idea of man.* For this, and nothing else, is what is meant by a universal idea of man. It is only a change of label when this awareness is called a "peculiar feeling" and the label, moreover, does not fit the facts of the case. So much for the "typical-image theory" of universal ideas.

9. The Word-Image Theory. Still another form of the im-

[7]Cf. *Grundriss der Psychologie* (3rd ed.), p. 315.

age theory of universal ideas takes cognizance of the fact that many persons have no object images worthy of the name. The only images such persons can detect when thinking even of sensible objects, are those of the words which are the conventional signs of these objects. It is assumed by sensationalists that, in the case of such persons at least, the universal idea, say, of man, is nothing else than *an auditory, visual, or kinesthetic image of the word "man."*

We do not deny the important rôle which word-images play in the experience of every person, particularly of those who lack object images worthy of the name. But the known facts and in particular the data ascertained in the experimental investigation of this matter (see pp. 183 sqq.), do not warrant the foregoing hypothesis of sensationalists. In fact, these data are irreconcilable with such an hypothesis. What really took place in these experiments was that the result of positive abstraction, the universal idea, became gradually but firmly associated with a definite nonsense syllable. Thus the nonsense syllable was gradually transformed into a "name" of the common feature abstracted. This transformation involved nothing mysterious and alchemistic. It consisted in this that the nonsense syllable became an arbitrary sign of the common feature abstracted. The same transformation occurs in the experience of every child when it learns its mother tongue and in the experience of every adult that learns a foreign language. For every word of every language is, of itself, but a nonsense syllable. It is simply doing violence to the facts as they occur in our experience and to the data ascertained in experimental investigations, to identify the image of the sign with the knowledge of the common feature signified. Really the word-image theory of universal ideas amounts to the denial that there is any idea at all corresponding to common words: it is nominalism pure and simple. *As long as it is true that we are not always beating the air when we use common words so long the word-image theory of universal ideas is sadly out of joint with facts.*

10. The Reproductive-Tendency Theory. Another attempt of sensationalists to evade our argument against the image theory of universal ideas may be called the "reproductive-tendency theory" of universal ideas. We have seen many different individuals of the same class, say, of four-footed animals. The visual experience of each particular animal leaves a trace in our brain and the combined effect of all these traces constitutes the "reproductive tendency" to a blurred image of a four-footed animal. In many persons this reproductive tendency fails to result in an actual image worthy of the name. It remains forever a potential image, that is, a purely physiological condition. *This potential image, however, constitutes, according to sensationalists, what we call a universal idea of a four-footed animal.*

We do not deny that a reproductive tendency such as is here described, exists in our brain and that, in many persons at least, it fails to result in an actual image of any kind. The existence of such a reproductive tendency is a matter of *inference* as we have explained in the chapter on Memory. Probably such "bottled-up images" have also an effect on our behavior. This, again, is a matter of inference or of legitimate hypothesis Such an hypothesis may be of value in dealing with certain obscure phenomena where a subject can give us no introspective report as to what guides him in his behavior. We have dealt with these matters in the chapter on Attention (see pp. 217 sqq.). But at present we are not concerned with the explanation of such obscure phenomena. We are dealing with facts which have been observed under controlled conditions, namely, those which have been ascertained in the experimental investigation of the process of generalizing abstraction.

The reader will recall from Chapter XIV (pp. 314 sqq.) that experimental conditions were created which force the process of generalizing abstraction and its result, the universal idea on our attention. Similar conditions exist in the case of every scientist whenever he attempts to classify objects. We know from the introspective reports of the subjects and from our own experience whenever we classify objects, what *guides* us in accomplishing our task, namely, *the contents of a universal idea arrived at by a process of generalizing abstraction.* Whenever we meet an object to which the contents of a definite universal idea or category can be applied without change, we assign the proper place for that object in accordance with the contents of a universal idea which are here and now in the very focus of attention. An appeal to "bottled-up images" in explanation of our work of classification is wide of the mark. Whatever "bottled-up images" may be capable of accomplishing for us in the discussion of psychological problems, these images have nothing to do with the data ascertained in the Würzburg experiments or with the facts of classification known to every scientist.

11. The "Common Image" of the Schoolmen. Before dismissing the image theory of universal ideas it may be well to point out *the grain of truth* which is contained in all the various forms of this theory. Though no image is a universal idea, still, under certain conditions it may be *an analogous imitation of a universal idea.* The great schoolmen of the past recognized this fact and called such an analogous imitation of a universal idea a "common image." It was postulated by them in the explanation of animal behavior. If animals lack intelligence, they cannot have universal ideas, just as they cannot be said to judge. The schoolmen, however, insisted that animals give evidence of analogous imitations of these and other intellectual operations. We have explained in the chapter on Instinct what is meant by an analogous imitation of a judgment in animals. Here is the appropriate place for explaining the analogous imitation of universal ideas as they are ascribed to animals, namely, "common images." Happily we can ascertain what is meant by this term from our own experience.

Suppose that we see an individual man. We experience this individual as he appears to our sense of vision here and now, and, insofar as we have an actual sensation of him. When in the absence of this individual, we revive the sensory experience we had of him in the past, we have, insofar, an image of him: we become again aware of this individual, namely, as he has appeared to our sense of vision on a former occasion.

Now suppose, further, that this individual has a twin brother who looks exactly like him. The image of one will fit the other, not because my image represents the common essence of both, but because the sensible appearance of one is exactly like that of the other. Every Ford machine has a "twin brother"; so has every shoe, every spade, etc. And all such "twins" are of the kind that in the language of the biologist should be designated as "identical twins," that is, they look exactly alike in every detail. Hence, even if our image of an individual Ford machine be as complete and detailed as it possibly can be, a perfect replica of the original sensation, this image would fit all other Ford machines of the same type and model. And if we have only a blurred image of a Ford machine, this image will in a fashion also fit automobiles of a different make. Roughly speaking, all automobiles look alike; so do bones, the all-important thing in a dog's experience, and all mice, the all-important thing in a cat's life. Hence, the dog need not know anything about the common nature of bones, nor need the cat be endowed with insight as to what the true inwardness of a mouse is, or as to the useful purpose a mouse can serve in the process of a cat's nutrition. *A "common image" of a bone and a "common image" of a mouse such as we have just described, are a better equipment for the instinctive life of a dog and cat respectively, than the knowledge of the common nature of bones and of mice respectively would be.* Hence, the schoolmen of old concluded that "common images" are the nearest approach to universal ideas that occur in the life of an animal. For that matter, a "common image" is also useful in the instinctive life of man, but it fails to perform the functions of his rational life. So much for the grain of truth contained in the image theory of universal ideas.

12. Further Tests of the Two Rival Hypotheses. In addition to the considerations set forth in our three tests of the two rival hypotheses, we may briefly mention other considerations

which occur frequently in the literature dealing with the Würzburg researches. Thus, for instance, it is pointed out that according to the introspective reports of the subjects *the clearness of an
idea does not depend on the clearness of an image that may be
present*. On the contrary, the idea or knowledge concerning the
nature of an object was frequently clear-cut and stood out boldly
in the foreground of attention while the accompanying image
was very hazy and had to be picked out laboriously from the
neglected background of attention. Vice versa, the image of an
object was sometimes clear and detailed while the knowledge as
to the nature of the object imaged was very hazy. These experimental data are unintelligible, if our ideas are images.[8]

It is pointed out, too, *that images and thoughts do not always
coincide in time*. Frequently the subjects knew with precision
what the nature of a definite object was, before any image of the
object arose. The reverse also occurred: the subjects had an image of an object, before they grasped the nature of the object
thus imaged.[9] This rules out at least the *object images* as the
constituent features of our ideas.

*As to word-images it is pointed out that they may vary
without affecting the idea expressed in the very least*. Thus it
makes no difference whether we imagine the German words
or their English equivalents: in both cases the contents of
our idea are identically the same. In the Würzburg hypothesis
there is no difficulty whatever to understand why for every German word there is an English equivalent. *A word is but an arbitrary sign for the contents of a definite idea, and the image of
a word is but the revival of our sensory experience of this arbitrary sign*. It is a mere accident of birth or a matter of free choice
whether we make use of one sign or another. Persons born in
the Fatherland use one sign, those of English parentage use another to designate the contents of identically the same idea. It is
for this reason that for every German word there is an English
equivalent. What this equivalence of corresponding words in

---

[8] Cf., for instance, *Arch. f. d. ges. Psych.*, VIII, p. 293.
[9] Cf. *op. cit.*, pp. 249 sqq.

two languages may consist in, if we assume that the image of a word is the idea itself, sensationalists have failed to tell us. In short, *sensationalists cannot give a rational account of the fact that thought, and only the thought, can be accurately translated from one language into any other language.*

Vice versa, the image of a definite word, say, "bar," may remain identically the same while the idea connected with that image may vary enormously. The word *bar* is equivocal, and there are many other words in every language which are just as equivocal. The object denoted by such a word can be gathered only from its context or from the circumstances in which it is used. When we speak of musical matters the word *bar* denotes a thing totally different from what it does when we speak of the Eighteenth Amendment, and another, again, when we discuss the profession of a lawyer, etc. In the hypothesis of the Würzburg school there is no difficulty whatever in explaining *the remarkable change in our internal experience which occurs when we actually pronounce or imagine the word "bar" now in one context, then in another.* What occurs is a change of *thought* and not of image. From this the Würzburg experimentalists conclude that the image of the word is not the thought.[10] The instructed reader will note that this argument of the Würzburg experimentalists is but the modern form of the classic argument of Aristotelian psychology.

Sensationalists have nothing to offer in explanation of the facts mentioned except speculations of an alchemistic kind known as *"the psychology of meaning,"* and these speculations have brought disrepute on the introspective method in psychology. Behaviorists rightly insist that introspective psychology as carried on by sensationalists and structuralists, has reached the point of stagnation and that the first thing to be done is, to get rid of all the jargon of sensationalists concerning the "structure of conscious states" and the irreducible elements of sensation into which these structures can be analyzed by psychological experts. *In the Würzburg*

---

[10] Cf., for instance, *op. cit.,* p. 293.

school no such scandal occurred as that of the "psychology of meaning." Its position has always been that of refined common sense. As long as science is but refined common sense, the facts of the Würzburg school must be recognized and the interpretation of these facts can only be that of the Würzburg hypothesis: thoughts are not images and cannot be reduced to sensations as their constitutive elements.

13. The Famous "Unpicturable Contents of Conscious Processes." One of the considerations on which the Würzburg experimentalists insist very much in their discussions of the image theory of thought, is that connected with their famous distinction between *anschauliche* and *unanschauliche Bewustseinsinhalte*. These terms can be rendered into English accurately by circumlocutions, but it is difficult to find a single word in the English language which is the exact equivalent for *anschaulich* and its opposite *unanschaulich*. The term *"Bewustseinsinhalte"* is readily enough translated but it is one of those compound German words that have perspective; it simply means "contents of our conscious processes." The strangeness of these German words is probably the principal reason why the famous distinction of the Würzburg experimentalists is neglected, if they are not passed over with a joke just like their "atrocious *Bewustseinslagen*." There is nothing atrocious about *Bewustseinslagen* except that the word has five syllables and is something of a jawbreaker. In plain English it means "mental attitudes" such as doubt, certainty, suspicion, etc. These attitudes will come up for consideration in connection with judgment. Nor is there anything atrocious about *anschauliche* and *unanschauliche Bewustseinsinhalte*. If the word *anschaulich* is to be rendered by a single English word, we suggest *picturable* as its equivalent; *unanschaulich* means *unpicturable*.

This premised, the famous argument of the Würzburg school runs something like this: The contents of every image are "picturable." *You can actually draw the contents of your image of, say a house,* and the picture you thus draw will be complete or fragmentary, distinct or hazy, according as your actual image is complete or fragmentary, distinct or hazy; a pencil may suffice for "picturing" the contents of your image or you may need all the paraphernalia of a painter in water colors. Over and against the "picturable" contents of all images are the contents of other conscious processes which are "unpicturable." We have already explained that the common nature of several individuals, the content of a universal idea, is "unpicturable," even though every individual to whom these contents can be applied is picturable. The most prominent, however, among the "unpicturable contents of a conscious process" are those of which we become aware when we are thinking of nonentities which, for the purpose of thought, are represented after the manner of real entities. Thus, for instance, a musician knows with absolute precision what is meant by a *pause* and, at least in the beginning of his musical career, he is guided by the contents of this idea in his musical performances. Now try to draw the contents of this idea with pen or pencil on a piece of paper. This is plainly impossible for the simple reason that the content of your idea is the negation of a physical reality. You may indeed be able to picture this physical reality, but it is not this reality which is the content of your thought; it is its negation that you think of and which guides you, at least in the beginning, in a musical performance. Whenever, then, we are guided by the actual knowledge of what a "pause" is, we have an actual conscious process whose contents are "unpicturable." Consequently such a conscious process cannot possibly be an image.

Here, again, the Würzburg experimentalists make use of an argument that is time-honored in the history of psychology. The great schoolmen designated all the "unpicturable contents of conscious processes" like that of the idea of a "pause" by the name of "creations of the mind" (*entia rationis cum fundamento in re*). Whenever we think of negations, privations, or logical relations, the contents of our idea are a "creation of the mind," and the conscious process by which we become aware of such creations of the mind, cannot be images for the simple reason that these creations of the mind are "unpicturable." In a nutshell, then, the classic argument of the great schoolmen and the famous argument of the Würzburg school against the image theory of ideas, is as follows: *The contents of every image are "picturable." But the contents of many of our ideas are plainly not "picturable." Hence, at least many of our ideas are not images.*

14. "Symbolical Images" and the Psychology of "Meaning." In answer to this argument, sensationalists drag us again into their metaphysical darkroom of the "psychology of meaning." A semblance of justification for this mode of procedure is afforded by the well-known fact that in dealing with "unpicturable" things *we frequently make use of metaphors and figures of speech.* These metaphors deal directly with sensible objects that can be pictured and the sensible things thus pictured are symbols of the contents that are unpicturable. Accordingly, it is said that all ideas of unpicturable things are really "symbolical images." After describing the image of a picturable symbol, sensationalists always wind up with the flourish: "and this image *means* this or that unpicturable thing."

The first and most obvious rejoinder to this answer of sensationalists is that *they mistake the image of a symbol for the knowledge of the thing symbolized.*

But there is another rejoinder which makes the appeal to the "meaning" of symbolical images a real *boomerang.* Let us suppose that the image of this or that sensible object *means* a definite unpicturable thing. Obviously, the sensible object thus imaged cannot be a symbol and have this or that meaning *except for him who understands the meaning of this symbol,* that is, unless he has, *over and above the image of the symbol, also the knowledge of the thing symbolized.* By the very fact, then, that we sometimes experience images which are symbolical, we know the *further* fact that we have also an idea of the thing symbolized. Accordingly, by describing the image of the symbol we are not describing "the existential aspect" of our idea but an *accessory* of that idea *just as is maintained in the Würzburg hypothesis.*

References for Further Reading

J. Froebes, S.J., *Lehrbuch der Experimentellen Psychologie*, Vol. I (1923), pp. 417-436.

H. Gruender, S.J., *Introductory Course in Experimental Psychology*, pp. 273-285.

K. Buehler, *Tatsachen u. Probleme*, etc., in *Arch. f. d. ges. Psych.*, IX (1907), pp. 297 sqq.

H. J. Watt, *The Economy and Training of Memory*, Chap. VI.

Chapter XVI

THOUGHT
(Concluded)

1. A Preliminary and Noncommittal Description of Judgment. The experimental investigation of judgment has not been very extensive. Some of the researches, moreover, that have been undertaken were hampered by the lack of a sufficiently clear preliminary description of judgment or by a faulty description of it If we know only vaguely what we mean to investigate, the results of our investigation will be likewise vague. And if we start with a description of judgment which is plainly too wide, that is, which also fits processes that in common usage are not known by the name of judgment, we must not be surprised if we arrive at results which are out of touch with our experience as it actually occurs in everyday life. And if we begin with theoretic bias as to what our conscious life really ought to be and as to the facts we ought to find, the results of our investigation will be tainted by this bias, and it will vitiate even the phenomenal description of the facts. Thus, for instance, it has been claimed on the basis of an experimental investigation of judgment that internal experience reveals no conscious process peculiar to judgment. It has also been claimed — and this, again, on the basis of experiment — that what we call judgment is frequently no conscious process at all but a purely physiological transaction; our neuromuscular equipment "judges" for us.

Before we can form an estimate as to the real value of these and similar results of experiment, and before we state positively what facts have been ascertained by experiment concerning judgment, and how these facts are to be interpreted, we must begin with a purely preliminary and noncommittal description of "judgment," and this description should fit the common usage of this term. True, vocables are arbitrary signs of things, and anyone, if he so chooses, may use any word to designate anything whatever. This holds also of the word *judgment*. But if we wish to be understood by others and remain in touch with the problems of everyday life, we must not in the very beginning of our discussion recede from the common usage of the term by which we designate its subject. *The very purpose of our present discussion is to investigate the nature of that conscious process which common usage designates by the term judgment.*

Surely we do not recede from such usage if we say that in a trial by jury those appointed to judge, namely, the members of the jury, manifest a judgment when they give their verdict concerning the guilt of the prisoner. In fact, such a "judgment" is an ideal instance of what common usage designates by the term. All the peculiarities of such a judgment stand out most boldly and every step in the process of its formation is public property. Anyone who desires to do so, can reëxamine every step, just as this can be done with every scientific procedure. Hence, it will be well for us to consider what in a trial by jury is meant by a judgment and how it is arrived at.

Whatever the legal form may be in which the verdict of the jury is announced, each member of the jury is at liberty to manifest his judgment in any one of many different ways. He may do so, for instance, by the simple word *guilty* or even by a nod of his head. It is, however, only from the circumstances in which this word is pronounced or the nod occurs, that they are seen to be signs of a judgment. The clearest and most unmistakable sign of a judgment is a declarative sentence such as "Mr. Jones is a murderer in the first degree." All other forms of expressing a judgment can be reduced to a declarative sentence, and it is by thus reducing them that all doubt is removed as to the conscious process in the minds of the speakers Accordingly, we can say that *a judgment is that conscious process which we manifest by a declarative sentence.*

The declarative sentence mentioned contains three elements known respectively as the *subject* ("Mr. Jones"), the *predicate*

("a murderer in the first degree"), and the *copula* "is." By the
subject of this sentence the speaker manifests his idea of a definite individual, namely, the prisoner in the dock and known by
the name of "Mr. Jones." By the predicate he manifests a universal idea or category whose contents are most accurately defined
by law, namely, "a murderer in the first degree." The speaker
joins the subject and predicate by the copula "is" and thus manifests the conscious attitude which he has here and now as the
result of the judicial procedure and with reference to the two
ideas mentioned. In this instance *his conscious attitude is that of
affirmation.* He "affirms" that the predicate as defined by law is
verified in the individual denoted by the subject. In the language
of the schools this is expressed by saying that *he affirms the "objective identity" of the two ideas mentioned.* The two ideas are
not identical in content. Far from it, nor is this affirmed by the
speaker. But the contents of the universal idea as defined by law
are verified in the individual denoted by the subject. This relation between two ideas is known by the name of "objective identity" and it is this relation which is "affirmed" by the speaker.

What the mental attitude of "affirmation" is in purely empirical
terms is best described by contrasting it with a totally different
attitude which each member of the jury might have arrived at
as a result of the judicial procedure and with reference to identically the same two ideas, namely, *the attitude of "negation."*
These two mental attitudes are *most clearly distinguished in the
experience of every man.* There are many conventional signs for
manifesting either of these two mental attitudes. Thus we may
manifest them in the form of an introspective report making the
"Ego" the subject of a complex sentence by saying "I affirm" or
"I deny," and then we indicate the object of these mental attitudes by a dependent sentence such as "that Mr. Jones is a murderer in the first degree." But *when we use a simple declarative
sentence like that previously quoted, the copula "is" is the conventional sign both for the mental attitude of "affirmation" and
for the "objective identity" affirmed.* In a simple negative sentence the mental attitude of "negation" is manifested by the par-

ticle "not." This particle modifies the copula "is." We thus indicate that it is the "objective identity" of the two ideas joined which we deny.

It will be noted, then, that with reference to identically the same two ideas of subject and predicate we may have two radically different attitudes, namely, either that of affirmation or that of negation. And *it is the fact that we take definitely one of these two attitudes that constitutes "judgment" proper*. Hence it is that Aristotle, when speaking of judgment in opposition to a simple idea, characterizes the former most pithily by describing it as *"affirmation or negation."*[1] The mere idea of "Mr. Jones" is no judgment, nor is the idea of "a murderer in the first degree." Either of these ideas can be present in our mind without the conscious attitude of affirmation or negation. It is the absence of both of these conscious attitudes that distinguishes a mere idea from a judgment. Hence *an idea, in opposition to judgment, may be defined as the mere knowledge of an object without any affirmation or negation.*

It will be noted, further, that judgment occurs in connection with the association of two ideas. But the mere association of two ideas, that is, the fact that two ideas are aroused simultaneously or in immediate succession in our mind, does not constitute judgment. The two ideas of "Mr. Jones" and "a murderer in the first degree" have been associated in the very beginning of the trial. But then the constituted judges, the members of the jury, had a mental attitude which is totally different from both affirmation and negation and which is popularly described as that of "an open mind." Whatever else may be meant by the attitude of "an open mind," it means in purely empirical terms that the members of the jury neither affirm nor deny "that Mr Jones is a murderer in the first degree." Each member of the jury was explicitly asked whether he had the attitude of "an open mind," for without it he would have been disqualified as a member of the jury.

---

[1] *De Anima*, III, 8.

In the course of the trial, as a result of the evidence given, the initial attitude of "an open mind" gradually gives way to a great variety of other mental attitudes. Such are, for instance, the attitudes of doubt and suspicion. We are not concerned here with the analysis of these various attitudes. For the present we merely note the fact that there are mental attitudes which precede judgment as this term is understood in a trial by jury. All these attitudes have reference to identically the same two ideas, say, that of "Mr. Jones" and that of "a murderer in the first degree." It is only when a member of the jury combines these two ideas by way of "affirmation" or separates them by way of "negation," that he is said to pronounce a "judgment."

What we said concerning the association of two ideas, holds likewise of their dissociation. In the very process of abstraction explained in Chapter XIV there occurs what may be rightly called a dissociation of two ideas. Thus in isolating abstraction we separate the idea of a feature of an individual, say, his "goodness," from the idea of the individual himself. But when we thus dissociate these two ideas, we do not deny that the individual has this feature, nor do we affirm that the abstracted feature exists by itself. Hence the adage *abstrahentium non est mendacium,* that is, "when we abstract we are not guilty of a lie." It is only when we dissociate or separate two ideas by way of "negation" that we may be guilty of a lie or are said to "judge," as common sense understands that term. Accordingly, if we insist on describing judgment in terms of association or dissociation, we must describe it as *the association of two ideas by way of affirmation or their dissociation by way of negation.*

From all this it will be seen that the analysis of a "judgment" as common sense understands that term, reveals undoubtedly the existence of a conscious process which is peculiar to judgment, namely, the conscious attitude of affirmation or negation. *The experimental investigation of judgment, then, must deal with the conscious attitude of affirmation or negation.* If it fails to do so, it misses the point at issue; it does not deal with that process which common usage designates by the term "judgment."

2. The problems presented by the conscious attitudes of affirmation and negation are numerous, and many sciences besides psychology are interested in them. Thus dialectics, the theory of knowledge, ethics, sociology, philology, in short, all sciences comprehended under the term "mental sciences" are interested in some phase or other of the conscious attitudes of affirmation and negation.

So important are these conscious attitudes that even the physical sciences are interested in them. True, physicists and chemists are not concerned with these attitudes directly, but *indirectly* they are. For they are interested in the *methods* by which they come to "affirm" or "deny" this or that concerning the object which they are investigating for its own sake. All sciences, moreover, are looking for *truth* and wish to avoid *error*. It is the peculiarity of "affirmation" or "negation" that it may be erroneous. We may attribute to an object a predicate which that object has not, or we may deny of that object a predicate which it has; this is error. The possibility of error will arise whenever the attitude of affirmation or negation is not called for by the conscious processes which precede it, or rather, by the contents of these processes. Whatever terminology the physicist or chemist may use in discussing the methods by which he arrives at a particular judgment, in reality he is examining the contents of the conscious processes which precede the conscious attitude of affirmation or negation.

Even behaviorists, their explicit denial to the contrary notwithstanding, are discussing conscious attitudes or *Bewustseinslagen*. They insist that there is something radically wrong with the methods of the structuralists in attacking their problems, in fact, with the problems themselves. They call for a reëxamination of the very premises of introspective psychology. Now, what are premises but judgments, and what are problems but judgments in the process of formation, and what are methods of science but conscious processes so controlled and acted upon as to lead to true judgments? But there is no judgment without the conscious attitude of affirmation or negation, and no judgment is true unless the attitude of affirmation or negation is called for by the contents of the conscious processes which precede it. Watson not only discusses in real earnest conscious attitudes whose existence he denies, but is, moreover, intensely interested in at least one philosophical problem concerning these *Bewustseinslagen*. In discussing the methods of the structuralists, he discusses in reality a phase of the theory of knowledge, though he claims to have no use whatever for any philosophical problem.

After all, the Würzburg experimentalists seem to have hit the nail on the head when they insisted on their famous Bewustseinslagen. These *Bewustseinslagen* are far from being as "atrocious" as some make them out to be. On the contrary, they are facts with which we are perfectly familiar and they call for an explanation.

3. The Experimental Investigation of Judgment and Its Difficulties. The field of investigation which is opened up to the experimental psychologist by the mere fact that there is such a conscious attitude as that of affirmation or negation, is very extensive. Thus, to mention only the most obvious problem that presents itself to the experimentalist, we may investigate the process by which we arrive at the attitude of affirmation or negation. Very little has been done in the psychological laboratory to elucidate this process.

One of the difficulties in carrying out experimental work of this kind is, that the manner in which we arrive at a judgment differs considerably from one case to another. Evidently, the process by which I arrive at the affirmation that twice two is four, or that grass is green, or that the instrument before me is a typewriter, differs very much from the process by which I come to affirm that the phenomena of simultaneous contrast are phenomena of inhibition, or that images are accompaniments of thought, or that "Mr. Jones is a murderer in the first degree."

Another and even more serious difficulty is that the process by which we arrive at a judgment is of no interest, at least to men in general, unless we take the truth of that judgment into consideration. A process which leads to error, and a method of procedure which leaves us in the dark as to whether we have arrived at truth or error, are of no interest unless we can point out why this process leads to error and why the method of procedure is barren of results. From this it will be seen that *the problem of truth and error is inseparable from the investigation of the process by which we arrive at a judgment*. But the problem of truth and error is a philosophical problem, and must be discussed — and has been most ably discussed — along philosophical lines Most experimentalists, however, are afraid of entering the domain proper to the philosopher. *If we insist on avoiding the domain of the philosopher altogether, we must abstain from inquiring into the process by which we arrive at a judgment*. This is the real reason why so little has been done in the psychological laboratory to elucidate the process by which we arrive at a judgment.

Experimental psychologists seem to be afraid that, if they take the logician's account of judgment into consideration, there remains no work for them to do. For in logic, the oldest and most firmly established of all branches of human knowledge, everything is settled as to how we must proceed if we are to arrive at a true judgment. Consequently it might seem that the experimental psychologist can only repeat what logic says on the subject of his inquiry. But this is far from being the case. To begin with, logical considerations are not the only conscious processes which lead up to a definite judgment; bias of the most varied kind only too frequently interferes with these logical considerations. The wish is in many instances the father of the thought. There remains, then, something very real to be described by the experimentalist. The same is true, even if all bias is excluded. For *the logical arrangement* of the conscious processes that lead to truth, is one thing, and *the workshop conditions* under which we actually arrive at a true judgment, are another. Frequently it is by mere accident that an investigator discovers a truth, and it is intensely interesting to see how he actually arrives at a true judgment. The history of every natural science describes a great many examples of such accidental discoveries of truth.

The obvious inference from these historical facts is that *logic really supplies only the test tube* by which we can ascertain whether we are on the right path and why we are right. For this purpose the jumble of processes as they actually occur in the workshop must be arranged in a logical form. Moreover, to a great extent, the processes as they actually occur, seem only a jumble. A flash of insight may bring order into this jumble, and then every one of these processes may fit into some orderly arrangement of thoughts such as is described by the logician. By the peaceful coöperation of the experimental psychologist and the logician, then, *each would supplement the work of the other.* As a matter of fact, however, such peaceful coöperation is conspicuous by its absence. Sensationalists, in particular, object most vigorously against what they call the mixing up of logical with psychological considerations. Hence, no laboratory data worth mentioning are available for a detailed description of the great variety of processes by which we arrive at a judgment. For the present, then, we must be satisfied with briefly indicating those antecedents of a judgment which are suggested by our empirical description of it.

4. The Conscious Antecedents of a Judgment. We cannot associate two ideas by way of affirmation or separate them by way of negation, unless we have these two ideas. *The first step,* then, in the formation of a judgment is *the acquisition of the two ideas,* namely, of subject and predicate. The manner in which we acquire them differs from one judgment to another. It should be noted, however, that *one of these ideas, that of the predicate, must be in every instance a universal one,* and must be acquired, originally at least, by a process of generalizing abstraction. We have pointed out in Chapter XIV how this process is apt to be lost sight of (see p. 315).

The next step is to compare the contents of the two ideas. Our mental attitude in doing so is that of a questioner, an attitude usually expressed by an interrogatory sentence. We wish to ascertain whether the ideas of subject and predicate are objectively identical or not; that is to say, we wish to learn whether the contents of the predicate are verified in the object denoted by the subject. For it is this objective identity which we are going to affirm or deny in the judgment and we will do so *because* we have perceived this identity or nonidentity.

On comparing the two ideas, one of three contingencies arises. Either we perceive clearly the objective identity of the two ideas; or we perceive clearly their nonidentity or objective diversity; or finally, we fail to perceive clearly either their identity or diversity.

The first contingency arises whenever we compare the subject and predicate of a self-evident proposition such as "twice two is four." So immediate and overwhelming is the perception of the objective identity of subject and predicate, that the attitude of affirmation follows this perception immediately and without hesitation. The same occurs whenever our judgment takes the form of a simple report of a fact observed. In this case the idea of the subject is furnished by immediate experience, and the idea of the predicate by simply focusing our attention on a definite feature of that subject. This we explained when dealing with the process of generalizing abstraction. The objective identity of these two ideas is likewise a matter of immediate experience. So rapidly do all these processes follow one another that they seem to merge into one. The result is that *perceiving seems identical with judging,* as a popular expression has it. What is true in this popular expression is that *no appreciable time elapses between the perception of objective identity and its affirmation, and that we are powerless to withhold the attitude of affirmation.* But the two processes are not identical. As a matter of fact, the clear perception of the objective identity furnishes the "evidence" on which the unhesitating attitude of affirmation rests. The unhesitating attitude of affirmation itself is called "certitude."

The second contingency arises when we compare, for instance, the idea of "twice two" with that of "five." The perception of their nonidentity or objective diversity is so clear and unmistakable that without any hesitation we assume the attitude of negation. It is in this manner that we arrive at some of the negative principles which lie at the basis of all human knowledge. The same occurs when our judgment takes the form of a negative report concerning the data of our immediate experience.

The third contingency arises in the vast majority of cases, namely, whenever we compare the subject and predicate of a proposition that is *neither self-evident,* like an axiom, *nor immediately evident from experience.* An instance in point is the proposition: "The number of stars is even" or "The number of stars is odd." No matter how we have acquired the ideas of subject and predicate, and no matter how clear the ideas themselves may be, *the simple comparison of their contents will not lead us to the clear perception of their objective identity or to that of their objective diversity.* In fact, there is not even a semblance of either perception. The result is that our mental attitude remains exactly what it was before the comparison, namely *the attitude of a questioner,* usually called that of *doubt.* If this attitude is to be replaced by that of affirmation or negation, the evidence on which this attitude must rest must come from *some third thing connected with the contents of the two ideas.* In the instance mentioned there is absolutely nothing thus connected with the ideas that would lead even to an obscure perception of their objective identity or diversity. Hence, we fail to arrive at a judgment.

We are, however, not always in the hopeless condition of the instance mentioned. Frequently there is some third thing connected with the two ideas which may lead to the perception of their identity or nonidentity. When the issue is a question of *fact,* as in a trial by jury, *the testimony of the witnesses* may lead to this result. The historian makes use of substantially the same method in arriving at his judgments. Frequently, however, the process is very complicated, particularly if the evidence of the witnesses is of the circumstantial kind. *Before the judgment in question is arrived at, a great many other judgments must be formed, and thus the whole process becomes one of inference or reasoning*. From this it will be seen that it is impossible to give a complete account of judgment without taking the reasoning process into consideration.

5. Reasoning and Discursive Thinking. As a matter of fact, reasoning is an antecedent of *most* of our judgments. It takes two main forms, known respectively as *deductive* and *inductive* reasoning. *The syllogism by which deductive reasoning is most clearly expressed, is no essential feature of it.* We frequently express deductive reasoning in other ways, as, for instance, by *a causal proposition.* What is *essential* is that *we perceive the objective identity or diversity of two ideas (S and P) only indirectly, namely, by comparing the content of each of these ideas with that of the same third, known as the middle term (M).* This mode of procedure is, of itself, extremely simple. What complicates it in our experience is that frequently many such processes must follow one another in orderly sequence before the identity or diversity of the two ideas in question is clearly perceived. Such an orderly sequence of processes is called in the terminology of the schoolmen *a discourse (discursus)*, but is also known collectively as a reasoning process. Thus understood, a reasoning process is sometimes far from simple. Here a simplification of the process is desirable, if not imperative. It consists in adhering to strict syllogistic form and in *the orderly arrangement of the various syllogisms into a unit of a higher order.* It is by means of deductive reasoning that the mathematician arrives at his theorems. The philosopher makes use of the same method in arriving at many of his judgments. So does the busy worker in the scientific laboratory, even though he be inclined to disclaim the fact.

If the modes of procedure thus far described do not lead to the *clear* perception of the objective identity or diversity of two ideas, there is still another mode which may do so. It is a process with which scientists are very familiar. *In order to have a starting point for experiment and investigation,* we may *at random* either affirm or deny the objective identity of two ideas, but we do so only with hesitation. *Such a provisional and hesitating at-*

titude of affirmation or negation is known as an hypothesis, and the investigation of which it is the starting point, is known as *the inductive method* or as *inductive reasoning.* We have explained this process at some length in Chapter XIV under the heading of "the four steps in the common-sense method of science as applied to the problem of the thought processes" (p. 328). To this explanation the student is here referred. The experimental investigation of the reasoning process will be dealt with in a later section of the present chapter.

6. Bias — Determining Tendencies — Influence of the Will on Our Judgments. Our account of the conscious antecedents of judgment would be incomplete if we did not refer briefly to one that is only too often present and which may vitiate all the modes of procedure described. This antecedent is known as bias. If we are honest with ourselves we can describe it from our own experience as *a desire, not of truth, but of justifying a judgment already formed without sufficient evidence.* In all such cases judgment becomes *voluntary,* and this aspect of judgment belongs to the chapter on the Will.

Even in the absence of bias our will is an important factor of many of our judgments. The very attitude of a questioner which leads us to compare the contents of two ideas, involves "the desire of truth" and any desire is a will activity. The influence of the will manifests itself also in the "determining tendencies" which figure so largely in the experimental investigations of the Würzburg school. We have dealt with something very akin to this when in the chapter on Attention we explained *expectant attention* and *Einstellung.*

It should be noted, further, that the attitude of affirmation or negation arises *with necessity* only when the identity or diversity of two ideas is *evident,* that is, clearly perceived. But frequently the modes of procedure explained lead only to an *obscure* perception of identity or diversity. Sometimes, in fact, we have an obscure perception of *both* identity and diversity. In all such cases the very attitude of affirmation or negation, in which judgment proper consists, is *voluntary* and arises only with *hesitation.*

Such *a voluntary and hesitating attitude of affirmation or negation is called a "probable judgment" or an "opinion."* In our experience it is readily distinguished from the unhesitating attitude of affirmation or negation which is beyond our control and
which is called "certitude." A great many of our judgments are
only opinions and sometimes a matter of free choice. It is for
this reason that *some psychologists have mistaken "consent" for
"assent."* "Consent" is really an act of the will and figures largely
in the discussion of the experimental demonstration of free will.
"Assent," on the other hand, is but another name for the attitude
of affirmation or negation and is clearly of the intellectual order.
What is true, then, in the voluntaristic account of judgment is,
that "assent" is frequently due to "consent," but the two processes are not identical.

Lastly, it should be mentioned that we may also affirm the objective identity or diversity of two ideas *simply because others
claim to have perceived this identity or diversity.* In other words,
we may rely in our judgments exclusively on the doctrinal testimony of some expert. The attitude of affirmation or negation
in such an instance is known as "belief." We all "believe" a great
many things, and this is true also of scientists for the simple
reason that *no one can investigate every problem for himself.* If
we make sure that the expert on whom we rely has the knowledge which he manifests and that he has no intention to deceive
us, then it can be said that we ourselves arrive at the perception
of the objective identity or diversity of two ideas indirectly,
namely, by a reasoning process. But sometimes we have no certainty concerning the antecedents of "belief" and *then* our belief
is really an *opinion.*

7. **The Image Theory of Judgment and Its Experimental Basis.** The fundamental assumption that sensations are the
structural units of all our thought processes is applied by sensationalists to judgment in very much the same way as it is to
the idea. The principal difference between the two thought processes is said to be that an *idea* is a case of *simultaneous* association, whereas a *judgment* is one of *successive* association. Accord-

ingly a judgment may be represented by the formula $(s + s + s) + (s + s + s)$. If this formula is correct, judgment involves two groups of elementary sensations, indicated by the parentheses, namely, the "ideas" of subject and predicate. The sign of addition $(+)$ connecting the elementary sensations of each group, denotes their *simultaneous* association or "intimate fusion," and it is by this simultaneous association that the "ideas" of subject and predicate arise. The same sign $(+)$ joining the two groups of sensations denotes a process of *successive* association, and it is this successive association of the two groups of sensations that constitutes judgment. It comes to the same thing when judgment is said to be *an association after disjunction*. We begin, so the account runs, with an "aggregate idea" $(s + s + s + s + s + s)$. This is separated into two groups. The latter are then joined again by a new "fusion" and it is this "fusion" of the two groups of sensations after their separation which constitutes judgment.

If we ask on what experimental evidence this theoretic account of judgment rests, sensationalists answer *by simply describing the images they experience when they are judging*. The obvious criticism is that sensationalists in thus appealing to their introspective data are missing the point at issue. The question is not, whether we experience images when we are judging. No one denies that we experience, frequently at least, such images. The question is rather, *whether images, if present, constitute judgment*. This question is not answered by a simple description of the images present.

When the discussion takes this turn, sensationalists introduce their famous distinction between the *existential aspect* of a thought process and what they call its *meaning*. Of all elusive terms, "meaning" is the most elusive, so that no one really knows exactly what "meaning" means. One thing, however, seems to be known about it, namely, that it is that mysterious something that the logician deals with. The experimental psychologist, we are told, has directly nothing to do with this mysterious something; he rather deals with facts as he finds them, and this is known as the "existential aspect" of our conscious processes. And what must we do in order to describe the "existential aspect" of any particular conscious process, say, of a judgment? Sensationalists answer that we describe it by simply describing the images which we have when judging and by analyzing these images into their component sensations.

The obvious answer is that *sensationalists in making this statement are begging the question*. Instead of giving us an experimental demonstration of their theoretic assumption, they merely restate it. When common-sense methods are used in describing the "existential aspect" of a definite thought process, we get not even a semblance of an experimental basis for the theoretic assumption of sensationalists. Common sense describes the "existential aspect" of a definite thought, that is, the mere fact that we have a definite thought, by indicating its *object*. We have no other way of distinguishing one thought from another. But common-sense methods are not wanted in the laboratories of the sensationalists. Their work must be done by "experts," skilled in teasing out of their consciousness images and analyzing them into their component sensations.

The insistence on the skill of the expert observers strikes us as peculiarly odd, since the work done by these experts is extremely easy. We have only to watch them at work to convince ourselves of this. All they do is to describe some imagery, relevant or irrelevant, that they have when "judging." It makes no difference what image they report, for *nobody can control them and no two observers agree in their report*. If an expert left out this or that detail of his imagery, or if he added one that was absent, nobody would be the wiser. Any child can do that sort of work. Of course, a child would not be accurate in his report, whereas a psychological "expert" is, as a matter of fact, remarkably accurate. He shows this, for instance, by stating that the imagery he experienced *"passed swiftly down the visual field from the northwest to the southwest."* This done, all that is necessary to complete the "experimental demonstration" of the sensationalistic theory is to end up with a flourish: "And this *means*" this or that.

This performance of the "experts" was known as "ideating meaning." To *"ideate"* means to *imagine,* and *"meaning"* — *well, really no one knows what it means.* So easy was this task of "ideating meanings" that it became quite a pastime in the laboratories of sensationalists.

Among other things, sensationalists "ideated" also the "meaning of affirmation." This is of particular interest to us, as, according to our empirical account of judgment, the conscious attitude of affirmation or negation constitutes the very essence of judgment. If sensationalists can account for this in terms of sensation, we have an experimental demonstration of their theory as applied to judgment. We quote Titchener: "I represent the meaning of affirmation, for instance, by the image of a little nick, felt at the back of the neck — an experience which, in sensation, is complicated by pressures and pulls from the scalp and throat."[2] Of course, we take Titchener's word for it that he actually had an image of a little nick felt at the back of his neck, while he actually affirmed something. Nobody will care to challenge the truth of his statement, particularly as it makes no difference whether it is true or not, just as it makes no difference whether, while judging, he felt "a quiver of the stomach" or whether he heard Yankee Doodle as played by some organ grinder in front of his laboratory. We take it, then, that he actually had the image he reports. *But what Titchener has failed to prove is, that the image of the nick, felt at the back of his neck, constitutes his attitude of affirmation, and that by describing this image he has described the "existential aspect" of his judgment.*

All we get by way of "experimental proof" for this assertion is, that "meaning" arises by the intimate fusion of sensations; that a single sensation has no "meaning"; that it takes at least two sensations to make a "meaning." All these are mere assertions that are incapable of being either proved or disproved for the simple reasons that nobody knows what "meaning means." As a matter of fact, Titchener, instead of proving his contention

---

[2] *Lectures on the Experimental Psychology of Thought Processes,* p. 22, quoted by permission of Macmillan Co., publishers.

has succeeded only in bringing disrepute on the introspective method in psychology His metaphysical darkroom of the "psychology of meaning" is in the history of modern science a real scandal, and serious-minded psychologists are still suffering from the disastrous effects of this scandal. It was the utter disgust with this scandal that is responsible for the origin of a new party among psychologists, known as "behaviorists." We cannot go all the way with Watson but we must give him credit for his scathing criticism of sensationalists and structuralists when dealing with the thought processes.

What we said concerning the distinction between the "existential aspect" of a thought process and its "meaning," holds likewise of another distinction which has come into vogue, namely, that between *"experience"* and *"analyzed experience."* It is but another way of covering up the fact that no experimental basis has ever been found for the theory of sensationalism. A good deal of dust can be raised by this distinction, and it comes in handy when facts are discussed as common sense knows them from experience, not only facts concerning ideas and judgments but facts also concerning the acts of the will We shall have occasion to revert to this when dealing with the will, and with free will in particular.

8. Various Tests of the Image Theory of Judgment. The conclusion which we have so far reached in our investigation of the image theory of judgment, can be summarized in one phrase, namely, *not proved*. We might rest our case here, but we shall not do so. For, though the experimental investigation of judgment has not been very extensive, we have quite a number of data of experience which enable us to test the image theory of judgment.

To begin with, our empirical description of judgment contains such data. They are common property and cannot be lightly brushed aside. We have stated exactly the conditions under which these data were ascertained, and anyone who cares to do so can verify them as often as he pleases. Every natural science makes use of such data. Provided, then, we follow in psychology the common-sense method of investigation, customary in all other natural sciences, we are in a position to test the image theory of judgment in the light of facts

What helps us considerably in applying such tests is that we can draw on a good deal of material that has come to light in the experimental investigation of the Würzburg school concerning ideas, the process of abstraction, and its result, the universal idea For *though ideas are not judgments, still they are embodied in judgments,* and no judgment occurs without them. Hence, the various tests which we applied to the image theory of ideas, are of great value to us in testing the image theory of judgment.

From our empirical description of judgment it is clear that *every judgment supposes two ideas and that at least one of these ideas must be a universal one,* namely, the idea designated by the predicate. In the case of a universal judgment, moreover, the idea of the subject, too, is universal. But we have seen that *the image theory of ideas and of universal ideas in particular is hopelessly inadequate when we face the facts fairly and squarely.* We have examined every variation of the image theory of ideas that has been proposed, and the result of our tests was invariably the same. There is no need of repeating here what we said on this subject in Chapter XV The reader is referred to that chapter. *By the mere fact, then, that every judgment supposes two ideas and that at least one of them must be universal, the image theory of judgment is out of the question.*

We saw, further, that one of the conscious antecedents of judgment is the perception of the objective identity or diversity of the ideas of subject and predicate. In fact, of all the conscious antecedents of judgment, this perception is the most important. For it is the perceived objective identity which we affirm, and we affirm it, because we have perceived it. Even when biased we claim at least to have such a perception and to be guided by it. And when we deny the objective identity of two ideas (or affirm their objective diversity), we do so because we have perceived, or claim to have perceived, this objective diversity. This premised, a little consideration suffices to show that *the image theory of judgment is inadequate to account for the most important ante-cedent of judgment, the perception of objective identity or that of objective diversity.* The content of either perception is plainly a logical relation and belongs to that class of contents which have been aptly designated by the experimentalists of the Würzburg school as *unanschaulich* or *unpicturable.* It is for this reason that the perception of objective identity or diversity cannot possibly be an image. An image is of its very nature but a revival and associa-tion of former sensations. *Hence, the contents of an image can never transcend the contents of the sensations of which it is the revival.* As Watson puts it, an image is but a "ghost" of a sensa-tion. The Würzburg experimentalists express the same thing when they say that the contents of every image can be pictured. Thus we can make an actual drawing of the contents of every visual image. But *we cannot make a drawing of a logical relation.* We can neither sense nor imagine it: we can only *know* it. *By the mere fact, then, that every judgment supposes the perception of a logical relation, the image theory of judgment is plainly inadequate.*

We have seen, further, that the very essence of judgment con-sists in the conscious attitude of affirmation or negation and that every theory of judgment which fails to account for these two attitudes, fails to explain judgment. Hence, the experimentalists of the Würzburg school stress these and all other conscious atti-tudes or *Bewustseinslagen* in their tests of the image theory of thought. It will not do to dispose of these *Bewustseinslagen* by calling them "atrocious." There is nothing atrocious about them. For we are perfectly familiar with such conscious attitudes as "doubt," "suspicion," "affirmation," and "negation." They occur a hundred times over in our daily experience and we distinguish them clearly from one another both inside and outside the lab-oratory. No experimental psychologist can question the fact that we have such a conscious attitude as that of "affirmation" or "negation." The only question with him can be whether these attitudes can be accounted for in terms of sensations (and feel-ings). And this question we can answer definitely in the light of the data in our possession. For *whatever else may have to be said about the conscious attitude of affirmation or negation, it involves essentially an awareness of a logical relation,* namely, that of the objective identity or diversity of two ideas. This we know, not by way of theoretic construction, but as a result of plain observation. We are not always beating the air when we use declarative sentences. At times, at least, we know with accuracy what we affirm or deny. And we affirm or deny the objective identity of two ideas. Accordingly, though the conscious attitude of affirmation or negation is not identical with the awareness of a logical relation, it involves essentially such an awareness. And a logical relation is of its nature *unanschaulich* or *unpicturable.* *By the mere fact, then, that the conscious attitude of affirmation or negation involves essentially the awareness of a logical relation, it cannot be accounted for in terms of sensations (and feelings).*

We can imagine a bodily attitude of ours and in particular any one of those bodily attitudes which are the sensible signs of the act of affirmation or negation. Thus we can undoubtedly have an image of a nick felt at the back of our neck. Similarly, we may have an image, visual or kinesthetic, of a shake of the head. We can also imagine the conventional signs of either affirmation or negation such as the word *yes* or *no.* But a *bodily attitude* is one thing and a *conscious attitude* is another. Similarly, a *sensible sign* of affirmation is one thing, and *the conscious attitude of affirmation itself* is another. The image theory of judgment, in whatever form it is proposed, mistakes a bodily attitude for a conscious attitude, and the image of a sensible sign for the thought process signified. All the vagaries concerning the nature of judgment which have been stated on the basis of experimental investigation, and to which we referred in the very beginning of this chapter, find their explanation here. In one word, then, *the image theory of judgment, in whatever form it is proposed, is hopelessly inadequate to deal with the essential feature of judgment.*

In our empirical description of judgment we stated, further, that, if we insist on calling a judgment an association of ideas, we must qualify this statement by calling it an association of ideas by way of affirmation. And if we call certain judgments a dissociation of ideas, our account of these judgments is incomplete unless we add that they are a dissociation of ideas by way of negation. In other words, *the mere association of two ideas is not an affirmative judgment, and the mere dissociation of two ideas is not a negative judgment* It is not difficult to create conditions under which a mere association of two ideas is clearly distinguished from a judgment. In some of the earliest investigations of the Würzburg school such conditions have been created and the said distinction has been clearly ascertained.[3] In fact, no elaborate laboratory devices are needed in order to ascertain what Messer ascertained in the investigation referred to. What is more important than anything else for such an experimental demonstration is, that we understand clearly what common usage denotes by the term "judgment" and what psychologists mean by the process of association and that of dissociation. The first requisite has been sufficiently dealt with in the first section of the present chapter. As to the second requisite, a few words of explanation suffice.

By the term "association" the psychologists denote the fact that, when two distinguishable contents of our experience have at any time occurred together or in immediate succession, one of them, on recurring, tends to revive the other. In literal strictness it is this tendency — also known as "reproductive tendency" — which is properly called "association." Of course, we know of such a reproductive tendency only by inference, as we have explained in in the chapter on Memory. We infer the existence of such a tendency from the fact that, as a matter of fact, and under certain conditions, the contents of one conscious process actually revive the contents of another

This brings us to *the second meaning of association.* It denotes *the actual revival of one conscious process by another as a result of a reproductive tendency* And thus we understand the term

---

[3] Cf. A. Messer, *Arch. f. d. ges. Psych.*. VIII (1906). pp. 95 sqq.

"association" in our present discussion. It should be added that the said reproductive tendency is sometimes not strong enough for the actual revival of one idea by another. *Such a failure of one idea to arouse another previously connected with it is called "dissociation."*

This being clearly understood, it is not difficult to test the statement of sensationalists that judgment is merely a matter of successive association or of association after disjunction. The letters of the alphabet, for instance, have occurred frequently in our experience in their fixed conventional order. As a result of the reproductive tendency thus created, the letter *a* when seen, heard, imagined or thought of, tends to arouse my thought of *b,* and frequently it succeeds in doing so. Similarly, and for a similar reason, the thought of number 4 tends to arouse the thought of number 5, and frequently this tendency is effective. But the actual revival of the idea of *b* by that of *a* is one thing, and the judgment that *a* is *b,* is quite another. We are simply incapable of affirming such a thing, just as we are incapable of affirming that 4 is 5. We may indeed deny that 4 is 5. But the mere fact that the idea of 5 is aroused by that of 4, is no such denial. *Provided, then, that we understand by judgment what common usage denotes by the term, and provided we know what psychologists mean by association, we cannot mistake the one process for the other*

There are other tests which might be applied to the image theory of judgment, but those mentioned amply suffice to show that this theory does not fit the facts as they actually occur.

9. The experimental investigation of reasoning, like that of judgment, has been hampered by a vague and faulty preliminary definition of the process under investigation. Thus. for instance, *reasoning has been defined as that process which enables us to proceed from the knowledge in our possession to the acquisition of new knowledge without the aid of perception.* This preliminary definition is both too narrow and too wide and has led to some curious results.

The definition is too narrow. For all inductive reasoning, making use, as it does, of perception and experimental procedure, is hereby ruled out. In fact, some forms of deductive reasoning are likewise ruled out. For frequently one of the premises of deductive reasoning expresses a fact of experience and the knowledge of this fact is acquired by perception. The part played by this perception in the acquisition of new knowledge is not fully described by the logician's account of reasoning and the syllogistic form in which he expresses it. *The orderly arrangement of the premises as made by the logician, is one thing, and the actual sequence of psychological events as they occur in our experience, is another,* as we had occasion to point out when discussing the antecedents of judgment (see p. 367). Thus, for instance, we frequently invert the "major" and "minor" premises. That is to say, the proposition with which we start and which, for convenience' sake, we call "major," may in reality be what the logician calls the "minor." A particular proposition stating simply a fact of experience, can never be what the logician calls the "major," but it may be the actual starting point of our deductive reasoning. If such is the case, the foregoing descriptive definition of reasoning is true. For then we can, and frequently do, arrive at the new knowledge expressed in the conclusion without the aid of further perception, simply by means of an *a priori* principle which, for convenience' sake, we call the "minor."

But the order of psychological events may also coincide with their logical arrangement. That is to say, the knowledge in our possession at the start may be a general truth, and for the purposes of present discussion it makes no difference how we acquired it. *From this knowledge in our possession we are frequently led to the new knowledge expressed in the conclusion precisely by the perception of a fact of experience which we express in our "minor."* Without the aid of this perception we should never have reached the new knowledge expressed in the conclusion. No one can deny that in the case mentioned we go through a reasoning process, but *the foregoing preliminary definition of reasoning does not apply in this case.*

In a word, *the artificial character of the syllogism must not be exaggerated,* as is done by some psychologists. What is true in this exaggeration is just what we have stated repeatedly, namely, that *the syllogism does not always express the sequence of psychological events as they actually occur in our experience.* But it is not true that the real nature of reasoning is obscured and buried by the syllogism. Far from it. We refer the reader here to the purely empirical description of deductive reasoning which we gave when discussing the antecedents of judgment. Aristotle's empirical description of deductive reasoning is crystal clear and fits every form of it that occurs in our experience. This description has never been improved upon by any one of Aristotle's successors and least of all by any worker in the modern psychological laboratory. On the contrary, *by some modern descriptions of reasoning the nature of the process has been obscured beyond recognition and turned into a "riddle."* So much for the fact that the above preliminary definition of reasoning is *too narrow.*

The definition is also too wide. For it is also applicable to processes which, in common usage, are not known by the name of reasoning. Thus, from the knowledge in my possession that A exists, I can *without the aid of perception* arrive at the "new" knowledge that A can exist. *Ab esse ad posse valet illatio,* as an old adage has it. But such an inference has from time immemorial been known as an "immediate inference" in order to distinguish it from "mediate inference" or *reasoning proper.* This distinction is ignored in the foregoing preliminary definition of reasoning. More than that. For in the further explanation of this definition *some psychologists have explicitly stated that there is no difference between "mediate" and "immediate" inference.* This is far from correct.

Suppose, for instance, that some scientist questions the possibility of a certain phenomenon. A brother scientist settles that doubt by simply producing that phenomenon in the laboratory and describing the conditions under which he did so. In such a case nobody would say that the "possibility" of that phenomenon has been proved by reasoning. In the common-sense language, customary in all natural sciences, we should rather say that the "possibility" of the phenomenon has been "proved experimentally" and without any inference whatever. It is only in the precise language of the schoolmen that we say that, in literal strictness, the *fact* has been proved experimentally and that our knowledge of its *possibility* is an "immediate inference" from this fact. When the scientist speaks of "inference" he means a process totally different from that designated by the philosopher as "immediate inference." We make an "immediate inference" when in our "conclusion" we merely state *explicitly* what we have stated *implicitly* in our "premise." Thus, when I state a *fact*, I formally imply its *possibility* and only state the same explicitly in my "conclusion." But in the case of reasoning proper, something totally different happens. If we are to describe in purely empirical terms what really occurs in reasoning, we must describe its two forms, deductive and inductive, separately, as we have done when describing the antecedents of judgment. From that description it is clear that *reasoning is nothing else than an indirect way of arriving at the perception of the objective identity of two ideas.* When we reason inductively the road by which we arrive at this perception is rather circuitous; in the case of deductive reasoning in its simplest form our road is rather short. We simply compare the contents of the two ideas with that of the same third, and thus we come to perceive the objective identity of the two ideas themselves. When our reasoning takes the complex form of a "discourse," we go through a whole series of simple reasoning processes and our road is beset with many dangers. What is common to all these various forms of reasoning is that we arrive at the principal antecedent of a definite judgment, namely, the perception of the objective identity of two ideas, only *indirectly* This constitutes the *very essence of reasoning* and *this is completely ignored in the foregoing preliminary definition of reasoning*

As to the curious results to which the preliminary definition has led, it may suffice to point out the following. *It has been claimed that the data obtained in the experimental investigation of reasoning warrant the statement that all reasoning can be reduced to the formula: "A over B; therefore B under A."* Of course, such a statement is in complete accord with the *vague* definition of reasoning which was the starting point of the experimental investigation But the formula stated is far removed from reasoning as we know it from experience. It makes no difference whether I state that "A is over B" or that "B is under A"; in both cases I state *identically* the same thing only from a different point of view, and *such statements have been known from time immemorial as "equivalent."* Nobody would call such a sequence of propositions an inference or reasoning proper.

Unfortunately the experimental investigation of reasoning has been further hampered by certain *theoretic prepossessions concerning the perception of relations.* A few words on this subject are in place here.

10. The Perception of Relations and the Reasoning Process. There is no doubt that the perception of relations is of the utmost importance in the experimental investigation of the thought processes and in the discussion of reasoning in particular. We have given due emphasis to the perception of relations when discussing the image theory of ideas. We emphasized the perception of relations again when testing the image theory of judgment, and our empirical definition of reasoning puts all emphasis desirable on the perception of relations So far there is no disagreement. But *some psychologists of the Würzburg school have exaggerated the importance of the perception of relations to such an extent that it is for them the alpha and omega of all intellectual cognitions.* And the experimental investigation of reasoning has been hampered considerably by this exaggeration of the perception of relations.

A little consideration suffices to show that *the perception of relations is not the alpha and omega of all thought processes.* Before I perceive intellectually the relation between A and B, I must first have an *intellectual* cognition of both A and B, and *this intellectual cognition of A and B cannot, in turn, consist in the perception of a relation.* We simply have no starting point for our perception of a relation unless the terms correlated are first cognized absolutely and in themselves. From this it will be seen that we cannot make the perception of a relation the *alpha* and *omega* of all thought processes without being forced into a *new theory of the perception of relations*. And such a "new theory" has been actually proposed by some Würzburg psychologists, and thus some of their investigations have been hampered considerably by *metaphysical speculations*. For further criticism of the exaggeration of the perception of relations the reader is referred to Dr. Willwoll's monograph *Begriffsbildung,* p. 142.

11. The image theory of reasoning can be readily tested in the light of the facts which we have ascertained in our empirical investigation of all the thought processes. When discussing the antecedents of judgment we found that we could not do so without taking the reasoning process into consideration. Accordingly, we gave a description of both deductive and inductive reasoning as they actually occur in our experience. From this description it is clear that deductive reasoning is, by its very nature, but an indirect way of arriving at the perception of the objective identity of two ideas, namely, by comparing the contents of each with that of the same third. To this simple mode of procedure the complex form of reasoning, known as "discursive thinking," can be reduced. When describing the process of inductive reasoning, we found that deductive reasoning is part of the sequence of psychological events which constitute the common-sense method of scientific inquiry (p. 330). From this it is clear that also inductive reasoning is but an indirect way of arriving at the perception of the objective identity of two ideas. In short, *reasoning is intimately bound up with judgment in that it furnishes the most important antecedent of many of our judgments. Accordingly, by the very fact that the image theory cannot account for judgment, as we have seen, it is inadequate when applied to reasoning.*

Reasoning is intimately bound up with judgment for another reason. Though reasoning is the antecedent of many of our judgments, it is not, and cannot be, the antecedent of *all* our judgments. Before we arrive at the judgment expressed in a conclusion, we must have formed at least two other judgments, namely, those expressed by our premises. In the case of discursive thinking and inductive reasoning many judgments are prerequisite, before we reach that designated as the conclusion. From this it will be seen that *reasoning, though an antecedent of a definite judgment, supposes other judgments* and it supposes all the other conscious processes without which judgment does not occur. Prominent among the latter are the perception of logical relations and the formation of universal ideas by the process of generalizing abstraction. *By the mere fact, then, that the image theory cannot account for the perception of logical relations and for the process of generalizing abstraction, this theory is inadequate when applied to reasoning.*

12. The Function of Images in Thinking. We must now complete our account of the thought processes by indicating the function which images have in thinking. For it is a fact that, frequently at least, we have images when we are thinking. So plain is this fact that Aristotle expressed it very succinctly by stating without any qualification that, though thought is not identified with images, it never occurs without images. *Possibly the need of images for thinking is exaggerated by Aristotle,* and we prefer to say instead that *without sensations, either actual or revived, no thought ever occurs.* This formula is correct whether we admit the universal need of images or not and, as we have explained before, the question of "imageless thought" is, after all, a *minor* issue in our controversy with sensationalists (cf. Chap. XIV, p. 322). The real issue is whether images, if present, constitute thought, and this we deny on the basis of experimental investigation. *Our formula, moreover, has the further advantage that it suggests the function which images really have in our thinking.*

Images are of their very nature but revivals and associations of former sensations Hence, it is natural to expect that, *in thinking, images have the same function as sensations.* At least we can use this as a working hypothesis which can be tested very readily. It is this very hypothesis that Aristotle expressed when he said, "As without sensations a man would not learn or understand anything, so at the very time when he is actually thinking he must have an image before him For mental images are like present sensations, except that they are immaterial,' that is, aroused in the absence of the material objects which caused the former sensations (cf. our comment on this passage of Aristotle, p. 321).

If we examine the part which different sensations play in the formation of a definite thought, we arrive at the obvious distinction between sensations which are *helps,* and others that are *hindrances* in the performance of a definite intellectual task. Thus the sensations aroused by an apple are the starting point for my thought of an apple. Without these sensations I should never have arrived at the first-hand knowledge as to what an apple is. But identically the same sensations aroused by identically the same apple do not help me in the very least to solve a mathematical problem which confronts me here and now; on the contrary, as far as the performance of this intellectual task is concerned, the sensations aroused by the apple are rather hindrances, usually designated by the name of *distractions.* The same is true of a host of other sensations If an organ grinder insists on playing Yankee Doodle right under my window while I am trying to solve a mathematical problem or to carry on research work on electricity, the auditory sensations thus forced on my attention are decidedly a hindrance in the performance of my intellectual task.

Associations once formed tend to persist. Suppose, then, that I actually solve my mathematical problem or my problem of electrical research under the conditions just mentioned. The result may be that whenever in future I think of these problems, the image of an apple arises in my mind or the tune of Yankee Doodle insists on running through my head. *Evidently we are dealing here with images that are totally irrelevant to the thought I have.* Such images tend to divert or "distract" our attention from the object which should occupy the focus of attention and they make voluntary attention to that object difficult (cf. p. 233). The disturbing influence of irrelevant images is the greater, the more our voluntary control is in abeyance, as in drowsiness, dreams, and fever delirium. Insanity has its origin here. A person is insane, not because he has no intellectual processes, but because the rational sequence of these processes is broken up by the disturbing influence of irrelevant images.

Dismissing now all irrelevant images let us try to find out *what help we really derive from relevant images.* Here again the hypothesis that, in thinking, *images have the same function as sensations,* suggests the answer. Evidently the help I derive from actual sensations differs as one intellectual task differs from another. We said that the sensations aroused by an apple are *the starting point* of our knowledge as to what an apple really is. A good photograph of an apple will arouse substantially the same visual sensations as the apple itself and, in the absence of the apple, these sensations will assist us in acquiring the knowledge of what an apple really is. Hence a photograph of an apple may be used as an illustration in a book. *This suggests the statement that sometimes images perform the same function in thinking as an illustration in a book.* And we find this statement confirmed by our experience both inside and outside the psychological laboratory.[4]

When I am trying to understand how a radio receiving set really works, I am greatly assisted by a good diagram of it. This diagram really consists of arbitrary symbols of the various parts of a radio set and of their interconnection. The sensations aroused by these symbols may be of greater help to me than the sensations aroused by the radio parts themselves. What the diagram does for me when I actually see it, may also be done by a visual image of it. Many of our images have a similar function and they are known as *symbolical images.*

Every word of every language is, of itself, but a nonsense syllable or a combination of nonsense syllables. Their "meaning" does not arise by a mysterious fusion of sensations. It is by the

---

[4] Cf. T. V. Moore, *The Process of Abstraction*, p. 95.

arbitrary convention among men that a definite word becomes the sign of a definite object and is capable of arousing the thought of that object. What a word does for me when I actually hear or see it, may also be done by an auditory, visual, or kinesthetic image of that word. As words are more frequently used in the acquisition and communication of thought than any other symbols, it is natural to expect that word-images should play a rather important rôle in the performance of intellectual tasks of all kinds. Their function is that of *arbitrary symbols*.

In trying to understand the nature of something that is new to us we are helped considerably by the similarities which exist between that thing and some familiar object of our experience. Thus physicists in trying to make clear to a beginner what is meant by voltage, amperage, and ohmage, compare these electrical phenomena with those that occur when a current of water passes through a pipe. They say that voltage corresponds to the pressure which is exerted by a column of water in a pipe. This pressure can be felt and thus by our own experience we can find out that this pressure is the greater, the greater the height from which the water comes. Amperage is compared with the volume of water that the pipe can carry. We can ascertain this volume by simply measuring the diameter of the pipe and we understand very readily that, the greater the diameter of the pipe, the greater is the volume of water it carries. Ohmage is likened to the resistance which the inner walls of the pipe offer to the flow of water. In this process of learning we really begin with the sensations aroused by a familiar object. Provided, then, that there exist some analogies between this familiar object and the new thing which we try to understand and that these analogies are understood, we arrive at a good preliminary knowledge concerning the nature of that new thing. And we may improve the knowledge thus acquired by following out the comparison in greater detail. What the actual sensations aroused by a water pipe can do for us in acquiring and perfecting the concepts of voltage, amperage, and ohmage, can also be accomplished by the *revival* of these sensations, that is, by an image of a water pipe. Evidently such an image is again of the *symbolical* kind. It differs, however, from the symbolical images previously mentioned in one important respect. When I imagine a diagram of a radio set or simply the words *radio set,* in both cases I imagine something that is but an *arbitrary* sign of the object I think of. But when I imagine a water pipe under the conditions and in the manner mentioned, I imagine something that has some *real analogies* with the object of my thought: I imagine something that *by its very nature* can be used as a symbol of the object of my thought. Symbolical images, then, are of two kinds, *arbitrary* and *natural*. It is particularly with reference to symbolical images of the natural kind that we speak of *"the scientific use of the imagination."* Though scientific inquiry is considerably more than the use of imagination, no scientific inquiry is ever made without the use of imagination. If Helmholtz, for instance, had not had an image of a piano, he would never have formulated his "piano" theory of hearing. The "telephone" theory of hearing, proposed by others, has a similar origin. The same is true of a host of other theories in all departments of scientific inquiry.

The function of images in thinking is also revealed by the figures of speech we use When we use a metaphor we liken one object to another by speaking of it as if it were that other; *we try to arouse in the mind of the hearer or reader the image of one object and by this means to assist him in acquiring the concept of another object*. It is worthy of note that many technical terms are originally figures of speech. Thus the mathematician "extracts roots," the philosopher "abstracts" universals and "conceives" ideas, the moral philosopher has his "rule" of conduct, the physicist has his "anodes" and "kathodes"; the chemist his "ions," and so forth. Once we have acquired the knowledge of the objects designated by such technical terms, we are apt to lose sight of the figures of speech these terms really imply. If, however, we direct our attention to these figures of speech then *word-images of this kind may be said to perform the function of both arbitrary and natural symbols.*

13. **The phenomena of aphasia throw additional light on**

the important function which images of all kinds have in thinking. Aphasia occurs in three forms usually designated as (1) motor aphasia; (2) visual aphasia or mental blindness; and (3) auditory aphasia or mental deafness.

Motor aphasia does not mean the paralysis of the organs of articulation or the inability to think, but the inability to recall the words by which our thoughts are expressed. In the chapter on Imagination we pointed out that we cannot execute any voluntary movement unless we have a kinesthetic, auditory, or visual image of that movement. Word-images are such images of movements, namely, those concerned in the pronunciation (or the writing) of words. If, then, through some brain injury, the image of the word, say, *knife,* does not arise when we are thinking of a knife, we cannot manifest our idea of a knife, at least not by that conventional sign. From this it will be seen that the function of word-images is not fully described by calling them variable accompaniments of thought. They have another and rather important function: they make it possible for us to manifest our thoughts by signs which of all others are the easiest and most unmistakable: spoken and written words. And it makes no difference which of the many variable forms the word-image has; every one of them can serve this important function.

Frequently, motor aphasia is not complete and then the person thus afflicted may say "something to cut with." When the images which are the antecedents of writing are lost, we speak of "agraphia." As we have stated in Chapter XV (p. 319), motor aphasics have been used in experiments on the process of generalizing abstraction and on the transformation of nonsense syllables into signs of thought. The student will gather from all this that the sensationalistic hypothesis derives no argument from the facts of motor aphasia and that these facts are in complete accord with our account of the thought processes.

Instead of going into elaborate details concerning "visual aphasia" or "mental blindness" we prefer to give the reader an experimental demonstration of the condition in which a visual aphasic finds himself. Simply read the following sentence: *Hurtig mit*

Donnergepolter entrollt ihm der tückische Marmor. Or try this:
Dunderkitken no mal, wat kollert der Racke von Kiesling. Both
sentences express the same thought and are translations of a
famous passage in Latin literature. The first sentence is in high
German, the second in low German or "platt." The probability
is that many readers only see the words and fail to understand
them. The only difference between such readers and visual
aphasics is this: The various sensory associations that are necessary in order to understand the thought expressed by these words,
have never been formed in the experience of these readers, whereas in the case of visual aphasics, they have been formed and are
now broken as a result of some injury to the brain. While the
visual aphasic is utterly unable to understand a written sentence,
even one which he himself has written, he will understand identically the same sentence when it is spoken. Accordingly, sensationalists derive no argument from the phenomena of visual
aphasia; on the contrary, these phenomena, provided they are
accurately described, confirm in every detail our account of the
thought processes and of the important function which images
of all kinds have in thinking.

If the reader desires an experimental demonstration of the
condition in which an auditory aphasic or mentally deaf person
is, he need only listen to a conversation carried on in a foreign
language. Not only does he fail to understand the thoughts expressed by the sounds he hears, but he may fail even to discriminate between the various sounds as they follow one another.
The whole conversation may create in him only the general and
confused impression of strange sounds. In spite of all this he
may be able to guess at the meaning of the strange sounds he
hears, namely, from the gestures made by the speakers or from
the situation in which they are. This is with absolute precision
the condition in which a mentally deaf person finds himself
when spoken to. The only difference between the reader under
these conditions and the mentally deaf person is this: The reader
has never known the language which is spoken and hence the
various sensory associations which are necessary to understand

the thoughts expressed in that language have never been formed. In the case of the mentally deaf, however, these associations have been formed but are now broken. In both cases the result is the same: failure to understand what is said. When the reader is in a railroad station he hears a confused medley of clicks made or listened to by the telegraph operator. To the latter these clicks are as truly a system of conventional signs of definite thoughts as spoken English is to the reader. While the reader is utterly unable to decipher the telegraphic message denoted by the clicks or even to tell where one word begins and the other ends, he understands identically the same message when it is presented to him by a messenger boy in typewritten symbols. Substantially the same thing happens in the case of a mentally deaf person. While he does not understand the thought expressed by a spoken sentence, he will understand identically the same thought when it is expressed by written symbols. From this it will be seen that the phenomena of auditory aphasia fit with precision into our account of thought and its relation to images, but are hopelessly at variance with the hypothesis of sensationalists and structuralists.

There is, however, one point in connection with the phenomena of aphasia that needs emphasis. It brings us back to the statement that, in thinking, images have the same function as actual sensations. Many of the images we have in thinking receive but slight and passing attention, and from the fact that we cannot ascertain images in thinking, it does not follow that absolutely none were there. For they might be in the dim background of our attention and still they might perform an important function in thinking. They may be the hook to which by habit a definite thought is attached. Take away the hook and you take away the condition without which the thought does not arise. In this regard our images are like actual sensations. Many of our sensations receive but slight and passing attention; others are so completely ignored that we are apt to think that they serve no function whatever in our everyday life. But this is far from correct. An instance in point are the sensations that arise from walking, namely, when the sole of the foot comes in contact with the ground. As you discuss a philosophical problem while walking with your friend in a garden, the sensations of touch mentioned never reach the focus of your attention. But suppose, now, that by some injury to the spinal cord, the afferent fibers leading from the sole of the foot to the central nervous system are put out of commission. This occurs in a pathological condition known as *locomotor ataxia*. The result of this condition is that the sensations which normally arise from the stimulation of the sole of the foot, are lacking. And the further result is that peculiarly awkward walk of such patients. They never know whether they have touched ground or not. The said sensations of touch, though usually completely ignored, are an important link in the series of events which we call walking The very phenomena of aphasia would seem to show that something similar is true of images. Though many of them are utterly neglected when present, their complete absence may have disastrous effects, and the various phenomena of aphasia mentioned are instances in point.

References for Further Reading

J. Froebes, S.J., *Lehrbuch der Experimentellen Psychologie*, 3d edit. (1929), Vol. II, pp. 176–189.

J. Lindworsky, S.J., *Experimentelle Psychologie* (1921), pp. 189–192, 194–199.

J. Lindworsky, S.J., "Revision einer Relationstheorie" in *Arch. f. d. ges. Psych.*, Vol. XLVIII, pp. 248–289.

Chapter XVII

THE WILL

1. A Preliminary Description of Willing or Internal Acts of the Will. Our rational life is not fully described by enumerating the three conscious processes which we investigated when dealing with thought, namely, ideas, judgments, and reasoning processes. For our very thoughts lead to other experiences which are generally considered to be even of greater importance for our rational life than the thoughts themselves. These experiences are known as acts of willing or acts of the rational appetite or internal acts of the will.

Such acts are numerous and varied and can be readily described in terms of common sense. Thus, for instance, we love our parents, because, after God, they are our greatest benefactors; we love God for His own sake, irrespective of the benefits He has bestowed upon us in the past or may bestow upon us in the future; we hate the pains and discomforts of a serious surgical operation, but we resolve to undergo that operation, because it is the only means of saving our life; we should like to buy some work of art because of the esthetic pleasure it would afford us, but we make up our minds to forego these pleasures because the expenditure involved would interfere with our duties toward those who depend upon us; we find ourselves powerfully attracted to an object we happen to see and we may deliberately yield to the sensory pleasures thus forced upon us; in other cases we disapprove of the sensory pleasures similarly forced on us, because they would put us in danger of sin; we find ourselves in two minds about a resolution taken previously and we may change our resolution because of the unforeseen difficulties which now arise in its execution; at another time and in a similar predicament we may decide to abide by our former resolution, be-

cause it is unwise to change a resolution when the time of action
has arrived; we experience an impulse to meet an insult with an
angry word, but, on remembering the old advice to count ten
before uttering an angry word, we resist the impulse, because,
apart from considerations of virtue, our mode of procedure is
more conducive to health, and so forth, and so on.

The various experiences here described and designated by such
terms as *loving, desiring, resolving, changing or renewing a former resolution, choosing, consenting, approving, disapproving,
deliberately yielding, or resisting,* etc., are subjects proper to our
present investigation. All of them come under the general heading of *conscious attitudes* or *Bewustseinslagen.* They differ from
the conscious attitudes of affirmation and negation discussed in
Chapter XVI, by a feature which is common to all internal acts
of the will and which is absent from the attitudes of affirmation
and negation. We express this common feature by a figure of
speech readily understood by everyone. Comparing our conscious
attitudes to bodily attitudes we say that all internal acts of the
will involve *a conscious "inclination" toward an object intellectually apprehended as good, or a conscious "aversion" from an
object intellectually apprehended as evil.* The conscious attitude
of affirmation or negation involves, of itself, no such conscious
inclination or such conscious aversion.

The internal acts of the will, then, belong to our rational life,
not in the sense that they *are* intellectual cognitions, but in the
sense that they *suppose* intellectual cognitions We cannot even
describe the various acts of the will and differentiate them from
one another in purely empirical terms without specifying the
rational considerations which give rise to them. These rational
considerations are known as *motives.*

2. Internal Acts of the Will and "Higher Emotions."
Some of the experiences which are mentioned above as typical
acts of the will, are classified by some psychologists under the
heading of "higher emotions." It makes no difference by what
name we call such experiences as "love," "hatred," and "esthetic
enjoyment." All these experiences are based on intellectual con-

siderations, as we suppose. When we "love" God or "enjoy" a work of art, we experience a conscious inclination toward an object intellectually apprehended as good; and when we "hate" sin, we experience a conscious aversion from an object intellectually apprehended as evil. Consequently, these experiences come plainly under our preliminary definition of willing. In this regard there is no difference between an act of "love," "hatred," and "esthetic enjoyment," on the one hand, and the "resolve" to do something and an act of "choice," on the other.

Accordingly, if we adopt the terminology of the psychologists just referred to, we must say that *the subject proper to our investigation includes also "higher emotions."* The latter differ radically from those emotional excitements and sensory impulses which, according to our account (pp. 286 sqq.), are the antecedents of instinctive actions of animals. It is true that higher emotions also are frequently accompanied by characteristic changes in breathing, circulation of the blood, heartbeat, and other organic functions, just as the "coarser" emotions of instinctive life are. This is probably the reason why "love," "hatred," "esthetic enjoyment," and other intense acts of the will are classified under "higher emotions." But this terminology must not be understood in the sense that the coarser emotions of instinctive life shade imperceptibly into those of "higher emotions." There is no foundation for such a statement. All internal acts of the will, the "higher emotions" included, are clearly distinguished from all acts of the sensory appetite by this, that *the former are based on rational considerations, the latter on sensations aroused by sensible objects or by the revivals of such sensations.*

3. The Nature and Importance of the Motive. From what has been said it is clear that an act of the will does not arise without a motive. An internal act of the will is of its very nature a conscious inclination toward an object intellectually apprehended as good or a conscious aversion from an object intellectually apprehended as evil. It is the goodness of an object thus apprehended which causes the conscious "inclination" toward that object; and it is the evil connected with an object similarly apprehended which causes the conscious "aversion" from that object. This is usually expressed by saying that the goodness of an object or the evil connected with it "moves" us to an act of the will or is the "motive" of that act of the will.

It should be noted, however, that *the motive of an internal act of the will may be masked in various ways,* so that an empirical description of that act does not seem to contain its motive. We may, for instance, renew a former resolution without explicitly rehearsing the reasons which first prompted it. In fact, we may explicitly refuse to reconsider the pros and cons of a former resolution and decide to abide by it, in spite of the difficulties which now arise in its execution. In such instances the absence of a motive is merely apparent. For I cannot renew a former resolution *without becoming aware that on a former occasion I have made that resolution and have thus assumed a definite obligation, task or "Aufgabe."* The very thought that on a former occasion I have assumed an obligation on reasonable grounds constitutes the *motive* for the present renewal of my resolution.

It should be noted, further, that the motive of an act of the will, say, a desire, is not necessarily something really distinct from the object of the desire. We may desire an object *for its own sake* or we may do so exclusively because that object is the *means* of obtaining something else which we desire for its own sake. In either case the object is intellectually apprehended as good and in either case it is the goodness thus apprehended which causes the desire.

Lastly it should be noted that also such an act of the will as *"consenting to a desire" has a motive.* But the motive of this "consent" is *not necessarily something distinct from the motive of the "desire" itself.* We may, and frequently do, "consent" to a "desire" without waiting for a *new* motive In such instances we "consent" to a "desire" for identically the same motive that originally prompted the desire. What really differentiates a desire before consent from the same desire after consent is that the former is *indeliberate,* the latter is *deliberate.*

As the distinction between deliberate and indeliberate desire is very important for our subsequent discussions, it may be well to explain it more fully in purely empirical terms of common sense. When two conflicting motives are presented to us, say, those of "pleasure" and "duty," each of these motives arouses a desire, one of a pleasurable action, the other of the performance of a duty Each of these desires is indeliberate, because it occurs independently of any consent of ours and is fully accounted for by mentioning its respective motive. When we consent to either of these conflicting desires, we experience an active interposition of the Ego through which the issue of the conflict is decided. *For this interposition of the Ego we need no new motive* but only the ability to decide the issue of the conflict by "consenting to one of the desires." Thus the active interposition of the Ego becomes an additional factor of this desire. *But the motive for this interposition of the Ego is identically* the same as that of the desire to which we consent.

The same is true, even if we have a *new* motive for a desire before consenting to it. For this new motive, of itself, only strengthens a previous indeliberate desire. But *strengthening a previous desire* is one thing, and *consenting* to it is quite another. The strengthening of a desire is fully accounted for by mentioning its additional motive. But the consent to this strengthened desire is not thus accounted for. It involves a new factor of that desire: the active interposition of the Ego by which that desire becomes in a unique sense our "own." But the *motive of this consent is identically the same as that of the strengthened desire to which we consent*. If this be kept in mind, much quibbling will be avoided in the discussion of free will.

What we have said concerning the distinction between a deliberate and indeliberate desire holds likewise of acts of "love," "hatred," "resolve," and other acts of the will Each of these acts is indeliberate or deliberate according as it occurs *before* or *after* the active interposition of the Ego known as "consent."

The reader who has carefully followed our empirical and common-sense description of the various acts of the will and their motives, need not be told explicitly that *the simplest act of the will is a complex experience:* it is inextricably connected with intellectual cognitions and, in particular, with judgments and with all the other conscious processes which precede judgment. Whether acts of the will are also complex in the sense that they can be reduced to simpler processes, such as sensations, is a matter of *theory* with which at present we are not concerned.

4. **Voluntary Actions or External Acts of the Will and their Gradual Mechanization; Reaction Experiments.** Just as thoughts give rise to those conscious attitudes known as internal acts of the will, so the latter, in turn, give rise to *characteristic bodily attitudes* known as voluntary actions or external actions of the will. Though these bodily attitudes are no *direct* concern of ours in the present investigation, still they are of interest to us because of their connection with the internal acts of the will, and have been investigated experimentally in what are known as "reaction experiments." In fact, "reaction experiments" figure largely also in the experimental investigation of the will itself.

As many of our bodily reactions are due to internal acts of the will and are manifestations of the latter, it is perfectly legitimate to use "reaction experiments" in the investigation of the will itself. The proviso, of course, is that the experimental arrangements be such that *the internal act of the will becomes the principal object of observation and introspective report* This proviso was overlooked in the earliest investigations of the will, as will be explained later.

Reaction experiments have confirmed a fact well known to the schoolmen of old but now designated by a new term, namely, the "gradual mechanization of voluntary actions." The schoolmen expressed the same thing by saying that external actions may be voluntary in three ways, namely, (1) *actually,* (2) *virtually,* and (3) *habitually.* It is the neglect of these distinctions which is responsible for the fact that the earliest investigations of the will by means of the reaction experiments failed to throw light on the nature of the internal act of the will and led to conclusions which are out of touch with the facts of everyday experience.

In acquiring a new motor skill, such as piano playing or typewriting, every one of the successive movements required is, at first, considered separately and willed explicitly. *An external action performed under the influence of an act of the will here and now present is called by the schoolmen an actually voluntary action.* In modern psychology it is sometimes known as a *"volitional act."*

The internal act of the will under whose influence the external action is performed is sometimes known as the *fiat* of the will. The schoolmen called it the *imperium voluntatis* (the command of the will). So prominent in our experience is this *imperium* of the will that every language has a special form to designate it. Grammarians say that we use the *imperative mood* which is readily distinguished by everyone from the *indicative mood.*

It should be noted, however, that the *fiat* of the will, though essential for an actually voluntary movement, does not, of itself, suffice to bring about the actual movement; *we need, over and above this fiat, an image of the movement to be performed,* as we have explained in the chapter on Imagination (p. 177). Thus *the kinesthetic image is the necessary link between the fiat of the will and the actual movement.* We have pointed out in Chapter XVI that every word-image, whatever form it may take, performs this important function in the actual communication of our thoughts by means of speech. It is precisely the absence of word-images which causes "motor aphasia" and makes it impossible for a person thus afflicted to say what he wants to say (see p. 392).

It should be noted, further, that *an image of a movement is, of itself, capable of producing that movement,* as we have explained in the chapter on Imagination. In fact, the "initial movement" or the first beginnings of the movement will occur in spite of an internal act of the will to the contrary, provided we persist in imagining the movement. It is owing to this fact that the various forms of "automatic writing," as by means of the Ouija board, become possible (see p. 180). *A movement performed in the absence of the fiat of the will and due exclusively to the image of the movement, is called an ideo-motor action* and is, under normal conditions, readily distinguished from a *"volitional act"* or an "actually voluntary" movement. This distinction is neglected by those psychologists who identify the "image of the movement" with the act of the will itself.

Even the mere sight of a familiar movement when it occurs in others may cause us to imitate that movement involuntarily. It is for this reason that yawning and smiling are "catching." *A movement touched off by an actual sensation is known as a "sensori-motor action."* This again is readily distinguished from an "actually voluntary" movement.

The more frequently an external action or a series of external actions is performed, *the less attention is required to the thoughts and to the act of the will* which originally guided the performance of that action or series of actions. *A neural organization is acquired by the mere repetition of an action.* The more perfect this neural organization is, that is, the deeper the "neural grooves" are which are acquired by practice, the more will the series of external actions take care of itself. When the neural organization is perfect, all thoughts concerning the details of that series and the act of the will to perform these details drop out entirely. In fact, we can perform a very complicated series of actions while thinking of something totally different. When this occurs, our external action is due exclusively to a physiological "habit." It can be called "voluntary" only in the sense that *an act of the will was the starting point of the formation of this habit.* The schoolmen expressed this by calling such external actions "habitually voluntary." Modern psychologists designate such actions sometimes by the name of "secondarily" automatic actions in order to distinguish them from those automatic actions which are due to a congenital neural organization, namely, physiological reflexes. The latter are known as "primarily" automatic actions.

It has been said that a man at the age of thirty is in a plaster cast; that he is a mere bundle of habits; that all his actions are a matter of routine. These popular statements are vast exaggerations, if the terms employed are understood in the sense of a "physiological habit" pure and simple. It is true, however, that a goodly portion of what are commonly called "routine" actions are "secondarily" automatic and only "habitually voluntary." In accordance with the facts explained, *the schoolmen defined an "habitually voluntary" action as one that is due to a past action of the will to which, however, we no longer pay any attention.*

Between the two end stages, the "actually" voluntary, and the "habitually" voluntary action, there occur many transitional stages and they are properly designated by the term "gradual mechanization of voluntary actions." As long as the neural organization is not perfect, it must be supplemented by the thought of the action or some of its details and by the will to perform that action or these details. Sometimes we explicitly renew our intention to perform the action or to carry out a definite detail of it. This has been observed also in the psychological laboratory. In fact, conditions were created which were favorable for such an explicit renewal of intention. In the absence of such a renewal of intention we are only dimly aware of the "task" or *Aufgabe* which guides us. In such instances it is rather by inference that we know of the existence of thoughts and acts of the will guiding us in the performance of our task, namely, from the fact that we actually carry out the "task" or *Aufgabe*. We have explained this more fully in the chapter on Attention when dealing with "subconscious" thoughts and activities. The schoolmen of old meant to describe precisely such a condition when they called certain actions *virtually voluntary*. They understand by that term *an external action which is performed under the influence of a past act of the will, though the latter is only dimly attended to.* Modern psychologists describe identically the same condition when they speak of *determining tendencies* which guide us in the performance of the *Aufgabe*. When we ask why this "influence" of a past action of the will or the "determining tendency" which proceeds from it consists in, the explanation given by the schoolmen differs only in terminology from that of modern psychologists. It involves two elements, namely, (1) *an imperfect neural organization,* and (2) *slight attention to the thoughts and the act of the will* guiding us in the performance of an assumed task. As these two elements are a matter of inference, it is not surprising that the distinction between an "habitually" and "virtually" voluntary action, though ideally very clear, is practically rather difficult and was always considered such by the schoolmen.

5. The First Experimental Investigations of the Will and their Results. The experimental investigation of the will was begun about thirty years ago. It yielded at first results which seemed little in accord with the purely empirical description of willing which we have given in the first section of this chapter. The mode of procedure was as follows. The subject of the experiment was asked to perform a simple voluntary action such as pressing a telegraph key (the "reaction key") or to pronounce a definite word in accordance with the instruction to be given by the experimenter. The instruction differed from one series of experiments to another but was the same for all experiments of the same series. It was given before each series was begun Thus, for instance, the instruction before a definite series of experiments was something like this: "At a preliminary signal fixate a definite spot on the instrument before you. A word printed on a white card will appear in this spot. As soon as you have read the word, find a rime for it and pronounce the riming word Do this as quickly as possible. Immediately upon pronouncing the riming word ascertain by introspection the conscious antecedents of your reaction and describe them with accuracy." The stimulus words exposed were frequently nonsense syllables consisting of a vowel between two consonants so that the task of riming was very easy. Thus, if the word shown was DOM, the rime might be ROM. Before another series of experiments another simple task was agreed upon, as for instance, to transpose the consonants of the nonsense syllable shown. In this case the correct reaction to

DOM would be MOD. Whatever the details of the task were in a definite series of experiments, *these details were agreed upon before that series of experiments was begun.*

Elaborate devices were used to *measure* with precision the "reaction time," that is, the time which elapsed between the presentation of the stimulus and the reaction of the subject. When the stimulus was presented, an electrical contact was made and it was broken by the reaction. In the case of a verbal reaction various means were used for breaking the electrical contact. Thus, for instance, a light lever was fastened to the jaw or the teeth of the subject, or he had to speak into a funnel. When the electrical contact was made, a timepiece resembling a stop watch, and called a chronoscope, began to work; when the contact was broken, the hands of the chronoscope were stopped. The principal difference between such an elaborate timepiece and an ordinary stop watch is that the former measures the time in *thousandths* of a second, while the latter does so in *tenths* of a second. A thousandth of a second is known in the psychological laboratory by the name of *sigma*. Thus it might be found that the subject needed 175 sigmas for riming and 225 sigmas for transposing the consonants of a nonsense syllable.

Immediately upon reacting the subject described the conscious processes which occurred during the "reaction time" and were still fresh in his immediate memory. In other words, he gave an introspective report of the conscious antecedents of his "voluntary" action. It was found that, the more the subjects became accustomed to the experimental procedure, the less they were able to discover an internal act of the will as common sense understands this term. The subjects reported images of the movement to be performed, also various sensations of tension in the muscles to be employed in the reaction. But *the internal act of the will of which common sense speaks was frequently conspicuous by its absence.* After a good deal of laboratory practice, in fact, the "correct reaction" was "touched off" by the mere sight of the stimulus.

From these experimental data it was concluded that there is no internal experience which is specific for "willing"; that what we call "willing" is really nothing else than an image of the movement to be performed or the sensations of tension in the muscles to be employed; that we can perform a "voluntary" action without "willing" it at all; that sometimes our nervous system "wills" for us. In short, experiment had failed to confirm the common-sense view of the internal act of the will.

The reader who has carefully followed what we have said concerning the gradual mechanization of voluntary actions will understand that the introspective data obtained in the simple reaction experiments described were to be expected: *they could have been foretold from the teaching of the old schoolmen concerning the conscious antecedents of an external action which is only virtually or even habitually voluntary.* The internal act of the will on which the experiments were supposed to throw light, really occurred *before* a definite series of reaction experiments was performed, namely, when the subjects agreed to carry out the instructions of the experimenter and resolved, for instance, to find a rime for a word, as soon as that word would appear before them in accordance with the agreement made. *All the reactions of the subjects were at best virtually voluntary; some, in fact, only habitually so:* they were due to a past action of the will to which during the "reaction time" they paid at best only slight attention or none at all. No wonder that the subjects did not discover a conscious process which did not occur during the "reaction time" or was, at best, only in the dim background of their attention.

Accordingly, the conclusions concerning the nature of the internal act of the will based on the introspective data mentioned, *are not warranted by these data* but are due to a *fault in the experimental arrangement.* The reaction experiments described were not properly designed, if they were expected to furnish information concerning the internal act of the will. The experimental arrangements were such as to throw light on the speed of reaction rather than on the act of the will to which the reactions were due. *Considered as experiments on the will itself, these reaction experiments missed the essential feature of a scientific experiment.*

As was explained in Chapter I, experiment is controlled observation. It differs from uncontrolled observation not precisely by this that we use instruments of precision; the latter may be very irrelevant for the purposes of our observation and may become positive hindrances, namely, if they divert our attention from the phenomenon to be observed. *To "observe" means to direct our explicit attention upon a phenomenon when it occurs.* In uncontrolled observation we wait until the phenomenon occurs; *in controlled observation we produce artificially the very phenomenon to be observed.* We do this by creating the conditions under which the phenomenon is expected to occur and directing our attention upon it when it occurs. We exercise further control by varying the conditions arbitrarily and noting attentively what occurs under these changed conditions. We then describe all our experiences in purely empirical terms together with the conditions under which we had the experiences. An observation thus made is public property and is "controlled" not only by the experimenter who first creates the conditions of a definite phenomenon but by anyone who cares to repeat the experiment.

Accordingly, if reaction experiments are to furnish an exact description of the conscious processes which common sense designates by the term "willing," then such conditions must be created that these conscious processes occur *during* the "reaction time." Then these conscious processes can be observed and described while they are still fresh in immediate memory and anybody who cares to do so can repeat the experiment and verify for himself the data obtained. This was neglected in the first experiments on the will. *It was a mistake to call them experiments on the will; they were rather experiments so designed as to ascertain the speed of reaction.* There was, in fact, a premium placed on the speed of reaction and on this point the reaction experiments furnished valuable information. But this information[1] is irrelevant for the purposes of our present discussion.

6. The Experiments of Ach. It need not be stated explicitly that not all psychologists accepted the conclusions based on the results of the experiments of the will so far described. The mistake made was recognized by Narciss Ach. He tried to remedy matters by introducing a new mode of procedure and this led to the distinction between the "fore period" of a reaction experiment, its "main period" and its "after period." The "fore period" extends from the preliminary signal to the presentation of the stimulus; the "main period" from the presentation of the stimulus to the reaction of the subject; the "after period" follows the reaction and is devoted to the introspective report of the subject. Ach tried to create such conditions as would favor the occurrence of the internal act of the will during the "main period." If he succeeded in this, the act of the will would become the main object of observation and introspective report during the "after period."[2]

In a preliminary series of experiments the subjects were requested to memorize pairs of nonsense syllables such as DOM and ZIB. A number of such pairs were repeated by each subject 120 times. *Thus a laboratory-controlled habit was established in the subjects to answer the first of each pair of syllables with the other of the pair.* On seeing, for instance, the syllable DOM, the subjects had a strong tendency to react with the word ZIB.

After these preliminaries a series of reaction experiments were performed which were similar to those described on page 405, but differed from them in one important respect. The task which the subjects were requested to perform was so devised by the experimenter as to *conflict with the habit acquired by the memorizing of the nonsense syllables.*[3] Thus for instance, in one series of experiments the task was to find a rime for the nonsense syllable shown, and the nonsense syllable shown was one of those mem-

---

[1] Cf. N. Ach, *Ueber die Willenstätigkeit und das Denken*, p. 6.
[2] Cf. N. Ach, *Ueber den Willensakt und das Temperament*, pp. 7–18.
[3] *Op. cit.,* pp. 19 sqq

orized during the preliminary experiments. The riming was to be done as quickly as possible. Each subject agreed to carry out these instructions. It should be noted that this agreement occurred *before* the series of reaction experiments began.

The introspective reports showed that *the subjects frequently reacted in accordance with the laboratory-controlled habit and failed to carry out the resolution made to answer the nonsense syllable shown with a rime.* These failures to react in accordance with the previous resolution were expected by Ach; in fact, they were intended by him (*op. cit.,* p. 40). Accordingly, he called them *intendierte Fehlreaktionen* ("intended faulty reactions").[4]

The faulty reactions caused a good deal of annoyance to the subjects and made them sometimes very angry. Thus one of the subjects burst out quite spontaneously *"Dies ist doch eine Affenschande"* ("this is a downright shame"). The further result of these failures was that the subjects made a *vigorous resolve* before the next experiment to perform the assumed task.[5] Thus a very lively act of the will reached the very focus of the attention of the subjects. This occurred generally during the *"fore period"* of the reaction experiment. The experience, however, was sufficiently fresh in the immediate memory that it could be described in empirical terms. *In this manner Ach succeeded in getting an empirical description of a vigorous act of the will under controlled conditions.*

The introspective reports of the subjects show that the internal act of the will was clearly distinguished from the other conscious processes which were likewise present. In the act of the will *the activity of the Ego was the most prominent feature* and this was absent in all the other conscious processes. The activity of the Ego was empirically described as *the determination proceeding from the Ego to carry out the previously assumed task* and not to be misled by a conflicting habit. So vigorous was the active interposition of the *Ego* that it was accompanied by characteris-

---

[4] Cf. *op. cit.,* p. 61.
[5] *Op. cit.,* p. 52.

tic bodily attitudes such as energetic gestures and the pronunciation of the word *rime* in the imperative mood or the sentence
ich will wirklich ("I really will"). No one mistook these gestures
and verbal expressions for the act of the will itself; these bodily
attitudes were but *the outward signs* of the conscious attitude
of the Ego-in-action.

The subjects reported also the sensations which reached the
focus of their attention, namely, external sensations caused by
the sensible objects attended to, and a great variety of kinesthetic
and other organic sensations arising from changes within their
body. Some of these sensations, particularly those of muscular
tension (*Spannungsempfindungen*), were indeed the result of
active attention and outward signs of the latter.[6] But none of
the sensations reported contained, of themselves, the activity of
the Ego which characterized the act of the will itself: *the Ego
did not originate these sensory experiences as it originated the
determination to carry out the assumed task* All sensory experiences were rather forced on the Ego: the subjects found themselves having the various sensations. But *there was something
dynamic about the internal act of the will:* the subjects, in observing it, became aware of the Ego-in-action

The subjects reported also the *Zielvorstellung,* that is, the
knowledge of the action to be performed. But this knowledge
did not take the form of an image of the expected movement,
for the simple reason that *the subjects did not know what movement in particular they were going to make.* They became aware
of the instruction received and of the additional fact that they
had agreed to carry out this instruction The instruction was indeed very definite in the sense that the subjects had no choice
between various modes of reaction, as between riming and tran-
sporting the consonants; but it was *indefinite* in the sense that
the instruction was *expressed in general terms* and was applicable
in identically the same sense to a great variety of responses. Thus,

[6]*Ibid.,* pp. 238 sqq.

for instance, the instruction was to pronounce a rime for any word that might be shown. Accordingly, it could not be said, as has been said by sensationalists, that the act of the will is but an image of the expected movement. In the experiments of Ach the *Zielvorstellung* was plainly of the *intellectual* order. Nor could this intellectual cognition be mistaken for the act of the will, for *the former was not originated by the Ego-in-action as was the latter.* The same holds of the additional knowledge of the subjects that they had agreed to perform the task and that by doing so they had taken upon themselves an obligation. The subjects became aware of this obligation by saying to themselves *"ich soll reimen"* ("I ought to rime"). *But this knowledge "I ought" was most readily distinguished from the experience "I will."* The latter experience contained the Ego here and now in action, while the former was forced on the subjects by the evident fact that in the past they had assumed a definite obligation. The knowledge "I ought" rather expressed the *motive* for the renewal of the former resolution or for the act "I will."[7] Accordingly, the internal act of the will cannot be identified with intellectual cognition without doing violence to the facts observed in the experiments of Ach.

Lastly, the subjects reported also various emotional experiences, such as the affection of anger due to the faulty reactions. The latter arose so spontaneously and without any active interposition of the Ego that none of the subjects mistook them for the act of the will itself. From the numerous data obtained by Ach on emotional experiences he rightly concludes that *the emotion theory of the will is untenable.*[8]

It is true that all the experiences described dealt with the Ego and could not be reported without expressing the Ego as their subject. The act of the will, however, differed from the other experiences in this, that *the Ego was apprehended not merely as the subject but as the originator of that experience.* When the

[7] Cf. *op. cit.*, p. 244.
[8] *Op. cit.*, p. 246 and pp. 307 sqq.

subjects observed the act of the will, they became aware of the Ego-in-action, and this Ego-in-action was *not a matter of inference but a datum of immediate experience.*[9]

From these introspective data Ach concluded that all attempts to identify the internal act of the will with cognitive processes, sensory or intellectual, or to reduce the act of the will to a combination of such processes, is plainly impossible: *the act of the will is an experience totally different from all other conscious processes.*[10]

7. Various Criticisms of Ach's Experiments. Sensationalists have challenged the results obtained by Ach on theoretic grounds and on the basis of other experiments. We shall deal with these objections later.

Though the subjects of Ach undoubtedly described a true act of the will, it cannot be said that their description fits every act of the will. The active interposition of the Ego which was the most prominent feature in the will acts observed, does *not* occur in those acts of the will which are *indeliberate.* The most ardent defender of free will admits that many acts of the will are indeliberate. It is precisely because such acts of the will occur independently of any "consent" or "active interposition of the Ego" that we describe them by saying that we are *drawn* toward an object or are *attracted* by it. Such acts of the will were not described by the subjects of Ach. *It is interesting to note, then, that the subjects of Ach really gave an empirical description of a deliberate act of the will and emphasized that feature of it which is of the greatest importance in the discussion of free will.* It is unfortunate, however, that Ach designated the vigorous act actually observed by the name *"primary act"* of the will.[11] Surely the vigorous act described is *not* "primary" in the sense that it is the *prototype* of every internal act of the will. Ach opposes this "primary" act of the will to a *weak* act of the will which

[9]*Op. cit.,* p. 241.
[10]*Op. cit.,* pp. 247, 248.
[11]*Op. cit.,* p. 238.

414 EXPERIMENTAL PSYCHOLOGY

came likewise under observation. It should be noted, however, that the two acts of the will thus opposed differ only *in degree of intensity.*

Nor can it be said that the vigorous act of the will observed was the most perfect of all the deliberate acts of the will that occur in our experience. Undoubtedly we experience a *more perfect* act of the will when *by the active interposition of the Ego we decide the issue between conflicting motives.* There occurred, indeed, a conflict in the experiments of Ach but it was *not a conflict between different motives:* it was only a conflict between a *laboratory-controlled habit* and the *determining tendency* which resulted from a previous act of the will. The subjects of Ach had no motive whatever against carrying out their former resolve, say, to rime. They were only too anxious to carry out their former resolve but forgot about it when the time of re-action arrived. In the "fore period" of the experiment the subjects merely renewed their former resolve without even re-hearsing the motives which had prompted the original agreement made with the experimenter. Of course, they renewed the resolve for identically the same motives that prompted the original agreement, but these motives were at best only dimly attended to. From this point of view, then, the vigorous act of the will described, though deliberate, should rather be called a "secondary" act of the will.

There is another criticism which applies to the experiments of Ach He thought that his experimental procedure enabled him to *measure the strength of the act of the will by its "associative equivalent"* (*"das associative Aequivalent der Determination"*).[12] When the pairs of nonsense syllables had been repeated only a few times, the resolve to rime triumphed over the reproductive tendency created by memorizing the nonsense syllables. When, however, the syllables were repeated 120 times, the laboratory-controlled habit triumphed, at least frequently. Hence it may be asked, *how often can the nonsense syllables be repeated with-*

----

[12]*Op. cit.,* p. 43.

out interfering with the efficacy of the resolve? If such a number of repetitions can be ascertained, it is, according to Ach, a
measure for the *strength* of the act of the will.

It may suffice here to say that *all attempts to measure the
strength of the will in the manner indicated are, to say the very
least, very doubtful.* This is the conclusion at which Dr R Mc-
Carthy arrives in his *Measurement of Conation* (p. 102). He
finds that, whenever he created the experimental conditions of
Ach, the results were like those of Ach. When, however, he
created such conditions as would *direct the attention of the observers in the "main period" to the task assumed,* there was no
difficulty in carrying out their resolve in spite of the laboratory-
controlled habit, no matter how strong the latter was.[13] Similar
results were obtained by other investigators, particularly C. Rux
in his *Beitrag zur Lehre von der Determination.*[14]

Dr. McCarthy adds a useful theoretic remark concerning the
breaking of a habit which may find a place here. "Theoretically,"
he says, "any habit can be broken automatically *by fixating the
attention on an antagonistic course of action.* But when the habit
is a physical one, when an organic craving clamors for the satisfaction or the discharge of one set of neurons incites another set
to react, other considerations enter in. In such circumstances the
difficulty is to get the individual to concentrate his attention on
the opposing course of action In our experiments such concentration was brief and easy In ordinary life the period of conflict
is long; the organic cravings draw attention to themselves, thus
draining it away from the realization of the ideal, or ambition,
or course of action, to which the habit is opposed."[15]

That attention is an important factor in overcoming a habit
was found incidentally also by Ach Thus, whenever the knowledge of the task reached the focus of attention in the "main period," the reaction of the subject was in accordance with their pre-

[13]*Op. cit.,* p. 103.
[14]Referred to in *op. cit.,* p. 75.
[15]*Op. cit.,* p. 103, footnote.

vious resolve.[16] But *Ach did not control this factor of the right reaction.* This was accomplished by the modification of the experimental procedure introduced by Dr. McCarthy. The subjects of Ach "knew in advance exactly what they were expected to do with the approaching stimulus. We kept ours in ignorance of their specific task until they had seen the stimulus."[17] The stimuli were presented in different colors. "If they were red they instructed the subject to rime the stimulus. If they were green, he was to transpose," etc.[18] It was thus that the attention of the subjects was controlled in the "main period" of the experiment and the contrary habit was effectively overcome. From this it will be seen that *Ach, in discussing the "associative equivalent" of an act of the will, leaves the most important factor of breaking a habit out of consideration, namely, attention.*

8. The Experimental Investigation of the Process of Choosing. If there is any conscious process which can be called an internal act of the will as common sense understands that term, it is the act of choice. Prof. A. Michotte, of Louvain University, and his pupil Prüm were the first to investigate this process experimentally.[19] Their mode of procedure was similar to that of Ach, except that it was so devised as to favor the occurrence of an act of choice during the "main period" of a reaction experiment. The subjects were instructed that after a preliminary signal two numbers would be presented to them. If the numbers shown were of four digits, the subjects were requested to choose between addition and subtraction, and that for a serious motive; if the numbers shown were smaller, the subjects had to decide on reasonable grounds whether they wanted to multiply or divide. The further instruction was to make the choice as quickly as possible.

The subjects agreed to carry out these instructions and it is important to note this fact. For *by making this agreement the*

---

[16] Ach, *op. cit.*, pp. 49 and 53.

[17] McCarthy, *op. cit.* p. 9.

[18] *Loc. cit.*

[19] Cf. *Étude Exp. sur la Choix Volontaire*, 1910.

subjects assumed three distinct and rather unusual obligations, and these obligations limited their process of choosing considerably. The first obligation was to make a deliberate choice between two rather *trifling* alternatives: the subjects were not free to reject both alternatives. The second obligation was to decide upon one of the trifling alternatives only when they had a *serious motive* for this decision. The third obligation was to *speed up this process of choosing* as much as possible. In our everyday experience we rarely, if ever, make choices that are limited by obligations like those mentioned.

Immediately after reaching a decision the subjects pressed down the "reaction key" and thereby recorded the speed of their choice. Then they observed retrospectively all the conscious processes that occurred during the "reaction time" and in particular the process which occurred at the critical moment of the decision itself.

Before discussing the results obtained by Michotte and Prüm it may be well to describe the *modifications* in the experimental procedure which were introduced by H. M. Wells in a similar research carried out in the University of London.[20] The alternatives of choice were not as trifling as those of Michotte and Prüm. The subjects were requested to choose between two liquids of different tastes and to drink the chosen liquid immediately. Eight such liquids were prepared in uniformly the same way. Some of them were pleasant, others, very unpleasant, others again quite indifferent. All of them were colorless and practically odorless. In a series of preliminary experiments the taste of each liquid became firmly associated with a definite nonsense syllable. Thus, each of eight nonsense syllables was gradually transformed into a "name" by which a liquid of a definite well-known taste was designated. In each experiment two of these nonsense syllables were presented to the subject and two glasses containing the corresponding liquids were placed on the table just beneath the spot where the nonsense syllables appeared. The instruction was:

---

[20]Cf. "The Phenomenology of Acts of Choice," *British Journal of Psychology,* Monograph Supplement, XI.

"You are to choose, for a serious motive, between these two tastes, and drink the one you have chosen. React as quickly as possible."[21]

Here again it should be noted that *the subjects by accepting this instruction assumed definite obligations and that these obligations limited their choice considerably.* It should be noted, further, that the instruction, to choose for a serious motive, was normally interpreted by the subjects of Wells to mean to "choose the best."[22] "But in the earlier experiments subject A interpreted this as an obligation to choose for an ethical motive. He therefore often forced himself to take the more unpleasant alternative for this reason."[23]

The most interesting choices observed and reported by the subjects of both experimental researches are those between two alternatives which were in every regard equal: equally easy, equally pleasant or equally unpleasant, or equally indifferent. In all these cases the very instruction to "choose for a serious motive" caused considerable difficulty. What serious motive can there be for preferring addition to subtraction or subtraction to addition, when both operations are equally easy, and when the only reason for performing either operation is the obligation assumed by accepting the instruction, and when this obligation is satisfied just as well by adding as by subtracting? Similarly, what serious motive can there be for preferring one drink to another when both are equally indifferent to taste or when one liquid is just as unpleasant as the other and when the only motive for drinking either liquid is the obligation assumed by accepting the instruction and when this obligation is satisfied just as well by drinking one liquid as by drinking the other?

In all these instances, then, there was *no objective difference* whatever between the two alternatives, or, if there was, the subjects were not aware of it. *Nor was there, prior to the actual*

---

[21]*Op. cit.,* pp. 5-10.
[22]*Op. cit.,* p. 83.
[23]*Op. cit.,* p. 85.

choice, any subjective difference between the two alternatives, that is, the value which the two alternatives had for the subjects before choice, was identically the same, or, if there was such a difference, the subjects were not aware of it.

Accordingly, if the instruction "to choose for a serious motive" is interpreted to mean that choice must be made only *after* the motive for one alternative is strengthened, then *it is impossible to make a choice which satisfies this instruction.* If, however, this instruction is interpreted to mean that choice must be made only *after careful consideration of both alternatives,* then choice between two equal alternatives is possible, provided we have the ability to settle the issue between conflicting motives by the active interposition of the Ego. Then the Ego-in-action could turn the balance in favor of one of the hitherto equal motives and thus add subjective strength to this motive. Common sense has always maintained that we have the power of "Self-determination" and that we make use of it in every voluntary choice. In every instance of such a choice "I decide" which motive is to prevail: this is what common sense understands by voluntary choice. *The experimental conditions created by Michotte, Prüm, and Wells, though otherwise rather unusual, afford an excellent opportunity to test the correctness of the common-sense view concerning voluntary choice.*

Some philosophers have asserted on metaphysical grounds that choice between two equal alternatives is impossible It has been said that in the face of two equal alternatives we should be in a predicament like that of Buridan's ass, who — sad to relate — starved to death between two bundles of hay What the experience of asses may be when placed between two bundles of hay. we can only know by inference. Whatever may be true about Buridan's ass, ordinary asses, somehow or other, do not die when placed between two bundles of hay, but they cannot give us an introspective report as to how they extricate themselves from their predicament. Nor are we particularly interested in their experience, as it is not precisely asinine experience which we are discussing at present. What occurs in human experience had best be settled by the introspective report of those who have been placed in such a predicament.

The subjects of Michotte and Prüm as well as those of H. M. Wells frequently extricated themselves from such a predicament *by the active interposition of the Ego* The Ego-in-action was clearly observed by the subjects and it was by the Ego-in-action that one of the hitherto equal motives was strengthened and the choice was effected. "This," H. M Wells says, "was the most interesting and frequent type of motive strengthening. It occurred during choices in which two negative, or two otherwise 'equal,' motives developed. We have previously stated that this type of motivation occurred when the values of the alternatives stood in the relation of 'likeness.' The figures given in . . . Table XV show the frequency with which a motive was made or strengthened by the 'Self.' "[24]

For our subsequent discussion of free will it is important to note that in all these cases *it was not the "strengthened motive" which determined the choice, but it was the choice which strengthened the motive.* It should be noted, further, that the subjects in all these cases had indeed *no new motive* for making their choice, but it cannot be said that they chose without a serious motive. *The old motive which was strengthened by the active interposition of the Ego was the serious motive.*

The active interposition of the Ego was likewise observed when choice was made between two unequal alternatives. The *judgment* "this operation is easier" or "this liquid is more pleasant" was an experience totally different from *the active interposition of the Ego* by which the easier or more pleasant alternative was chosen. Of course, the "Ego-in-action" was more plainly in evidence when the more unpleasant alternative was chosen for an ethical reason.[25] "Subject A sometimes voluntarily strengthened the motive for taking an unpleasant alternative in this

---

[24] *Op. cit.*, p. 84.
[25] *Op. cit.*, pp. 84 sqq., and p. 147 n. 7.

manner, even when he had the option of taking a pleasanter one."[26]

All voluntary choices as they actually occurred in the research of H. M. Wells confirm what we said on page 400 about the nature and importance of the motive. "The 'Self' makes one of the motives its own, and in the process of tending toward one end in preference to another we shall show, by quotations from our protocols, that we have a direct lived and cognized experience of the 'Self-in-action.' "[27]

Attention plays an important rôle in choice, but "the order in which the alternatives in the choice present themselves has no ascertainable influence on the ultimate selection; nor does a high degree of consciousness for one of the alternatives necessarily determine its acceptance by the 'Self.' "[28] It should be borne in mind, however, that *attention itself may be either voluntary or involuntary.* "The alternative to which the 'Self' directs attention rises to the focus of awareness, while the other fades."[29] It was in this manner that a difficult choice was sometimes hastened. In all these cases "the mental set to 'choose for a serious motive' has been suppressed by a fresh voluntary decision to inhibit further discussion of motives by a deliberate concentration on *one* course of action only."[30] It need not be stated explicitly that *this is but another way of saying that choice was effected by the active interposition of the Ego.*

9. **The Sensationalistic Account of the Process of Choosing.** The data obtained by Ach. Michotte, and Prüm caused a good deal of discussion. Raymond H. Wheeler undertook to verify these data for himself. In his *Experimental Investigation of the Process of Choosing*[31] he comes to a totally different conclusion. "In a voluntary choice," he says, "there is

[26]*Ibid.,* p. 87.
[27]*Ibid.,* p. 75; cf. also p. 141.
[28]*Ibid.,* p. 147, n. 10.
[29]*Ibid.,* p. 89.
[30]*Op. cit.,* p. 89.
[31]*University of Oregon Publication,* Vol. I. 1919-1922, n. 2, p. 51.

no consciousness of activity as such, no awareness of an immediate and unanalyzable self and no conscious conative of striving
process. . . . Each reagent was familiar with the descriptions of
these various contents which have been attributed, in the literature, to the volitional consciousness (Ach, Michotte, Calkins).
All agreed that in their most genuine and difficult acts of choosing such experiences as might be termed 'feelings of mental activity,' 'immediate consciousness of the self,' 'elemental awareness
of the self,' 'consciousness of willing,' etc., could be analyzed into organic and kinesthetic processes, with occasional visual, auditory, or verbal accompaniments."

All the subjects of Wheeler had theoretic convictions concerning the very facts they observed. According to the current theory
of sensationalism, the Ego is but a bundle of sensations, and sensations are the constitutive elements of all our conscious processes.
It is perfectly natural, therefore, that the subjects of Wheeler *interpreted* their experiences as they did. The important thing to
note, however, is that it is a matter of utter indifference to psychology as a science how the subjects of Wheeler *interpreted* the
facts observed The subject in a psychological experiment acts as
an observer. His task is to gather facts and to describe them
without any theoretic bias. This is the first step in every natural
science. When this first step was taken in chemistry, the observers were not asked how they *interpreted* the facts observed:
this is a matter of utter indifference to the science of chemistry.
The observers simply described the facts observed in purely empirical terms of common sense and they stated the conditions
under which these facts were observed. Facts thus observed and
described are public property inasmuch as they can be verified
by anybody who cares to do so. It was only when this mode of
procedure was adopted that chemistry began to be a natural
science and then its progress was rapid.

The same mode of procedure must be adopted in psychology
if it is to be considered a natural science. The first step in experimental psychology is to gather facts and to state them without
any theoretic bias. *As long as we take the theoretic interpreta-*

*tions of the observers into consideration, we are not gathering
facts that are public property;* we are, rather, gathering theoretic
opinions concerning facts. Such a gathering of opinions is known
by the name of a *symposium.* What Wheeler calls "an experimental investigation of the process of choosing" is in reality only
a *symposium* on this process. That such is the case, is clear from
the following statement of Wheeler, in which *all italics are ours.*

"Different observers," he says, *"interpreted* their final decisions
in different ways. J described his decisions as 'attitudes of acceptance'; B described his as 'kinesthetic sets' toward the stimulus
in question; A called his decisions 'esthetic judgments'; E and C
interpreted their decisions as 'adjustments to hear the music' . . . ;
D called his final decisions 'muscular jerks'; F spoke of her final
decisions as 'motor attitudes.' It is not difficult to trace the reason why our different reagents varied in their terminology. *Certain terms can obviously be traced to their psychological training or belief,* others to the way in which their experiences appeared to them, i.e., the localization of sensations, the order of
appearance, etc., but the significant feature of all their terms is
the fact that each was essentially kinesthetic, that each expressed
the recognition on the part of the reagent that the vital feature
of his choosing was its kinesthetic content."[32] This passage speaks
for itself and needs no further comment.

What is more important than the interpretations which found
their way into the very description of the facts observed is the
surprising statement which Wheeler makes concerning the observers A and D in particular. "Neither D nor A," he says, "are
conscious of the self or of a feeling of activity during the act of
choosing. In fact, such experiences never appear to them even
in kinesthetic or organic complexes."[33] It will be best to quote
one of the introspective reports of both A and D. The instruction of the experimenter was that the subject was to choose which
of two musical selections indicated on a card was to be played

[32]*Ibid.,* pp. 26, 27.
[33]*Ibid.,* p. 31.

by a Victrola; but if he cared for neither selection, he might reject both.[34]

A describes his experiences during the fore period as follows: "During the hearing of the instructions I tended to repeat each sentence in vocal-motor-auditory imagery. When the experimenter announced that he was going to give me primitive music I had the vocal-motor-auditory: 'Oh! Primitive music; (I) like primitive music; choose (the) one (I) prefer; (the) don't want either (alternative) won't happen.' This was followed by the vocal-motor-auditory: 'Probably don't know either; good, (I am) interested in primitive music; hurry up and present them to me.' During this time I was conscious of rather intensive strains about the brows, shoulders and chest; and as the time approached for the exposure of the stimuli (alternatives) these strains increased in their intensity and at the same time became widespread. . . .

["Here the reagent is assuming a favorable attitude toward certain anticipated alternatives and the motor preparedness to proceed in the act of choosing is greater than is required for mere fixation of attention. The reagent is unconsciously tending to choose in an anticipatory fashion and expresses this tendency in his eagerness for the exposure of the alternatives, in the widespread muscular tenseness and in his desire for the early exposure of the alternatives."][35]

The reader should note how certain sentences in this report are printed, as for instance: "(I) like," "(I) prefer," etc. Wheeler explains this by the following note: "Parentheses denote the reagent's own interpretation of his experiences; brackets indicate explanations or interpretations added by the writer."[36] As, therefore, *the reference to the Ego appears in parentheses,* Wheeler is perfectly justified in stating that A is not aware of the self when he "likes," "prefers," etc.

D describes his experiences during the "main period" as follows. "I first perceived the 'Evening Star' title and as my eye

---

[34]*Ibid.*, p. 4.
[35]*Ibid.*, pp. 5, 6.
[36]*Ibid.*, p. 5.

glanced along the card I repeated each word in auditory imagery. This was accompanied by a rapid onset of pleasantness, together with a feeling of familiarity. . . . I then read the other title and very much the same series of experiences developed; then followed the vocal-motor: 'Well, both are good; both poetic; which do I want? This is going to be a difficult choice; both are good, I am sure.' For a short time I was aware of strains about the jaws, eyes, and in the throat; then followed the verbal process: 'Now let me see the first title again.' I turned to the upper card; I read it over carefully and came to the name, Wagner, which I had not noticed before; then I was aware of a kinesthetic 'jerk' which seemed to pervade my whole body; I noted kinesthetic tensions and incipient movements of leaning forward, slightly; my line of regard remained fixed upon the composer's name; sensations came in of moving my body slightly forward and upward; at this juncture appeared the verbal process: 'Well, I know this is good; better take the one you are certain of'; this was accompanied by marked pleasantness. I then turned to the experimenter and said: 'I will take this one.' "[37]

The reader will note that *the frequent references to the Ego in this report are not eliminated by parentheses.* Wheeler explains this by the following general remark about A and D. "Both stated, upon questioning, that they were conscious of themselves or of mental activity after the final decision had taken place and relaxation had occurred, but agreed that this awareness was merely retrospective and interpretative and that under these latter conditions the awareness was one which the experimenter suggested by his questions and was not one which was characteristic of their acts of choosing."[38] From this it will be seen that Wheeler is perfectly justified in stating that the subjects A and D were not even aware of the Ego when they chose.

Such is the famous evidence on which the sensationalistic account of the process of choosing rests. *It is exactly on a par with*

[37] *Ibid.,* p 17.
[38] *Ibid.,* p. 31.

the experimental proof that Titchener gave of his sensationalistic account of the perception of a relation. He simply described "a flashing picture of a bald crown, with a fringe of hair below, and a massive black shoulder, the whole passing swiftly down the visual field from northwest to southeast."[39] This done, he testified, as a psychological expert, that in his experience this image constituted the perception of a definite logical relation. Nobody will deny that Titchener actually had this odd image when, on the occasion described, he was thinking of a definite logical relation. *What Titchener has failed to show is that this image constitutes the knowledge of that relation.* Similarly, the observers of Wheeler simply described the various kinesthetic sensations and images they had when they made a definite choice and then testified, as psychological experts, that these sensations and images constituted their choice. Nobody will deny that subject D, for instance, "was aware of a kinesthetic 'jerk'" and that he "noted kinesthetic tensions and incipient movements of leaning forward," when he actually made a definite choice; nor will anybody question the fact that subject A "was conscious of rather intensive strains about the brows, shoulders and chest," when he reached his decision. *What subjects D and A and all the other subjects of Wheeler and Wheeler himself have failed to show is, that these kinesthetic sensations and images constitute the choice or final decision.*

Titchener called such a description of images an *analysis of a thought process,* and Wheeler called it an *analysis of the process of choosing.* Hence, in answering the obvious objections raised against his experimental proof, Wheeler distinguished between "analyzed" and "unanalyzed experience."[40] Here *a protest is in place against the abuse of the scientific term analysis.* In all other natural sciences an *analysis* made under controlled conditions is *public property,* and that for two reasons. The first is, that *everyone who cares to do so, can make the analysis described over*

---

[39] *Thought Processes,* p. 185, quoted by permission of the Macmillan Co., publishers.

[40] *Psychological Review* (1922).

again, the second is, that *everyone can test this analysis by a corresponding "synthesis."* Chemists do not simply rely on the testimony of this or that chemical expert that water can be analyzed into H_2O. Many a chemist has actually tested the accuracy of this analysis in the two ways mentioned and it is only because this analysis is public property that it is accepted in the science of chemistry. *What Wheeler calls an "analysis" of a definite act of choice is incapable of being verified by other observers; nor can any other observer synthesize the particular choice,* say, of subject A, by combining again the "rather intensive strains about the brows, shoulders, and chest" into which this subject analyzed his particular choice; nor will anybody succeed in reconstructing the particular choice of subject D by combining again the "kinesthetic 'jerk'" and the "kinesthetic tensions and incipient movements of leaning forward" into which this expert analyzed his particular choice. *Accordingly, it is only by an abuse of a scientific term that Wheeler can call the theoretic interpretations of his subjects an "analysis" of their act of choice.*

In conclusion it is well to state that one of the aims of the experimental research of H. M. Wells, described in the previous section of this chapter, was to verify the statements of Wheeler. And the verdict of H. M. Wells is as follows: "We find no justification for Wheeler's statement that consciousness of 'Self-activity' can be analyzed into the basal elements of kinesthetic and organic sensations and images. We find that consciousness of 'Self-activity' is absolutely distinct and different from the kinesthetic and organic phenomena which may or may not be present together with it."[41]

10. The Problem of Free Will. Our account of the will would be incomplete without a discussion of the problem of free will. This problem has ever been the battle ground of metaphysical speculations. As experimental psychologists we have nothing to do with these speculations. *We shall discuss the problem of free will exclusively on the basis of facts that can be veri-*

---

[41]H. M. Wells. *op cit.*, p. 147, n. 9.

fied by anyone who cares to do so. The first requisite for such a discussion is to state clearly what is meant by free will. This is all the more necessary as, in the metaphysical discussions referred to, the very nature of free will has been turned into a *caricature* by those who deny free will.

Free will, as common sense understands this term, may be defined as *the power of self-determination,* or more accurately, as *the ability to settle the issue between conflicting motives by the active interposition of the Ego.* The schoolmen express identically the same thing when they define free will as *the ability we have, when all conditions for action are given, to determine actively (that is, by the active interposition of the Ego), whether we shall act or abstain from acting, whether we shall do this or that.*

From these definitions it will be seen that the problem of free will is *primarily a question of fact* and the central fact on which the whole discussion of free will hinges, is *the active interposition of the Ego by which the issue between conflicting motives is settled.* Common sense, on the basis of everyday experience, has always maintained that, frequently at least, such an active interposition of the Ego occurs. This fact is usually expressed by such phrases as "I consent," "I determine," "I decide," "I approve," "I disapprove," "I accept," "I yield," "I agree," "I resolve," "I make up my mind," etc. *In all these phrases not only the Ego is expressed but also the "Ego-in-action."* The term most frequently used to denote the active interposition of the Ego is "consent." It is by the presence or absence of "consent" that an unsophisticated man distinguishes acts of the will that are deliberate or free from those that are indeliberate or not-free.

Aristotle has described the most central fact of free will with all the accuracy desirable when he says that "man is the *origin* and the *parent* of his actions, as of his children."[42] If man's will is free, "virtue also must be in our own power; and in like manner vice. for *wherever we have the power to do, we have also the*

---

[42] *Nicom. Eth.,* III, 5, translated by Browne, p. 67.

*power not to do; and wherever we have the power not to do,
we have also the power to do."*[43]

In the language of the schoolmen the function of the Ego in
deciding the issue between two conflicting motives is likened to
that of an *arbitrator;* hence, free will is succinctly called *arbitrium* (arbitry). The nature of free will and the conditions requisite for its exercise could not be better described than by this
comparison. An arbitrator hears and considers carefully the conflicting claims of the two contending parties. It is, however, not
the relative weight of the conflicting claims that decides the issue; for this relative weight is the very matter of dispute. It is
the arbitrator who decides and, by doing so, *assigns the relative
weight* of the conflicting claims. His decision is not doctrinal
like that of a scientific expert, or advisory like that of a consul-
tor: it is authoritative and final. Whatever may have been the
relative weight of the conflicting claims before the authoritative
decision, after this decision all dispute ceases *This is an exact
picture of what occurs in free choice.* The contending parties are
the two alternatives, and the conflicting claims of the parties
correspond to the conflicting motives for the alternatives. The
Ego is the arbitrator who takes cognizance of the conflicting
motives. But *it is not the relative weight of the motives which
decides the issue; the Ego decides and, by doing so, assigns the
relative weight of the motives.* His decision is not doctrinal but
authoritative and final. Whatever may have been the relative
weight of the conflicting motives before the authoritative decision, after this decision the internal conflict ceases. This is what
the doctrine of free will implies.

From this it will be seen that the doctrine of free will does
not assert that all internal acts of the will are free. The most
ardent defender of free will admits that *many acts of the will
are impulsive.* Such are all our conscious inclinations and aversions which occur prior to consent They are fully accounted for
by mentioning their motives. Only when the conditions for free

[43] *Op. cit.,* p. 66.

choice are given, is the act of the will free. The most essential condition for freedom of choice is the attentive consideration of the motives for both alternatives of choice. *This weighing of conflicting motives is known as deliberation.* It may be completely absent. When present, it *admits of degrees:* we may be more or less clearly aware of the conflicting motives. It is for this reason, and for this reason alone, that freedom of choice admits of degrees: an act of the will may be more or less "deliberate."

The very *minimum* of deliberation requisite for the exercise of free will occurs when, without explicitly considering the motives pro and con, we are aware that *on a former occasion we have considered these motives and have assumed or recognized a definite obligation.* Under these conditions the *renewal* of a former deliberate resolution is far from being "inconsiderate"; on the contrary, it is eminently reasonable. It is characteristic of a man of principle who deliberately stands by decisions he "has considered" carefully. Accordingly, such a renewal of a former resolution is undoubtedly free: it consists in *the active interposition of the Ego approving a former deliberate choice.* From this it will be seen that "deliberation," the essential requisite for the exercise of free will, does not necessarily imply "hesitation." It cannot be said, however, that an unhesitating renewal of a former resolution is an *ideal* example of the exercise of free will.

There are certain conditions under which there occurs no deliberation at all. Such are the states of sleep, dreams, fever delirium, and hypnosis; hence, under these conditions, the power of choice is in complete abeyance. When we are drowsy or under the influence of violent emotions we are at least incapable of such an exercise of freedom as would make us gravely responsible for our strivings and doings. The same is true in the state of abstraction or "absent-mindedness." In general it may be stated that as long as an object occupies only the dim background or margin of attention, we cannot exercise our freedom with regard to *that* object.

It should be noted, however, that an object but dimly attended to may indeed arouse an act of the will but this act is impulsive.

In psychoanalytic literature such dim, impulsive strivings are known as "subconscious urges," "subconscious phobias," "complexes," etc. It need not be stated explicitly that we know of such subconscious aversions and inclinations only by *inference,* namely, from certain modes of outward behavior which cannot be accounted for without such subconscious antecedents. Though the discussion of these subconscious antecedents has been frequently mixed with speculations that are unsound, still there remains a grain of truth in these discussions which must be admitted. And admitting this grain of truth means that we grant that *subconscious strivings may issue in external actions and may thus become a great hindrance in the practical use we make of our freedom of choice.*

For the present the most important thing to note is that the problem of free will, as we have formulated it, *is not directly concerned with the control we have over our external behavior.* It may suffice here to state that at best our external actions are free only by *extrinsic denomination,* insofar as they depend on an internal act of the will which is really free. A good many of our external actions occur independently of any internal act of the will. With regard to those actions which depend on an internal act of the will, we have stated in the fourth section of this chapter that they may be voluntary in three ways; namely, actually, virtually, and habitually. We add here that this is true whether the internal act of the will which is the starting point of these actions is free or impulsive, whether it is conscious or subconscious.

In the sixth section of this chapter we noted, further, that *the most vigorous act of the will may be inefficacious as far as its external execution is concerned.* Ach has demonstrated experimentally and to the great annoyance of his subjects that *a laboratory-controlled habit may triumph over a most vigorous resolve.* A physiological habit, then, may interfere with the execution of our internal acts of the will even though the latter arise under ideal conditions of free choice. What can be done by a physiological habit can also be done by a pathological condition.

A blood clot somewhere in our nervous system may result in our failure to do what we have freely resolved to do. No wonder, then, that "subconscious urges" and "complexes" of all kinds may likewise interfere with the external execution of our resolves, even though the latter be perfectly free.

From this it will be seen that *we should complicate the problem of free will enormously if we formulated it in such a way as to include also the control we have over our external actions.* We avoid these complications by restricting our problem to the *internal* acts of the will. And the fact on which our whole discussion hinges is *the active interposition of the Ego* by which the issue between conflicting motives is decided. Nor are we concerned with doubtful cases of such an interposition of the Ego but only with such cases as are clear and unmistakable. *The discussion of all doubtful cases we leave to "abnormal psychology" and to "dynamic psychology."*

It is worthy of note, however, that not all psychologists formulate the problem of free will as we do. Not only do they include in their question the control we have over our external behavior but *they so formulate it as to make it a problem of metaphysics.* No wonder that they find that the problem of free will is too complex to be answered on the basis of experiment. Some psychologists grant at most that experiment has revealed nothing against the doctrine of free will. As we understand the problem of free will, is simply *a question of fact* exactly on a par with any other problem that is discussed in experimental psychology or in any other natural science.

11. Free Will in the Light of Controlled Observation. The reader who has carefully followed our discussion of the various experimental investigations of the will, cannot have failed to note that all these investigations dealt with the *central fact* on which the whole discussion of the principal problem of free will hinges: *the active interposition of the Ego.* Ach ascertained this fact in the case of a deliberate resolution or rather a deliberate renewal of such a resolution. Michotte, Prüm, and Wells ascertained the same fact in the case of a deliberate choice. All the acts of the will which were described on the basis of controlled observation were characterized by the active interposition of the Ego.

In the interpretation of these data we do not rely on the theoretic convictions of the subjects as to whether man's will is free or not. The present writer is not aware that any such convictions were expressed. But if they were, they do not enter into our present discussion.

Neither do we rely on the conclusions reached by the experimenters on the basis of the introspective data obtained. As a matter of fact, Michotte, Prüm, and Wells express no conclusion concerning the doctrine of free will. As to Ach it should be noted that in the seventh section of this chapter *we voiced several serious objections to the conclusions which he actually draws from his experiments.* We add here that though he did not mean to investigate the problem of free will, he broached it incidentally in the introduction to his investigation *Ueber den Willensakt und das Temperament,* pages 2–4. It may suffice here to say that *Ach does not formulate the question as we do or reach the same conclusion as we do.*

We rely exclusively on the *data* ascertained by controlled observation. These data are *public property* and can be verified by anyone who cares to do so by creating the conditions under which the facts were observed. These facts are that, *frequently at least, it was the active interposition of the Ego by which the issue between conflicting motives was settled.* This was most clearly ascertained *when the two alternatives were equal in every regard;* it was likewise ascertained when the two alternatives were unequal. Even when choice was made in favor of the alternative which was easier or more pleasant — and this occurred frequently — the mere *judgment* "this is easier" or "this is more pleasant" was an experience totally different from *the active interposition of the Ego* by which the issue between the two conflicting motives was settled. *From these data we draw the obvious conclusion that we have the ability to settle the issue between two conflicting motives, equal or unequal, by the active interposition of the Ego.* And this ability is what common sense designates as free will. In short, *controlled observation has confirmed the common-sense doctrine of free will.*

Many are the attempts made to invalidate this simple experimental proof of free will. It has been said that the question of free will cannot possibly be settled by an appeal to the data of introspection. For free will, by its very nature, is an *ability* or a *power* we have under certain conditions. But introspection does not reveal any ability or power of ours. The object of introspection is *present internal facts;* but no ability or power of ours is a present internal fact. Introspection reveals *what we do here and now;* it does not reveal what we *can* do; still less does introspection reveal that while doing a thing we were *able to leave it undone.* According to Aristotle this constitutes the very essence of freedom that "wherever we have the power to do, we have also the power not to do." Accordingly, there cannot possibly be a simple experimental proof of free will.

This difficulty is a very old one and has been proposed and discussed by the stanchest defenders of free will — the schoolmen. Accordingly, we shall answer it first in the precise language of the schoolmen; then we shall express the same answer in the common-sense language customary in natural sciences. We grant, then, that in literal strictness free will is not a matter of immediate experience: it is not a present internal fact, as the schoolmen understand these terms when defining the object of introspection or "psychological reflection." Free will, precisely because it is an *ability* or *power* of ours, can only be a matter of inference. But inference is of two kinds, immediate and mediate. We explained this at length when discussing the reasoning process, and to this explanation the reader is referred (p. 383). This premised, we admit that in literal strictness *we experience only the fact that here and now we settle the issue between conflicting motives by the active interposition of the Ego.* From this we infer that we have the *ability* to do so. This inference, however, is *immediate* and far removed from that indirect way of arriving at a judgment which alone is designated by the term "reasoning process."

In the language customary in natural sciences we should rather say that our mode of procedure is in literal strictness *an experimental proof of free will.* If the possibility of a certain phenomenon is questioned, and a scientist succeeds in actually producing that phenomenon in the laboratory, that scientist is said to have proved *experimentally* the *possibility* of that phenomenon. This has been done in the case of free will. Accordingly, in the terminology of natural sciences it must be said that we have experimental proof of man's free will.

We add that in literal strictness *neither the necessity nor the freedom of any conscious process of ours is an immediate datum of our internal experience.* But we know the necessity of certain conscious processes in *exactly the same way* as we know the freedom of others: the former occur *prior to consent* and independently of it; the latter *depend on our consent.* And this consent is but another name for *the active interposition of the Ego.* This consideration disposes of another difficulty frequently urged, namely, that introspectively considered a free act of the will looks exactly like an impulsive act: each must be described as a conscious inclination toward an object intellectually apprehended as good or as a conscious aversion from an object intellectually apprehended as evil. Hence, introspectively we cannot tell the one from the other.

The answer is that in the one case we *consent* to the conscious inclination or aversion, and in the other we *do not.* In this manner we distinguish most clearly acts of the will that are free from those that are impulsive. At times, indeed, consent is a matter of doubt and then it is doubtful whether the act of the will was free or impulsive. *If the person concerned cannot settle this doubt, nobody else can.* We admit, then, that there are doubtful cases of the exercise of free will just as there are doubtful cases of any other fact recognized in natural sciences.

It has been said that our choice is always in favor of "the greater seeming good" and that "the stronger motive always prevails." We answer that "the greater seeming good" and "the stronger motive" are ambiguous terms. If the contention is that our choice is always in favor of that motive which *prior to consent is stronger,* we deny this statement. It is a sweeping generalization not borne out by the facts observed inside or outside the laboratory. If, however, by "the stronger motive" we mean *the one which is actually adopted by the active interposition of the Ego or consent,* then, of course, it is universally true that the stronger motive prevails. But such a statement is mere *tautology:* that motive prevails which prevails.

The same difficulty is also proposed in a different form. It is pointed out that we frequently express our choice by the practical judgment "this is better" or "this is to be done." From this it is inferred that *choice is terminated in every instance by such a practical judgment.* If such is the case, choice is a matter of judgment and not one determined by the active interposition of the Ego. Even Aristotle's description of a voluntary choice is appealed to. According to him, choice is arrived at by what he calls a *practical syllogism.* "The major premise," he says, "is universal . . . while the minor has to do with a particular fact: for, while the former asserts that such and such a person ought to do such and such an act, the latter asserts that a particular act is one of the sort and that I am such a person. Now it is the latter judgment which at once moves to action, not the universal."[44]

The answer is that *a practical judgment* as we know it from our experience and as Aristotle understands it, is a totally different thing from *a theoretic judgment* such as a theorem of geometry. The truth of such a theorem depends exclusively on its objective evidence, and this evidence is furnished by a theoretic syllogism or a series of such syllogisms. The truth of the practical judgment by which we express our choice depends exclusively on *the consent of the Ego.* The practical syllogism which leads to the conclusion "this is to be done" or "this is better" does not

---

[44] *De Anima,* translated by Hicks, p. 157.

express *the objective proof* for this conclusion but only *a motive* for its acceptance by the Ego. *The whole efficacy of the practical syllogism of which Aristotle speaks is derived from the active interposition of the Ego.* Accordingly, whenever we express our voluntary choice by the practical judgment "this is better" or "this is to be done," *this judgment supposes consent or the active interposition of the Ego and expresses the very fact of this consent;* it means in every instance "this is what I want" or "this is my choice." The schoolmen stated all this by saying that, though the practical judgment (*judicium ultimo-practicum*) precedes external actions and determines the latter, it does not determine the internal act of choice; on the contrary, *the act of choice determines the practical judgment.*

Somehow or other the solution here given leaves a serious doubt in the minds of some. For *at times the theoretic judgment "this is better" terminates our choice.* This plain fact, rather than anything else, gives point to the above difficulty against free will. Thus I may deliberately decide to reach a definite end as best I can, and then consider the various means to reach that end. Under these conditions all that is needed to terminate my choice is the *objective proof* that a definite means is the best to accomplish my purpose. This proof can be furnished by a *theoretic syllogism.* The purely theoretic conviction I thus reach necessarily terminates my choice. And if it does so, how can it be said that my choice is free?

The answer is that the necessity of this choice is not that of an impulsive act but one that arises from the logical impossibility of making two contradictory suppositions. The former necessity is known in the terminology of the schoolman as *antecedent necessity,* because an impulsive act is inexorably determined by its antecedents; the latter is known as *consequent necessity* and is best understood by the time-honored example used by the schoolmen. Let us suppose that Socrates here and now is sitting. Of course, he can arise at any time he pleases, but *supposing that he is sitting, he sits with metaphysical necessity,* for it is unthinkable that he should be sitting and not sitting at the same time. This applies to our case.

We *suppose* that somebody has resolved to reach a definite end *as best he can,* and we *suppose* that here and now he does not change his former resolution. *This resolution of his implies the will to use the best means to that end, as soon as that means becomes known to him.* Of course, he remains free to refuse it, when it becomes known to him. But he cannot refuse it without changing his former resolution. Hence, *the knowledge he acquires concerning the best means to a definite end, is an excellent touchstone to the sincerity of his former resolve.* If, then, we suppose, as we do, that he here and now persists in his former resolution, the objective judgment "this is the best means to the end I am resolved to reach" necessarily terminates his choice. If it does not, *our supposition is wrong,* namely, that he persists in his former resolution. Thus the whole difficulty against free will resolves itself into a *quibble.*

As to *the oft-repeated objection that free will implies "willing without a motive,"* we have said enough in the third section of this chapter. The objection rests on a *misrepresentation* of the doctrine of free will. The same is true of a number of other objections which we here pass over in silence.

Psychologists behavioristically inclined point out that we can *foretell* the behavior of our fellow men from the knowledge we have of their character, habits, intellectual convictions, native and acquired tendencies. In fact, *society is entirely built on the certainty with which we can foretell how a man will act under given conditions,* as for instance, that he will pay his bills and that a cook will not poison the dinner he prepares, etc. But if man's will were free, we could never be sure about these things. By admitting the doctrine of free will, then, we take away the very foundations of society and make all human behavior a matter of caprice.

We admit that it is indeed impossible to foretell the future free actions of our fellow men with *absolute* certainty. We can, however, do so, frequently at least, with that degree of assurance which is required for prudent action. Such an assurance is known as *moral certainty in the wider sense of the term*. It does not exclude the *possibility* of error but only its *probability*. It is such a certainty on which society is built and this certainty is in perfect accord with the doctrine of free will. For though free will excludes the regularity which obtains in the domain of physics, chemistry, and biology, it does not exclude *all* regularity; on the contrary, *it makes the regularity of moral conduct possible*. It is just because we are endowed with free will that *we are capable of observing the moral law and of mastering the instinctive and acquired tendencies which militate against this law*. By the very fact that we make use of our free will in accordance with the laws of God and country, our conduct will evidence a regularity. A behavioristic psychologist may interpret this regularity in terms of stimulus and response; but those who observe the laws know from their internal experience that it is only by the active interposition of the Ego that this very regularly is brought about.

12. **Free Will and "the Scientific Definition of Mind."**
We said before that the problem of free will has ever been the battle ground of metaphysical speculation. This is as true today as it was before experimental procedure was applied to psychological problems. No doubt, the ultimate explanation of free will presents rather puzzling metaphysical problems. *So does the ultimate explanation of every phenomenon in nature,* even such a simple phenomenon as that of motion. Zeno of old proved to his own satisfaction from the true inwardness of things that motion is impossible. Du Bois-Reymond, though not doubting the fact of motion, declared its origin one of his seven world riddles. The metaphysical difficulties of Zeno are solved *ambulando* (by walking), that is, by a simple appeal to the plain fact of motion. *Ten thousand difficulties like those of Zeno do not make a doubt as to the possibility of motion*. And the difficulties voiced by Du Bois-Reymond only prove that not all problems can be solved by the methods of experimental science All problems concerning the ultimate nature and origin of things are philosophical problems and must be solved by the methods of philosophy.

Our attitude, then, with regard to the metaphysical difficulties against free will is, that *we leave them entirely to philosophy.* Whatever the solution of these difficulties may be, *ten thousand of them do not make a doubt.* Such should be the attitude of all experimentalists. For the facts on which the doctrine of free will rests are plain and in the possession of all. No laboratory equipment is required to create the conditions under which these facts can be ascertained by anyone as often as he desires. In spite of all this, metaphysical speculations constitute to this day the *greatest* difficulty against the doctrine of free will. Modern psychologists find it impossible to square the facts of free will with their metaphysical assumptions concerning the ultimate nature and source of our whole conscious life. Hence, they make every effort to explain away these facts in accordance with their metaphysical assumptions.

Titchener probably has voiced the attitude of many contemporary psychologists when he concludes his discussion of the experimental evidence for free will as follows: "As psychologists, therefore, we cannot accept the freedom of the will unless (1) we throw away our scientific definition of mind, and return to the popular notions held about it. And further, (2) as psychologists, we are able to explain, by means of nervous tendencies, certain phenomena of choice which are commonly supposed to furnish a basis for the belief in freedom."[45]

It is undoubtedly true that free will is irreconcilable with the theoretic assumptions which enter into what Titchener calls "the scientific definition of mind." The obvious inference we draw from this is: *So much the worse for these theoretic assumptions.* For, after all. theories must fit facts and not *vice versa,* that is, facts must not be explained away so as to make them fit theoretic assumptions. *And what of it, if the explanation of facts lead us to notions concerning the ultimate nature and source of our conscious life which are in perfect accord with common sense?* All

---

[45] *A Primer of Psychology,* pp. 255, 256, quoted by permission of the Macmillan Co., publishers.

other natural sciences boast of the fact that their findings are in accord with common sense and that scientific inquiry itself is really nothing but a refinement of common sense. Why should psychology be in this regard so different from all other sciences? *Modern psychologists cannot point to a single fact which would invalidate the common-sense view of Aristotle and the schoolmen concerning the ultimate source of our conscious life.* Neither has any experimental procedure succeeded in throwing doubt on any of the basic facts on which the schoolmen built their doctrine. In a word, experimental work, mixed as it is with metaphysical assumptions concerning the nature of "mind," has never succeeded in creating a "psychology without a soul." Watson has stated this with all the emphasis desirable; so, at least, we interpret the following passage: "In the late sixties an attempt was made to make an experimental science of psychology. The boast was voiced that the psychology growing out of this attempt had become a science without a soul — that is, a natural science. Notwithstanding the establishment of many laboratories both here and abroad, it has never been able to substantiate this claim."[46] It is refreshing to hear an out-and-out materialist like Watson say that the boast of "psychology without a soul" is an empty one.

We have so far abstained from all metaphysical discussions and we shall do so now. Those readers who are interested in the philosophic discussion concerning the ultimate nature and source of our conscious life, are referred to a book published by the present writer in 1912 and entitled *Psychology Without a Soul, A Criticism.* In this book *all the metaphysical assumptions which enter into what Titchener calls "the scientific definition of mind" are dealt with at a great length.* And the conclusion reached is: Psychology as taught by the neo-scholastics has absolutely nothing to fear from the findings of experimentalists. Whatever else the experimentalists have to say against *"the old-fashioned psychology"* is metaphysical speculation of a rather crude sort.

---

[46] *Psychology* (2d ed.), p. 1.

References for Further Reading

Narciss Ach, *Ueber die Willenstätigkeit und das Denken* (1905).

Narciss Ach, *Ueber den Willensakt und das Temperament* (1910).

Raphael C. McCarthy, S.J., *The Measurement of Conation* (1926).

J. Lindworsky, S.J., *Der Wille* (1923).

J. Lindworsky, S.J., *Experimentelle Psychologie* (1921), pp. 147–151; 224–258.

J. Froebes, S.J., *Lehrbuch der Experimentellen Psychologie* (3d ed.), Vol. II, pp. 368–435.

H. M. Wells, "The Phenomenology of Acts of Choice," *British Journal of Psychology*, Monogr. Suppl. XI.

INDEX

Abnormal color-vision, defined, 51

Abnormal psychology, 432

Absent-mindedness and free will, 430

Abstraction, experimental investigation of, how devised, 314; generalizing vs isolating, 314; the process of, 310; two phases of, 311, 312

Accessory structures of the sense-organs. 29

Accident *and* insight, 268; *without* insight, 268

Accommodation, active and passive, 134; movements, can be artificially dissociated from fixation movements. 156

Ach, experiments of, 409

Ach's experiments, various criticisms of, 413, 414, 415

Active interposition of the Ego, 410; as expressed by the man in the street, 428, in the experiments of Wells, 420; in the light of controlled observation, 433

Activities, subconscious, 219

Acuity, of vision, 122; of binocular depth-vision, 149; of depth-vision irreconcilable with local-sign theory, 151; of depth-vision the same as the acuity of the monocular perception of direction, 152

Adequate vs. inadequate stimuli, 29

Advancement of knowledge by original research, too narrow a definition of intelligence, 301

Afferent neuron, part of the reflex arc, 246

After period, 409; *see* reaction experiments

Analogous imitation, in animals, of recognition, 296; of judgment in animals, 298

Analogy, argument from, 6, 243, 248

Analysis, abuse of the term, 426; of clang-tint by attention; method of

procedure, 222; scientific, can be tested by a corresponding synthesis. 427

'Analyzed" and "unanalyzed" experience, 376; *see* analysis, abuse of the term

Anthropomorphism, naïve, not implied in our explanation of instinct, 285

Anti-instinctive attitude of modern psychology, 240

Antinomies, of animal behavior, a stumblingblock of intelligence theory, disappear in our hypothesis, 286

Aphasia, the phenomena of, throw light on function of images, 391

Aphasics, subjects in experiments on generalizing abstraction, 319

Apparent, lateral displacement of objects, 132; size of objects, 128

Arbitrium, 429

Argument from analogy, 6, 243, 248

Aristotle, on free will, 428, 429

Artificial character of syllogism, exaggerated, 383

Assent vs. consent, 372

Association, "after disjunction," 373; rational, the most powerful means of recall, 315; simultaneous and successive, 373; two accepted meanings of, 380

Associations, intellectual vs. sensory; superiority of intellectual, over sensory, 204

"Associative equivalent" of the determination, 414

Assumptions, unwarranted, of modern psychology, 11

Attention, 213; an important factor in breaking a habit, 415; definition of, 217; the normal range of, in binocular vision, 143; the physiological theory of, 237; the span of, 227

Auditory, aphasia, 392, 393; sensations, the importance of, 82